CW00688101

NOT OUT OF MALAWI

BY

ENID WATERFIELD

Dedicated To

Wendy and Ben

First Published in Great Britain in 2008
by Plaintiles Publishing,

A CIP Catalogue of this book is available from the British Library

ISBN 978-0-9559030-0-7

Printed and bound in Great Britain by Biddles Ltd, King's Lynn, Norfolk

Produced and presented by Corinne Dennis & Barry Wilson

Front cover, frontispiece, drawings and maps
by Ken Waterfield, unless acknowledged separately.

ACKNOWLEDGMENTS
First of all to my husband, for all his help and encouragement, but for him there
would be no story. Secondly to our daughter Corinne for practical help beyond
the call of duty, and to our good friends Barry and Barbara Wilson who in spite
of their heavy work schedule took time to drag me into the computer age. Thanks
especially to Tom Williamson for reading and correcting the manuscript. Also to
Catherine Bishop, David Bishop, Doreen Ridley and John Whicher who likewise
encouraged me. And to Mark Waterfield for legal advice. Last but not least I
acknowledge the help of the late Elspeth Huxley, a good friend, who on hearing
of my intention to write some African memoirs for the family, urged me to write
it 'as if for publication'.

AUTHENTICATION
The time, place, events described in this narrative are authentic; the more important
facts may be verified even at this late date. The people too are actual. Their true
names have been used in all cases but a few, which have been altered to avoid any
offence or possible embarrassment. Conversations are, obviously, not verbatim,
but the occasions having been documented in my diaries, therefore give a true
reflection of what was actually said.

ABOUT THE BOOK

This narrative is an attempt to describe as accurately as possible, the formative years of a young couple embarking on marriage in a remote corner of a remote country of Africa; in the pre-plastic, pre-mobile phone, days of the early 1950s. The stated aim of the husband, an Agricultural Assistant in the British Colonial Service, was to improve the lot of the impoverished people who lived there; by means of better farming practice.

ABOUT THE AUTHOR

Enid Waterfield born 1927, was brought up in Hertfordshire and educated in the air-raid shelters of Watford. She trained as a librarian and followed that career for some years. She and her husband live in Dorset. They have been married for fifty-four years and have four children.

ILLUSTRATIONS

Every effort has been made to contact copyright holders for permission to include the photographs and other images in this publication and, where possible, the copyright owner for each photo is stated in the photo or image details. Any copyright holders we have been unable to reach or to whom inaccurate acknowledgment has been made are invited to contact: corinne@corinnedennis.co.uk

CONTENTS

FOREW0RD

'A land where it seemed always afternoon.'
This is the impression that lives on. Which is strange when the conscious mind more readily recalls brilliant early mornings washed by rain, or else the limpid nights, the moonflower by the back door casting a scent so sickly and powerful that to sleep under it would be death. Or so the people said. Powerful too is the sense of disbelief that it really happened at all. But this is not surprising, 'The past is another country', literally in this case, and the girl who sojourned there long since fled. Only when documents, diaries, old photographs come unexpectedly to light does memory return with undiminished clarity .

But to the facts. Nyasaland, Central Africa in the early 1950s, a British Protectorate since 1891. A small country, long and thin, running North/South, with a lake following much of its length, bounded by Northern Rhodesia (Zambia) to the North West, Mozambique to the South and East, and by Tanganyika (Tanzania) to the North. It had a population of some 3,000,000 Africans, a smattering of Asians, mostly traders, and circa 3000 Europeans. The last were made up mainly of British administrators in the form of Provincial and District Commissioners and their aides, wholly committed to their work, paternalistic, popular even, plus officials of various Government Departments - Agriculture, Veterinary, Health, Education, the ubiquitous Public Works and others.
Last but by no means least, was the handful of Scots missionaries whose influence from early days far outweighed their number.
Bribery was unknown, Apartheid - the colour bar that obtained in South Africa - had no place here. The British Government acknowledged that the land belonged to the African people and white settlement was not permitted. No matter how long serving, how devoted an English Colonial Servant might be, on reaching retirement age he must pack his bags and leave the country in which he may have spent most of his life. An unusual face of Imperialism perhaps.
Colonialism has long been a dirty word. And yet... After all this time Britain has good relations with many, probably most, of its former territories, most of which chose to remain within the British Commonwealth.
In the case of Nyasaland the designation Protectorate was no idle euphemism. It had come about, belatedly, as a result of the great explorer David Livingstone and others having alerted Parliament in England of the miserable state of affairs in the country around the middle of the 19th century. For as well as inter-tribal warfare involving slaying and slaughter of 0ld Testament propensities, the country had for generations been ravaged by the depredations of Arab slavers, its people suffering grievously.
The Protectorate having been proclaimed it took many years more actually to

put an end to slavery. But as the 20th century progressed the slave trade was stamped out, internal strife was controlled, the Pax Britannia held sway. By the 1950s schools and hospitals were well established. If the crops failed and famine threatened, Government brought in food from Rhodesia. Identifiable Aids had not yet appeared.

A halcyon period? Hardly for poverty was still endemic, the impoverished land too overworked to support a growing population. Indeed there was criticism from armchair idealists in the West who indignantly demanded that living standards be brought up to those of England, without specifying how this was to be achieved.

Certainly the country had but a curtailed railway, virtually no tarmac roads, no telephones, or houses with running water or electricity, which might have been, and indeed was, annoying to expatriates, but which impinged on the local people hardly at all. So, halcyon days for them certainly, by comparison with what had gone before.

For the British there was sunshine, beautiful scenery, the delights of Lake Nyasa and above all, there were friendly people among whom to live and work. People who were, by the stated policy of the British Government, being supported in self help and encouraged to train for posts of responsibility in the administration and departmental running of the country, with a view to eventual self rule.

Whatever the merits or otherwise of such a regime, it was not in any case destined to last. The Wind of Change was blowing through Africa, the concept of Independence was gathering pace. It came to Nyasaland well ahead of the time scale envisaged by the British.

This however is no historical treatise. Rather it is an attempt to chronicle the vanished way of life of one junior Colonial Servant who, newly married, embarked on an agricultural career in a remote and mountainous enclave where African people struggled to support themselves on ever deteriorating land. Common sense people, industrious of necessity, Thomas Hardy's Wessex villagers would have recognised them at once and hailed them as kindred spirits. Across the years I salute them.

CHAPTER 1

LUX IN TENEBRIS

"What made you go there in the first place? I asked, "And how did you get the job?"

We were sprawled across the bed at our Chesham flat three months after our wedding, on a typical English summer day. Which is to say, persistent light drizzle deterred any desire to venture out. Ken was on leave after a four year tour of duty overseas and had just remarked that this was not real rain. He added,

"Just wait till you come across the African variety."

Which was what, at a rather late stage, had sparked off my question. Now he said, "Oh, when I was a boy I used to collect stamps. Colonials mainly, they were the most exotic. The Nyasaland ones were the best, with zebra grazing, and fishermen in dug-out canoes. Things like that. Then there was the motto you know, 'Lux in Tenebris' - Light in Darkness. Only these days it's usually known by expatriates as 'Hold on to the Soap'. I'd always thought it would be good to go there."

"But how did you actually...?"

"'Well when I was working as a farm labourer I saw that Government was advertising for agricultural assistants there. And for Tanganyika and Uganda as a matter of fact. But their stamps weren't so inspiring, at least not to me. Didn't expect to get selected though."

This was hardly surprising for his Curriculum Vitae could not have been very encouraging to the mandarins in Whitehall before whom he was summoned to appear.

"I see from your application Mr Waterfield, that your early education was devoted almost exclusively to — er — Art." said one disdainfully.

It was true. On winning an art scholarship he had in the manner of the time, been plucked out of mainstream education at the tender age of thirteen to attend art college, where he and his peers spent the next three years high up in an airy, glass roofed studio. The year being 1940 they had presented a prime target for German bombers in the 1939/45 war.

Between times of diving down to the air raid shelter, they studied still life with Mr Jackson, the master waiting to join the army, whose main pleasure in life was putting put his arm round the girls when leaning over their donkey benches to help them with their perspective. Technical crafts such as metal work, printing etc, also on the curriculum, were under the guidance of Juicy Mellon who was too old to be called up. Or put his arm round the girls for that matter.

Nor was the first job listed on the CV more reassuring, for Ken, the war still raging, had been employed as a book-jacket designer for a firm of publishers in London. Coincidentally his office was near the very one in which this peacetime interview was being conducted. Indeed there was a fair chance that he and his interrogators had dodged the same missiles, which may or may not, have accorded some sort of bond. On the other hand the experience was hardly a recommendation for the matter in hand: doubtless most of the panel were looking decidedly sceptical.

Be that as it may they would have been slightly cheered as they read on.

In the 1940s and for many years after, the one communication that youths could rely on receiving on their 18th birthday, was the one from King George VI ordering them to report for military service. Thus it was that Ken left the publishers and spent the next three years in the Royal Engineers, acquiring much knowledge, technical and worldly, most of it unknown to the world of Art. Probably the younger mandarins were themselves war veterans and this was something to which they could relate.

The last item on the CV was also more promising, for on deciding he could not face the prospect of spending a lifetime in a London office, he had taken up a course at a farm institute. Hence his introduction to agriculture. This made everyone look happier. One member of the panel said.

"Well you would of course have to work on your own quite a bit - should your application be successful that is - so it might be fortunate that you have this -er - painting hobby."

In the light of subsequent knowledge this could have been roughly translated as,

"You'll probably have to spend weeks alone in some God forsaken hellhole. The last chap there shot himself in the foot. Not accidentally. So you'd jolly well better have something to occupy you if you don't want to end up the same way."

Everyone brightened further at this; lunch was in sight, one or two started shuffling papers in preparation for leaving. But then one older man who had not yet spoken leaned forward, and steepling his fingers said,

"Tell me Mr Waterfield, why exactly are you applying for this post?"

There was a pregnant pause while Ken mentally reviewed the considerations which had brought him to this point.

A boyhood interest in Nyasaland stamps seemed hardly convincing.

He could have said his artistic training did not seem likely to promise an exciting career. He could have said that, without a farming background or else vast capital, he was unlikely ever to have a farm of his own. He could have said that he 'wished to help people' - although that was also true.

"So what did you say?"

"I said that my girl had turned me down so I had decided to go off to Darkest Africa."

"Very funny." I said. By the 1950s this Victorianism had long since gone out of fashion.

"Anyway I hadn't turned you down exactly, only prevaricated a bit. No seriously, what did you actually say?"

"Oh I said something about wanting to travel. And the post seemed to offer the possibility of advancement. Something of that sort. They seemed to like it, anyway I got the job. Isn't it about teatime?".

"No it isn't, I said firmly, "Tell me what you actually do there."

At once his face took on the abstracted look I was later to know well.

"It's not easy to explain because the job takes in so many minor matters, not all of them directly concerned with agriculture, not all of them official even, but important just the same. Local people come with their problems for instance."
"Such as?"
"Well, such as giving them a lift to go and see their sick father. Or advancing money on their pay for children's school fees, or perhaps dealing with a witchcraft complaint. Not an easy one that.
We go on ulendo - safari - a lot of the time, on foot as I've told you, because there aren't many roads in North Nyasa, and the few there are are pretty rough. No tarmac of course, so when we do drive it knocks hell out of vehicles. And as there are no professional mechanics around we have to do our own motor maintenance. That's very time consuming.
"Then there's a fair amount of building work too, storage sheds and the odd barn, things like that. Perhaps a basic house. There are never enough houses to go round."
By this time I was wondering how the real, agricultural, work fitted into the scheme of things, but instead I asked suspiciously,
"HOW basic?"
"They're more like huts really, he admitted, "Mud and thatch, no running water or electricity of course. Or proper ceilings, or floors for that matter..."
As I found out later, he was not joking.
"But of course all this is incidental to the main agricultural work."
"Which is?" I prompted.
He thought for a moment,
"It has two main strands. Firstly there's the preservation and conservation of the land, and secondly there's the introduction of a cash crop - coffee in my case - to try to raise living standards. The people are desperately poor; they have no money, just a little land and a few cattle, but virtually nothing else."
The concept of conservation, so all pervasive a generation later, was virtually unknown at this time and I needed him to explain it. He said,
"It's a question of taking care of the land. As you know I'm based mainly in the Misuku Hills in the far North of the country. It's a small enclave, about 15 miles across I suppose, at an altitude of some 6000 feet. The countryside is all broken hills and steep sided valleys, and that causes all sorts of problems. It's bounded by mountains so there's no room for expansion and land pressure is tremendous.
Every possible inch is cultivated, and there's the rub. Every rainy season the soil on the hillsides gets washed away, causing severe erosion, already some of them have been reduced to barren rock. All over the area crop yields are getting poorer each year. So the Agricultural Department has brought in measures to check this."
"What are they?"
"We get the people to plant contoured strips at intervals on the steeper slopes to stop the loss of soil."
"Does it work?"
" It does, but it takes time. And of course involves extra labour."
"Not popular then?"
"You could say that. Hated in fact. And so is the ban on stream bank cultivation."

"Why is that banned? I would have imagined the soil there to be very fertile."

"So it is. But unfortunately it can cause flooding. If banks give way whole crops are sometimes washed out. Occasionally a family might lose its entire food supply and be left with nothing to eat."

I was silent as I considered this direct manifestation of cause and effect. It was true that in England food had been severely rationed during the war, (and indeed bread remained so into the 1950s,) but the cause - an enemy blockade of our shores which prevented the food supplies getting through - had been at a distance and not before our very eyes. Besides, although people were often hungry, no-one actually starved. At last I said,

"Tell me about the other strand."

"What? Oh yes, the cash crop. In some parts of the country they grow tea, that's a well established industry. In other parts it's tobacco, or rice. In Misuku we're pioneering coffee. As I said, the people are very poor, they rely on subsistence cultivation. So the aim is to give them a small source of income as back-up."

"You mean they have no money at all?" I put in incredulously.

If the stark, direct cause of starvation was new to me, the concept of a wholly non-cash economy was inconceivable.

"They must need money for some things, I went on, "Clothes, and saucepans for instance. All the things they can't make or grow for themselves."

"It's amazing how inventive they are. But yes, he conceded, "In practice most have a little I suppose. You see the young men go off to work in the gold mines in South Africa and send money home. But that's another story. And yes, you're right they can't get far without any money at all. Government helps them with loans for hoes, shovels etc to tend their gardens, so in theory they can make a bit on what they grow. But that's not enough to pay for things like school fees if they want to educate their children, which not many of them are able to in Misuku. Then they have to pay their poll tax..."

"Poll tax?"

"A tax on their huts. A bit like the rates that County Councils in England impose on people's houses."

I was to learn later that this imposition was hated quite as violently in Nyasaland as was its counterpart in England during the 1990s. At the time I remarked merely that making money just to pay taxes must surely be one of the greatest disincentives of all time.

"Well there it is, he said, "In a good season there's food to carry them over. In a really poor one Government brings in supplies from Southern Rhodesia which always has surplus food. So it's not all bad. And about the coffee; it's a beautiful crop. Misuku is beautiful too, wait till you see it, And the people are friendly, and..."

I privately thought that in view of what he had told me, this last part was just as well. He would have expatiated further but I had had enough for one day. The rain, real or not, had stopped at last so I said,

"It really is teatime now. And look the sun's shining and we can go for a walk afterwards."

PART OF A SUBMITTED REPORT OF KEN'S EARLIER WORK AND A MENTION OF THE COFFEE COOPERATIVE.

Duties Performed.
(a) Soil and Water Conservation.
Surveyed and supervised construction of 'bench terraces', contour and graded bunds, (a type of storm drain,) contour box ridges, and gully erosion control by means of check-dams and cut bunds. This work carried out in intensively cultivated hill area.
Earth dams constructed to impound storm water and extend effective grazing area. Resting and replanting of overgrazed pastures, afforestation of steep, eroded hillsides. Demarcation limits of stream bank cultivation.
(b) Irrigation
An official survey carried out for Nyasaland Government of a 700 acre estate in the Southern Province, and two plane-table surveys carried out for the Colonial Development Corporation on pilot projects on their Vipya tung oil estates in the Northern Province.
© Experimental Work.
Randomised variety trials established throughout Karonga District for maize, coffee, cotton and groundnuts. Fertiliser trials laid down for maize and coffee.
Coffee
I was for several years in charge of the African coffee growing scheme in the Misuku Hills. During that period production of seedlings from Agricultural Department nurseries rose from 7000 thousand annually to 120,000. Production of clean coffee rose from 2 tons annually to over 100 tons. The coffee was planted on bench terraces at 9ft x 9ft spacing, with Albizia shade trees, and Napier Fodder for wind breaks and mulch. Pruning was to multiple stem.

CHAPTER 2

OHMS

Ken had come home in early summer and we had married at once. The weeks and months passed most pleasantly, so pleasantly in fact that the time once over, rapidly acquired a sense of unreality, Only when summer gave way to a spiteful Autumn and Ken's leave, seemingly so endless in prospect, began to gallop full tilt to its close, did the need to face the future become urgent. Official letters designated 'On Her Majesty's Service', some from Whitehall, some direct from Nyasaland emblazoned with the aforementioned stamps, appeared on the doormat, reinforcing the need to be practical.

"We must make a list of the things to take out with us, said Ken, "I've got a certain amount of stuff there already of course, but not enough for both of us."

"Can't we buy it when we get there? I ventured, "It seems rather a long way to take it all." He laughed,

"The shops are pretty basic. And not exactly round the corner. (Another mastery of understatement as it turned out.) "No we'll have a day in London. We'll go to the Army and Navy Store in Victoria, they've got everything there."

He was right. This vast emporium had served several generations of the Heaven Born and was stocked from floor to ceiling, not only with everything one could think of, but with a great deal more beside. There were grand pianos especially adapted to tropical conditions, pith helmets trailing red flannel spine pads, tiffin boxes, cut glass decanters decked with necklaces designated port, whiskey, etc, moustache cups, mosquito boots and many other intriguing artefacts. Almost all of them male orientated. Pausing to sneer in disbelief in front of something unidentifiable but labelled 'Collapsible Bath', I was brought up sharply by Ken,

"Come on. No need to waste time here, I've already got one of those."

It was a memorable day. Only by exercising the greatest restraint did we manage to leave merely with two trunks, a camp bed for me - Ken already had one of those as well - which looked, and indeed proved to be, hideously uncomfortable, but which was apparently, "The type easiest for the carriers to manage and that's the main thing", plus a double mosquito net. Of this last Ken explained that Government provided single nets only. And single beds too for that matter, a state of affairs he intended to rectify as soon as possible.

"Let us roll all our strength and all / Our sweetness up into one ball / And tear our pleasures with rough strife / Thorough the iron gates of life."

Said the poet to his coy mistress. Well, we had been doing that all the summer. Now it was time to tear ourselves from the pleasures and roll up all our worldly goods into the two trunks, which must then be labelled 'Not wanted on Voyage' and sent in advance to the boat which would carry us far away.

A nightmare scene ensued, one that was to become all too familiar in the years ahead. That is to say a vast sea of belongings was soon piled up in the middle of the room. How could we have accumulated so much in just six months of married life? The trunks which had appeared so capacious when empty - indeed the larger one had looked big enough to accommodate a corpse should one wish to - were now woefully inadequate. Many and bitter were the demarcation disputes.

Looking at my pile Ken said,

"You won't need your wedding dress for a start."

"Don't be silly, I'm not leaving that behind."

It was of beautiful pale blue silk and I had visions of wearing it at splendid receptions graced by ambassadors, and their wives dripping diamonds.

"Or those red high heeled shoes." he went on cruelly.

"But I never wear flat..."

"Or that hideous vase."

"But it was a wedding present!"

"Never mind, we won't need it."

"I shall, I said firmly "What about the huge art books you're taking? We won't really need them either."

"That's different."

So it went on. Finally I said heatedly,

"It's not fair. You have got lots of things out there already, I haven't." And getting really worked up added, "I'm sick of packing. Sick of the whole business."

At last when the trunks were full to overflowing, Ken sat on the lids and managed to snap the locks. An uncomfortable amount of detritus remained, either to be thrown out or left with long suffering relatives.

After this the days tumbled over each other in a hectic round of leave-taking of family, friends, and of the dear, familiar places. Also with last minute practicalities, not least in my case, a smallpox vaccination and an assortment of injections against strange diseases. So much so that I began to feel ill. Ken who had been through it all before, said,

"Sometimes there are side effects."

"Did they make you feel sick?"

"Well no, not sick exactly, just a bit groggy. Perhaps you'd better go and see the doctor. Just in case."

The doctor looked at me keenly and asked how long I had been married. Then in stead of scribbling a prescription for some elixir which would cure me at once, as I had hoped, he said,

"Just hop on the couch will you."

After a bit he announced,

"Just as I suspected. Early pregnancy. Where did you say you were going? Oh yes, Nyasaland. Hm, well, take it easy. And see a doctor regularly."

Both strictures in the event, impossible to fulfil.

Of course the possibility of pregnancy had not escaped me. How could it have done given the circumstances? But having always enjoyed perfect health it had never occurred to me it would feel like an illness. Ken withstood the shock bravely.

"Of course there will be a doctor on the boat, he said, "And in Nyasaland too."
I later discovered the latter to be about as plentiful as lamp posts in the desert.
"You'll be fine, he went on, "Better not tell the relatives though. It would only add
to their worries."

Lying as it did at the heart of Central Africa, Nyasaland had never been readily
accessible. Indeed its existence was unknown to Europeans until the 1850s. By
the 1950s it was still to most people including myself, remote as the dark side of
the moon.
The great missionary/explorer David Livingstone, 1813 -1873, was the first white
man to gaze on the still waters of Lake Nyasa, and he surely, could have had no
idea of its extent in those early days. He had sailed from England to Quilimané,
Mozambique, on the south east coast of Africa in March 1858, and set out from
the delta river- mouth of the Zambezi to explore its upper reaches and tributaries.
Trekking over the great flood plain he and his party had taken to canoes where
possible, hauling them up rapids, proceeding on foot to carry them whenever the
difficult and dangerous river was un-navigable. Thus they reached the confluence
of the Zambezi and the Shiré[1] River which, indirectly, drains Lake Nyasa at its
Southern tip. A hazardous journey lasting several months.

On his return to England, after alerting Parliament of the state of affairs in
Nyasaland, Livingstone went on to inspire a number of his compatriots in
Scotland to follow in his footsteps to set up missions in this far off part of Africa.
They must have been a hardy, self-sufficient breed; they achieved their purpose
of disseminating Christianity among the African people whom they regarded as
benighted heathens, but at great personal cost. Many of their number left their
bones in the unhealthy sites chosen for the great work, their numbers decimated
by a tiny adversary whose deadly effect was unknown to Livingstone, or to anyone
else at the time. Namely the malarial mosquito.

For a long time Livingstone's route was the only way of reaching Nyasaland -
and that during the dry season only. Nevertheless the Scots missionaries were
followed by a handful of traders, a few British army officers, notably Captain
Lugard of whom more later, and by an assortment of adventurers and erstwhile
soldiers eager for excitement, All of them did their best to protect the people from
the Arab slavers.
This was at the height of the great Victorian age of invention and innovation when
the British Empire had begun to spread its tentacles, eventually to encompass a
quarter of the world's surface.

As a result of Cecil Rhodes' dream, a Cape to Cairo railway had soon begun to
snake its way across Africa, but it had little bearing on Nyasaland. Not until 1934

---

[1] Pronunciation: the é throughout does not exactly convey the correct sound, but is the
nearest approximation available. Similarly the b is usually soft as in Katobo, pronounced
Katowo.

was that country opened up when the Zambezi was spanned by a bridge 12,100 feet long, at Sena, Mozambique, and a rail link established between the Indian Ocean port of Beira and landlocked Nyasaland. This was the route we ourselves would essentially be taking.

The railway was not the only form of progress however. Sometime between the World Wars of 1914-18 and 1939-45 an air service had been established in the form of two Short Sunderland flying boats which took turns to skim swan-like out of Southampton Water, alighting perhaps a week later if the gods were kind, on Lake Nyasa at its southern tip.[2] En route they would make scheduled stops on any convenient stretch of water and sometimes unscheduled ones as well, when hurricanes, typhoons, sandstorms or other Acts of God forced them down on some obscure lake or exotic lagoon. In which case passengers would arrive at their destination not only late but with tempers frayed and moral fibre sorely tested.

The flying boats had been pensioned off by the time Ken joined the Colonial Service, replaced by more conventional planes, but the air travel option was confined to senior officers, of whom he assuredly was not one. Which is how we came to find ourselves, I still nauseous, on the deck of the SS Rhodesia Castle, a Union Castle liner, one of a fleet carrying passengers and mail, which left Southampton promptly at 4PM every Thursday afternoon. With luck it would disengorge us some six weeks later at Beira, Mozambique.

We had arrived none too early, one murky November afternoon after a long train journey, to the throbbing of the ship's engines beneath our feet. Other passengers, mostly Government officials like Ken, some of them with their families, crowded the rail. As the hands of a clock on the jetty crept towards four o'clock activity became frenzied. New arrivals hastened up companionways, the lethargic dockers loading cargo quickened their pace, taxis zoomed up with late comers, the vibration below became more urgent. Finally gang planks were removed, somewhere a band played.

At 4PM precisely the boat began imperceptibly to move off. Flimsy, coloured streamers thrown down to loved ones lining the quay tautened, tightened, snapped symbolically. The gap widened, very soon warehouses, docks, people, were lost in fog and the gathering dusk.

The cabins on the SS Rhodesia Castle were arranged in tranche of three, outer, middle and inner. Outer cabins had direct access to a porthole, the inner had no porthole at all. Allocation was according to status, the outer ones were for senior government officers and their wives, the inner for luckless single men. Ours reflecting Ken's junior position, was a middle cabin. It was very small, accommodating two bunk beds with a shelf above, a small wardrobe and a locker. Leading off was a narrow corridor, some 8feet long, forming the long arm of an L, at the end of which was a porthole with a wash basin beneath.

---

[2] These facts have not been verified.

As the marine equivalent of a pied á terre it was adequate, but would not have been ideal for anyone with a tendency toward claustrophobia. Indeed it was very stuffy, the porthole being too far off to be effective. Ken said it would be better once we got out into open sea, and anyway it was a vast improvement on the hellhole of the inner cabin he had shared, perforce, with a complete stranger on his first voyage out, which was why he had got married in the first place.

When night came I lay awake on the lower bunk to the grumbling of the engines, the unfamiliar rocking motion, the slapping of sea against the side. Snapshots of the day's events flickered before my eyes. First and foremost the trauma of parting with loved ones. Ours was a close knit family and I felt it keenly - though I did not fully appreciate my mother's pain until many years later, when the role was reversed and we bade goodbye to our own daughter bound for the same destination.

On this night as I tossed and turned, the scene etched most strongly on my mind was of my father, mother and much loved sister, flanked by her two young children, strung out on the platform of the local railway station, hands joined as in the frieze of a child's cut-out. Wretched as I was I never doubted as the train slid away, that on our return the tableau would be re-enacted in reverse. Everyone would be their place, but instead of the stoicism of parting would be the certainty of a joyous reunion.

In this, as in so many things over the next few years, I was wrong. My father died while we were away. He had been a soldier in the 1914 -1918 war, some ten years before my birth, seeing action in France, volunteering as a stretcher bearer 'because he did not want to kill anyone.'

On the edge of sleep the images persisted. My sister had said it was worse for the ones left behind and in this instance she was probably right, for despite myself, the demands of the journey had soon taken over.

In London we had changed trains for the express that would take us across the lovely countryside of Hampshire to Southampton. Southampton! A name to conjure with, it had for centuries been the world's major sea port, in the eyes of the British at least. In the first half of the 20th century it was still the hub of world shipping.

Lying awake I relived the hustle and bustle of our arrival. Time pressing, Ken made a mad dash for a taxi to take us from the train to the docks. The driver wove his way skilfully through narrow streets with wartime scars still showing, to the quayside, where boats of all shapes and sizes loomed, finally dropping us off at exactly the right spot. At this point I myself dropped off.

In contrast to the cabins, the public rooms - saloons - were unexpectedly spacious as I discovered next day. There was a huge dining room, where Ken made a hearty breakfast and I toyed with a bread roll, several large lounges, one of which by dint of having a bookcase or two along one wall, was designated 'Library'. The saloons gave access to upper or lower decks by means of sliding doors.

On one deck was a swimming pool, empty and sad in the raw November air, on another there was space enough for sports, deck tennis, badminton, even a form of cricket which would be taken up enthusiastically once we reached more clement latitudes.

So big did the boat seem, it brought back to me the trauma of transition to the senior school in town, from the intimacy of the village mixed infants, and it was several days before the geography became fixed in my mind. By which time the voyage was well under way with the serious business of contests, competitions for the said sports, as well as chess, bridge, and table tennis tournaments, and games for the children.

In the evenings there was dancing to the ship's band, Bingo, and sometimes impromptu cabarets or concerts. Only the faint hearted, or nauseous like myself, failed to participate. That is until a Force Ten gale struck in the Bay of Biscay, when even the hale and hearty were laid low. Ken, one of the few not affected, reported that the dining room was virtually empty.

We sailed into calmer waters at last but still I lay on my bunk hoping to die, the thought of food utterly revolting.

Finally with admonishments and inducements from Ken, I tottered to my feet and spent the days lounging on deck, drinking in the sun that was now gaining strength, watching the frenetic activity of the games players, and energetic individuals who felt impelled to take their daily 100 brisk turns around the deck. When the swimming pool was filled I sometimes made a great effort and joined Ken for a swim. But mostly, to the scorn of those around, I lay in a long chair thankful for having nothing more strenuous to do than observe the romances, licit or otherwise, burgeoning like hybrids in a hothouse.

In this connection we once met an Assistant District Commissioner and his wife, who had embarked at Southampton as strangers, got engaged at Cape Town and married at Port Elizabeth, all in a matter of four or five weeks,. But that came later; it is doubtful whether many of the liaisons I was witnessing would last in the same manner.

These days at sea were punctuated by meals of gargantuan proportions during which all activities, even the romantics ones, were suspended. Ken, having experienced it before had become blasé about the cornucopia of plenty set out before us but to me it was quite incredible. In common with all children in wartime Britain, food rationing had been part of everyday life. We had never known anything else and were brought up on the plainest diet imaginable. Sweet things were especially scarce. If by some miracle Spotted Dick was served up for dessert at school dinner, we were hard put to it not to lick the pattern off the plate, or would have been, but that the plates too were plain, the colour of cold porridge.

It was therefore a particularly cruel irony to me that, surrounded by sumptuous fare, pregnancy/sea sickness meant that I could not eat any of it.

The day began with early tea and biscuits brought in by a cabin steward, after which came breakfast in the dining room. Ken and I shared a table with a mature, very pleasant couple, Colonel & Mrs Apthorpe, also bound for Nyasaland where he was a Provincial Chief of Police. Unfortunately, after a week or so the Colonel was laid low with chicken pox, although in truth he was no chicken. Which left

Mrs. Apthorpe, a former nursing sister, to keep her end up at the dining table. She summed up my pregnancy at a glance as I sat sipping fruit juice, and assured me the sickness would go off after three months. But I had trouble believing her.

In mid morning in case anyone should be assailed with pangs of malnutrition, there was another Epicurean interlude when cups of hot Bovril, and snacks, were served on deck - to be replaced by tubs of ice cream once the weather grew warmer. A lavish lunch at noon was followed by 4 o'clock tea, with sandwiches thin to the point of transparency, and platesful of fancy biscuits. As for dinner at 7PM... But this I could not face, opting to spend the time lying face down on my bunk until Ken came back.

Then we would go up on deck again, deserted but for romantic couples half hidden in unlikely crannies. In the balmy nights of the approaching tropics this was the best time of all.

Of early ports of call there remain only the haziest memories. Rotterdam, where Ken bought me a watch - they were still in short supply in England due to the war. Las Palmas where all signs of winter had magically vanished and young boys in dinghies alongside dived into translucent waters for coins thrown down by passengers from the ship's rail high above. Ascension Island, another lonely outpost of Empire, with regular calls by Union Castle liners like our own, its only physical link with the outside world.

It was at Ascension that two of our onboard acquaintances disembarked, the husband to take up a job with the Cable & Wireless Company, and the wife to occupy herself as best she could. I was tactless enough to tell the latter I could hardly imagine a worse fate for a woman than being cast adrift on such an island 'swilled by the wild and wasteful ocean'. She said there was reportedly a vibrant ex-patriot community on the Island, and anyway, if she did not like it she could always leave on the next boat going back to England. For good measure she added pointedly that at least it would not be as bad as living in the wilds of Africa.

We also put in at St. Helena, that lonely hunk of rock in mid ocean where Napoleon Bonaparte had dragged out his last bitter years, unresigned, plotting his escape, schemes which came to nothing. Ken & I climbed up to the house in which he had lived; it had been left as it was during his lifetime, with various artefacts and a collection of memorabilia. Surveying the scene one could only guess at The Little General's thoughts, emotions...

The only other event to break the routine of the voyage was the seemingly inevitable 'Crossing the Line' ceremony when King Neptune ruled the swimming pool, his minions man-handling and close-shaving all the male passengers who had not passed that way before. They, and un-travelled women, who were spared the ceremonial thank God, were then presented with scrolls suitably embellished.

After this the sea which had behaved impeccably following the excesses of the Bay of Biscay, began to heave once more, heralding the long, lazily powerful Cape Rollers and the imminence of landfall.

Cape Town at last.

How to describe the impact of Africa? Nothing in my previous experience had prepared me for it. No pictures, no travellers' tales, not even Ken's accounts could do justice to the pulsating colour, from the brilliant sky, the patterned clothes of the people, to the flamboyant flowers and trees lining the streets, or to the sounds, the smells. All new, all suffused in sunlight. Behind the town Table Mountain rose up to form a dramatic backdrop, I loved it all.

One of Ken's inducements on the boat to counter my ignoble lethargy had been the promise of,

"A spot of lotus eating as soon as we reach land".

By which he meant we would enjoy all the blandishments of civilisation in a near perfect setting. There was also the prospect of lazing on golden sands, with no fog coming down, no spiteful cold wind blowing up, which alas was only too likely on the shores of home.

In spite of everything we lived life to the full. Early each morning we went ashore to sample the delights of the town. Then spent long lazy afternoons on one of the beautiful beaches along the coast, wandering into the sea whenever we felt like it, returning to the Rhodesia Castle at dusk with sand in every crevice of our bodies. Ardently we prayed for some Act of God that would delay the boat's departure.

Of course it did not happen. All too soon we were snatched away, 'The boat had somewhere to get to and sailed calmly on'.

Very soon we found ourselves at Port Elizabeth, at East London, pleasant towns both, then on to Durban. Surely it too must be anti-climax after Cape Town? But no, it was beautiful, and English enough to make one feel at home at once. We climbed up to the University, or perhaps one of its colleges, standing high above the town overlooking the splendid sea. What a privilege to be a student in such a place.

Durban was the last port of call in South African waters. The next was Lourenco Marques, Mozambique, (Portuguese East Africa) before Beira - our point of disembarkation.

CHAPTER 3

THE LONGEST CHRISTMAS

Perversely it was at Beira, patently unsuited to lotus eating in any way, shape or form, - this much was apparent from the boat - that we were destined to linger. Here was no sparkling city backed up by splendid scenery, but a nondescript port set on a swampy plain. The ship lay a few hundred yards offshore and even up on deck there no refreshing breeze to alleviate the humidity. Also we had had the misfortune to arrive on Christmas Eve.

Whether the multiracial band of dockers on the distant quay appreciated the significance of the occasion was open to question, but that did not stop them taking full advantage of it. Some were carousing, others slept in shade. Not a vessel moved in the harbour.

The Rhodesia Castle which had steadily disgorged passengers at all the South African ports, so that only a handful remained, lay idle as a painted ship upon a painted ocean, ostracised as if plague had broken out on board. Our cabin was an inferno, the porthole at the end of the narrow corridor too far from the bunks to provide any fresh-air. That and the silence of the engines, lack of the motion we had become accustomed to, combined to make sleep virtually impossible. All entertainment had come to an end once we arrived at Cape Town. The swimming pool had been drained for cleaning. The Apthorpes and other newly made friends had sensibly disembarked long since.

In the circumstances it was no wonder that thoughts turned to the Christmas festivities going on at home in England. Here there was nothing to do but endure, self pity set in like an illness.

The ship's officers did their best. The air conditioned dining room was decked with paper chains and tinsel, dejected looking rather than jolly, which stirred listlessly every time someone passed. Recorded carols played somewhere in the background. On Christmas Day there was traditional fare, turkey, Christmas pudding, mince pies, even crackers and paper hats. Briefly the party spirit was rekindled, but no-one's heart was in it, everyone chafed to get away.

The state of affairs threatened to lengthen to eternity, or at least until after the New Year, with a rumour circulating that the dockers were planning a strike over the whole period.

Mercifully for our sanity it did not happen. On the fifth day of our incarceration we were woken from a restless sleep at dawn by the slap of bare feet on the deck above and the sound of voices raised in alien tongues. A glance through the porthole confirmed that small boats, hitherto frieze-framed at the dock side, were now roused to purposeful action. Bigger boats too were stirring.

We got up at once and made for the cool dining room. But when I ventured to hope this might be our last meal on board I was doomed to disappointment. Ken, who had made overland journeys before, said,

"No, We'd better arrange to stay here tonight in case there's no train today. There's only one a week, or it might be two a week by now, but we must be prepared for another delay. We must go ashore at once and find out. And buy the tickets."

We went up on deck where the cargo being unloaded with surprising speed. In short time we were ferried ashore in a small boat, very much hoping to find our heavy luggage, hitherto stowed away in the ship's hold, awaiting us on the quay. It was not; I waited in shade. Ken pushed his way through the surging throng of dockers, vendors, onlookers, to try and locate the two large trunks last seen by us standing on the sitting room floor of our Chesham flat in England amid a sea of detritus, waiting to be despatched. It seemed a lifetime ago.

He was gone some time. When he returned he said,

"I've found them. They're in one of the sheds over there, so that's alright. But there's a snag. The train to Blantyre isn't due for two days. We might have to put up at a hotel for a couple of nights."

I looked around at the sleazy warehouses, the grubby stalls selling all kinds of comestibles, and at the un-enticing prospect of the town beyond. Visualising the sort of place in which we might find ourselves, our airless cabin - which at least was always clean - suddenly seemed highly desirable. I said,

"Couldn't we just stay on board?"

"Well, he replied, "We'll certainly give it a go. It depends on when the boat will be sailing. I'll look into it as soon as we get back. But first of all the train tickets."

He hailed one of the many run-down taxis. A glimpse of the town as we rattled over bumpy roads, did nothing to increase my desire to stay in it.

The railway station was a seething mass of bodies and assorted livestock. Such was the crush and the heat that once more I headed for the scant shade while Ken fought his way to the ticket office. Where were all these people going? I wondered. The train was not due for another two days, surely they were not preparing to stick it out till then? But no, of course there would be other trains, local or long distance, coming or going in all directions, not just to Nyasaland.

When Ken returned with the tickets we lost no time in getting back to the boat. And here we had a bit of luck. On investigation we found rumours had surfaced that the strike had been resumed, lading new cargo might it seemed, be delayed after all. Consequently no-one raised any objection to our continued presence and we returned thankfully to our cabin.

CHAPTER 4

IN THE STEPS OF DAVID LIVINGSTONE

Two days later the railway station again. We had got up early and packed our hand luggage. According to a syndrome I was beginning to recognise, it had multiplied several times over the course of the voyage. For who could resist the fripperies offered by hawkers at every port, or the variety of goods on display in the well stocked shops of South Africa? Consequently our cases, full to overflowing, were necessarily supplemented by two or three woven baskets.

After eating in the cool dining room for the last time, we said our farewells to the ship's officers - old friends by now - then went below to check that we had left nothing behind.

With unexpected nostalgia I looked round the cramped cabin which had been our refuge for the past six weeks. With all its limitations it had been a physical and psychological haven and suddenly I felt reluctant to leave. But Ken shut the door decisively and we made our way up on deck where a few near naked strike breakers were unloading the last of the heavy luggage.

On shore again Ken collected our trunks from the warehouse and had them piled into another ancient taxi.

The scene at the station was identical with that of our previous visit. Indeed the crowd could have been composed of the very same people, all milling about with bundles; live chickens and a goat or two added to the clamour. Vendors with trays slung round their necks, hawked portions of steaming food wrapped in banana leaves, the aroma mingling with the aura of sweat and bad sanitation, the heat, the noise, the smell were all engulfing. Ken chose a porter from the importuning multitude, and with difficulty followed him to see our luggage loaded on to the train.

I had plenty of time to observe everything from the back of the platform. Over the top of the crowd, or when it parted momentarily, it was just possible to see the powerful, wood burning locomotive, which over the next twenty four hours, would haul the train from sea level to the heights of Nyasaland. To me it was an embodiment of one of the Hornby clockwork model locos with which my brother and his friends had played so passionately during my growing up. So much so I would not have been surprised to see a giant key sticking out of its side... Clearly the heat was getting to me. But a non stop procession of women head-loaded with bundles of firewood and/or water pots, threading its way through the throng to energise this hungry, thirsty monster, was real enough.

The sun climbed higher, the heat increased as shade became non-existent. The noise level also climbed, taking on a sense of urgency as the time of departure drew near.

Carriages had begun to fill up with African passengers, those already aboard leaned down from the windows to take leave of loved ones on the platform, surely stifling those inside. Porters pushed their way through the press with freight for the luggage van, vendors still regaled their wares with practiced persistence. Bodies coalesced, parted, sometimes with brief struggles, the engine began to belch black smoke.

Ken came back, it was time to take our places. We fought our way to the two first class carriages at the front and climbed up; unlike the rest of the long train they were almost deserted. A corridor gave access to two or four berth compartments, most of them unoccupied. We found our reservations in one of the former. It was furnished with two seats which when extended, doubled as bunks. The window was heavily gauzed with rusting anti-mosquito wire, beneath it was a wash basin. There was just enough room for our hand luggage on the overhead rack.

"Well this isn't too bad is it?" said Ken cheerily.

And indeed it was not. For it was private, quiet too, and although a good deal hotter, and far less salubrious, it was reminiscent of the coupé on the trans-continental express that had taken us across Europe on our honeymoon. Of which we had fond memories.

We arranged our belongings, Ken pushed the window open to its full extent and we settled down. He said,

"The last time I was here I'd already been on a train for five days. On my first tour I came out on a mail boat to Cape Town. Only two weeks by sea. Unfortunately that was the last port of call, the boat off-loaded there and sailed back to England. So I had to go the rest of the way by train. Not just me of course, that was the way most people went. The rail link to Nyasaland is indirect from Cape Town and it meant going North, half way across Africa. Well it seemed like that anyway. But it was wonderful to see so much of the countryside. I'd never been out of England before, except to Germany in the army, and that was no picnic really, so you can imagine the impact it made on me. We crossed the Karoo to Johannesburg, through Bechuanaland to Southern Rhodesia, and right up to Salisbury, before coming south again.

"I shared a compartment with three other chaps. I was the youngest. Somewhere along the line a mad woman got on, or she might have been alcoholic. Either way she continually threatened to jump off the train and I had to keep her supplied with cups of tea while the others took turns to restrain her."

"What happened to her? " I asked.

"Oh, one of the men was attached to the British South African Police and he eventually managed to hand her over to the authorities at Salisbury I believe, but luckily that did not concern me. I had to get another train down here to Beira. So this is a bit of déja vue you might say.

"Come to think of it" - he looked round at the shabby upholstery and dingy paint work - "It could have been this very train. I was pretty glad to get to Nyasaland at last I can tell you! "

So absorbed had I been in this story, especially the bit about the mad woman, that I was unprepared for a powerful snort of steam which rose high above the train then settled like a fog, obscuring everything. The locomotive erupted into life, a whistle sounded. With a lurch the train slid invisibly out of the station.

What a relief to be on the move again! To catch what breeze there was, sit back and watch the passing scene. We quickly cleared the town and set off across the flood plain. The country being flat, held nothing spectacular, but as this was my first sight of African life as lived by thousands of people, I found it absorbing. Dotting the landscape like mushrooms were villages and settlements of thatched huts set among banana palms, all of them having an air of impermanence about them. Not surprisingly, for the countless small rivers and streams at present making their way sluggishly toward the sea, were in the rainy season, regularly devoured by the Zambezi river, before it emptied itself into the Mozambique Channel further north and flooded the whole area.

We stopped at several wayside halts to deposit or pick up traders laden with goods. Those alighting swiftly hoisted up their head-loads of town goods and set off briskly for some invisible destination in the interior, their forms diminished by the immensity of the plain even before the train set off again.

The torpid afternoon wore away. The sun started to dip with a speed which still surprised me. Very soon there was little daylight left.

When it was quite dark we made our way to the dining car. There were only four other occupants, all men, conversing in what I took to be Portuguese, they greeted us civilly before turning back to their own affairs. The menu gave promise of a splendid meal and Ken took full advantage of it. More to the point as far as I was concerned, a plentiful array of bottled fruit juices was also on offer. After the meal was over we sat on a while. One or two more travellers drifted in, we had desultory conversations with the English speakers.

When we returned to our compartment we found the seats extended into beds and made up with sheets and pillows - blankets would have been quite superfluous - and with mosquito nets, which decidedly were not. The curtain had been drawn across the window, excluding any breeze. But this was too much. Once we had turned in, with nets securely tucked round us, we pulled the curtain back again. The mesmeric clatter of wheels over un-welded rails made sleep irresistible...

Not an undisturbed sleep however. First a drunk lurching along the corridor on his way back from the bar. Then a series of whistle-stops seemingly in the middle of nowhere, lit by flaring torch brands. The light of which revealed more women trudging to and fro with their loads of firewood and water for the engine. Several years later we were to repeat this journey in reverse. By which time the monster had been replaced by a diesel locomotive which, if less impressive, was less dirty, gave a smoother ride, and above all, did the journey in half the time. But what, I wondered, became of the toiling women who had been put out of business?

Later still this route, and the railway in particular, became part of the notorious Beira Corridor, with people living in the vicinity falling victim to FRELIMO guerrillas during Mozambique's Independence struggle against the Portuguese. Independence achieved, Mozambique elected to join the British Commonwealth, although it had never been British territory.

At each halt we fell asleep again as soon as the train moved off. I woke finally to the first sign of dawn, the sky streaked with bars of saffron and magenta, early sunlight showing through. I lay watching the psychedelic drama unfold while Ken slept on. Finally he stirred, yawned, and said,

"We should get a glimpse of the Zambezi soon. We cross it at Sena."

Ah the Zambezi. No-one in England could fail to be stirred at mention of this mighty river. Its very name conjured up feats of heroism and daring.

David Livingstone who had discovered it, enduring much danger and hardship as already mentioned, wrote an account of his exploits in, 'Narrative of an Expedition to the Zambezi and its Tributaries,' 1865.

Then there were writers, Rider Haggard, John Buchan and others, whose African novels had caused a generation of children to lose sleep reading in bed by torchlight. No doubt to the detriment of our school work. An incident from one of these books had impressed me deeply. The hero, harassed by hostile hordes bent on his destruction, had won them over by noticing in his diary as he scrawled a last goodbye message, that an eclipse of the moon was due. He turned the occasion to good account by forecasting the phenomenon, ostensibly as a demonstration of his own powers over the elements. I very much hoped that no such display of resourcefulness would be necessary in this era.

The actuality of the river did not disappoint. From a sliver of silver away in the distance, it grew as we approached, to the dimensions of a gigantic snake snugly coiled in the confines of its bed, the railway broadly following its curves at a flood safe distance. At this season the Zambezi, which by the 1950s formed the frontier between Mozambique and Nyasaland, was perhaps half a mile wide and looked placid enough. But during the rains its lower reaches were reputed to expand to a width of five miles; no wonder it had proved such a formidable barrier to the early explorers.

The train slowed and we cruised gently into Sena at the head of the bridge said to be the longest in Africa, if not the world. Sena therefore had strategic importance. More significantly at the time it was virtually the only place of any size we had come across since leaving Beira.

On the platform was the usual crowd of food vendors and curio sellers, people coming and going. Clearly we would be halting for some time. All along the line passengers, including ourselves, climbed stiffly down like prisoners released from detention. We stood, witnessing not only the customary procession of women with their offerings for the hungry, thirsty engine, but also the appearance of a secondary locomotive en route for attachment to the rear of the long train to assist with gradients to come. It passed us on a siding with a lot of steam, the huge driving shaft along its side moving in rhythmic concert with the wheels.

Suddenly there was a shudder along the line, the train jerked forward. Panic. Would we all be left behind? A false alarm, it was merely the newcomer being coupled on out of sight.

Back on board, the sun fully risen, the compartment was very hot. The heat however claimed our attention only fleetingly, for we moved off in the wrong direction. Should we have changed trains? But no, it seemed reverse shunting on land was necessary to get both engines in position to tackle the bridge and the ensuing climb.

After a mile or so a halt, then the train moved forward once more with much huffing and puffing. Amid clouds of steam we dawdled over mud flats, until a change in the tenor of the wheels told us the train had reached the bridge itself. The Zambezi lay a long way below, giving one the sensation of being in a small plane flying far too low, far too slowly, for comfort and safety. A feeling accentuated if one looked out of the window, momentarily in my case, at the rest of the carriages snaking behind us on a bend, its tail out of sight.

Once more the syncopation of the wheels reverted to a more solid sound, and we knew the river was behind us. The bridge receded and we settled down to eat oranges bought at Sena, as the two locomotives attacked the first gradient.

The morning wore on. Water to the wash basin had given out, the efforts of the head-loaded women at Sena notwithstanding; luckily the restaurant car still had a good supply of fruit juice.

We reached Port Herald, the point of entry to Nyasaland, and I knew I should feel excited. But in truth, what with the heat, dust and grime, it was difficult to feel anything at all. However British customs officers came on board, welcomed us and stamped our passports, so there was in fact a sense of being on home territory.

After Port Herald the gradients were more pronounced, both engines laboured now, the going correspondingly slow. We crossed the Shiré river at some stage, which again caused me to think of Livingstone and his travail at this point. Once more there were wayside halts, local people with their loads took short or longer rides.

Now the elevated country was well wooded, beautiful with the hills and valleys that formed part of the Shiré Highlands; somewhere away in the distance, sensed rather than seen, the fabled Mlangé Plateau reared up to a height of some 10,000 feet.

Finally, in late afternoon, twenty-four hours after leaving Beira, tired, with parched bodies, dirty, gritty eyed, we reached our destination at last.

CHAPTER 5

AT BLANTYRE [1]

"Blantyre is a charming spot in the heart of the Shiré Highlands. It consist of a series of houses in the form of a rectangle, most admirably built of sun dried bricks, with sawn-wood joists, and very neat thatches. The foundations of the houses are raised some four or five feet above the surrounding ground, and the broad verandahs are paved with burnt bricks. The interior of the square is a very prettily laid out garden, irrigated by water channels brought from a distant brook. One side of the rectangle is open and on this side was the site now occupied by the magnificent brick church, designed and built by the Rev. Clement Scott. ... Nearby at Mandala stands a fine house in which live Messrs John and Fred Moir - the joint managers of the African Lakes Company - and their wives."

These words are not mine. They were written by Captain Lugard, 1858-1945, some sixty years before our arrival.[2] Captain Lugard was among the foremost of my heroes, being not only a man of action, but of passion as well. A professional soldier from his youth, he had served with distinction in India, Burma and other places. He was regarded as a confirmed bachelor and something of a misogynist. Until 1886 that is, when stationed in Lucknow, he fell hopelessly in love with a young and beautiful divorcée. For a short time he blissfully enjoyed her favours, rather to the detriment of his army career which hitherto had been his whole life. Useless for his friends to point out the effect that such an alliance would have on that career - being involved in a divorce - even if one were the innocent party - warranted instant dismissal, not to mention social ostracism. Useless too to point out that the woman was unworthy of such a sacrifice. No doubt the friends did both, but such was the strength of Lugard's passion, he paid no heed. The whole regiment must have been relieved therefore, when he and his troops were despatched to deal with yet another skirmish in Burma.
On his return to India however, finding his beloved had left for England, his feelings undimmed, he sought, and obtained, home leave and followed her. One can only guess at his state of mind during the long and arduous voyage.
On arrival at last he lost no time in making his way to London, to seek her out with the intention of throwing himself at her feet and declaring his love. Brushing past a timid housemaid who told him her mistress was 'not at home', he charged upstairs. to her bedroom. Only to surprise her inflagrenté with another man.

For a time those close to him feared for his reason. At last they persuaded him that a change of scene would be beneficial. In his autobiography he says merely

---

[1] Named after the Scottish birthplace of David Livingstone.
[2] See Frederick Dealty Lugard, 'The Rise Of Our East African Empire.' published 1893.

that his health had been impaired by the rigours of active service in India, but on setting out to sea once more, he privately admitted to intimates that his purpose was to lay down his life in some noble cause.

At this time the British Empire 'on which the sun never set', could not have been short of such causes, or of places in which to carry out the intention. He could take his pick, and was not long in making a choice. It was at Gibraltar that he heard first hand of the ravages of the slave trade on the natives of Central Africa, and realised at once that here lay his destiny. Hence his protracted arrival in Blantyre in 1888.

From Blantyre he proceeded upcountry, by boat on Lake Nyasa - there being no roads - to Karonga at the Northern tip - which by lucky chance was the very place for which we ourselves were bound.

At Karonga after weeks of skirmishes between the British garrison and the Arab slavers, Lugard was badly wounded. Fortunately by this time thoughts of suicide had faded and he fought hard to recover, and went on to have a long and illustrious career. There is no doubt it was largely due to him and his compatriots that slavery in Nyasaland was checked and finally stamped out, with the formation of the Protectorate in the 1890s.

How could one fail to be inspired by such a man? How could one not be excited at the prospect of following in his footsteps?

EXTRACT FROM CAPTAIN LUGARD'S OBITUARY, 14th edition Encyclopaedia Britannica. (Possibly taken from The Times April 1945.)

"Frederick John Dealtry Lugard, Baron Lugard of Abinger, born 1858, administrator who played a major part in Britain's colonial history between 1888 and 1945, serving in East Africa, West Africa and Hong Kong. Became Governor of Nigeria 1912-19. Knighted in 1901 and raised to the peerage in 1928." (Previously served in Afghanistan, Sudan and Burma.)

"An officer with a promising career ahead of him in British India, he experienced a catastrophic love affair with a married woman. Highly strung and undermined by Burma fever, he sought oblivion by following the explorer David Livingstone's lead in fighting Arab slavers in eastern Africa. In 1888 he was severely wounded while leading an attack upon a slaver's stockade near Lake Nyasa. But he had found his life's work in service for Africa and for Britain - work that he saw as having a mutually beneficial purpose..."

Ryalls Hotel in Blantyre in which we were to stay a few days before proceeding upcountry, was another notable name to me because of Ken's fond memories of visits to it during his first tour. The first night I spent there however passed in total oblivion.

We had been met off the train by Ken's friend Arthur Tomes, who had driven us from Limbé the railhead, to his house on the outskirts of town. Arthur and his wife Billie, had befriended Ken on his first arrival in the country when he spent some time in the South undergoing training. Kindred spirits from the start, they had been his salvation, generating sanity-saving hilarity in circumstances so dire -

heat, flies, isolation and sickness - as to bring on madness or chronic alcoholism. I missed meeting Billie on this occasion as she had preceded Arthur on home leave, but we met later and formed a friendship which endures to the present day.

Meanwhile Arthur gave us baths and a sketchy supper, amid familiar signs of packing, as he too prepared to leave. Afterwards I drowsed while he and Ken talked endlessly, catching up with news and gossip, rousing myself only superficially when he drove us to the hotel.

In the morning, as on board ship, we were woken in the most civilised manner by a discreet tap on the door and a servant bearing a tray of tea. It was delightful to lie back relishing the lack of motion of train or boat, and know that, for a few days at least, we would not be going anywhere. Our room gave on to a common verandah running the length of a long, single storey building. Purple bouganvillea trailed over the balustrade, beyond it was a garden fresh with flowers and shrubs, with the glimpse of a flight of steps leading up to a road. Decidedly things were looking up, another interlude of lotus eating perhaps.

Not for Ken though. Over a leisurely breakfast in a dining room appointed in true colonial style, with sumptuous food on hand for anyone able to enjoy it, he said, "I've got a lot to do today. You'll be alright here on your own won't you? Take it easy. It'll do you good to rest for a bit."

It was a question which would become quite rhetorical over the years.

"First of all, he went on, "I must pick up my van from Arthur. He's been looking after it. Using it as well no doubt, so it will need servicing. I must buy a few spares as well before we head north. Then there are various customs formalities. Also I must go and report to the Agricultural Department's headquarters in Zomba. But that can wait till tomorrow."

He left. I found it pleasant to have nothing more strenuous to do than decide whether to sit in the lounge with its potted palms and elderly magazines, or in the garden with an iced drink at hand.. Either option commanded a good view of the passing scene, but I chose the latter for the air was still fresh and cool, and the trees shady.

It was immediately apparent to me why Ken had found the place so congenial. As I soon realised Ryalls was the epicentre of Blantyre, and therefore of the whole country, the place to which ninety nine percent of the expatriate population of Nyasaland gravitated at some time or other. People based in the town used it as a club, visiting officials stayed there as a matter of course, as did people like ourselves in transit to and from leave. Others based on outstations in the region cheerfully drove a hundred miles or so over earth roads to enjoy a social weekend there.

By lunchtime I had struck up several acquaintanceships, all of them men, who clearly felt it their bounden duty to alleviate the loneliness of an unaccompanied female. Disquietingly, those who knew the country registered dismay at hearing we were destined for Karonga, though they did not specify why.

Next day Ken set off for Zomba, the administrative capital of the country some

30 miles away. Situated at the foot of the mountain from which it took its name, it was reputed to be a beautiful town.

"I would take you along, he said, "But there's bound to be a lot of hanging about in offices, and there's nowhere for you to wait in comfort. I hope to see Dick Kettlewell at the Agricultural headquarters, he's the Director now, in over-all charge. He was formerly Provincial Agricultural Officer for the North - well, I've told you that already. He knows me, and will understand why it's important for me to go back to Karonga and Misuku, to continue the work already begun. But I expect he's away a lot, or has meetings to attend, or simply be too busy to see anyone. Then things could be a bit rough."

By this time I had realised two things. Firstly, contrary to my assumption that Ken would return automatically to his previous work, such were the vagaries of officialdom, he could just as likely be posted somewhere quite different. To some fetid swamp on the Lower River perhaps, or else to what would for him be nearly as bad, a semi suburban station attached to one of the townships. Secondly I knew that Dick Kettlewell, of whom I had heard a great deal, held the key to our future.

Unlike some PAOs, Dick had spent much of his time in the North getting out and about, familiarising himself with the difficulties peculiar to the region and supporting his field officers up to the hilt, Ken among them. A meeting with him therefore, was crucial.

Left to myself again, further restored by a good night's sleep, I decided to go out and explore the town. That it would be vastly different from the Blantyre of Captain Lugard's day was only to be expected. Although it was said that hyenas, and even the occasional lion, could still be seen strolling the streets after dark, scavenging scraps left by daytime food stalls.

The road was broad and lined with flowering trees, their foliage quivering in the morning breeze, cast dappled shade on the people below. Apart from shops there were traders whose wares spilled out on to the road, which did not appear to matter as there was little traffic. Customers gathered round haggling, arguing with much banter. Groups of old men sat apart in quieter spots gossiping, women with babies on their backs, and head-loads of various kinds, threaded their way between. As in South Africa an exuberance of colour predominated.

Suddenly there was a church which might have been, but probably was not, the 'magnificent brick built church designed by the Rev Clement Scott.' of which Captain Lugard had written, and marvelled again at the faith and determination of those early disseminators of the Christian religion. Of the 'fine house in which lived Messrs John and Fred Moir of the African Lakes Company', there was no sign. Perhaps it had suffered the ravages of time, or perhaps I was in the wrong area. I was most happy however, to see that the name 'Mandala', also mentioned by Lord Lugard, had survived. The word meant spectacles. Had one of the Moir brothers been short sighted? c/f Mandala in Buddhism a circle; also used in the psychology of Jung to indicate wholeness. Be that as it may, there it was, writ large over a large glass-fronted emporium which would have looked quite at home in London's West End. Below the name in slightly smaller letters was the legend 'African Lakes Company'.

The town also boasted two dress shops, a Bata shoe store, a hairdressing salon, a branch of Barclays Dominion, Colonial and Overseas Bank, and a commercial motor repair garage. There were also a good many Indian stores with cavernous interiors, the contents of which could only be guessed at.

All in all despite the heat, for the morning was by now advanced, I quite agreed with Lugard's assessment that, indeed "Blantyre in the heart of the Shiré Highlands was a charming spot."

Afternoon tea at Ryalls was a ritual harking back to a more gracious era. Little tables dotted about the garden were set with eye-searing white table-cloths, starched napkins, elegant crockery and silver ware. Waiters, also in white, hovered with plates of tiny sandwiches or sugary cakes. A far cry from the austerity of 1950s England. I was enjoying this pleasurable occasion, sipping tea and chatting to nearby acquaintances, when Ken returned from Zomba. I poured him tea and cautiously, for he looked hot and irritable, asked how he had got on. He finished the cup before replying.

"Oh, alright I suppose. I had to go to Admin first to sort out my pay and allowances and various other things. I was right about the hanging about. Good job you didn't come."

By now I was becoming familiar with Ken's aversion to bureaucracy.

"Then I went to the Agricultural. Department, but Dick wasn't there. Gone on home leave apparently. So I had to see some stuffed shirt who'd never heard of me and looked the type who'd never ventured off the tarmac of Zomba. But he got out my file. And luckily, thank God, Dick had left a note authorising my return to the North."

Though The North was but a terrifying abstraction to me as yet, I knew it was where Ken wished to be, and gave a sigh of relief.

"So it's alright then?

"Should be. But he didn't specify exact details. So this chap told me to report to the Provincial Agric Officer at Mzimba - that's the H/Q of the Northern Province. The chances are I'll be sent back to Karonga. You'll like it there.."

Recalling the reactions of my new acquaintances at mention of this place, I was not so sure. But I thought of Captain Lugard and secure in the knowledge that at least there would be no marauding Arab slavers to contend with, felt better.

Over dinner that night, refreshed and revived, Ken announced,

"We'll leave early the day after tomorrow, so in the morning you must go and buy provisions. There aren't many decent shops in the North." (a mastery of understatement as I found out later.) "So make out a list of stuff to last us for three months. Go to Mandala, they sell just about everything. Oh, and be sure to include some seeds, got to get a garden going"

Accordingly I set out for Mandala next morning before the sun was too hot, the pleasurable link with history somewhat dimmed by the responsibility of my task.

True I had made a list, but never having lived more than five minutes away from the village shop where any omission could be rectified in a jiffy, it was of very little use. Moreover in the months after our marriage, my attempts at housekeeping in England had been sketchy in the extreme, so that even to plan three weeks ahead would have taxed me to the limit. As for three months... It began to look as if we would be experiencing severe privations, starvation even, because of my incompetence. Fortunately Ken had promised to join me after going to the bank and I decided to leave most of it to him.

Meanwhile I spent the time happily buying seeds. There was no lack of choice. Morning Glories, marigolds, cannas, gerbera and a host of others, would according to the packets, ensure our garden becoming a veritable Chelsea Flower Show of colour. To be on the safe side I bought several varieties of each kind and felt pretty pleased with myself. Some four months and circa 600 miles later, Ken was less pleased when it transpired that what he had in mind was vegetable seeds.

On this day however, he came soon enough and began ordering bulk supplies of flour, sugar, tins of dried milk, butter, jam, meat, as well as things hitherto available to me at the drop of a hat and therefore taken entirely for granted. Indeed I was glad he was on hand, and made notes for future reference.

CHAPTER 6

UP COUNTRY

Another matter claiming Ken's attention during these days in Blantyre had been to try and trace his former cook/houseboy John. John was of the Yau tribe local to the South, who had made his way to the North and worked satisfactorily for Ken for some years in Karonga. In the course of his journey to Blantyre, as he went on leave Ken had dropped him off near his home, retaining him on half pay and the promise of his job back later if he wished. However, in spite of general enquiries at the hotel and one or two places round about, of John there was no sign.

"He most likely took another job and left the area, said Ken, "We'll have to take on someone else. It's not so easy to get trained staff in the North."

Another understatement, as I soon discovered.

There was no shortage of hopefuls hanging about the hotel. All of them claimed to be experienced; to prove it some of them had work books with entries signed by erstwhile employers, describing their previous jobs.

Until that moment servants had figured in my life not at all and once more I left the matter to Ken. He settled on one, James, not much more than a boy really, who spoke reasonable English, and claimed he could cook, clean the house, and in short, 'do everything.' Despite his youthful appearance his work book had one or two entries backing up his claim. Starting as a kitchen boy and working his way up, he had come by good references. I was impressed by this, and decidedly dashed when one of the few women I had met assured me that most of the entries in the work books were forged. Whether this was true or not I never discovered for we never afterwards lived in an area where work books were current. Ken told James of our destination, and asked if he were willing to travel that far. He said he was, a decision he was to regret bitterly.

We were to make an Early Start next morning. - the capital letters warranted by the significance the phrase came to assume in our lives over the next few years. To me at that time, it meant something like 7AM, to Ken it meant dawn, or sooner. Accordingly, with the help of a hotel porter, he had loaded up the van the night before and what with the two trunks, suitcases, detritus of the journey so far, and the bulk supplies delivered by Mandala, it was soon full to overflowing.

Even in pre-dawn darkness next day morning tea was forthcoming; by the time we were dressed, breakfast with the usual impeccable service was already under way in the dining room. We ate hastily then made last minute preparations for the journey. I fearing this would be the last of the lotus eating for some time, followed Ken outside. He was making last minute adjustments to the stowage and looking out for James who had promised to meet us in the hotel forecourt. A chilly dawn was breaking, I heard Ken address a shadowy figure,

"Good, there you are. Where's your katundu?"(luggage)

27

The figure shrank back in alarm, it seemed we had almost kidnapped the night watchman hovering in hope of a tip. Fortunately at this point another form loomed and James was identified. His katundu consisted of a cloth bundle securely knotted. He wedged it in among the rest of the stuff in the van, then climbed up after it, finding a space for himself with difficulty.

It was not entirely accurate to say we would be following in Captain Lugard's footsteps as we set off that morning. For he had travelled to Karonga by the only means possible at the time, namely on the waters of Lake Nyasa. For not only were roads nonexistent, but the Interior was a cauldron of tribes warring with the slavers, with other tribes and occasionally with Europeans.

Which was why Lugard and his companions had gone up on the SS Ilala, reputed to be the first steamer on lake water on the whole of the African continent. Lugard writes,

"The little steamer the Ilala was brought out by Mr E D Young RN in 1875. It was about 65feet in length and its carrying capacity was some 3tons."
He goes on,
"The hold was full of (gun)powder, rifles and other necessaries and all the available deck space was taken up with firewood for the engine. In addition to which...we numbered eighteen white men...several native servants and others, and the native crew of the steamer; therefore there was hardly standing room on board."

Here one is tempted to say it was lucky no Health and Safety Officer was around to witness their departure, or any other official to look out for the Plimsoll Line which had been instituted in 1876, and point out the likely consequence should a spark from the engine come in contact with the contents of the hold...

By the 1950s the long, thin country of Nyasaland was served by a network of minor roads and tracks, and a major land route running almost its entire length, from Blantyre in the south to the frontier post of Fort Hill in the north, thence into Tanganyika. It was referred to by us and others, not entirely accurately, as The Great North Road. I remarked to Ken that with only one road to choose from we could hardly lose our way. He laughed and replied that would be the least of our problems. Which left me wondering apprehensively what these might be. Lion? Elephant? Surely not hostile hordes as in Lugard's day? This last was an attempt at a feeble joke, for in truth, now that it came to it I was nervous at the prospect of venturing so far from civilisation as I knew it.

"Don't be silly. he said, "The state of the road is quite enough to contend with. We haven't seen much rain since we arrived, but we're still in the middle of the wet season. The surface can turn from dust to mud in an instant. Culverts get washed out, bridges go occasionally, and fissures occur frequently after flooding.

Then there's the van itself. Should be alright now as it's just been serviced. But if a hidden boulder should hit the sump..." Seeing my expression, he added, "Don't worry though, there's always someone around to help out, the locals are very friendly."

So much for hostile hordes. Even so, as we proceeded northward, even without floods or breakdowns, the road surface was such that he might well have added miscarriage to the list of possible disasters.

Nothing of this was apparent however on the first stretch of our 500mile journey. The morning was still fresh and cool as we set off, so that it was pleasant to bowl along the tarmac road linking Blantyre with Zomba. Altitude and plentiful rainfall ensured that the countryside was green and fecund, quite able to support the many small villages along the way. Villages that were just coming to life, with chickens scratching in the dust, women crouching over some task. Here and there a man still wrapped in his sleeping blanket stretched and yawned in preparation for the day. From the open door at the back of the van, James exchanged pleasantries with all and sundry whenever we slowed down.

When we reached its outskirts Zomba was also waking to the day. I had the impression of more homesteads and more trees, with spacious houses dotted among them. This was all I saw, as the road soon veered away from the town and suddenly, without warning, we plunged into a ploughed furrow. Ken said matter of factly,

"Well, that's the last of the tarmac for some time."

So it proved. Apart from a few miles in Lilongwe, as I found out, we would not see tarred roads again for many a long day. Earth roads, dusty or muddy according to the season, became the norm in the ensuing months and years, with memories of smooth roads fading, as in a dream..

We jolted on, speed much reduced, encountering few vehicles, enveloped in a cloud of dust whenever we did. Just as we ourselves choked other travellers, especially the unfortunates trudging the roadside, most of them women with heavy loads on their heads.

Now the villages were full of life. Near naked children played in the compounds of thatched huts, women pounded maize in pairs with mortar and pestle. Here and there a tailor treddled his sewing machine in the shade of a tree.

The line of the hills away in the distance receded as we made our way down to the Shiré River and the Liwondé ferry. I had no conception of what this crossing might be like, or how wide the river. If my mind had formed a conscious image the scene would have been on the lines of a Mississipi showboat, with shades of Mark Twain.

The reality was altogether different. The Shiré here was roughly the width of the Thames at Richmond, and the ferry a flat bedded barge hauled manually across by convicts hauling overhand on a cable fixed to both banks. Whether the criminal fraternity of the country in general was possessed of superior physique, or whether this section of it had benefited from the fresh air and exercise, is a moot point; suffice it to say, that as we waited our turn on the near bank, they presented a magnificent spectacle. Bare to the waist, they chanted a deep refrain rhythmically as the barge slewed across flowing water. The bank attained, the mooring secured, they broke ranks and flung themselves down in the shade, laughing and talking, waiting for the barge to be re-loaded with vehicles for the return journey.

From the Shiré the road took a north/westerly direction through scrubby bush country, less populous, until we reached Balaka, a small and isolated Government outstation where, by coincidence, Billie and Arthur Tomes had once had the misfortune to be posted. Hot and dry, with few if any amenities, its only redeeming feature was its position as terminus of the railway from the south, so that one could, in theory at least, hop on a train for a few days in Blantyre whenever insanity threatened.

A few miles later we came to a disinfectant checkpoint in the form of a long, corrugated shed resembling an aircraft hangar, through which vehicles must drive to be sprayed against the sleeping sickness carried by the tsetse fly. It was said that some travellers cursed the procedure as an unnecessary delay and circumvented it by blazing a trail through the bush. Captain Lugard and his compatriots would have been only too thankful for anything that could relieve them of what was a keen danger to them.

As was malaria, thought at the time to be caused by a miasma, literally 'bad air', hence the name. Mosquitos were a deadly trial in the 19th century; it would be some years before their menace was recognised and a prophylactic found.

As we emerged from the shed into sunlight once more, I wondered idly why members of our own generation, myself included, should feel superior in this knowledge to the stalwarts of those days, when we ourselves could claim no credit for the discovery.

We jolted along in heat and dust and I reflected ruefully that at least Lugard and his men had been spared bumpy roads on their journey north. Overcrowded, overloaded and hazardous as the Ilala undoubtedly was, it afforded the opportunity of admiring the passing scene from the smooth waters of the lake. And for the Europeans to indulge in their favourite sport of shooting crocodiles, and going ashore in the evening to 'bag something for the pot'.

Ken broke in on these musings,

"We'll be coming to Dedza pretty soon."

"Is there a hotel?" I asked hopefully, visualising a long drink and a bathroom. He laughed,

"Nothing like that I'm afraid. It's only a small settlement Not much more than the Boma really, with houses for Government staff, the DC, ADC, and their clerks, and perhaps a PWD."

"Boma?" I queried.

"That's the name for the District Commissioner's headquarters. Formerly it denoted the stockade of a chief, or a cattle kraal, Nowadays the Boma, with a capital B, is the hub of all Government stations, with the DC heading local administration. It's fair to say that without the DCs and ADCs, the country would probably grind to a halt. The same system more or less applies all over the Empire I shouldn't wonder."

I was getting confused with initials, and in fact only gradually over time, came to understand the whole picture of an administrative structure by which large numbers of people could be governed by very few.

"More to the point just now, Ken continued, " I knew an ADC in Karonga who was later posted to Dedza. He'll surely give us lunch if he's still there. We'll call in and see."

As Ken had indicated, Dedza was merely a group of offices, above one of which - the Boma presumably, fluttered the Union Jack. One or two European houses interspersed with a number of thatched huts, were set with pleasing irregularity among trees, bluegums mostly. I was reminded of an English clump village set round a village green - a space of beaten earth in this case; a church spire would not have seemed out of place. Further off the land reverted to bush, at the edge of which small boys languidly tended cattle.

Ken knocked on the open door of the Boma and went in. The incumbent was not his former colleague, we were told that he was on leave. No matter, the stranger in charge said he would be happy to give us lunch. He called a uniformed African messenger to go to his house and tell the cook to expect two visitors.

I later found that DC's houses varied in size and splendour according to the size of the administrative area of responsibility. This one was quite small, sparsely furnished, but cool and our requirements were easily satisfied.

This was my first experience of the casual hospitality meted out to total strangers and to travellers one would most likely never see again, that obtained all over the country. Ken having grown used to it, took it for granted, and said that everyone responded in kind. I found it very encouraging. Especially as in this case, our host offered us a bed for the night as well. But Ken explained we must push on to Lilongwe, in order to reach Mzimba in good time the following day. After a good lunch therefore we gave our goodbyes and thanks, and started off again.

The rest of the journey took us through nondescript country, was without incident and we reached our destination in an unexpected shower of golden rain against a sunset sky.

Lilongwe's only hotel was as comfortable as Ryalls, though not so big. In fact we saw little of it on this occasion and I registered merely a handsome dining room and a comfortable bed. Subsequently I came to know it rather too well.

Sleep came quickly but almost immediately I woke up screaming. A rattlesnake reared up at the foot of the bed. Came paralysingly closer, closer... Then snapped its jaw with a tremendous crash. I woke up terrified. Ken spoke soothingly, got out of his single bed and into mine and comforted me. Gradually the snake resolved itself into the branching bentwood hatstand in the corner of the room. The rattling sound was a shutter flapping in high wind, the crash of jaws a thunderclap.

We lay in each other's arms as the tropical storm rumbled on, sometimes faintly, sometimes with lightning and thunder assaulting the senses simultaneously. It subsided toward dawn; we both slept through the morning tea ritual. Waking later to a brilliant morning, the only reminders of the storm were the dripping tendrils of bouganvillea trailing across the window and the freshness of the garden beyond. For once an early start was not called for.

As Ken had already mentioned, Lilongwe was the administrative headquarters and principle town of the Central Province. It was smaller than Blantyre or Zomba, but boasted all the amenities and institutions needed to support, satisfy and amuse the expatriate British community. Which is to say, there were one or two European shops, a Club where numerous cultural, sporting and social activities abounded, with tennis courts, cricket pitch and a golf course. There was a school for primary children, and African and European hospitals - the latter the only one in either of the Central or Northern Provinces. Never mind that it was some 450miles from where we would be living, it was here in Lilongwe that our baby would be born. Obviously it was necessary to pay it a visit.

Unlike the doctor on board ship, this one was brisk, kindly, and overworked. Not because the white population was unduly sickly, but because the larger African hospital nearby for which he was also responsible, took up most of his time.

"How do you feel?" he asked me.

Making the most of rare medical attention, I said firmly,

"I feel sick. All the time. Not just in the morning, but all day, every day. And if I wake up in the night."

It was no exaggeration. I could not eat, I had lost weight and my hope that the nausea would disappear once we reached dry land had not been fulfilled. The doctor was sympathetic but not unduly concerned. Once more hopes of a miracle cure faded as he said,

"Ah well, it takes some women that way. It usually goes off after a few months. I'll give you a thorough examination... Then, "Good, good, everything quite normal. But you must try to get some food down. Take plenty of fluids and come and see me every month."

Ken explained that we would be living in the far North, the doctor said,

"Well I'm sure there's a doctor in Karonga."

At which Ken looked doubtful and I thought privately that even if there were not, the effects of the journey on such roads would cancel out any benefit that a medical consultation might afford.

"Now, when did you say the baby was due?"

"Er..."

But what with the frenetic activity of packing up to leave, the trauma of leaving home and loved ones and friends seemingly so long ago, and the rigours of the voyage, I could give him but a hazy approximation. He sighed and said,

"From my examination I'd say you are about three months into the pregnancy." He made a few notes on a pad, "That would put the birth around the end of June. Now go and give the details to Matron and she'll book you in for that period."

It was after 10 o'clock when we left Lilongwe, there was no time to be lost if we were to arrive in Mzimba in time for Ken to see the Provincial Agricultural Officer in Mzimba, before he left his office, as he hoped.

In the back of the van, James had rearranged the luggage to suit himself, regardless of the fact that at least one suitcase would topple on to our heads should we need to make an emergency stop.

We very soon came to the end of Lilongwe's only tarred road and rejoined the earth one of the previous day. The surface was not noticeably different except that at intervals wide stretches had been graded and smoothed by the Public Works Department and had gangs of workmen out who saluted us whenever we came across them. Traffic became more sporadic as we proceeded northwards. Which was just as well for the road narrowed, and was severely cambered to ditches at either edge so that drivers, Ken among them, tended to hold to the middle, praying not to meet another vehicle head on. Fortunately there were no sharp bends.

The rain came without warning, the real rain of Africa of which Ken had spoken so graphically in England. It pounded the roof of the van and obscured the windows. In an instant dust was churned to mud, the road became a quagmire. Ken ploughed on - a mistake. We skidded to one side and slid half into a ditch now running with water.

There was nothing to be done but sit it out and wait. Drops penetrated the cab, water dripped down necks, arms and legs, we mopped ourselves up ineffectually with our handkerchiefs. This went on for about half an hour, then the leaden sky lifted, the rain stopped, the sun regained its strength again. It took another half hour of Ken's and James' efforts get us on the road again.

Cautiously we moved off, only to be halted again a few miles further on. Here was no road at all, in its place a fast flowing river - the run off from saturated hills on either hand. Again we waited, so far we had covered only 30miles or so, Mzimba was still a long way off. After this flash flood had subsided however, things improved, there was no more rain and the surface quickly dried out. We pressed on, meeting virtually no other traffic, riding out the punishment of corrugations as dust gradually replaced mud once more.

At some unknown stage we crossed into the Northern Province and went on without further delay, to reach Mzimba in late afternoon.

Mzimba was the Provincial H/Q of the North, as Lilongwe was to the Central, but there any resemblance ended. Ken had warned me there would be no more hotels, henceforth we must stay in Government rest-houses.

"Although it's the main town of the Province, it's quite small, he said, "Mostly it's taken up with administrative and departmental offices. The Provincial Officer is in over all charge, then there's his ADC, and other Provincial Heads. It's the Provincial Agricultural Officer I'm hoping to see, as I told you. There are staff houses as well of course. Most of the officers are married, some have children as well, but they are mostly away at boarding school. Then there are a couple of Indian stores that sell most things. And a big Public Works Department depot. That's about all really."

"No restaurant? I queried, No club?"

Oh, naturally there's a club. But no restaurant, nothing like that."

We drove along the only street - no tarmac. Ken said,

"I'll drop you off at the rest-house, then go and see if the PAO is still at his desk. He might be, although it's a bit late,"

Rest-houses were, as I came to find, built to a general pattern, with a front verandah (khondé) furnished with so-called easy chairs of wood and hide. The khondé led through to a communal sitting/dining room flanked by a bedroom on each side. There was also a basic bathroom. The kitchen, indiscernible at first, was a rectangular hut out at the back where a cook, assisted by many hangers on, cooked the food provided by travellers themselves.

Rest-houses were staffed by Africans, but often supervised by volunteer wives of Government officers, who had the unenviable, unpaid, unsung task of waging war with cockroaches, finding reliable staff and in short, conducting a constant battle to maintain an acceptable standard of hygiene and comfort.

Our room was spartan, with two iron framed single beds and minimum furniture. I called James to bring tea. As dusk threatened imminent darkness I groped unsuccessfully for a light switch; as I did so there was a knock at the door and James came in with an oil lamp. I drank my tea thoughtfully, realising that, like tarmac, electricity was now a thing of the past.

Ken came back having caught the PAO just as he was leaving his office. He said, "That was lucky. He hadn't time to talk just then, but he's invited us to supper at his house. I've told you about him, he's a good type, gets about the District unlike some. He even came up to see me one time in Misuku, and I showed him round. You'll like him."

Irritably I thought this unlikely. The invitation dismayed me, for one way and another - the hospital visit, the atrocious journey and general malaise - it had been a trying day, and a meeting with Ken's boss was not a happy prospect. On the other hand neither was the alternative. An evening at the rest-house would entail rummaging in the van, in near darkness, to locate the food box almost certainly buried under everything else. The box would then have to be unloaded to find tinned food to provide some kind of supper: mentally I made a note to have it at the ready on future journeys. In any case however, it seemed we had little choice, the invitation was it seemed more of a summons, an offer we could not refuse.

Robert Smith and his wife Margaret lived in some style as befitted his rank as the head of the Agricultural Department for the Northern Province. A tasteful lounge showed the unmistakable influence of the London Army and Navy Emporium. Especially memorable were the oil lamps which though unremarkable in themselves, were here shrouded with frilly lampshades which caused them to shed pleasing pools of light, Also Robert dispensed drinks from decanters hung with silver necklace name- tags. I wondered dubiously if Ken and I would ever attain such elegance.

Introductions were made, the drinks served, desultory conversation struck up. I was overawed and silent, Ken never a natural purveyor of small talk, our hosts must have found it heavy going. Especially when we moved through to a formal dining room to an excellent supper served by a servant in spotless white kanzu, and I could eat nothing. Ken was appreciative however; he ate heartily and revived accordingly, but my lack of appetite was not unnoticed by Margaret.

When it was over Robert's talk became more business-like. Stirring his coffee briskly, he said,

"By the way Ken, you'll be based at Fort Hill this tour."

There was a hush, I sensed Ken's sudden tension. Then he exclaimed,

"Fort Hill! Why on earth Fort Hill?"

"Well, it makes sense, said Robert equably. "Your work is mainly in the hills, and

it's not too far from Misuku, which is where the development work is."
"But we can't live at Fort Hill. It's a dreadful place, bang in the middle of the
WENELA recruitment compound! There are no other Europeans there, virtually
no one who speaks English. I couldn't leave Enid there - she's pregnant by the way
- while I'm away in the hills." Here Margaret shot Robert an 'I told you so' look.
"Why can't I go back to Karonga as before? Enid would have company there."
He added as if it clinched the matter,
"Andrew and Jess Williamson are there."
Robert said,
"Karonga is Andrew's patch as you know, and so is the lake shore. Yours is
the hill region, you can't cover it as well from Karonga. Besides, there's no
accommodation there."
"What about my old house?"
"Seconded to the Cotton Board. One of their officers is already installed."
Ken was silent. He had anticipated a battle over housing, such matters were
routine, but not over location. The prospect of being sent to Fort Hill had never
even occurred to him. At last he said,
"What about the Misuku house? Why can't we live there? That's where most of
my work is after all."
"That's not a house, it's a mud shack."
"I could work on it." Ken put in swiftly. But Robert went on -
"Misuku is far too remote. Enid's pregnant you say? There's no road, how would
you even get there in the first place?"
"Enid's a very good walker..."
I was startled, not to mention gratified, at this unexpected accolade, the more so
as it seemed likely to be my only qualification likely to come in useful in this new
life. Robert was not impressed; he replied reasonably enough,
"Well, she wouldn't have company there either would she while you were away
on ulendo?" (safari)
"No, but I wouldn't have to be away so much from there, and anyway she could
come with me..."
The argument looked set to run, but Robert fell silent. At last he said,
"Well, you must go to Fort Hill for the time being. After that we'll have to see."
Not surprisingly the evening fell apart after that. We left as soon as decency
allowed, my thanks to Margaret over effusive to cover Ken's perfunctory ones.

For a second night sleep eluded us. At the rest-house the narrow beds did not allow
the comfort of proximity. Separated by more than the three foot space between us,
Ken was isolated in his own Slough of Despond. Across the void I asked,
"Is Fort Hill really as bad as that? And what is WENELA?"
"It's a terrible place, he said, "It's an outpost right on the Northern border with
Rhodesia, largely ignored by the rest of the country. WENELA is an African
labour recruitment organisation. There's a big compound there with an air strip.
Men, teenagers mostly, come from all parts to sign up for three year contracts
to work in the South African gold mines. Mostly village boys who have no idea
what they're letting themselves in for. They're flown out on Dakotas, then housed

in single sex compounds at the other end, and they have to work long hours underground. Partly they do it for status, a rite of passage as it were, but mainly so they can send money back to their people.

They're subject to all manner of exploitation along the line. And there's more trouble even when they're flown back to Fort Hill at the end of it."

"What sort of trouble is that then?"

"The WENELA compound is full of prostitutes and thieves, and swindlers of all kinds, all ready to fleece them of whatever they have. And there are beer stalls, and constant fights and brawls. I couldn't possibly take you to live there."

"But what will you do? You can't disobey orders can you?"

He did not answer for a long time. Then just as I thought he had gone to sleep, he said,

"I know exactly what I'm going to do. But don't think about it now, I'll tell you in the morning as we go along."

With that he got up and pushed his bed next to mine, threw an arm across me and we slept at last.

Next morning found us heading north once more. Traffic, sparse the day before, was now virtually nonexistent. We passed through scattered villages and the few people we came across invariably stopped what they were doing and waved. There was no rain and we were able to give ourselves to the matter in hand. I asked,

"Well what have you decided?"

"That we'll make for Karonga. We'll stay there a while. There or thereabout. If necessary we'll camp at Mpata a few miles out. There's a hut there, not too bad. And when I go on ulendo I'll take you back to Karonga and you can stay with Jess, or the DC, or whoever. Someone will always put you up. When you're feeling stronger you can come with me to Misuku."

This sounded alright, Karonga was the place I had assumed we would be based, though the 'pass the parcel' aspect was not too appealing. I was anxious also at the thought of his flouting official orders.

"But won't you get into trouble? For not going to Fort Hill I mean? Sacked even?"

He gave a short laugh.

"You have to do something dire to get sacked I assure you. Like fiddling the cash, or taking bribes."

"But Robert..."

"Don't worry. It's hard enough for Government to recruit staff in the first place. And getting people to stay is even more difficult. Rather than push them out, the powers that be turn a blind eye. As for Robert, he and Margaret are going on leave as you know... "

Indeed the early part of the disastrous evening had been taken up with their talk of little else.

"So he won't be bothering us. And whoever takes over from him will have far more important things on his mind. It'll be months, if ever, before the new PAO gets to visit the North."

I pondered this, remembered also Ken's account of his interview with the mandarins in Whitehall. Clearly they had not been exactly inundated with applicants wishing to bury themselves in some far flung corner of the British Empire.

Again I had the feeling of being overtaken by events, I knew Ken's mind was made up. Thus it was that, faced later with the choice of keeping to the main road to Fort Hill, or branching off on a minor one leading to Livingstonia Mission and thence to Karonga, he chose the latter, and the die was cast.

The road to Livingstonia was not noticeably wider than a farm track, with barely room enough for vehicles to pass. We met none however, and very few people. As we neared Livingstonia Mission which, Ken said, lay off the track, we began to lose altitude and the heat grew.

Presently we stopped to eat dry sandwiches by a narrow waterfall half hidden in an exuberance of undergrowth and creeper, as it rushed on down to the lake shore far below. The only sounds apart from the water, were the orchestration of cicadas and the buzz of mosquitos.

As we ate I tried unsuccessfully to visualise the lives of the doughty missionaries in the early days.

Livingstonia Mission had been established in the hills in the middle of the nineteenth century after its original site on the lake shore had proved unsuitable. True, the lake was a natural highway, a line of communication with the rest of the country, but not only had the good Scots missionaries shared it with the Arab slavers in their dhows, but with warring tribes in canoes, none of them friendly toward newcomers. Then there was the heat, humidity, and billions of mosquitos which David Livingstone had failed to mention in his religious rallies in Scotland. A goodly number of the faithful left their bones there. Once relocated to its present site however, the Mission flourished. Here the redoubtable Dr Laws and his wife, with other largely forgotten heroes, set about building a hospital and a school for the local people. Later came a splendid cathedral that rivalled, or even surpassed, the 'fine church at Mandala'. Another superb act of faith, or folie de grandeur, according to one's viewpoint. In a landscape of low mud huts, one can only conjecture the reaction of the local people and others who flocked to the Mission, at the sight of a building soaring skyward to unimaginable heights.

Several years later in Misuku I came across a very old man who had spent his youth at Livingstonia. He told me,

"Before I came to that place, I worshipped the sprits of the ancestors in the forest. But there I heard about God."

Livingstone is on record as saying wryly, that in all the years of his wanderings and teaching in Africa, he had made only one true convert. Perhaps, indirectly, this old man was the second.

Through the years the Mission had become a centre of excellence for training in practical skills. Bringing me back to the present, Ken said,

"Parents send their children from miles away to the school in the hope they'll become Government clerks, or even teachers. Some do, but the emphasis has always been on the training of artisans. There's a great demand for skilled workers and they can always get jobs. Most of the PWD builders and carpenters are mission trained. Nowadays they teach mechanics as well - that's pretty popular

as you may imagine."
"I'd love to go there, I said, "Can we call in ?"
"Better not. It would make us late getting to Karonga. We must get on, we'll go there another time."

The dirt road was now steep as well as narrow, with a surface of shale and stones. When we came to the Livingstonia Escarpment, about which I had heard much from Ken, the land fell away sharply to reveal the first of a series of hairpin bends, twenty-three in all. Some were so tight, and the track so narrow, it was not possible to get the truck round in one operation, so that a driver must reverse and try again. James and I got out to walk on down and round, skidding on scree, sliding perilously near the edge with its steep drop. Nor was the sight of an overturned lorry on a bend below particularly reassuring. We caught up with Ken at the bottom; my legs were trembling with nervous exertion, he sought to distract me by saying,
"We should see the Lake pretty soon. Near a point where Livingstone once had his tent ripped by a lion."
I looked round apprehensively. He laughed and added,
"We're unlikely to see one these days."

Unlike the Zambezi, Lake Nyasa had not figured unduly in my youthful imagination. Captain Lugard had regarded it either as a convenient means of travel, or as a troublesome means of access whence the slavers might launch an attack at any time. It was not therefore until Ken's letters, emblazoned with the aforementioned stamps, came dropping through the letterbox of home, that a romantic interest had begun to dawn. Now I was keenly looking forward to seeing it. Alas, the moment of sighting it shimmering in a haze of blue and silver far below, coincided with a nosebleed brought on by loss of altitude, so that I viewed it that first time with blood pouring down my face.
When we reached the lake shore at last the heat hit us like a wall. The lake itself was hidden by the reeds and tall elephant grass that lined the track apparently running parallel to the shore-line. A track now flat and smooth, throwing up alluvial dust that percolated every crevice of the van. We passed through a high concentration of villages, inevitable in such a fertile region, set among bamboos and banana plantations. And, just as Ken had said, the people were friendly, smiling, sending us on our way with salutations. Until the sun which had hung interminably overhead all day, began its hurried descent. Soon we were cocooned in stifling darkness, the world reduced to our wavering headlights, pin-points of stars, the flare of an occasional cooking fire... And in this way, hot, tired, thirsty, bloodstained, we came to Karonga at last.

CHAPTER 7

BUGLES AT DAWN

Hot, humid, remote. Why then did our arrival in Karonga have a feeling of déja vu, almost of homecoming about it? Was it because of Captain Lugard? Hardly. Certainly he had found adventure and purpose there enough to wrench his mind from his own troubles, but clearly he had not been enamoured of the place. Was it because of Ken's letters then? But they had been largely unflattering.

"It's hellish hot here, he had written in letters home, "And everything is pretty basic."

After marriage he had told me more,

"Most people loathe Karonga, and can't get away fast enough. No-one stays long if they have any choice. Well, hardly anyone. But some like it."

"Including you?" I suggested.

"Well, yes, I suppose so. For one thing it's right on the lake, which is wonderful for swimming, or bird watching on the lake shore. For painting too, if one has the time and energy. But of course it depends a lot on who else is stationed there with you. There are only about a dozen Europeans at any one time, so it's important that everyone gets on well. Andrew and Jess have been there for eight years. Well you've met them haven't you? Jess will be a tower of strength to you."

None of this could account for my affinity with the place, a feeling which, though subsequently tried by various vicissitudes and privations, never entirely left me.

The rest-house was similar to the one at Mzimba and, thank God, one of the two rooms was vacant. Ken had previously said airily that if both were occupied, he had a choice of friends we could pitch up on, no problem. But the thought of meeting his colleagues in my bedraggled state was less than appealing.

Since leaving Blantyre the list of the necessities missing from every day life, tarmac roads, shops, telephones, electricity, to name but a few, had grown longer at each stop. Running water and conventional sanitation were the latest casualties. And the need for a bath was paramount. To my relief there was a long, free-standing bath in the bathroom, which James and one of the staff filled with cans of lukewarm water. Ken carried long drinks through and slowly our parched bodies revived.

Afterwards we sat on the khondé which doubled as a dining room, with more drinks, and waited for supper to appear. It consisted of tinned corned-beef accompanied by rice. Frustrated mosquitos pinged against rusting wire gauze, the oil lamp sputtered, adding its own heat to general airlessness.

Our bedroom was even hotter. We lay on regulation cast iron beds with lumpy mattresses, stuffed I learned, with locally grown cotton, not entirely successfully parted from the congenital seed bolls. Each bed was firmly netted in. In Karonga there was no question of tossing nets aside to get more air, the threat of malaria was only too real. Mercifully however, the place was quiet, only the sound of a distant drum, like a heart beat, disturbed the silence.

"A beer drink probably. " Ken said drowsily.

We fell asleep at once but it was to be a short night. All too soon we were woken up by the Last Trump. Naturally this ultimate phenomenon had given no indication of its coming, but a strict religious upbringing ensured that I had no difficulty in recognising it instantly. Its clamour filled the air, assaulted the senses, bombarded the eardrums, cancelled out the universe. I knew without doubt that even now sheep were being sorted from goats, the righteous ascending into Heaven, the unrighteous, myself clearly among them, remaining below to enjoy eternal torment.

Cautiously I opened my eyes. Two things were immediately apparent; one was the eerie light quite in keeping with the occasion, which now filled the room, the other that I had not been widowed by the happening. Ken however was not taking it lying down. He leapt naked from his bed, strode across the room, poured water into a washing basin from an enormous enamel jug on the floor, and proceeded to splash it over himself.

The cacophony stopped abruptly as it had begun but still I lay shaking. At last I whispered,

"But what was it?"

"Reveillé, he replied briefly, then, "Got to go. I'll get James to bring you tea."

"What! Is it morning already?"

But he had gone. I crept to the window and peered through the wire gauze. Some 30yards away was a space of beaten earth like that outside the Boma at Dedza. To one side was a row of wooden offices, in front of which was a squad of African soldiers, very smart, standing to attention. Two of the number were raising the Union Jack atop a tall flag staff, the bugler who had woken us so cruelly, standing to one side. The flag hoisted and saluted, the Askari all turned and marched briskly away in a cloud of dust.

This ritual, and its counterpart at dusk, with the flag lowered to strains of the Last Post, was no idle ceremony, but the summons to work for all Government personnel. No matter what their status, race or creed, they disregarded at their peril. When James - Christian according to his workbook - came in with the tea I observed him closely for signs of agitation, wondering if he too had been shaken. But no. No doubt the occasion was common to all Government stations, young as he was, he would have heard it all before.

When I got out of bed for the second time I found the ewer of water impossible to lift on to the wash stand. So I stood the basin on the floor and tipped water into it, reflecting as I did so that in all probability it would be small details that would trip me up at every hand from now on. I dressed and went out to the back khondé which looked across to the parade ground and the group of buildings seen from our room. Beyond and around were many tall trees, some of them in flower. Half hidden among them were one or two European houses, which as I later learned were the ones allocated to single men.

Already there was a heat haze, the Union Jack hung limply at its mast. Near at hand was the rest-house kitchen whence came sounds of animated conversation, James' voice mingling with the others. On the ground sat several women in colourful cloths, most of them with babies on their backs, or at the breast, and toddlers playing at their feet. They called out when they saw me, I responded by waving a hand then turned to have breakfast.

As I finished eating another dust cloud heralded a small figure on a push bike. As it drew nearer I recognised Jess Williamson whom I had already met, with her husband Andrew, in England. Their home leave had partially overlapped Ken's, and they had given us tea in the caravan in which they were touring, enjoying lush green English countryside by way of a change from the tawny landscape of Karonga's lake shore. Andrew had been Best Man at our wedding, their young son Tom was also present.

Truth to tell, I had not known what to make of Jess, simply because I had never met anyone like her before. In an English setting both she and Andrew stood out. Not only because of their tropical tan, but also for an indefinable aura of being subtly different from the people I was used to. I had been daunted by their erudition, their wide experience of the world. They in turn must have been appalled at my ignorance and unsuitability for the life I was about to embrace, and fearful for Ken.

Nor would this morning encounter do much to correct their first impression, Jess taking in at a glance signs of fatigue and weakness which the short night's sleep had done little to eradicate.

Jess was intellectual by nature, and scientific by training. One of the few women Cambridge graduates of her day, she had taught in England, India and Australia, before going on to Nyasaland in the 1930s to take part in a dietary survey. Which is how she met Andrew, who was engaged on agriculture in the same region. During an outbreak of rabies, a shortage of medical supplies meant they must share a hypodermic syringe with which to vaccinate themselves over the obligatory twelve days. The needle must have been very blunt at the end of it. Perhaps it was her fortitude and toughness that impressed Andrew, at any rate he proposed shortly after, was accepted and they married quite soon.

Such a brief biography can convey little or nothing of Jess' character, of her intense energy and drive, does no justice to her magnanimity and kindness; her inquiring mind enlarged one's own, she instructed unconsciously by example. She was a mine of local information, and a tower of strength to me in those early days in Karonga, just as Ken had foretold. She also had the endearing quality of sometimes being wrong. From the first inauspicious meeting in England, our friendship took root and blossomed. It ended only with her death some forty-five years later.

On this particular morning at the rest-house she listened patiently while I expatiated on my woes, and fears that I would not be able to cope with the practicalities of this new life. Fighting rising panic, I said,

"I mean, well, food for instance. When there are no shops!"

"Yes, it is difficult for newcomers at first," she agreed, "But in Karonga it would be difficult to starve, the land being so fertile."

"But milk, I replied, thinking of my unborn child, "And potatoes..."

Potatoes had been our war time staple, not even rationed, when everything was, so that the prospect of life without them was unthinkable.

"Milk is a problem certainly, she conceded, "Occasionally we get some fresh, well fairly fresh, from the locals, but mainly we rely on tinned milk powder. No potatoes either, but rice is plentiful, cheap too because it's grown here. Fresh vegetables largely have to be grown by ourselves, which is quite difficult in the dry season. On the other hand there's always plenty of fruit, mangos, pawpaw, bananas of course, and tomatoes, all very good. You can get them in the market, and sometimes women bring them round to the door as well. They kill meat here twice a week. Then there are always chickens...

"And it's not quite true to say there are no shops. There are two Indian stores, Andanis and Khaterias, they sell all the basics, including paraffin. We all have paraffin fridges by the way."

She spoke so reasonably, so sensibly, that Karonga began to sound like a cornucopia of plenty. Which of course it was, it was merely a case of readjusting one's perceptions.

"Come to lunch tomorrow, she added, getting up, "About twelve."

When she had gone James informed me a woman outside had corn cobs for sale. I went out prepared to haggle. 'Never pay the asking price' was the general dictum, the new regime must begin. Even so, as Ken came back at this point, I gladly handed the transaction over to him and watched with surprise as it was conducted with banter, even laughter, and the price reduced to about half.

"Jess came to see me, I told him when it was over, "She cycled. In all this heat!"

He did not comment on this, knowing Jess' habits of old, but said,

"I've just come from their place. It's at Baka, a locality about a couple of miles out. Andrew's office is there and they live in a house near it. I used to live in the only other one, the Cloverleaf next door that I thought we'd be going back to. But it's true enough, there's a Cotton Board chap there now. I told Andrew what I thought of that. He said it was all fixed when he got back from leave, and in any case it was only on a temporary basis as the Cotton Board is putting up a new one there. In fact building has started. But that doesn't help us at present, and I think he should move out for us and - "

"Jess has invited us to lunch tomorrow." I put in hastily, not wanting to go over all that again.

"Yes, she told me. I had coffee with them. Then I came back to report to the DC, but he was out." Changing the subject he added, "This afternoon we'll go over to the tennis court. Everyone is sure to be there and you can meet the whole station."

As he left after lunch he urged me to rest,

"I'll be back soon after three, that's the end of the working day. Officially at least"

42

To me it seemed rather a short day until I recalled the early start, designed of
course, to maximise the cool of morning and make the most of the few hours of
daylight remaining in the evening. In actual fact most expatriate officers worked
longer hours I found.

After tea therefore we walked across to the tennis court. It was situated a little
beyond the parade ground, but was completely hidden by tall bamboos which,
Ken said, had been planted as stakes to fence it off, but which had started to
sprout immediately. Once inside the enclosure the sensation was as being in an
airy, quivering bower, wholly delightful, the slender bamboos swaying gently in
an almost imperceptible breeze, their leaves casting a quavering pattern of light
and shade on the ground.

On court an energetic game of doubles was being contested, Andrew and Jess
two of the protagonists. Slightly less energetically urchins acted as ball boys for
pennies. Ken introduced me to two men sitting out. One was a Forestry officer
who first engaged me in conversation. The other was the Veterinary officer, Dick
Isaacs, a New Zealander - the first I had ever met. He asked about our leave and
how we spent our time in England. He had never visited it, he said, but hoped to do
so when his leave came round. In return I asked about his work. He said it would
take a long time to cover all aspects, but one of the most important was dipping
cattle against tics and other parasites, to boost resistance to diseases.

"Cattle are the people's currency, he said, "All important. When a man takes a
wife he must pay the libola - bride price - of so many cows, to the girl's family. If
one of the animals is sickly, or dies soon after, as sometimes happens, there are all
manner of disputes. Cases often go before the DC.

"You would expect the locals to welcome any sort of treatment for their animals,
but in actual fact dipping is unpopular, especially in country districts."

I was more interested in the marriage custom than the dipping, and wished to
know more.

"Isn't it a bit unfair, I ventured, "On poorer people I mean, who haven't many
cows?"

"Yes it's a burden. Rich old men with big cattle kraals often have several wives,
the younger ones must wait until their family can deliver. Still at least it means
marriage is taken seriously."

At this interesting point the game ended, and I did not learn till later that Vet
Officers also had the unenviable job of shooting rabid dogs, mercifully rare,
dissecting them for laboratory examination, and quickly getting suspected contacts
to hospital for injections. Or that they liaised with the Game Wardens responsible
for regulating the killing of lion, leopard and elephant under licence. As opposed
to illegal hunting by villagers who claimed that their cattle, and even their people,
were being preyed on, which indeed was sometimes the case.

The tennis players strolled over to where we were sitting. Andrew renewed our
acquaintanceship with a wave of the hand, then he and Jess left, saying they would
see us next day at noon. The other players introduced themselves. One was Noel
Harvey the ADC, the other an official visitor, a guest of the DC and his wife,

neither of whom were present. I made some excuse for not making up a foursome in the next game. Instead Ken played singles with the Forestry Officer and I had an interesting talk to Noel, and liked him in spite of Ken having told me I would. We strolled back to the rest-house in gathering dusk, to strains of the Last Post.

I was having a bath when Ken came in with a note.
"The DC's back, he said, "He has sent a messenger over with a note inviting us to supper tonight."
I had mixed feelings about this, remembering the evening with the PAO and his wife in Mzimba. But when I voiced my fears, Ken said,
"Oh no, it won't be like that. Although the DC is responsible for administration and civil order and is the most senior officer on the station, he wouldn't interfere in Departmental matters. At least, only if anyone did something illegal, or was in danger in some way. Both rare occurrences."

It was dark when we made our way to the DC's house, so I gained little impression of what it would be like, beyond noting its bulk. Standing black against the sky, large and impressive, it was the first two storey building I had seen since leaving Blantyre.. Sue Maynard, the DC's wife, was also large and impressive. I later got to know her well. Not only was she kind, but resourceful as well. Subsequently I witnessed her breaking up a mob of drunken locals on the lake shore one night, when her husband was away, because the noise was keeping her children awake.
The DC himself at first gave the impression of being less impressive, so that one might think their roles could well have been reversed. But other qualities made up for this as he was fair, genial, and got on well with the local people.
Noel and the official visitor were also present that evening. There was no tension, altogether it was very pleasant. I very much hoped lunch with the Williamsons next day, a Sunday, would prove likewise.

The Agricultural Department station out at Baka comprised a few acres of land for crop trials, two European houses with big gardens, one of them Andrew and Jess' home for several years, and the one next door, the so called Cloverleaf, which Ken regarded as his, but now occupied by the Cotton Board official. In line beyond was a building site that would perhaps, in time become another dwelling. There was also a complex of sheds, and Andrew's office. At the back were brick built, rectangular houses for African staff and a small homestead of huts which had grown up to accommodate their many relatives. As we turned off a dusty road lined with blue-gums on to an even dustier track leading to the houses, I could see a grassy patch and a flower bed with shrubs and climbers. This was Jess' garden.

Inside the house bright rugs were islands of colour on the polished stone floor. Book-shelves lined the walls, above them hung Indian paintings collected by Jess when she was teaching there. A vase of gerbera from the garden, delicate, beautiful, stood on a low table. I complimented Jess on the flowers.
"Ah well, she said, "We're still getting some rain, it's a different story in the dry."
Andrew said,

"Steve should have come to lunch as well, but he's away on ulendo."

Knowing Steve to be the Cotton Board man living in the Cloverleaf, I privately thought this was just as well as Ken might have taken issue with him. Whether Andrew should have fought harder to retain the house for the Agricultural Department as Ken believed, or whether the deal had been struck during his - Andrew's - absence, was a moot point, the outcome was the same.

Andrew, technically Ken's superior officer, had been a wild man in his youth and was still a law unto himself. Which perhaps was why he had not risen further in his career. Infuriating at times, he could be equally kind at others, and was always a staunch friend to us. He it was who had just lent us the then enormous sum of £50 to pay the income tax bill waiting for us on our arrival in Karonga.
Here it should be explained that a 'Pay As You Earn' system of paying tax had not yet found its way to Nyasaland. Salaries were paid in full and the tax clawed back once a year, A tax bill could strike at any time, accompanied by a stern warning of the penalty incurred for late payment. Needless to say, what with delays on the voyage, expenses of the overland journey - only some of which could be reclaimed - the Waterfield coffers were bare by the time we reached Karonga. Not only was Andrew's loan crucial, but he never once reminded us of it, even though it must be admitted, repayment was somewhat tardy. Such friends are rare, their kindness and generosity never forgotten.

Jess dispensed iced lemonade made with local lemons, skilfully steering the conversation away from contentious matters as she did so. I was learning to respect her common sense as well as her erudition, so it was all the more alarming when, by now knowing of the impending enlargement of our family, she listened to Ken's intention of our going to live in the Misuku Hills and expostulated,
"But you can't go and live in Misuku now!"
There was a short silence, then Andrew said,
"What does it matter where they live so long as Ken covers the District and gets the work done?"
She threw him an exasperated glance. Over the years she had accompanied Andrew on ulendo to Misuku, so knew what she was talking about.
"That's all very well. But he can't take Enid there just now. It's a wonderful place, but quite impossible for a pregnant woman. There's no road for a start, she added, unconsciously repeating the PAOs protests. "They would have to walk in, it's at least fifty miles!"
Ken countered with the same arguments he had put to Robert, and got much the same answers. Jess was not impressed,
"There are no other Europeans there either as you know. Supposing Enid needed a doctor?"
"We'd only be there for about three months initially, Ken said, "We'd come back here well before the baby was due."
The conversation went back and forth, Ken could be intractable on occasion, Jess remained unconvinced.

In spite of heat, dust, mosquitos, nausea, and the limitations of the rest-house, the next few days were enjoyable. Ken, blasted out of bed every morning by reveillé, left early for work. I went back to sleep, getting up in leisurely fashion a good deal later. Overtaken by lassitude, and the sense of detachment which sometimes assails women in pregnancy, I spent most of the day lazing about on the khondé. Nor was I lonely. Jess going about her morning activities made a habit of calling, often with gifts of home grown fruit or vegetables. Then the unattached men on the station, known collectively as The Bachelors, although not all of them were, who had come to introduce themselves on my second day, often dropped in to seek female company over a cup of coffee. Ken returned briefly each day for lunch at twelve.

After tea when the day's work was over and the fragile breeze had struck up, everyone converged on the tennis court, there to decide whether to take up the game, or go down to the lake to swim

The lake shore was stranded with fine sand too hot to walk on barefoot. At its hinterland one or two tall trees casting blessed shade, were interspersed with thorny bushes hung with the nests of weaver birds. Butcher birds too were evident, fish eagles hung in the sky.

There were always groups of women at the water's edge drawing water or pounding washing, all the while exchanging badinage with the fishermen offshore in canoes - archetypes of the ones depicted on the stamps, casting their nets in the same manner.

Otherwise the beach quivering in heat, was ours alone. The body delighted in limpid water that caressed the body like silk, the mind was cleansed of care, even of memory. And afterwards to lie in the shade oblivious of time, until the fishermen began hauling in their nets...

Lotus eating with a vengeance.

Naturally it was too good to last. At the end of a week Ken came back from Andrew's office and said,

"I'm going on ulendo to Misuku on Monday. Then seeing my face he added, "Well you knew it had to happen."

"But I'm coming with you, You said I could. You said it would be alright."

"Not this time, he said gently, "You're not strong enough yet. You must build up your strength, it's an arduous journey. Besides, I must see about the house there, make it habitable you know.

"I'll be away about three weeks. You can stay with Jess the first week - Andrew is going on ulendo as well - although not with me. Then you can stay with Sue Maynard. It's all arranged."

The parcel passing had begun.

CHAPTER 8

PASSING THE PARCEL

It goes without saying that in circumstances not of their making, most women would make capital out of the pain of the first parting in their married life, and I was no exception. Yet it must be admitted this one was tempered by the hospitality and kindness I experienced from everyone on the station. Not just from Jess and Sue, but also from the bachelors to a man.

"I've got a spare room. Why don't you come and stay with me?"

"Come and have supper tonight. Or lunch tomorrow."

"Any time you feel like swimming on the lake shore I'll come and pick you up. Or take you to tennis. Or if you just feel like a bit of company..."

It could have been a lot worse.

Out at Baka, installed in Andrew's bedroom, I slept on in the mornings undisturbed by reveillé. The first sounds to reach me were the creak of the hand pumped well that supplied the whole complex with water, and the murmur of voices as Jess instructed the garden boy where to direct cans of water on to thirsty plants outside the window. When I finally appeared for breakfast she had already been busy for at least two hours.

On the face of it there was nothing much for a woman to do left on her own out at Baka, yet Jess was never idle, never bored. After breakfast there were the household chores to organise. Next, a knot of local people outside, mainly dependents of the African work force, waited for manquala - medicine. Then, except on the mornings when she had concerns in Karonga, came the matter of correspondence which she conducted on a grand scale. The twice weekly plane brought letters from all over the world. From friends made in the course of her global travels, from relatives at home, from scientific societies, and especially, from her ten year old son Tom, at boarding school in England. She also tended a vegetable plot at the back of the house, which during the rains supplemented their diet in very welcome fashion.

In addition Jess had two part time jobs which, several times a week, were what sent her sent her pedalling down to Karonga so early in the day on her elderly bicycle.

The first was as overseer for the storage of skins and hides of animals killed by locals for meat or any other reason. Once paid for and dried the skins were graded, despatched and sold, mainly to the Bata shoe conglomerate.

The second job carried great responsibility. It was to act as agent in Karonga for the Central African Airways Corporation. Among other tasks she had to supervise the refuelling of the Beaver: the small five seater, single engine plane which put down at Karonga twice weekly, by means of a hose pipe attached to a 44gallon drum of petrol. She must also check the passenger list and ensure the doors were securely shut before take off.

Last but by no means least, in addition to her famous Sunday lunches which were a blood transfusion to solitary bachelors, and hospitality to waifs and strays like myself, Jess was engaged on a magnum opus.

She was collecting and collating the edible and medicinal plants of the country, in the hope that knowledge of them might not be lost to future generations as more and more people became urbanised.

Needless to say she had mastered the local language, and had given it out that anyone bringing unusual plants would be rewarded. Thus it was that most mornings, in addition to the sick, there would be a few people waiting with their offerings. Her 'office', situated at the far end of the khondé, consisting of a desk made from orange boxes, was always covered with papers and files, with jam jars of water on the floor round about containing droopy plants. In the course of this pursuit she had earned the nickname of 'Dona Mwadyachiani', meaning 'What have you eaten today?'

The enterprise was regarded as an indulgence, not taken seriously by any of us on the station. Great was our surprise therefore when in due course it came to completion, and the results published.

In 1955 the first addition of 'Useful Plants of Nyasaland' by Jessie Williamson, MA Cantab, Dip Diet, London, appeared. Reprints with a supplement on fungi followed. (After Independence, in subsequent editions, the title was changed to 'Useful Plants of Malawi'.) It was widely used in schools, and is a definitive textbook on the subject to this day.

After lunch even Jess rested, which is to say she retreated to her room for half an hour with a book, after which one of the bachelors would drive up from Karonga for tea, then carry us off to tennis or to the lake. This probably happened routinely, for when Andrew was away Jess had no transport apart from the afore-mention cycle.

One afternoon she suggested instead that we take a stroll round Baka for a change. Among the cluster of huts at the back of the house nothing stirred, the men dozing in shade after their labours, the women resting from their chores before setting about preparing the evening meal. Jess knew them all of course, and they her. She responded to their greetings in kind and asked after their families. We made our way to the Cloverleaf house of which I had heard so much. It was shut up, Steve Witting the Cotton Board official, who lived there, still away. I remarked to Jess that Ken and I had not yet met this mysterious character, and had begun to doubt his existence. She laughed, and said,

"Oh, he's real enough I assure you. And very nice.

"But his work on the cotton along the shore takes up a lot of his time. The house is pretty, don't you think?"

I agreed, and felt sorry we would not be living there. Rather than the severe, straight lines of all the other Government houses, it seemed to have evolved out of three rondavels linked together by one central room. Hence its name. I peered in at a window, but could see little because of the mosquito gauze.

"Let's go and see how the new building next door is getting on, suggested Jess, "Steve is in charge of its construction. Progress is slow even when he's here, and non-existent when he's away."

I could see that such walls already achieved were of burnt brick. There was to be a corrugated iron roof and, even more impressive, an integral kitchen. AND piped running water - the first in Karonga. In short, it would be far more like my idea of a proper house and I was envious. Jess was not so sure.

"Yes, all very nice I suppose, especially the running water, if Steve gets a fool-proof system going that is. But tin roofs aren't nearly as cool as thatch, and very noisy in the rains. As for the inside kitchen, well, easier to supervise and keep clean - not that Steve would care about that - but a wood burning stove indoors - In this heat!"

The time spent with Jess passed very quickly; Andrew, who hated house guests, would soon be back and I must remove to the DC's residence.

My first sight of this house in daylight had quickened the pulse, so nearly did it correspond with the picture in Captain Lugard's book, of Messrs Moir's house at Mandala, in the 1880s. Indeed the caption could easily have been 'The DC's residence at Karonga'. It may even have been built by Fred Moir himself, for he and his brother had been joint managers of the African Lakes Company in Karonga, for several years toward the end of the 19th century. There were two discernible differences however. The Karonga house had no chimney, for who would need a fire in such heat? Secondly it had wire gauze to upper and lower khondés, vital in the lake shore region. Later I discovered that this house was one of two such remaining in the area. Perhaps Fred Moir's brother had lived in the second. Be that as it may, it was by now dilapidated, rat infested, but still occasionally inhabited by luckless bachelors, including Ken at one stage of his first tour, when no other accommodation was available.

There were no houses at all when Captain Lugard and his men arrived in Karonga in 1888. The place was besieged by slavers who were inflicting great cruelty on the people of the region. This is how he describes the conditions he found there,

"Karonga's - the trading station of the Lakes Company - was a very small stockade, made of upright poles two or three deep, and about 12ft long, forming an irregular enclosure open to the lake in the rear. Inside it was a mass of filthy native huts, built wherever the fancy of the occupant could find space: there was no passage or gangway, and huddled up among these native huts were those of the white men. Every hut had its fire, at which the natives cooked their food, and the wind blew the sparks and flames in every direction. Dried grass and drier thatches of the houses were on every side! How the place had escaped being burnt to the ground in a week was a miracle. Yet inside this small enclosure was a store containing a great quantity of bales of goods (for payment to the natives as wages and for food purchase), and, here, in Central Africa, of great value; and - yet more extraordinary - here, in the very midst of these open fires, and huts of reeds and dry grass, were many hundreds of pounds of (gun) powder, protected only by common wooden kegs, which often leaked, so that absolutely loose powder lay about! Had this taken fire, not a fragment of a white man would have been found within some distance of Karongas."

This then was the place in which Lugard, that man of passion, believed his life would be laid down in the service of mankind. There was much to be done first however. Being the sort of man he was, the first imperative was a complete reorganisation of the stockade. He goes on:-

"On arrival I found six more employés of the Lakes Company. Monteith was the senior, and had been in charge for six years. He never left his post, and had been there through the siege and subsequent attacks."

These extracts are taken from - Lugard, The Rise of Our East African Empire.
Altogether therefore, with the men who had accompanied Lugard from the South,
there must have been ten or twelve Europeans, among whom
"A thoroughly good feeling existed, notwithstanding that the two sections of the European community were of somewhat incongruous types."
Monteith later wrote his own account, 'Adventures in Nyasaland; a two year struggle with Arab slavers in Central Africa.' L. Monteith Fotheringham. pub. Sampson Low, 1891.
Lugard's qualities must have been recognised immediately by the men, for he was voted their leader. His account continues -

" MY LITTLE SPEECH"
"To promote this harmony, I said a few words to my comrades one evening, though anything like 'speechifying' is a duty I dread, and would prefer to shirk. I pointed out that our little campaign had four main objectives to achieve - viz, to suppress slave-raiding; to save the Wankhondé, who had helped us; to save the missions from extinction; and to vindicate British honour; that, in the face of a common danger, and in the hope of succeeding in a cause so worthy, we must give and take, and tolerate each other's foibles, for we could not afford to quarrel, when we might not know whether we might not shortly be standing by the grave of a man with whom we had differed on some petty triviality. I added, that my own position of command was held entirely under sufferance, and at their own desire, and I asked for a promise that all would loyally obey me, since it rested in each one's power to make my position a pleasant or an intolerable one. This promise they gave me heartily and unanimously."
He then began immediately to
"Construct a small fireproof magazine for the gunpowder just outside the stockade, and turned out all the natives except for a small guard... After some days there was a complete revolution in the appearance of Karonga's...Two large houses forming two sides of a hollow square, accommodated most of the men, and the third side consisted of three tents. The rough stockade was strengthened,

the guns overhauled and repaired, and neatly arranged with all ammunition and powder in the new, sun-dried brick magazine. Many sanitary arrangements were instituted..."

This done he set about planning a strategy of how best to drive out the 'Arab' slavers.[1]*

Among the hierarchy of slavers operating all over the country, the Karonga area was plagued by one Mlozi, whose headquarters were some 15miles off. Halfway between his stronghold and Karonga was another manned by one of Mlozi's lackeys. It was known as Kopa Kopa's. This was the first target of Lugard and his compatriots. Accordingly they made a hazardous reconnaissance of the area, then laid their plans for a night attack.

It was not a success. Almost certainly intelligence was faulty, that and the difficult terrain precluded the element of surprise. The enemy awaited them, heavy casualties were sustained and Lugard himself was injured. At first he thought he had been hit through the heart and mortally wounded; afterwards he found he

"...had received a very singular wound. The muzzle of the gun must have been placed a few inches from my body, for the coarse grains of 'trade powder' had entered the right arm... like a charge of shot, and could not be dislodged, while two big lumps of wadding were extracted from the wound." (It) "then struck my chest, apparently in a direct line for the heart, but glancing off a rib...came out at the top of my breast pocket."

For many weeks his arms were useless, he could not bend either of them, neither could he lie down. But clearly the experience dispelled all thoughts of suicide and he fought hard to recover. He describes his sufferings in detail, but concludes endearingly,

"As I write I feel continually how egotistic my narrative is, and at times am tempted to destroy the MSS, but this is the innate difficulty in telling a personal story. If I have interested my reader, and helped him to realise African life, and to appreciate some of the difficulties through which success has been achieved, I shall have gained my object."

As well as Lugard himself several of his colleagues had been injured, one fatally. They also had to contend with the natural hazards of climate and conditions, malaria and other types of fever, boils, rats, snakes and crocodiles. Also there was the very real threat of a counter-attack by the slavers. As soon as he was well enough Lugard addressed the men once more:-

"Next day, 17th, I called a meeting of all the Europeans, and told them that nothing could have exceeded the pluck they had shown, and that we had been baffled only by the impossible; that I had never seen a hotter ten minutes, even in 'MacNeil's zeriba' and I urged them not to be discouraged. Indeed by Mr Nicholl's account, we were within an ace of success, for the stockade had, he said, caught fire where he was, and, if our side had not received a check by my having been disabled, he was confident we should have carried it. I advised the strengthening of our

---

[1] Arab blood had long since intermingled with African.

stockade in case of a counter-attack by the Slavers at the full moon, and said I thought that, without disciplined troops, the stockades were impracticable unless we got a cannon, and I advised that this should be immediately procured. Mr Moir undertook to get one from England, and Mr Raw said he knew of one in South Africa which had been surreptitiously imported in a recent war, and which he could obtain very cheaply."

Eventually the SS Ilala made an appearance further along the coast and, "Almost everybody wished to leave on it" Messrs Moir and Raw were despatched to buy the cannon and several others also left. Lugard himself refused to leave in spite of urges of the others that he should go for medical treatment. He knew that if he did so the remaining few would not be able to withstand the slavers and the whole cause would be lost. So for the depleted garrison the days passed wearily. However as wounds healed things gradually improved. At last, on January 16th 1889, six months after the engagement at KopaKopa's, the Ilala came back once more, and with it the long awaited cannon. It was a severe disappointment, being antiquated, and lacking the proper ammunition. Nevertheless it was a tremendous morale booster. A gun company was formed at once. After much drilling and firing practice, another raid, successful but not conclusive, was made on KopaKopa's.

Lugard left Karonga shortly after this. He was still a serving officer in the British Army, and was at last mindful of his career. "I had overstayed my time in the extreme urgency of the case, and the loss of my commission would be a serious matter indeed to me..." On the evening of 12th March, at a touching ceremony, his colleagues presented him with a sword and a pair of binoculars. In his final account he wrote:-

"All were poor men - they were facing constant fever, and exposing their lives for a miserable pittance; yet everyone of them gave a large subscription. I value these gifts more than any other thing I possess."

On his return to London, it was largely due to his representations to Parliament that reforms began to take place, not only in Nyasaland but on a wider canvas. The first official step to eradicate slavery in North Nyasa came on October 2nd, 1889, when Mr Johnson, British Consul in Mozambique, arrived in Karonga and agreed a treaty with Mlozi. It was worthless because of being unsubstantiated, Mlozi carried on as before. But on May 15th, 1891, the British African Protectorate was formed. This time it was backed up by force. The name was changed to the Nyasaland Protectorate in 1907. The slavers' days were over, Lugard and his men were vindicated.

In the 1950s it was possible, in theory, that some very old people in the Karonga area at the time, might have early childhood memories of the portentous events of some sixty years before. If so, they would certainly have given verbatim accounts to their children and grand-children.

For myself, I believed no evidence, no direct link, would remain. I was wrong. On the very first day after our arrival in Karonga when Ken walked me over to the tennis court, I stopped short at the Boma. Outside the DC's office, hard by the parade ground, stood Captain Lugard's cannon. Minus its gun carriage now, but polished and well cared for. I had no doubt of its authenticity. I regaled the story to Ken at length, rather to his impatience, and would have expatiated further on the circumstances which had brought it there, but the heat compelled us to move on.

Many years later I was amazed to learn that Lugard - by then Lord Lugard, for he went to have a long and illustrious career - had lived on until 1945. Too late I realised that during my growing up, had I the temerity, I could have written to this living legend. Even perhaps have received a first hand account of those far off struggles...

The menage in the DC's household was very different from the one I had just left with Jess at Baka.

Apart from being the senior and most important officer on the station, Joe, and Sue his wife, were family people with two young children. In addition they must entertain a continual stream of visiting officials and other dignitaries and keep up a certain style, so that in spite of having numerous servants, Sue, like Jess, had little leisure. A sickly house guest like myself, must have been as welcome as frost in May.

Social life was lived on the upper khondé. It was wide and spacious, airy too to a certain extent, because although heavily gauzed with wire mesh like the rest of the house, it caught any breeze off the lake, which it overlooked at a slight distance. Here I spent languid days as inconspicuously as possible, watching the children tended by their ayah, making myself pleasant to visitors. In the grounds below, vendors of fruit or vegetables waited for Sue to appear, other people lingered in the hope of being taken on as domestics, and a phalanx of loungers hung around with nothing better to do, observers like myself.

For me however, the idle existence was about to change dramatically. One morning I woke to find the nausea which had plagued me since before leaving England several months before, had suddenly vanished. So much a part of my life had it become that I could not believe it, and lay still for a full hour anticipating its return. Only when I caught myself actually looking forward to breakfast did the miracle become reality. Sue, who had been a model of forbearance, was almost as pleased as I, even though she was barely able to keep up with my appetite over the next few days.

So invigorated was I that the need for stimulation and exercise, sadly lacking previously, reasserted itself. I determined to go out and explore my surroundings. Accordingly next day before the temperature climbed to outrageous excess, I set out with a shady umbrella, mentally saluting Lugard's cannon as I passed the Boma.

I knew that, in spite of being one of the oldest settlements in the country and having comparative accessibility by lake, Karonga had not expanded and developed as might have been expected. On land it was accessed from the main highway many miles away, by the lake-shore road, barely more than a track in some places, over which we had travelled. The township itself still had only one street, broad, lined with jacaranda and other trees bearing bean-like pods about a foot long, which rattled in the breeze and were known by local people as 'grandmothers tongues'.

There were various tracks leading off, to Baka, to the lake, to the rest-house, to the airfield and to the various European houses with large gardens. Road and tracks alike were very dusty. Beyond the township lay Mpata, some fifteen miles off, in Lugard's day a slaver's fortified stronghold, but now a peaceful village, with a small rest-house much patronised by Andrew whenever he felt in need of a change or a rest. Beyond Mpata the track climbed to the hills.

Being so fertile the whole of the Karonga region was densely populated, with many villages and homesteads nudging up to, interspersing with the European settlement.

The Boma was a collection of brick built offices, plus an open sided, thatched roof rondavel - the Court House where the DC and his Aide dispensed British justice. Whether fining or imprisoning perpetrators, but more often than not, leaving them with their illgotten gains, was a principle readily understood by people more used to wreaking vengeance and retribution on their enemies and recovering the loot, is a moot point. Be that as it may, they had their own ideas and took matters first to the local chief and to the DC only as a last resort.

Near the Boma was the Post Office, a one roomed building, suffocatingly hot, always crammed with people. Staffed by African officials, it was perfectly possible to spend a whole morning buying one of the exotic stamps which had drawn Ken to the country. Or so I was told by James one day when we were staying at the rest-house, having sent him there and he had failed to come back in time to cook lunch. The Post Office boasted a radio telephone which was, apart from surface mail, Karonga's only link with the outside world. It was used almost exclusively for official purposes, with telegrams despatched to their destinations in stages. Naturally this allowed for a certain amount of distortion along the line, like a game of Chinese Whispers, so that the contents might arrive in quite a different format. (c/f a celebrated telegram of the second World War sent off as "We are going to advance can you send us reinforcements?" which was, allegedly, received as "We are going to a dance can you send us three and four pence?")

Two other institutions completed the official involvement of the township. The first was the African hospital. (Europeans must make their own provision for medical treatment.), the second was the prison. Both had African staff, with sporadic attention from Mzimba.

It goes without saying that if British justice was little understood, Western medicine was incomprehensible to local people. Nevertheless the hospital was popular, it being well known that the Asungu[2] - Europeans - had access to strong magic. Although just as they went first to the local chiefs to settle their disputes, they went first to the Medicine Man for charms and fetishes. Only if or when his methods failed, did they go to hospital. Sometimes it was too late, so the magic did not always work.

One branch of medicine however, was unexpectedly popular. Young wives had taken to going to hospital to have their babies, not out of need, but for the prestige such births promoted among their peers, a newfangled idea almost certainly frowned on by the older women.

Prestige may also have played a part in going to prison, a rite of passage perhaps. Everyone knew that regular food was forthcoming, even in the dry season when many people in the hills went hungry. If it did not suit one's taste, wives who usually accompanied their husbands, camped in the compound and cooked other food to supplement prison diet. Indeed a smoke haze hung about the place continually.

As for hard labour, that was a laugh. Consisting as it usually did, of chopping wood for the DC's kitchen, or fetching water from the lake, it was not nearly as strenuous as breaking ground for their own gardens for instance. And as for drawing water, that was women's work, so it was naturally delegated to the aforesaid wives. All of which left the prisoners plenty of time for gambling games, kicking a ball about on a patch of earth the Asungu called a football pitch, or simply doing nothing at all.

Writing near the beginning of the 21st century, it seems unlikely the ravages of time, fluctuations in lake level, and economics, have permitted the Karonga of that time to survive. Probably all is forgotten as a dream. Remote to present day inhabitants as were the 1880s exploits of Captain Lugard and his men to those of us living there in the 1950s.

Thoughts of history however, were far from my mind on the bright morning of my new found freedom. I was making for Andanis to buy sewing cotton. Andanis was one of the Indian stores mentioned by Jess, the other being Khateria's. Both catered for Africans mainly, but with a nod to Europeans in the form of crates of bottled beer, the occasional bottle of whiskey, and a few luxuries such as tins of jam and butter, Even tinned chocolate, which one must eat with a spoon, the heat having taken its toll.

The way seemed longer than I had anticipated, but I reached my destination at last, and plunged from the glare of the sun into the dark, airless interior of the store. My new-found strength deserted me, replaced by near blindness; I was once again overcome by nausea and weakness. Someone came swimmingly toward me, Mr Andani presumably. He looked at me suspiciously, summed up the situation at a glance, drew up a wooden chair and barked out an order to an unseen assistant. I sat down thankfully, surrounded by swaying sacks of rice and

---

[2] Asungu is the plural for Europeans, singular is Msungu. To avoid confusion Asungu has been used throughout.

salt, cans of paraffin, stacks of hoes, spades, axes, lamps, and bales of cloth, the whole exuding a pungent odour which threatened to overwhelm me. Presently the assistant appeared with a tin mug of water. Had it been boiled? I neither knew nor cared but swallowed it gratefully. Somehow I completed my commerce and tottered out.

CHAPTER 9

'I WILL LIFT UP MINE EYES
UNTO THE HILLS...'

Ken came back a few days later and we returned to the rest-house.

"You're a different person." He told me.

"I feel it, I assured him, "I can't tell you."

"I hardly knew you when you came running to meet me. All the chaps were wondering what I'd seen in you."

We were sprawled across the single beds, pushed together once more, although it was not night time. Reunion, like revenge, was sweet.

I considered the back-handed compliment and decided to ignore it, but realised belatedly that the whole station, including the bachelors desperate to a man to get married, must have pitied him the gaunt, apathetic creature he had brought back from England with him.

Changing the subject, I asked how the ulendo had gone.

"It went well. Wonderful to be back in Misuku. Of course things had got slack with no-one there to supervise, otherwise it was pretty much as I'd left it. The coffee bushes on the nursery slopes were growing nicely."

"And the house?"

"Well that was pretty much the same as well, he conceded, "But, he brightened, "Most of the materials to finish it off are there, it's only a question of putting in the work. And I've made a start. I put the window frames in, and the glass is there too but it needs cutting and fixing."

I tried unsuccessfully to visualise it.

"Next time you go I'm coming with you." I said.

"We'll see." he replied.

In truth, although this was what I had been looking forward to, as the actuality drew near I was apprehensive. The trek would be long and arduous, that much I knew. No part of the route coincided with a road, we would be on foot the entire way. Moreover, Ken had told me we must climb from the lake at 1600 feet above sea level, to an altitude of about 6000feet. There were no European settlements en route, only camping places in African villages. Nor were there any Europeans once we arrived, apart from a couple of American missionaries about 8 to 10miles from where we would be living.

The episode at Andanis had shaken my confidence. I asked cautiously,

"I know it's a long way, but, er, just how far is it?"

"Well, of course it's never been mapped, or properly measured. The path winds all over the countryside because of the terrain, but it's reckoned to be about fifty miles. Or perhaps sixty. I do it over three days."

Unnoticed the day had slipped away. Dusk was falling; there was a soft tap on the door and James came in with a lamp. Across the parade ground the Askari sounded the Last Post.

Our exodus was not to take place for another three weeks, during which time I ate ravenously and regained strength. Ken resumed work with Andrew in Karonga and along the lake shore. I passed the time agreeably, as before but with more energy and enjoyment, so it was with something like regret rather than anticipation that I received Ken's announcement -

"We'll leave on Monday. We'll be staying in Misuku for three months, and must take plenty of provisions because we can't get anything there. We'll get them from Andanis. Two bags of rice - one for us and one for James, and a bag of salt. Then the usual things. Tins of meat, because they don't kill meat there and we can get only the odd stringy chicken. We can live off the land to some extent for fruit and vegetables, though they're seasonal so can't be relied on.

Then there are the household things we'll need. I left a few pots and pans there last time, but not much else so we'll need more. And there are the bedding rolls to go - the camp bed etc we bought at the Army and Navy Store - oh, and a blanket or two because the nights are cool."

"That'll make a nice change."

"Yes. We'll take one case each for personal things, the odd book and such, but remember, essentials only or there won't be enough carriers. Which reminds me, I must buy another lamp. But you can see to the rest can't you? For God's sake don't forget the tin opener, and when you're packing it all up, make sure the foodstuff won't get wet if we get rain on the way." [1]*

With the experience of the shopping expedition in Blantyre still fairly fresh in the mind, assessing our food requirements was the easiest part of the exercise. What is more my calculations would have been near the mark, had not some of the commodities, sugar especially, unaccountably shrunk on the journey.

At any rate, armed with recharged vitality I visited Mr Andani once more. He eyed me warily at first, but his eyes gladdened as the bill mounted up and his respect at my restored health grew in equal measure.

The rest of the preparations were less straightforward and necessitated opening up the trunks 'Not wanted on Voyage', which had languished in one of the Agricultural Department's sheds out at Baka ever since our arrival in Karonga.

Ken had them sent down to the rest-house and I tackled the task at once. Their contents had not been seen by us since their despatch from England on that dismal November day, and I knew exactly what would happen. Merely opening the lids was to be transported to the Chesham flat, seemingly so idyllic in summer in the first flush of married life, so cold and damp as winter set in. So real did the scene become that for an instant I actually felt the cold. Alas it did not last, but was rapidly replaced by memories of the wrangling over what to take, what to leave behind, and of the mound of detritus remaining in the middle of the floor.

At the very top of the bigger trunk lay my wedding dress, delicately swathed in tissue paper, awaiting the elegant occasion that I now suspected would never take

---

[1] Not so easy in pre-plastic days.

place. The temptation to put it on was well nigh irresistible and overcome only by lack of a suitable mirror, the only one in the room being a small shaving mirror set at man height on one wall.

I did not even try however, to resist the next challenge. Namely that of reading the newspapers in which everything else was wrapped. I spent a happy morning noting that Princess Margaret had a cold, studying the fashion features, poring over estate agents advertisements for residences only too desirable to anyone likely to be living, for the foreseeable future, in a mud hut without electricity, running water, or proper sanitation. Soon both trunks were empty, their contents strewn about the floor amid a sea of newspaper.

At this point I realised two things. One, I had not sorted out anything. Two, horror, Ken would soon be back for lunch. Scrunching my way over to the door, I called for James, hoping as I gave instructions for the meal that Ken would be too preoccupied with work, as he often was, to notice what he was eating.

After lunch, in the hottest part of the day, all thoughts of cold unimaginable, I set to work in earnest, quickly locating my bedding roll, a blanket or two and some cooking utensils. Now for the personal options.

We had been living out of suitcases for months, mine was full to bursting already, certainly inadequate for the bare essentials newly restored to my attention. Clearly the red high-heeled shoes would have to be left behind. Would Ken consider hair curlers essential? I thought not, but stuffed them in my bedding roll anyway. The pile grew. When the protesting case would take no more I tied the rest in a cloth bag, and hoped no-one would notice.

Next came the task of putting everything else back in the Revelation trunks. Once again they lived up to their name in that they seemed just as full as before in spite of what had been taken out. With an effort I managed to snap the locks shut by sitting on the lids just as Ken came back after work. He was pleased and impressed.

"Good, he said. "I've only managed to get twelve carriers, so everything must be divided into twelve loads. Are those trunks locked? They'll have to go back to Baka, can't leave them here. We must have an early night because it's vital that we get off to an early start in the morning."

"When is it not?" I sighed.

Acting as carrier was not a popular task among the Nkondé people of the lake shore of northern Nyasaland. Living was easy and the men undertook it, as far as one could judge, only in cases of severe financial embarrassment. This not just because it was arduous, but also because carrying (anything) was women's work. As the men saw it they should be able to send their wives along, they themselves naturally taking the money. For some obscure reason however, the Asungu - Europeans - refused to countenance this. In passing however, in my experience, male staff - domestics, capitaos - etc, had their own code of conduct regarding the hand luggage of the Asungu. These prestigious items must be carried by them alone, positively no European should be seen carrying so much as his or her own umbrella.

Roused from deep sleep by Ken next morning, even before reveillé had sounded, I lay for a moment listening to voices outside, bitterly regretting the impromptu send off party given for us by the bachelors the previous night.

This would not do. Venturing out at last in half light, another illusion was shattered. Books and magazine articles on the great explorers and missionaries all had black and white illustrations of the white man, pith helmeted, at the head of a column of smart, neatly dressed porters with equally neat wooden boxes on their heads, blazing a trail through trackless jungle. Clearly standards has slipped by the middle of the twentieth century. Our carriers were a motley crew. To be sure, four of them were decently covered - two of them seconded from the DC's complement wore khaki shorts, two others, trusties from the prison, wore broad arrowed trousers. The rest, sensibly in such heat, wore little at all.

Nor did our baggage approximate to the pictures in the books. The head-loads, divided into twelve, were lined up at the back of the rest-house. There were no neat boxes. The sack of salt packed in the collapsible canvas bath, the sacks of rice and the sugar in a lidded bucket, were free standing. Everything else, pots and pans, cans of paraffin, a lamp, bedding rolls etc, were grouped arbitrarily together, tied with bark twine. Only our bulging suitcases which, then as always in spite of Ken's remonstrances, were carried wrong side up, presented some sort of formality.

Neither was there any question of the men following us in good order. They knew the way, knew also they could accomplish the journey in half the time, arrive at their destination before the hottest part of the day, and enjoy the hospitality of the locals, long before we ourselves showed up. Now they stood like greyhounds in the slips straining upon the start, eyeing the loads keenly to assess the weight and/ or awkwardness of each.

When all was ready, the capitao gave the word. They surged forward, the tallest and strongest making for the lightest loads.

"Stop!" cried Ken.

They stopped, perplexed. Clearly the race had suffered a false start. Ken re-allocated loads more fairly. With much argument and jostling, one by one they adjusted their head rings, hoisted up their burdens and, still procrastinating, made off at a brisk pace.

We had been lucky. Two hydrologists staying intermittently at the rest-house, with whom we had become friendly, had offered to take us in their launch along the lake as far as Mweniteté, a village some miles off, their work for the day being in that direction; at Mweniteté we would disembark and strike off inland on foot. After a hasty breakfast therefore, accompanied by a capitao and coincidentally blasted on our way by the morning bugle, we started for the lake shore.

At the water line a lone figure - Jess - the friend I would miss most of all, had come to see us off. She said,

"Here are a couple of pawpaw for the journey. Most refreshing at midday"

She watched as we splashed our way through the shallows to the boat which waited, its engine already running, and waved us out of sight.

Daylight grew stronger, a slight breeze ruffled the water. The strand was fringed with palm fronds and bango reeds which parted every now and then to reveal clearings of small round huts. Already women were at work, some at the water's edge pounding clothes then spreading them out to dry on yellow sand; all paused to wave and call out greetings.

Early travellers in the area had rhapsodised on the scene unfolding before us, as well they might.

"It seemed a perfect Arcadia, wrote one, Joseph Thomson, in 1878, "I felt as if I had fallen on some enchanted place."

Surely it could have changed but little since then. Then as now, the place was not only beautiful, but fertile as well, the plain not only lush with crops but supporting herds of cattle also. The importance of the countless groves of banana palms can hardly be over estimated. That they provided a free, ever ready source of food, was but the beginning. The large, fibrous-fronded leaves were the building material of wattle and daub huts, thatch for roofs, used also for mats, baskets and perhaps other artefacts; in former times women had woven them into skirts. Indeed the very word Wankhondé meant 'banana'. Thus the Wankhondé had lived in the same fashion since time immemorial, easy going, peaceable people, as well they might be.

That is, until the advent of the slavers, nine years after Joseph Thomson's visit.

For we were now approaching the Khambwe Lagoon about three miles from Karonga, where the 1950s successor of the Ilala which had taken Captain Lugard to Karonga, anchored on its regular voyages up and down the lake.

There was no sign of it on this morning. The lagoon lay empty, innocently beautiful in sunlight, the villagers friendly and unconcerned as all the others we had encountered.

Yet it was here, on the 20th October, 1887, that the tranquillity had been shattered by what, surely, was one of the cruellest, unprovoked massacres in human history.

For generations, as already mentioned, Arab slavers had plagued the people of northern Nyasa, now they turned their attention to the Wankhondé. Betrayed by a neighbouring tribe, the villagers were drawn into a trap.

The story is taken up by L. Monteith Fotheringham,[2] the early overseer for the African Lakes Company, who was in Karonga when the obscenity occurred. He wrote:-

"...Next day we heard firing in the direction of the lagoon... The Arabs having drawn the Nkhondé into this trap, had now commenced their fiendish brutality..." He goes on,

"By a stealthy and rapid march they surrounded the lagoon before the natives were well aware of their presence. Immediately a scene of the wildest excitement prevailed. The war-whoops of the Ruga-Ruga smote the Wankhondé heart with terror. Armed only with spears, they were no match for the Arabs, who keeping at a safe distance, poured volley upon volley into the reeds, which were soon red

---

[2] L. Fortesque-Monteith, Adventures in Nyasaland 1888?

with the blood of the dying. Every black who jumped out of the lagoon was shot in the open, and not a native escaped who came within range of the Arab rifles. There was no outlet to the west side, and but small chance of escape on the north. The Arabs gradually moved forward, and the terror-stricken Wankhondé were forced into the swamp yard by yard. Maddened by their success, the Ruga-Ruga rushed upon the natives and drove them farther back, spearing those who stuck fast in the mud. Then they fired the reeds, and as the flames rose, the yells of the poor creatures behind might be heard far and near above the steady discharge of the guns. Now another enemy, more dreaded than the Arabs, rose against the natives in their dire extremity. This was the crocodile, who swung his hideous jaws out of the pool and made an easy prey of the bewildered blacks. Those who did not perish by the rifle or the spear were either burned to death or devoured by the innumerable crocodiles that infest the lagoon. Few succeeded in struggling through the slough to the other side. While the attack was in progress, the three Arab leaders, in order to gratify their morbid curiosity, climbed into trees, and with diabolical interest watched and regulated the work of extermination. Darkness only put an end to the slaughter. The native chiefs with the remnant of their people fled to the Songwe river, while the Arabs, who had captured a great many women and children, encamped at the lagoon."

Nothing of this was known to me until much later. On hearing of it I shuddered to reflect that the very reeds quivering at the water's edge, on the bright morning of our exodus, were engendered of the very ones growing there on that dreadful day, the crocodiles lurking offshore direct descendants of those glutted by the unexpected feast...

The lake was not always benign and tranquil. Sometimes a rain storm would raise a spiral of water far out, upsetting everything in its wake. A ferocious wind - the Mwera - would whip up waves which raced inland to bend and buckle bamboos and flatten banana plantations along the shore. I knew all this from Jess, Andrew & Tom, having been saved from near shipwreck one time, when sailing south on the Ilala in just such a storm.

We reached Mweniteté, our point of disembarkation. It looked and according to Ken was, a God forsaken place of mud flats, unsuited to human habitation. No village was in sight, only a sort of Dutch barn where the cotton was bought, and a rough shelter for the vendors when it rained. At a short distance stood a mud-brick hut, with thatched roof reaching almost to the ground, which housed the unlucky official responsible for the transactions. For two seasons that official had been Ken. He had spent frenetic days dealing with queues of people, each with a few pounds of cotton to sell, battling heat, rain, and malarial mosquitos the while, the solitude of his primitive hut during scant leisure hours broken only by occasional visits of a malachite kingfisher. His predecessor in the job had gone mad and shot himself in the foot. Literally.

Ken saved his sanity with a bit of sketching, and by cycling to Karonga on a push bike, for convivial weekends. This involved wading the flood plain and two swollen rivers, in company with other travellers, all shouting at the tops of their voices to keep off the crocodiles. Of which, more later.

Cotton growing was interspersed with rice or maize, according to the rains, and it was a long season. Which was why we had not yet met Steve Witting - the interloper (in Ken's view,) in the matter of the Cloverleaf house - whose job it now was.

There was no sign of him at Mweniteté however, no sign of anyone in fact, as the launch pulled in to shore.

We thanked our benefactors who clearly did not envy us, said our goodbyes, then climbed out of the boat and made our way ashore over hot sand. At the end of a rise we turned and waved. But they were already out of sight, our last link with civilisation had gone.

The Lufira river and many small streams spilled out their contents in the area of Mweniteté, flooding the whole plain before going on to stain the waters of Lake Nyasa up to a mile out. On this occasion there were no floods, only moist alluvial soil on which the people had planted a risky second crop. The risk came not just from flash floods, but also from hippos which were apt to come ponderously ashore at night to graze on young shoots. The going was easy enough although it was very hot. There was no shade. Where was the big umbrella we had bought at Andanis? I wondered, as we followed the capitao[3] on the narrow path parting young green rice; too late I remembered James had taken it from Ken - a status symbol as compensation for having to go with the carriers as there was no room in the boat.

"How far did you say we would be walking today?" I ventured when the path had broadened sufficiently for us to walk abreast

"About five or six miles, Ken replied, "Just far enough to break you in gently. There'll be a bit of shade once we clear the plain. It won't be quite so humid either. Tomorrow will be a lot farther I'm afraid, and the next day. About fifteen miles tomorrow, then perhaps seventeen miles the day after."

I was silent, never having walked that far in my life. He went on,

"The countryside is barren and inhospitable when we begin to climb. No villages at all until we come to camping places. It wouldn't be safe to camp in the middle of the bush."

"So there really are lion, and leopard?"

Well, leopard are the more likely. And other things." He did not specify what these might be, but added, "I don't suppose we'll see anything apart from monkeys though. And it will be cooler. And we'll be spending the last night with the Udds, the American missionaries I told you about. I sent a note up by a messenger, so they'll be expecting us. They're very kind. Their place is on the edge of Misuku, only about eight miles from Katobo. (He pronounced it Katowo.) Which as you know, is where we'll be living. You'll love it there." he finished enthusiastically.

We cleared the plain at last, the land rose slightly, bush and bamboo began to take over and an occasional tree. In the shade of one we sat down to eat curling

---

[3] capitao: overseer, African

sandwiches and Jess' pawpaw. The area was populous after this with villages of friendly people, not surprised to see us as the carriers had preceded us overland and in any case Europeans were common enough in the region, due to the relative proximity of Karonga.

Toward afternoon we reached the village of Mwaulambo our over-night destination. It was set among banana groves and boasted a mud brick church in which we would be sleeping. Thatched huts were grouped together around the customary space of beaten earth. The huts did not vary in size, only in number; the more huts in the group the greater number of a man's wives, a direct indication of his wealth and status, as I realised from the account given me by the Veterinary Officer on my very first day in Karonga.

There were more greetings, especially from the women, visiting white females obviously less common here. Children and young girls stood aside giggling, older boys took the opportunity to air their little English, chickens pecking about in the dust squawked out of the way without undue haste.

The capitao led us to the other side of the clearing where the Village Headman and the elders were waiting to receive us. They knew Ken of old, this being the route he habitually took to Misuku. Daylight was fading as the headman launched into a speech. In English he congratulated Ken on having bought a wife in England, he hoped he would beget many fine sons. Ken made a suitable response. The niceties over, a procession of women emerged from the shadows with gifts of fruit, a live chicken and a calabash of milk. Ken thanked them, then they escorted us to the Scots Mission church. In gathering dusk it was just possible to make out a rectangular building, before it a cooking fire threw figures of the assembled carriers and others into sharp relief. Among them was James, last seen in Karonga, very bad tempered at not going with us in the launch. Now he was a changed person. A personable youth with the added attraction of being a well travelled stranger, he was the centre of attention among the village girls. Ego fully restored he cheerfully set about making tea.

The church was quite dark inside. At first we could make out nothing but two small wind holes - windows would be a misnomer for there was no glass - set in one wall. When James came in with the lamp the uncertain light revealed the beaten earth floor of a long room. Obviously the interior was undivided. At one end was a low platform on which stood a rustic chair and table; on the wall behind a banner proclaiming Yesu Kristu was just discernible. Otherwise the place was empty but for pole bench seats running the length of the side walls. These were for the elderly who had, as in English churches in former times, 'gone to the wall.' Later I noticed a drum in one corner, used as Ken said, as a summons to worship, instead of a bell.

I knew that the Scots missionaries had travelled far and wide over the country establishing such churches, schools as well, in the charge of African pastors, or teachers, with an occasional visit from a member of the parent mission.

Our baggage was strewn all over the floor. Ken unearthed camp chairs and we sat and drank the tea thankfully. It was amazingly restorative, although in truth the undemanding walk had been no more arduous than a country ramble with friends at home. Refreshed, he said,

"Now I must go and make sure the carriers have food and somewhere to sleep. As I go I'll get James to come and give you a hand with the beds. Then you must tell him about supper."

Ken's bedding roll was faded and shabby, mine brand new. I noted with relief that the bundle of my bare essentials concealed in it had gone undetected. Each bed was a complicated arrangement of light, metal tubes which fitted into one another to form two six foot lengths, with a canvas stretcher slotted along each length to form the bed base, and lateral struts at intervals to keep the canvas taut. The whole structure was raised about nine inches off the ground by means of minute splayed legs. Other rods slotted into other holes to support a mosquito net; a thin, padded mattress and small square pillow, completed the ensemble. As Ken had said in the Army and Navy Store in London on that memorable day, they were light to carry. They proved to be quite as uncomfortable as I had envisaged. We put them up on the dais well away from the door and the wind holes in case it rained in the night, and dragged the rest of the bags and bundles up there as well.

When Ken came back we washed in water from the bucket and put on fresh clothes, then we sat outside. The cooking fire silhouetted James and his self appointed assistants, their torsos gleaming with sweat. At the edge of darkness women chattered, girls giggled.

Supper was surprisingly good. It consisted of the chicken presented by the headman, accompanied by plenty of rice, followed by a dessert of the bananas brought by the women.

As we ate I wondered aloud whether the early Colonials really did change into evening dress on safari in the bush and if they had planted the Union Jack outside their tent, as pictures in old copies of the Illustrated London News would have us believe. And if so, when had the practice disappeared? Ken said he had never come across it. Everyone he knew had some sort of bath (collapsible?), or dipped in a river or stream if possible, and changed into long trousers and mosquito boots, but that was as far as it went.

Afterwards we lay in our narrow beds cocooned by the nets, beyond which mosquitos hummed. It rained heavily in the night, it breached the roof thatch, drove in at the wind holes, made mud puddles on the uneven floor and trickled under the door. But we slept high and dry on the dais under the banner of Yesu Kristu.

CHAPTER 10

'DOES THE ROAD WIND UP HILL ALL THE WAY?
YES TO THE VERY END'

A shaft of sunlight under the door. Bare windows transformed into animated tapestries of leaves. Leaves that emitted high pitched sounds, for to misquote T. S. Eliot,
'The leaves were full of children, hidden, excitedly containing laughter.'
For a moment I could not think where I was. After a while when it became apparent that this was no dream I shrank further down in bed, glad of the dubious privacy of the mosquito net. Vaguely I recalled Eliot also saying something about mankind being able to withstand change only in small doses. How true, I reflected.
Ken was already up and out. I lay still, wondering how to get up unobserved, knowing it would soon become necessary to visit the chimbuzi. This was the pit latrine newly dug for us at a discreet distance, surrounded with a makeshift fence of banana fronds and leaves, the opening roughly screened off.
Presently James came in with tea. He said,
"There is trouble Madam"
I was not surprised, to my mind the whole exercise was fraught with trouble. I asked,
"What kind of trouble is this?"
"Those carriers are bad men, he replied, "The two men from the DC say they must return to Karonga."
As he spoke there was a sound of rusty metal bars being struck together. At once the chattering at the wind-holes stopped and was followed by the pounding of bare feet, the quivering leaves settled back into silence.
"It is the time for school to start Madam."
One problem solved at least. When I ventured outside Ken was in consultation with the village headman, a small crowd had gathered. It did indeed seem that three of the carriers - the two from the DC contingent and one casual - intended to leave and were clamouring to be paid. No argument Ken put forward could make them change their mind. Containing his temper as best he could, for time was pressing, he began negotiating for substitutes from the village. It was a difficult situation, all the villagers had been so friendly and helpful, coercion at this stage could only sour relations. Yet carriers we must have. Ken reiterated,
"I must have three strong men."
"But Sir, protested the headman, "There are no men here."
I looked around. Sure enough, apart from the elders the group was composed entirely of women and children, the men having summed up the situation had melted away. Ken was adamant. At length the headman said he would see what he could do, and shuffled off into the trees. To me Ken said,
"Have breakfast, you must keep up your strength. I'll grab some later. Can you and James pack up afterwards?"

He turned aside to supervise the remaining carriers, who were also protesting in anticipation of increased loads. Presently the headman returned with one old man and a puny looking boy.

"They don't look very strong." said Ken.

"Oh yes Sir. They are strong too much. But they can carry for one day only. Tomorrow they must return."

The loads were re-distributed to make up the shortfall. Ken picked up a camp chair while everyone looked on. James took it from him, horrified, then reluctantly moved off after the carriers. Ken took up another package, the capitao down from the hills - the one from Karonga had returned earlier - had the bucket containing the bag of sugar, I was not allowed to handle anything.

Ken thanked the headman for his people's hospitality and according to custom, discreetly paid him for the 'gifts' of food of the previous evening. Having done so he came back into the church to eat a hasty breakfast. Then we too set off for the interior, with the headman himself and a gaggle of young children escorting us the first half mile of courtesy.

As we passed the school, at some hidden signal singing arose strongly from within. The words, the language, were incomprehensible, but there was no mistaking the tune. 'Once in Royal David's City' hung on the air, out of context, out of season, heartrending...

At the edge of the village the headman bid us a gracious God Speed. We watched and listened as he and the little ones turned to retrace their steps, suspended between the fluting voices of the children at our backs, and the deeper tones of the carriers fading as they forged ahead. When silence fell we moved off.

Gradually we began to climb, the rich soil of Mwaulambo giving way to stonier ground, lush vegetation dwindling to scattered clumps of bamboo and bush. Through it we had glimpses of yesterday's path across the plain and the lake shining silver beyond. We paused now and again, ostensibly to admire the scene, but in reality for a brief rest, for already my legs attuned to the lake shore flats, were beginning to protest at the gradient.

After an hour or so we came to a sizeable stream, the first of many, and surprised the carriers bathing, their scant clothing strewn about the bank. They moved out of sight with much hilarity, I regarding them with envy, regretful of convention which confined us merely to dabbling our feet. Thereafter the countryside was a mass of tumbled hills and steep sided valleys forged out by streams rushing down to the plain. All must be crossed, by wading where possible, or by means of crude pole bridges, all the hillsides must be scaled. Constant ascent and descent was arduous, the overlying character of the land ever inclined upward.

Even the carriers, whom we glimpsed now and again above us, were finding it hard going, and reduced to silence for once. Occasionally a stream swollen with recent rain would cause us to detour up to a mile or more, to find another crossing place.

Now there were virtually no bamboos, only hillsides dense with bush and brachystegia trees trailing ghostly lichen. We met no other travellers, saw no sign of habitation - for who could live in such a barren place? The infuriating grating of cicadas enveloped us, otherwise the only sounds were of rushing water and the occasional screams of monkeys as they raced away from us.

Now I needed to rest frequently; once we took a short lunch break, but Ken continually reiterated the need to reach the village of Mwenikumbira before dusk.

At first the mere thought of being benighted in such a place lent strength to my failing legs, but as the day wore on the act of putting one foot before the other became totally mechanical, unconnected with conscious thought. Ken's insistent, urgent voice - "We're nearly there. Not far to go now" - came out of a void, made no impression.

A long time later, stopping yet again to drink, I registered a sliver of shade and it came to me dully that the fierce sun was slipping toward nightfall. Confusedly, quite without reason, I took this to mean we were reaching our destination. Miraculously so it proved. We heard shouts, saw people coming towards us...

Another village, another church. Camp beds already set up. No doubt there was another headman, another reception committee, more fraternising between carriers and locals. None of it existed for me. I collapsed on to a bed and slept instantly. Ken woke me later telling me I must eat. I ate from the spoon he held out to me, only half awake, then went back to sleep, dimly aware of Ken putting a blanket over me.

In the morning cool air blowing in at the wind hole. Grateful for the blanket, I knew then that the fifteen miles or so of broken country had indeed carried us to a considerable altitude.

Tottering outside eventually on stiff legs, it was immediately obvious that this village bore no resemblance to the previous one. Here was no fecund soil yielding crops almost without human effort, but millet gardens hacked out of stony hillsides, and plantain bananas so vital to survival, grown with difficulty. The people were leaner, tougher looking; the nsaru worn both by men and women, were uniformly black, accentuating their poverty, the harshness of their lives. Nevertheless they had indeed welcomed us and presented Ken with what gifts of food they had to spare.

Now Ken paid off the carriers returning to Mwaulambo. (I was relieved to see the old man and the boy had survived the ordeal.)

This time there was no trouble here in getting replacements, but competition rather for the rare chance of earning some money. The hilly slopes, the rough terrain, were nothing to these men, they had never known anything else. Therefore, once we had breakfasted and broken camp, when the headman and elders had been thanked for their hospitality and paid for the food, the customary leave taking was concluded and there was nothing to delay our early start.

CHAPTER 11

'THE HILL CALLED DIFFICULTY'

Ken had warned me this day's journey would be hardest of all.

"It's about seventeen miles. Perhaps a little more."

But at first in the freshness of morning the going was not hard at all, partly because the enervating heat of the lake shore was now behind us, and partly, surprisingly, once the stiffness of my legs had worn off it seemed that yesterday's trek had toned up the muscles. I was also buoyed up by the prospect of spending the night at the American mission station, the Udds being kind and hospitable by all accounts. After several hours however, with the sun directly overhead, in spite of the altitude it became hot once more. The terrain had not changed except that the hills and therefore the V sided valleys, were steeper, the streams more turbulent, the pole bridges more rickety. I climbed up from valley bottoms clinging to a stick which Ken ahead held down to me. Bush and brachystegia trees persisted, shade was scarce and my earlier optimism evaporated. All too soon I was asking,

"How much further?"

A short break by a stream came and went, Ken estimated we had covered about eight or nine miles. Only about half way! On again through a never ending afternoon, the hours punctuated by Ken's urging and assurances. At last he said,

"Look, we've struck the Udd's road!"

I looked dully but could make out no road. The only discernible difference from the path we had left was that the track on the scarred hillside was wider. Ken went on, "Yes, it goes right up to their place at Mubula. Ragnor himself made it with his labour force. A bit rough but quite serviceable. In the other direction it goes down to the Kalengé river, then to Kapoka and on to the road leading to Fort Hill."

The geography meant nothing to me, although it later became all important, but at least the fact of being on a designated road was encouraging. In a practical way too it was helpful, for we could now walk side by side and I could lean on Ken's arm. It was not a straight route however, it twisted and turned constantly to avoid boulders and the worst of the gradients. Much later Ragnor Udd told us he and Alice never ventured on it without saying a prayer first, and it was easy to understand why.

We climbed interminably upwards in silence. At last Ken said,

"Only a few more miles. This is the last hill."

The carriers had long since pulled away, out of sight, out of hearing, the capitao remained a few yards ahead of us.

The rain came without warning. Its vicious attack soaked us in seconds, landscape was blotted out, there was no shelter, nowhere to hide. Clinging together we stumbled blindly on, slipping, skidding on the mud and scree that cascaded down the hill. Finally my legs gave out and I sank to the ground. Ken knelt beside me, hugging me, protecting me from the worst of the onslaught. Thus we stayed for immeasurable time. Impossible to tell what words of comfort he was murmuring, possible only to cower in his arms, semiconscious, aware only of tenderness in the eye of disaster, wanting never to move again.

The rain eased at last and finally stopped, Ken drew me to my feet, fished a sodden handkerchief from his pocket, squeezed it out and dabbed my face on which rain, mud and tears mingled. He said gently,

"We must get on."

"I can't." My teeth were chattering, "I can't walk any more."

"You can! You must. We'll get chilled if we don't get moving. Besides it wouldn't do to linger here."

I looked around stupidly. We were alone, even the capitao was nowhere to be seen. The surrounding bush was silent, menacing, the very thought of what it hid gave a measure of impetus to the body. Slowly we moved off, Ken keeping up a stream of encouragement,

"Lucky the rain didn't come before or we might not have got across the streams. Look, the sun's coming out, we'll soon get dry again. It's not far to the Udds now."

In other circumstances the brilliance of every leaf, every blade of wet grass glistening in sunlight would have enchanted me. Now it seemed maddeningly excessive, heightened as if by fever. I said,

"I must rest."

"Alright. But not for long. We must get on. It'll be dark soon."

I resented this bitterly but putting one foot before the other automatically was marginally less strenuous than resisting.

Sunset came with terrifying swiftness, too soon to dry us out completely. Soon it was quite dark, no moon, no stars, nothing but blackness, primaeval in its totality. The path was invisible, there was a real danger of our straying from it and into the bush. Fear drove me on, at the point of collapse I clung to Ken. Hallucinations came in the form of shouts, lights dancing before the eyes. I heard Ken's voice once more as in a dream,

"Look, the Udds have sent down men with torch brands to guide us in!"...

Another blur of images. A lamp-lit room, a bathtub of hot water before a wood fire. Ken rubbing me dry. A bed...

CHAPTER 12

IN MISUKU

Daylight poured in at the window. I woke suddenly, with a sense of dread. But on the instance registered a familiar lurch of the stomach, and sank gratefully down in the soft bed. Where was I? In England perhaps? Wherever it was there seemed no good reason to get up. Sighing I turned over and went back to sleep.

It was hunger that woke me the second time. After a while Ken came in. He looked worried.

"Oh good, you're awake. How do you feel?"

Cautiously I flexed leg muscles, wriggled ankles and toes, pleased to find them still in working order.

"Stiff, " I said at last, And hungry. Where are we?"

"Yes, of course you would be. I didn't wake you up to eat last night, I thought sleep was more important. But apart from that? I mean... Well, how are you really?"

"I'm alright, I told him firmly, "Everything is alright."

He looked relieved.

"You're sure?"

"I'm sure."

"So that's alright then?"

"Yes, that's alright."

The disjointed conversation seemed to have stalled. I asked,

"Is there any food?"

"What? Oh yes, I'll go and see about it. Meanwhile drink this tea. It wouldn't do to get dehydrated. No need to hurry, he added, "Not far to go this morning."

These were the sweetest words I had heard for a long time and I sat up drinking cup after cup of the sweet tea, and looking about me. Obviously we were at the Udd's place. This was a proper bedroom, the first real home I had encountered since arriving in the country. There was a patchwork quilt on the bed and a hearth-rug in front of the fireplace. The walls were painted a pale blue, the window was glazed, and had pretty curtains. On the wall facing the bed was another text, embroidered this time, not 'Yesu Kristu', but 'Thou God Seest Me'

When Ken came back with the food - millet porridge, eggs and the miracle of newly baked bread - he told me the Udds were, in fact, away on home leave in the States and not expected back for some months. Last night's search party had been organised by our capitao who had gone on ahead of us.

"I thought I was hallucinating last night, I said, "Those lights. And the shouting."

"No, that was real enough. It was Samueli, the Udd's retainer who opened up their rest-house for us. And baked the bread."

I said it was lucky we had not known yesterday of the Udd's absence, or I might have given up long before. Ken said no I wouldn't, and it had turned out alright anyway, hadn't it?

Getting up and dressing at last I found James packed and ready to go. Ken paid off yesterday's carriers. There was no shortage of others to take over, some of them I came to know well as they were labourers from Katobo, the Agricultural Station of our destination. Ken said they had been sent by Sutherland, the head capitao, who was "A very good chap."

Also present was the seemingly inevitable crowd of onlookers, all talking excitedly. I too was in a state of excitement at the prospect of seeing Misuku at last and arriving at our future home, relieved too that the day's journey would be only eight miles or so. In truth I felt that would be quite enough.

We thanked Samueli heartily; he presented us with the rest of the bread and said the Udds had told him to welcome travellers in their absence, and do what he could for them. Ken made him discreet recompense and we parted with the utmost goodwill.

I had imagined the Udd's mission to be at the top of the mountain we had climbed the day before, so never ending had it seemed. It was not so, for at the start of the new day's journey the path continued to snake upwards. Fortunately however, although the countryside below remained broken, we now followed the lie of the land, went along the contours instead of traversing them, skirted the tops of the hills instead of climbing them, so the going was less arduous. Our immediate goal was the Mughessé Mountain ridge, estimated to be 6,000 feet above sea level, which formed one of the natural boundaries of Misuku. On the opposing horizon a smudge of blue shadow indicated its counterpart, Wilindi Ridge. Between these two, protected, self sufficing, snug, lay the entire bowl of land that made up Misuku.

Mughessé crowned with primaeval forest, was the source of many streams which watered villages and gave life to the countryside below. Near at hand, partly obscured, the land fell sharply away to stony, over-grazed areas. Very faintly the sound of cow bells drifted up to us.

It took us two hours to reach the summit. Instantly we were plunged into cool gloom as in a cathedral, the sky blotted out by the canopies of enormous trees through which a neglected path threaded its way. The boles were hidden by dense shrub, the trunks swathed in creeper, the whole place pulsated with the secret life of insects. At one point we came on huge, iridescent butterflies dipping down silently over a still pool. Enchanting. Enchanted as well apparently, for as we sat down to eat Samueli's sandwiches, the capitao accompanying us broke the spell, saying,

"Sir, this is not a good place."

It was known that lion and leopard lurked in the forest, but surely the size of our party would keep off predators? Nevertheless assuming this to be the reason, we soon moved off.

Much later I learned that the forest was the burial place of chiefs and the haunt of their spirits. No wonder the carriers had quickened their pace, no wonder that left to themselves, people shunned it entirely, preferring to keep to the path following the contour well below the tree line; though a longer way round, it was a good deal safer.

Abruptly we burst through to sunlight again and I had my first glimpse of Misuku. I caught my breath, Ken had not exaggerated. Below, as far as the eye could see, small hills tumbled over one another, separated by valleys of half concealed streams. Homesteads and villages nestled on every slope, the roofs of round thatched huts merged into the landscape like mushrooms in a meadow. Every possible inch of ground supported maize or millet gardens interspersed with groves of plantains, with here and there a stand of pines or blue-gums.

"Well?" said Ken cutting across my thoughts.

I drew another deep breath but could not reply. The Austrian landscape of our honeymoon had delighted me, Misuku was even more beautiful. Now we saw the belled cattle heard from above and saw the boys who tended them. Saw also women working on the high, stony, unrewarding slopes. Without exception they stopped to stare and call out greetings as we passed, it was a fair assumption that apart from Alice Udd to whom they may have gone for medicine, they had not seen a white woman for many a long day. If ever.

The pattern continued as we came down through the villages. Excited chatter preceded and followed us, women in the compounds pounding grain two by two, called out. Small children peered fearfully from doorways, men emerged from the shade of roof thatch to shake Ken's hand, make welcoming speeches, while others fell in with us as we went along, swelling the retinue. And it was in this manner that we came to Katobo at last.

CHAPTER 13

AT KATOBO

Like others in Nyasaland, the Government Agricultural Station at Katobo occupied African Trust Land. That is, land leased from the local people, with their agreement and cooperation. The aim was to demonstrate ways of checking erosion and improving the soil by means of conservation, to introduce new crops and/or improved strains of traditional ones and in general give help and advice.
The people of Misuku, the Asukwa - no doubt in common with their compatriots elsewhere - had naturally, parted only with a few exhausted acres no use to anybody, and watched and waited to see what the mad Asungu, the Europeans, would make of them. So far, apart from the embryo coffee bushes, little had happened at Katobo because of its remote position and lack of a resident supervisor. A state of affairs Ken intended to rectify.

Needless to say, none of this concerned me on that first day. Always susceptible to atmosphere my priorities, roughly, were place, people, house. Misuku itself was magnificent. The people were friendly just as Ken had said, now for the house. We had walked for about two hours since leaving the forest on Mughessé, and were still among the foothills when he announced,
"Nearly there now. We should see the house soon. Yes, look, there it is!"
I looked, but could see only the grass roofs of yet another village on the side of a hill. Would we be living in one of these huts? It seemed perfectly possible. But then, set slightly aside and marginally larger than the rest, was the rectangular structure, with a grass roof certainly, but with a hint of whitewash on the walls, that was destined to become our home for several years.
It was not exactly the house itself however that commanded attention as we walked on down, but the noise coming from it. A party? Certainly the sounds were festive enough. The capitao accompanying us shouted something. The laughter, the guffaws, stopped abruptly. In the hush that followed a startled face appeared at an unglazed window, then giggling and subdued chatter broke out again. Ken swore. To the capitao he said,
"I told you before I left last time that all this was to be finished by the time I returned. It should have been done weeks ago,"
"Sir, replied the capitao, "The women could not come. They were digging their gardens."
"I didn't hire women. The labourers should have done it, it's their job to do what's required."
"Yes Sir. But whitewash is women's work. Men cannot whitewash."
"Nonsense. Anyone can put whitewash on a wall."
He elbowed his way into the house, I looked in at the doorway. The rectangle was divided into two rooms, both of which were crowded with men and women, hence

the merriment. All were now working away assiduously, all wore black and white nsaru which had formerly been black only, the earth floor was patterned white with the prints of bare feet.

Disorientated, I turned away to look at what Ken had euphemistically referred to as the garden, but yet again was brought up short.

Someone, Oscar Wilde probably, once said that the most magnificent view in the world palled after half an hour. He was wrong. The vista first seen from the top of Mughessé, was here presented close at hand. Before, below, all about the house, the little hills and corresponding valleys were sown with different kinds of crops; in close proximity the intimacy of daily life was clearly evident among a multiplicity of homesteads. The scene was replicated as far as the eye could see, until brought up short by Wilindi Ridge rising up on the skyline.

In the ensuing years I never tired of this unexpected gift of beauty. It surprised me each morning as I parted the bedroom curtains, strike when in the middle of some daily chore, I caught sight of it through the open door, catch at the heart when coming on it from different aspects of the garden. Its moods changed with the seasons, with the day, the hour even.

Very occasionally, as if in punishment for some misdemeanour, the gift was withdrawn. A mist would envelope the countryside, the house islanded, isolated as a ship at sea, the labourers hanging about aimlessly, until the wheeling sun broke through to put everything to rights once more.

The house stood on a patch of ground levelled out of the hillside. In front of it was a grassy area some twelve feet wide, which seemed to have the potential of becoming a lawn. It gave way to a lower, more extensive terrace, beyond which the land fell away sharply. I discovered later that a path down the hidden hillside bordered the coffee garden to the valley bottom.

At the back of the house the upward slope continued. To one side, about 100yards off, another path on a localised ridge led to three or four rectangular huts, brick built and seemingly in much better condition than our own. These were houses for the capitaos and other African visitors.

When I had wandered round the house I returned to the front and investigated the lower terrace. It was a mass of tangled undergrowth. But when about a week later, we had become sufficiently organised to hire a garden boy, and had it cleared, we discovered dark red roses growing there. I was reminded then to ask Ken who had built the house in the first place. He said it had been started by one, Keen Hammerson, a Dane, who had moved on for some reason and never been heard of again.

"So he was the one who planted the roses?"

"I suppose so."

I pondered on this unusual man who considered roses more important than a house with doors or glazed windows but, alas, we never found out any more about him.

The frenetic activity inside continued, clearly it was better to keep out of the way. By this time I realised the house was not rectangular as I had first thought, but L shaped with another small room tacked on at the back. This room communicated with the bedroom but it also had an outer doorway, likewise door-less, and a window with no glass.

Also out at the back at a short distance from the house, was the round mud shack of a kitchen, outside which stood James looking disgusted. A little way up the hill was another, smaller, mud and thatch structure which I recognised with sinking heart as the chimbuzi -latrine.

I told James to bring tea, and watched as he sullenly picked up a bucket and made his way across to a water furrow running down the hillside past the house and on down to the stream, carrying with it the lifeline of our water supply.

Ken meanwhile had been paying off the carriers. One or two had been with us throughout the ulendo and were anxious to get back to Karonga. First however, there was the matter of poso, (sometimes called posho,). Poso meant food, or food money spent on the journey. Of which more, much more later. Suffice it to say at this point, that carriers were never satisfied with the payout, they invariably argued and complained bitterly and it always took a long time to settle the matter.

After a while the workers started to leave, though whether this was because the job was finished, or because it was the end of the working day, was not clear. Either way it was at last possible to go inside. The front doorway opened directly on to a sizeable room with a fireplace, obviously a sitting room/dining room. On the right was the doorway to the bedroom which as already noted, gave access to the small room at the back.

Apart from having no doors or glazed windows, the house had no ceiling and the underside of the thatch was clearly visible; the internal dividing walls rose to eaves level only. An earth floor prevailed throughout, there was no furniture. An acrid smell of whitewash hung over the entire place.

"Well it could have been worse, said Ken looking round. "Though I was jolly annoyed they hadn't finished the whitewashing before. But never mind, it'll soon dry, then the smell will go. And my first job tomorrow will be to put the glass in the windows. The glass is all here, it only needs fixing."

"But doors, I protested nervously, "I mean, there aren't any. And there are leopard up on Mughessé, you said so..."

"Oh, that's alright. Last time I was here I heard of a carpenter in one of the outlying villages and sent for him to make doors. He came and took details, so he should have them ready by now. He'll most likely be along tomorrow."

"But tonight?"

"Tonight we'll use this."

He indicated a rolled up mat tacked to the lintel above the front doorway. I privately thought that no self respecting leopard would be put off by such a flimsy defence, but he went on,

"The people always use mats like this. They don't have doors to their huts."

He turned away dismissively and added,

"Now we must check that all our stuff is under cover, especially the food. It may rain in the night. Try to organise some supper, I'll put the camp beds up. First of all though I must light the lamp."

Evening was coming on, when the sun dipped it seemed very cool after the heat of the day. A breeze got up, it shook the matted door, came in at the unprotected windows and sent wisps of straw floating down from the thatch. James managed a scrappy supper of tinned corned beef and rice; he would be better housed for the night in one of the capitaos' houses. After a while we went to the back room, covered the wind-hole with a towel, washed perfunctorily and unearthed a blanket. Ken had put the beds close together under the double mosquito net so high on his list of priorities. Here it was more a matter of privacy rather than need. From the outer doorway, matted as at the front, came an intense fragrance. I asked Ken what it was.

"It's the moonflower, he said sleepily, "The bush is just outside the door."
I turned over and, lion and leopard notwithstanding, slept soundly till morning.

As usual morning came too soon, again our sleep was cruelly interrupted. Of course there was no bugle and the assault on the ear drums was not in the same league as that of reveillé in Karonga, but it was strident enough to galvanise us into wakefulness. The brazen sound coincidentally set up a hullabaloo among unfamiliar birds. As in Karonga Ken leapt out of bed.
"Time to start work, he muttered, "Should have woken up before."
The work clanger, for such it proved to be, consisted of a length of piping suspended from the branch of a nearby tree in which the birds - hornbills in fact - roosted, was struck several times by an iron bar. For several years this work clanger was to rule our lives six morning a week, bringing labourers from all directions. Only on Sundays did we sleep on, hornbills notwithstanding.
I got up and dressed, then made my way to the kitchen to see about breakfast, but was halted by a semicircle of women sitting outside it, all with babies and/ or young children. Having witnessed Jess' ministrations to the sick at Baka, I realised with sinking heart why they had come. Pity rose up inside me, not at this stage because of their ailments, but because of awareness of my incompetence, my lack of ability to help them. It was too late to reflect Ken should have married someone quite different, too late to regret not having been a Girl Guide. To gain time I asked James to question the women on the nature of their illness. He replied sulkily,
"I do not understand these people."
This was only too likely given the multiplicity of the different dialects, different languages even, spoken in the country.
"Well, who else here can understand them and speak English as well? There must be somebody."
There was not. Ken had gone off to organise the work force, the women would have to wait. Somehow the fact that clearly they were used to waiting, made the matter worse.
Fortunately at this point Ken came back. To my surprise he was accompanied by a tall African stranger wearing a bush hat, immaculately laundered khaki shirt

and shorts, shoes AND socks. (By contrast, due to recent circumstances, Ken's khaki was decidedly rumpled, and he wore no socks.) Thus my first meeting with Sutherland Mlenga, the Head Capitao.

The post of Head Capitao was the most senior in the Agricultural Department's hierarchy of African staff. It involved day to day management of the labourers, supervision of all the District Capitaos, inspection of land use throughout the region, noting infringements of the Department's regulations, and many other matters. In addition he was in sole charge when no European supervisor was present. Small wonder then that such an influential figure was held in high regard by the people.

Ken introduced us and we shook hands. Sutherland apologised for not having been on hand to welcome us on our arrival, he had been on ulendo he explained, and word of our coming had not reached him in time. I noted with relief that he spoke excellent English and wondered if it would be in order to enlist his help with my own problem. I told Ken about the sick women, and did not need to spell it out. He said,

"Oh, Sutherland can help you with that. He can translate for you much better than I can. And anyway I must go and see about that glass."

"But I don't know anything about medicine..."

"Just do the best you can. If any of them seem really ill tell them to go to the Court. There's a Government dispensary there with an African dispenser."

He moved off, Sutherland interrogated the women rapidly.

"This one has a fever Madam. This one has a sore on her leg. That one says her baby has no teeth."

I dressed the sore with antiseptic powder from our first aid kit, and after some thought, crushed up aspirin and shared it out among the feverish, wishing I had thought to bring more. They received it in cupped hands as if for the Sacrament. There seemed little to be done for the baby with no teeth.

Like the work clanger, the morning sick parade was to become a regular early morning feature. Although my ministrations never went much beyond common sense and the most basic treatment, in the course of time I did at least become more competent, always conscious that the psychological effect of belief in the power of European nfiti - magic - far outweighed the physical benefits.

On that first morning however, appalled at this new responsibility, when Ken and I at last sat down to breakfast, I raised the subject again.

"If people keep coming like this for medicine there soon won't be anything left to treat them with. Or ourselves for that matter."

"Remind me to write a note for the chief medical orderly at the hospital in Karonga when I send the messenger down with the mail, he replied, "He'll send up the basics for you. At the moment most of these women will be coming mainly out of curiosity to see you, rather than because of real need."

"But the language problem..."

"Sutherland can go on translating for you each morning. If it doesn't take too long that is."

Having finished his breakfast Ken was more concerned with getting glass in the windows, and was just leaving, when James came in to announce that the bread was finished. This reminded me of the other pressing problem.

"What about the kitchen?" I demanded.

"The kitchen? What about it?" Ken was genuinely surprised.

"Have you ever been in it? No, I thought not. It's just a smoky hut with nothing in it but the few pots and pans we brought with us. No stove, no chimney, no door, no window, just a fire over three stones on the ground, like the African women have. I can tell you there won't be bread or anything else unless something is done about it."

He was silent. At last he said,

"I'll have a word with Sutherland about that too. He's sure to come up with something. Or you can see him if you like. Yes, that would be better because you know what you want."

Certainly I knew what I wanted, there seemed very little chance of getting it. I went outside again and found Sutherland waiting. I led him to the kitchen and explained the situation. He tut-tutted, and conferred with James. At last he said he would see what he could do.

Ken meanwhile had been unpacking the sheets of glass stored in another mud shack, along with other materials previously ordered from the Public Works Department in Mzimba. I did not know then of the laborious route taken to get them to Katobo. First they had been driven some hundreds of miles over bumpy earth roads, by a PWD lorry to Kapoka on the edge of Misuku, off-loaded there and brought in the 17 arduous miles to Kapoka by carriers on foot. Either the glass sheets all miraculously survived the journey intact, or the broken ones had been discretely discarded en route.

The PWD had also thoughtfully provided one small glass cutter. But no putty.

The window frames, already in situ, were of the English cottage type, which is to say they were divided into small squares, 12 to each casement. There were two casements to each window. The house had 4 windows, plus the one in the small back room...

It grew hotter as the day wore on, and so did Ken. Neither was he left to get on with the job without interruptions, the life of the station must go on and plenty of complications arising from his absence became apparent.

The glass cutter became more and more blunt. Several hours, two sore fingers and much swearing later, all the panes were cut. Ken, surrounded by shards of broken glass and outright breakages. At dusk he straightened up and said,

"Too late to do anything more now, fixing the panes in the windows will have to wait till tomorrow."

Meanwhile, throughout the day the place had been a hive of activity. Apart from the sick ones, there were other women, come to do more whitewashing, this time on the outside of the walls. Others with head-loads of firewood - James had complained bitterly at lack of this vital commodity - processed toward the kitchen across what would eventually become our garden. On the roof of the house two labourers were piling on more thatch.

Sitting outside on the top terrace, I was occupied with some sewing. In Karonga when we were preparing to leave, a surprising, and to me rather touching, item on Ken's list of bare essentials, was curtain material. Now the reason was all too obvious. Not only was the house open to all and sundry by day, but the rooms clearly visible after dark. The goldfish bowl syndrome with a vengeance. At the moment our only dubious privacy was a towel tacked across the wind hole in the back room where we slept.

Fortunately however there was no shortage of cotton cloth in Karonga. Messrs Andani and Khateria each had a goodly supply in their stores, all of it brightly coloured, mostly with big swirly patterns, very popular among local ladies. I had bought a bolt of red and white checked gingham, plus a good supply of needles and cotton thread. Now it was pleasant to sit in Misuku sunlight, not yet too hot, observing the activity around and in the homesteads below, pausing in my work now and then to look up and admire the scenery once more. Only the problem of the kitchen, lurking at the back of the mind, marred the pleasure.

At last I got up and crept unwillingly to the back of the house. There I had a surprise. At the kitchen doorway a slatted door stood propped open. Inside was a rough hewn table such as could be seen outside some of the village huts. A length of plank was pegged to the curving wall to make a shelf, On the floor stood three large gourds of water - another of James' grievances had been that lack of containers, which meant carrying water from the furrow each time he needed it. I also noticed a can, known as a debé, about 18inches high and 12inches cubed which had formerly held 4gallons of paraffin. I came to know afterwards that empty debés were highly sought after, were almost a form of currency, and put to a variety of uses. In the townships they were collected and hammered flat to make roofs for huts or small stores. In country districts they were mainly used for storage. In our case, with the top taken off, it would be used not only to heat our bath water, but placed its side on the fire on the floor, could serve as a primitive oven as well.

Last but not least there was a wooden chair which, one suspected, had come from Sutherland's own house. The sum total did not add up to much, but any change was an improvement and I was very pleased. Not so James. He sniffed, and remarked that a man must be found to cut the nkuni - firewood - and fetch the water.

He rose magnificently to the challenge however, and for breakfast next morning produced a perfect loaf of bread.

As if to prove the assertion that with one problem solved, the mind will find something else to worry about, as I continued my stitching after lunch, my thoughts reverted to our lack of doors. For the foreseeable future it looked as if we must sleep protected only by slatted mats. Suddenly a slight movement caused me to look up. A man stood uncertainly at the edge of the lower terrace. He was tall and wore an archaic bush hat, this and his grave expression gave him the look of Mr Arnolfini in Van Eyke's picture of that name. An impression instantly dispelled when he opened his mouth to speak and displayed teeth filed to a point. I exchanged greetings with him as best I could, and when he had shaken hands with me and with the labourers working nearby, he launched into a speech totally incomprehensible but for one word - carpenter. My delight at hearing this was tempered only by the fact that unless he had a possé of carriers waiting out of sight down the hill, he appeared to have brought no doors with him. I sent one of the men to fetch Ken, meanwhile the others began to question him, But here was another surprise, his speech was not understood by them either. He must have come from a far country. Ken came back shortly with Sutherland. Even he had difficulty. Ken asked him to enquire how long the carpenter would need to make four doors. A protracted discussion followed, then Sutherland said,

"Sir, this man says it will take fifteen days to make four doors."

"Tell him that is too long"

There was more discussion, then,

"Sir, he says this is long time work. First he must find a tree and cut it down and..."

"Alright, alright. Ask how long for the two outer doors."

Another pause,

"He says he can make one door in three days because he has the wood already. He says also that he has made one door already."

"Good, good. Tell him to bring both on the fourth day."

Next came the knotty question of the price. I left them to it and called James to bring tea.

By evening two of the curtains were finished. We threaded them through bamboo canes and tacked them up above the bedroom windows. What a transformation. Never had the closing of a curtain seemed so dramatic.

In spite of the slatted doors - I was becoming blasé about them - we moved the camp beds into the bedroom from the small back room. With that now empty, there was nothing to prevent us taking a bath there. Accordingly Ken told James to heat up water in the debé, then he set up the collapsible bath, the counterpart of which had seemed so quaint in the Army and Navy Store in London. It was roughly the size of a child's inflatable paddling pool, which is to say, it was about three and a half feet in diameter, with sides some ten inches high. James brought the water in.

"You can go first." said Ken generously.

With the cool night breeze fluttering in at the unglazed window covered inadequately by the towel, the prospect was less than inviting. I undressed quickly and lowered myself carefully. The bare earth floor struck chill through the canvas. It was no place to linger. I washed quickly then attempted to get out. Alas, an incautious movement caused the collapsible bath to live up to its name only too literally. One side drooped, the water overflowed and trickled across the floor in a muddy stream. As it had been, in James' words "too few" to start with, it was now only about an inch deep, and cooling rapidly. Shivering I called to Ken to come and take his turn. He was not best pleased. But I was dried and tucked up in the camp bed, secure under the mosquito net before he had finished cursing.

Ken spent most of the next day coaxing the panes of glass into their allotted squares, using nails to fix them in lieu of the putty the PWD had failed to send. Neither the individual panes nor the frames were truly accurate and it later transpired that every pane in every window took part in an orchestration of whistles, rattles and snare drums whenever a breeze got up. No matter. Though still door-less, we now had windows and as I finished my sewing, curtains to draw across them, a sure sign of progress.

Because the evenings were cool, we had been having a fire in the main room. Not as simple an operation as might be supposed as we had no paper to light it and the matches brought from Karonga had got wet on the journey. James brought in an armful of firewood and a few sticks. When he had arranged these to his satisfaction he carried in a spadeful of red hot embers from the kitchen, narrowly missing the new curtains as he did so. The twigs blazed up immediately, but the logs resisted. Only after much blowing and puffing did they burn at all, and when they did they sent billows of smoke out into the room.
"The wood's wet." said Ken disgustedly.
Indeed we had been getting rain every night, but I knew better.
"It isn't just the wood." I told him.
The chimney stack rose up in the room straight against the wall and out through the roof. We had lived in such a house as that once when I was child and the fire always smoked.
"Chimneys must have a bend, I went on authoritatively, "Two are even better, a sideways one and a back bend."
"It'll be alright with dry wood." he retorted.
It was not, the mud brick chimney continued to smoke. Ken said he would do something about it, "When I have time." And we both knew what that meant.
In the event the matter was taken out of his hands. A few nights later as we sat reading aloud to one another to an accompaniment of hissing rain, rattling windows and frequent lungsful of smoke, a chunk of mud slid down the chimney and landed on the hearth. More chunks followed until the entire stack collapsed, The fire was smothered, mud half filled the room, in the wall was a gaping hole.
There was much hilarity among the labourers when they turned up for work in the morning. Ken detailed two of them to clear up the mess and two more to plug the void. Once again James was disgusted. That was the end of our nightly fires for quite some time.

That the carpenter failed to appear on the fourth day surprised no-one. But on the sixth day as I was attempting to help the new garden boy clear a patch of brambles on the lower terrace, a strange sight presented itself. An unaccustomed object appeared horizontally over the rim of the garden. Beneath it, bent almost double, was the carpenter and another man. Both had the look of having carried the burden a long way.
They set down the door down with relief. I waited until they had recovered a little, then we exchanged the usual polite greetings. They were very pleased with themselves, and I with them. I sent a labourer to get Ken and Sutherland and told James to make them sweet tea. The carpenter and his mate drank it gratefully. Once again the men working nearby gathered round with interest, as incapable

of communicating as I was. James addressed them in Chinyanga, I tried English and even French. To no avail. Ken had said possibly they lived across the Songwe river, the Northern border of the country, and spoke a form of Swahili.

When they had finished the tea they got up and eyed the front doorway, calculating measurements, discussing the matter between them. I caught a word which sounded like inches, but subsequently turned out to be hinges.

Ken and Sutherland came back, the former also was pleased to see them, the more so as he actually had hinges to hand, and door knobs and accessories which had come up with the glass. (He had of course, ordered doors as well, but the PWD had its own whimsical sense of priorities.) The hinges forthcoming, the carpenter and his mate set to work. The door was a creditable piece of craftsmanship, the door frame, like the windows, less so. There followed a Pyramis and Thisbe interlude as they tried to surprise it into position.

It hung to their satisfaction at last, the door swung freely - in both directions. Ken went off to the store to get a piece of wood to make a jamb, sending for Sutherland again as he did so. A quantity of dusty timber was stacked against a wall of the store, presumably intended for completion of the house. A task which Keen Hammerson for reasons best known to himself, had not stayed to achieve. Ken came back not only with the required wood, but also with a marvellous idea.

But first the door. The jamb was fixed, the door opened and shut one way only. Door-knobs and a lock were added, the latter upside down, but this did not matter.

The job was completed to the satisfaction of everyone concerned, the carpenter, and his mate whom we came to refer to as The Walrus for literary reasons, clearly were looking forward to returning to their village well recompensed.

But here Ken's great idea came into play. Loath to part with such good workmen, he asked via Sutherland who had now rejoined us, if they knew how to make a bed. There was a pregnant pause. Then the carpenter said reluctantly that, yes, he had once made such a thing for an Nsungu - European - long ago, but... This was good enough for Ken. He led them off to the store, showed them the timber and explained what he wanted, for it goes without saying that it must be a double bed. Even Sutherland was hard put to explain this unknown requirement so Ken, employing his artistic talents, made a sketch. The carpenter looked dubious. At last he said doubtfully that he would try. But first of all he must return to his village, he would come back later, and bring the other door when he had made it and...

The vision of a comfortable bed faded. But Ken was not to be put off. He said, "Sutherland, tell these men I will give them a good price if they will stay here and start on it at once. I will get them a place to sleep, and also give them food."

The carpenter and his mate digested this, the idea of such precipitate action being unheard of. I held my breath. Finally, to general approval they agreed, the deal was on. Albeit it at a price.

Next morning even before the work clanger had sounded, we were woken by the noise of sawing and hammering. The Walrus and the Carpenter had slept in one the capitaos' empty houses, the promised food had been cooked by a labourer's wife. Both men were anxious to get the job done as soon as possible. When Ken went out to them before breakfast they had already cut the required lengths of wood and were now planing them.

The labourers arrived and the carpenter announced he would need a cow's skin. This item at least was easier to find in Misuku than it might have been in England, since most of the people had cattle. On the other hand the beasts were their currency, the gauge of their prestige, and they seldom killed them. It followed therefore that the animals died either from disease or from old age, which might, or might not affect the condition of the hide. Be that as it may, we were in no position to quibble and as the men bent to their task, a hide was soon forthcoming.

The two craftsmen worked till dusk, by which time the construction creditably resembled Ken's sketch. Next morning they cut the hide into strips and wove them crisscross over the frame to form the spring/base. The bed was finished. Except for a refinement insisted on by Ken, namely the drilling of holes in the tops of the uprights of head and foot to accommodate rods supporting the double the mosquito net.

As with the door, all planes and angles were true, though no measuring tools were in evidence.

Both men were pleased with result. Flattered too at the labourers' astonishment over the speed with which it had been accomplished. We ourselves were delighted. Ken paid them the agreed sum and we parted cordially, with handshakes all round, and Ken urging them to return as soon as possible with the rest of the doors.

Of course we had only the thin mattresses from the camp beds to put on the spring, and thereafter woke up with the squares of the hide patterning our bodies. But 'Oh the bliss of the double bed after the hurly-burly of the camping equivalent of the chaise longue.'!

CHAPTER 14

FOOD FOR THOUGHT

In the ensuing days life began to assume some sort of routine. Every day we looked for the return of the carpenter and his mate with the rest of the doors, but it was a matter of two weeks before they came and completed the work. By which time there was something more pressing to worry about.

We had survived a week and a half at Katobo when the body blow fell. One evening when supper was over, James coming in to take the plates, stood resolutely in the doorway. He said,
"Sir, I wish to leave."
I stared and sat bolt upright, Ken looked startled.
"What! But why? What's the trouble?" he said.
"I have no food."
"But that's impossible! I bought you a sack of rice before we left Karonga. You can't have eaten it all already."
"It is now finished." James replied sullenly.
It certainly was not possible that one person could have eaten a whole sack of rice in a fortnight. Had it mysteriously shrunk on the ulendo as had our own provisions? A distinct possibility. Or had he been selling it off to the locals?
"Well, I'll get you some more. Anyway there are other things growing here, potatoes for instance, and millet for porridge. I'll try and get you some. Meanwhile you can make bread for yourself as well as us."
It was true about the potatoes as I had been pleased to discover, but they were something of a novelty in the area and so far we had managed to buy only a few pounds. James said,
"I do not eat potatoes. Also I have no relish." (fresh green stuff.)
"But you can buy other things from the people. They have relish."
"I do not know these people. I do not speak their language."
Poor James, by now everything was wrong. Born and bred in the warm South where there was plenty of food, where markets and shops abounded, where there were job opportunities and, above all, his own people all around, it was small wonder that Misuku was alien to him. At first he had enjoyed the respect and status accorded to a stranger, but this, patently, was not sufficient compensation. Absorbed in my own problems I realised too late how isolated he had been. Not because the people were unfriendly, but simply because he could not communicate with them. Nor had the primitive conditions at Katobo done much to restore his morale or enhance his well-being.
Even so, Ken reasoned with him at length. It was no good, his mind was made up, he was desperate to get away. At last Ken saw that further remonstrance was useless, and said,

85

"Very well. On Tuesday I will give you your money and you can go to Karonga with the mail messenger."

James stood his ground. He said,

"I wish to go tomorrow."

"Tomorrow! But that's impossible. You don't know the way. Besides it would be far too dangerous to go alone."

"I do not wish to go to Karonga. Tomorrow there is a man who will walk to Fort Hill. I will walk with him. I wish to go to South Africa. I wish for work in the mines."

Fort Hill. The mines. We looked at him in consternation. He had heard, probably from a returned miner who had picked up some English, that many of the young men in Misuku went off to the South African mines. Heard too how they earned much pay and returned three years later full of money. It was impossible to impress on him the reality of the situation, of which he could have no conception, although Ken tried very hard, reiterating the conditions he had described to me on our journey from Mzuzu to Karonga. Nothing he said had any effect, James was adamant, he would go next day.

I spent a troubled night. Not entirely, not it must be admitted, even primarily on James' behalf, although that certainly weighed on my mind. No, what kept me awake was the realisation of what our own situation would be once he had gone. Belatedly I saw how much we relied on him for so many things. How could we manage without him?

How much of his work could I do myself I wondered? After all we lived very simply, still virtually maintaining a camping existence. Housework was nonexistent, for what could be done in a house with an earth floor, no ceiling and bits of grass constantly floating down from the underside of the thatch, white ants tunnelling down the walls?

What about the laundry? I could do that I supposed, so long as someone fetched water from the furrow, lit the kitchen fire and heated water in the debé for me. My heart sank at the prospect. Then there was the ironing, quite a different matter, and very important. Not just for the sake of appearance, but against ticks and other unpleasant creatures which laid their eggs on the washing when it was hung out to dry. Moreover the iron was a mediaeval monster which must be fed red hot charcoal. On the only occasion I had ever tried to use it one of the embers had dropped out on to one of Ken's shirts, the front naturally, and made what looked like a neat bullet hole exactly over the heart. All our clothes were of cotton, except for Ken's twill bush shirts and they presented an extra challenge.

In the watches of the night it was probably inevitable that my thoughts should now turn to Sutherland, not only because he had been a tower of strength already, but because his clothes were invariably spotless and immaculately pressed. Could I ask him who did them? Better not, I decided, in case he did them himself. But no, he would have a dhobi of course. A dhobi. That was the answer. With so many people eager for employment it should not be difficult to find and train one. One problem solved at least.

Reluctantly I now turned my mind to the most urgent matter of all, the one beside which all others paled into insignificance, the one which had lain on my mind, heavy as indigestion, ever since James had dropped his bomb-shell. We MUST have a cook. Above all we must have a cook who could make bread. Never had this humble commodity, hitherto taken for granted, seemed so unattainable or desirable. Oh the wicked waste that someone with the talent of conjuring up perfect loaves in diverse conditions, should elect to spend his time sweating away in the South African mines.

Apart from the bread I knew very well that producing three substantial meals a day was a task I definitely could not undertake myself. Not that I could not cook. What I could not do was spend my time crouching over a fire contained in three stones on the earth floor of a smoky mud hut. Nor did I intend to try. The solution was no nearer when a troubled sleep overtook me at last.

Early next morning James brought in tea for the last time. Later he prepared breakfast. We ate it with heavy hearts. When it was over Ken gave him his money. Presently he came to say goodbye, already looking more like the jaunty youth Ken had hired in Blantyre. Confidence restored, his belongings wrapped in his sleeping blanket slung over his shoulder on a stick in true Dick Whittington fashion, he was looking for adventure. His travelling companion waiting slightly to one side was also excited. We wished them well and said goodbye.

Ken turned away to talk to Sutherland but I stood and watched as they took the path round the hill, until the land dipped and they were lost to sight.

Did James go to Fort Hill and enlist for the mines? Achieve fame and fortune? Return home rich, a hero at last? Or did some chance encounter along the way - a lift on the main road from a PWD lorry going south perhaps - change his life in some other direction? We would never know. But the thought lingered in the mind, 'Hoping it might be so.'

It was not true that we were entirely without help in the kitchen. From the first Ken had detailed one of the labourers, Station Chabinga, to fetch water, chop wood, and act as general factotum. It was probable that he had been the first to arrive in the morning and, being as putty in James' hands, lit the fire for our early tea. In the brief era of our evening fires he had sometimes brought in the logs and got a blaze going. Clearly his accomplishments would have to be extended.

Naturally Sutherland knew of our predicament, naturally I enlisted his help once more. I told him we wanted to take on a boy to train as a dhobi, he said he would see about it. But when, despairingly, I mentioned our dire need for a cook, he looked dubious.

Depression set in with a vengeance when he had gone. A dhobi was one thing, not even Sutherland could conjure up a cook out of thin air. Once again I was mistaken. Meanwhile I prepared a basic lunch and later struggled to cook it in the pressure cooker on the (single burner) Primus stove bought in Blantyre. This spiteful beast was difficult to light, temperamental in operation and would go out at the least provocation.

We did not eat well that day. Even Ken became aware of the seriousness of the situation.

In the afternoon as the labourers were leaving, Sutherland returned. He said,
"Madam, these men say there is one man who was a cook."
My heart leapt.
"A cook? Who? Where?"
"Yes Madam, I also know that man. Sometimes he is a labourer. But in former times he worked in the kitchen of Mr Lilford."
"Mr Lilford? Who is he? Where does he live? No, never mind that... Can you find this man and bring him here?"
"Yes Madam. He is not present today. Tomorrow he will come."
I was very excited at this development. But when I told Ken the news and asked indignantly why I had not heard before of this unsuspected neighbour, he replied,
"Because he's been dead for at least twenty years."
"But who was he? Did he live near? What did he do?"
"I'll tell you if you let me. He lived here in Misuku, about five miles away over the hill. I only know that he grew coffee there and was killed by a lion."
"Killed by a lion? I echoed stupidly, "Poor man."
"Yes. That much is true, I had it from Andrew. All the rest is hearsay."
The gist of the story it seemed was that Lilford, a disreputable younger son of British nobility had, late in the 19th century, in time honoured tradition, been shipped off to the Colonies to make his fortune, and found his way to Nyasaland. In passing I wondered if he had come across Captain Lugard. Be that as it may he had somehow managed to acquire a few stony acres in Misuku before the prohibition on European settlement; perhaps by that time he had finished sowing his wild oats. At any rate he settled down and grew coffee. He had apparently been in Misuku for many years before dying of wounds sustained while hunting down a man-eating lion which had been troubling the villagers.
Ken cut across my contemplation of this romantic story -
"Don't expect too much from this so-called cook. The chap must be pretty old by now, most likely he will have forgotten anything he ever knew. Anyway he might not come."
The warning fell on deaf ears and in no way inhibited my vision of the delicious meals we would soon be enjoying, courtesy of this former employee of British aristocracy.

Reality returned soon enough. Next day Sutherland presented a Rip van Winkel figure in a rusty black nsaru who spoke not a word of English. Abashed, I collected myself sufficiently to ask sensible questions. Where did he live? He pointed vaguely down the hill. What was his name? William Chisumela was the answer. How long ago did he work for Mr Lilford? A foolish question. He would not have measured the years since. What sort of work had he done? Another exchange,
"He says Madam, said Sutherland, "That he helped the cook in the kitchen."
In other words he had been the kitchen boy. With sinking heart I put the ultimate question,
"Does he know how to make bread? Can he make it for us?
Clearly mention of this long forgotten item struck some sort of chord. After some

cogitation he said doubtfully that he would try. There was no need to consider the matter, no choice in fact. I took him on. I asked Sutherland to impress on him that he must come faithfully every day very early, to light the kitchen fire, and left it at that for the moment, afraid of scaring him off. There yet remained the communication problem but Sutherland said he would translate my needs for the day, when he came to help with the sick and suffering. I thanked him, knowing as I did so that the new regime would take a good deal more organisation on my part than hitherto employed. For good measure I also asked him to tell Station - an interested onlooker at this point - that he must work in the kitchen and help William as he had helped James, and also do other things which I would show him. He looked startled but after some consultation finally he too said he would try.

Next morning early I hurried out to the primitive kitchen and was pleasantly surprised. Not only was the fire burning nicely and the kettle boiling on it for morning tea, but William was dressed in clean shirt and shorts, no doubt with Sutherland's connivance, for standards must be maintained. Station was also there, the two of them good-naturedly parrying ribaldry from labourers turning up for the day's work.

As soon as Sutherland appeared I gave William instructions about the meals and said I would show him what he must do. Then I tackled the bread problem. William eyed the flour, the dried yeast, the baking tin, with the air of one commanded to spin gold out of flax. I explained how to reconstitute the dried yeast, suspecting that Mr Lilford's cook would have used fermented wild hops all those years ago. I stressed the need to leave the dough out in the sun until it had become big - not too sure of myself as I had never actually tried it. Should I stay and supervise him? Or should I leave it to him in the hope that memory of his earlier employment might reassert itself. I opted for the latter. It was a mistake.

In the evening after a fairly indigestible supper of stringy chicken, William appeared diffidently in the doorway holding out something that looked like a brick. Alas, it not only weighed, but felt, and in imagination, even smelt like a brick. He scanned our faces hopefully, having no idea if he had succeeded or failed in the task.

He never did master the art of bread making. It was the magic properties of the yeast that defeated him, and in truth, who could blame him? Certainly I knew I could do no better in such primitive conditions; during our remaining time in Misuku, every day after carefully sifting out the weevils from the sack of flour, I made up a basic scone mixture and gave it to William to cook in the debé. He for his part, learned to make tea, ground millet porridge for breakfast, and produce a boiled chicken for supper accompanied by rice and anything else we had managed to acquire. Also to make an omelette for lunch when we were fortunate enough to get eggs.

On the plus side I no longer minded going into the kitchen, for in place of a sullen James, both William and Station were good humoured and anxious to please.

They did not quite succeed in ruining our digestions although it was a near thing. Neither did I succeed in making cooks of them; I came firmly to the conclusion that

Mr Lilford had died not from his mauling by the lion, but from slow poisoning.

Finding a cook was by no means the only problem we had with food. Getting it at all was equally fraught. As related we had brought flour, rice and other basics with us from Karonga, somewhat reduced on our arrival, but with the departure of James the remainder no longer dwindled as if by magic. So we were unlikely actually to starve. Achieving a balanced diet was another matter. Ken's appetite, always hearty, was now the more so with all his physical and psychological activity. As for myself, by a cruel twist of fate, when faced with a cornucopia of plenty on board ship a combination of sea and pregnancy sickness had prevented my enjoying any of it, I was now perpetually hungry. The fruit so abundant in Karonga, did not grow at the altitude of Misuku. Ken assured me that oranges and other citrus did grow, but we never saw any. Perhaps it was the wrong time of year. Nor did we have any fresh vegetables until Ken gave it out that we would buy any the villagers had to sell, such as corn cobs, green beans etc. But here was another misunderstanding. Only potatoes were immediately edible. All other food stuff was grown to maturity by the villagers, hardened off in the sun then stored in nkokwe against rats and other predators. Nkokwe were miniscule round huts raised on stilts, in the manner that farmers' barns in England were raised on staddle-stones in former times. And for the same reason. In Misuku, as in many other places, the grain, the pulses were brought out in the dry and hungry season and pounded to flour, or meal, by the women to tide the family over until the rains came again. It goes without saying therefore, that our desire to eat young green beans and tender corn cobs, was not only incomprehensible to the people, but considered wickedly wasteful as well.

It might well be thought that starting up our own vegetable garden would have been a top priority, and so it was - or would have been. On the first day after our arrival, even before starting on the glass cutting, Ken had designated a plot to one side of the house, a little higher up the hill, and hired one of the labourers, Trisom, as garden boy. It was at this point that my heinous crime of buying flower seeds only, in Blantyre, came to light. Defending myself vigorously in what I considered to be a natural mistake and declaring it was no use crying over spilt milk, in the spirit of Keen Hammerson and the roses, I planted the flower seeds all round the house.

Ken meanwhile, lost no time in firing off urgent pleas to Jess and to Mr Andani, next time the mail messenger went to Karonga, to send up anything they had to rectify the situation. Jess sent what I took to be pumpkin seeds, but which turned out to be South African squash, and tomato plants. The latter were rather droopy by the time they reached us, but revived soon enough when planted. Tomatoes grew like weeds in Karonga, but were virtually unknown in Misuku. From Andanis came packets of lettuce seed, New Zealand spinach, French beans.

In due course the vegetable plot sprouted colourful packets set on little marker sticks. Unfortunately, apart from the tomatoes and squash which did well, and lettuce, that was all it did sprout for many weeks. By which time we were ready to leave.

By contrast the flower seeds germinated at once; the front garden soon became a riot of colour, with marigolds, gerbera, cannas etc, and morning glories leaping up the walls of the house.

We leaned heavily on canned goods. Butter, milk, cheese and meat, all came in tins. Of fresh meat there was nothing but scrawny chickens, lean and strong in the legs from scavenging scraps in the villages, bearing absolutely no resemblance to the succulent birds my father kept in the orchard at home. At the other end of this food cycle we would sometimes get eggs, noticeably from the women who came for medicine. Before using them, following Jess' example, I tested them for freshness by plunging them in cold water; a method not infallible. New laid ones sank, old ones were supposed to float. But more than once I came across a foetal chick when mixing up an omelette. In any case I felt guilty about taking eggs from the people, addled or not, and once when Sutherland was on hand, I suggested he tell the women they themselves should eat them, or give them to their children as a valuable source of protein.

"They will not eat them Madam." he said decidedly.

"Why not?"

"They say that if they eat eggs they will not get babies."

I considered this novel method of birth control then, the inference by this time plain for all to see, said,

"But I eat them myself."

"That is true Madam. But it is different for Europeans."

Two other factors were vital to our diet. The first came to us, surprisingly, by way of old Simbeyé the mail messenger who plied his trade regularly between Misuku and Karonga with letters official and personal. From the start Ken had extended his duties by getting him to bring back fresh fruit, vegetables, and even meat from the market there. That he seemed not to mind the extra burden surprised me until I came to know him better, and realised he never travelled alone, that there were always others on the route only too happy to carry things for him in the expectation of favours down the line. As he (they) took at least two and a half days over the return journey, the meat, wrapped in banana leaves bound round with bark twine, arrived decidedly gamey. I pressure cooked it at once on the Primus stove. The stock made delicious soup with all the restorative properties of beef tea. We ate as much of the flesh as we could and gave the rest to Station and William to share among all and sundry, every- one feasting while it was still palatable.

The second factor, by no means less important, was the sack of finger millet Sutherland had managed to get for us early on. Millet, known as mlési, was the staple diet of the people and we ate it as they did. That is, pounded to meal by the women, then mixed with water and made into porridge. Babies were of necessity weaned on mlesi porridge, surely not a good thing. For nutritious as it undoubtedly was, palatable it was not, and a good deal of coaxing must have gone into inducing them to eat it. As for ourselves, glad as we were of a substantial breakfast, not even the addition of sugar and reconstituted dried milk could make it enjoyable. Especially as in some part of its preparation - the pounding? The sack it came in? Conditions in the kitchen? - it was gritty. So that as with Hardy's Wessex villagers faced with a similar problem, it was advisable to eat it without actually bringing the jaws quite together...

CHAPTER 15

CHIEF DISTINCTION

Over-grazing and erosion had taken such a toll of the land at Katobo that it had become exhausted and good for nothing. Which of course was why the people had been willing to lease it to the Government in the first place. During his last tour when based in Karonga, between numerous other duties Ken had managed to get away to Misuku long enough to supervise the terracing, manuring and mulching of the steep sided valley below the house, and the planting of coffee seedlings. By the time of my arrival the young bushes were in their third year, their glossy dark leaves very pleasing to the eye. Moreover in the valley bottom bordering a stream was a nursery of seedlings intended for distribution among the villagers to enable them to open up their own coffee gardens. Of which more later.

Apart from Mr Lilford, coffee growing was not entirely new to the area. One man, Joseph Mkumbwa, had grown it successfully for some years, perhaps encouraged by Lilford himself, possibly with seed beans supplied by him. Joseph now had a flourishing garden near the Court of Chief MweniMisuku and was, by local standards, very rich, with numerous wives and children, so that his homestead was the size of a small village. Indeed it was difficult to understand why others had not followed his example.

Be that as it may, the Agricultural Department had now decided to establish a coffee cooperative in the area which would serve a double purpose. Firstly the cultivated terraces would help check erosion on the barren hillsides, secondly it would give the people the chance to grow a cash crop and decrease their total dependence on subsistence farming. It was this Ken felt, that justified his full time (albeit unofficial,) presence in Misuku.

The nursery now required daily inspection, for the seedlings had germinated well and the tender young plants were vulnerable. They must be protected from predators, large and small, as well as from the sun. Accordingly they were set in neat lines and shaded by tunnels formed by sticks about 18inches high, two feet apart, thatched over with banana leaves - the fore-runner of today's plastic tunnels. If the rain held off the seedlings must be watered morning and evening and a group of girls had been hired to tend them non stop in daylight hours, to prevent them drying out and withering. The girls, young and pretty, not yet married, moved with unhurried grace between stream and nursery, water pots on heads, well aware of the glances of the labourers working on the terraces above. All were clearly delighted at this rare chance to earn money, even though of course it must immediately be handed over to their fathers. In practice however, some of it returned to them in the form of the coloured nsaru they wore, or perhaps a beaded necklace. Which as the fathers well knew, would enhance the girls' chances in the marriage market.

Ken routinely inspected the nursery first thing in the morning and often in the afternoon as well when everyone had finished work, in which case I would go with him. It was pleasant to thread our way down the steep path bordering the terraces on which the bushes were beginning to shoot white blossom. Slightly less pleasant was the climb up again. But provided nothing untoward had happened to the all important seedlings, Ken always came back in good spirits, able to face William's indigestible supper with something like equanimity.

All the District Capitaos had orders to publicise the Coffee Cooperative as they went about their work so that people all over the region could not fail to know about it. Ken backed this up when he went on ulendo round the villages, holding meetings to extol the advantages of coffee growing, telling all potential growers that when the bushes came to bearing Government would buy the crop at a fair price.

"If you don't believe what can be done on land given up as useless, he said, "You can come to Katobo and see for yourselves."

This at least was a popular pastime, involving no work but rather a good day out, and many strangers turned up at the house in expectation of conducted tours.

"How long does it take for the bushes to bear?" I asked Ken.

"Aye, there's the rub", he replied, "Three years at least, four to get a decent crop."

In view of this, as well as all the hard work initially involved, it was easy to see why people were reluctant to commit themselves, and not difficult to deduce that the success or otherwise of the venture was still in the balance.

Ken now decided that a visit to the local chief - who had already given tacit approval for the scheme - might be profitable. Indeed he could do no other than pay it lip service, for although enjoying great prestige and influence over the local people, the authority of chiefs was limited. Jess had given me an inkling of the hierarchy. Local chiefs were responsible in the first instance to the Paramount chief of the whole region, who in turn must liaise with DCs, PCs and ultimately with the British Government in Zomba.

Misuku being small and somewhat insignificant, apparently warranted only a sub chief. Although not yet having seen the Court complex I knew it to comprise the open sided court-house where the sub-chief and elders dispensed their own brand of justice, a Dispensary in the charge of an African dispenser, a Scots' Mission church and a school. All around lived the elders and advisers and their extended families, plus numerous hangers on, so that the village grown up about the complex was bigger than that of Joseph Mkumbwa's.

"He seemed very interested when I went to see him, said Ken, "He's agreed to come here and see for himself what's going on. I've invited him for tea afterwards. The day after tomorrow."

"What? I cried, "But that's terrible!"

The thought of receiving such an august personage in such primitive conditions filled
me with alarm,

"We've only got two chairs. And two cups. What will he think?"

"Oh you don't need to worry, it'll be alright. Sutherland will help us out I'm sure"

An air of excitement filled the whole station at news of the visit. On the appointed day Station as well as William, had somehow acquired clean shirt and shorts. The afternoon being cool Ken wore a sleeveless pullover over his newly pressed khaki. I put on my best maternity dress, Sutherland of course, was smartest of all.

Ken went down to meet the Chief at the nursery; the working day was over but the labourers and the colourful girls lingered. I posted Trisom at the head of the path to alert us of their coming, then went to the kitchen to make sure that William had the kettle boiling on the stove. Half an hour later Trisom gave a shout, voices floated up to us then a straggle of men appeared over the rim of the garden.

I had not known what to expect of an African chief, but lodged somewhere in the subconscious was the thought of a tall imposing figure in colourful robes and feathered head-dress. In this I was disappointed, Sub Chief MweniMisuku was quite young, little more than a boy in fact. He wore long trousers and a sports jacket, the elders wore ordinary black nsaru, as did the bodyguard, their spears, one hoped, purely ceremonial. Their lord and master spoke no English, but shook hands as Ken introduced me. Through Sutherland he made a flowery speech declaring his pleasure at Mr Waterfield's coming to live among his people and teach them good ways of farming. (Ken had formerly crossed swords with him because of breaches in the Department's regulations.) He looked at me and said he prayed to God that He would give Mr Waterfield many fine sons.

There was more but I was preoccupied, hoping William would have the tea ready, and that Station would make no blunders. It came as a shock therefore when the oratory abruptly ceased, and at a sign, one of the men stepped forward and presented me with a depressed looking chicken. Disconcerted I took it awkwardly and struggled for control it as it squawked and flapped furiously. Stammering my thanks I handed it over to Trisom as soon as decently possible.

Ken led the way indoors and sat the Chief ceremoniously on a wooden chair borrowed, along with some enamel mugs, from Sutherland, who now stood in the background with the elders. Very nervously although I had practiced it assiduously with him beforehand, Station brought in the tea, also a plate of cakes made by me, and gently burnt by William.

While this was going on there were speeches from the others, Ken trying hard to turn the subject once more to the coffee cooperative.

When everything had been eaten and drunk and the talk finally over, the Chief stood up to leave. At the door he waved his retinue away and began talking urgently to Sutherland. What matter of import was this? Had we unwittingly breached some detail of etiquette that could ditch the whole scheme? Had the cakes affected his digestion already?

"Sir, said Sutherland at last, "Chief MweniMisuku wishes to know where he may buy such a thing as you are wearing."

Never one for paying much attention to sartorial matters Ken glanced down in surprise.

"What? Oh, my pullover. I didn't buy it, my wife knitted it."

There was a pause as this was considered, then more talk. Sutherland began again,

"Sir, Chief MweniMisuku wishes that his daughter might learn this knitting."
I gave a start.
"I would be delighted to teach her." I said, meaning it.
At this the Chief made his salutations and turned to go. His entourage regrouped behind him as they crossed the garden and one by one, disappeared down the path.
We ate the chicken for supper.
Over the weeks life took on a routine of sorts. That is to say Ken got up with the work clanger and went off to put in a couple of hours before breakfast. I got up in somewhat more leisurely fashion and went out to see what could be done for the sick people. After breakfast Ken would be out all the morning, usually coming back for lunch. Sometimes however he had to visit distant villages, in which case he did not return till nightfall. If Sutherland had gone with him or was absent for any other reason, there was no-one on hand who spoke English.
It was on such an afternoon, when the labourers had finished work and gone home, with William and Station away for a couple of hours, the whole place deserted, that I looked up from a book to find two young girls in colourful nsaru standing at the open doorway. Assuming they were girls from the coffee nursery needing medicine, my heart fell. Not because they were unwelcome, but because of knowing we would have little means of communication. Still at least I could give them a cordial welcome.
"Ndaga, I said, "Ndaga Mawomba."
The taller of the girls replied,
"Good afternoon."
Oh the joy of it. This must be an unaccustomed schoolgirl who knew a few English phrases. However to my surprise she went on in good English,
"My name is Katie Chanya. This one is the daughter of Chief MweniMisuku. We have come to knit."
Of course, the knitting. Events and the minor crises of everyday life at Katobo had driven the matter from my mind. Too late after the Chief's visit had I realised that knitting needles and wool had not figured as bare essentials likely to be vital to life in Misuku, and that what I had brought with me from England was still locked away in one of the trunks left at Karonga. I had immediately sought to rectify this by sending a note to Jess - an inveterate knitter of little coloured garments for African children - to send up what she could spare, but so far old Simbeyé had failed to return with any. I explained the situation to Katie Chanya, saying I would be happy to teach her and her friend to knit when the wool and the needles arrived. I also complimented her on her English, and asked how she came to speak it so well. She said,
"I am the daughter of the headmaster of the school. I also wish to become a teacher. My friend does not speak English."
It occurred to me that a chief's daughter, plump and pretty to boot, would have little need of English. We had some further conversation and I parted from them with genuine regret.

When the materials arrived Ken sent a messenger to the Court and the girls came again. We spent several afternoons together, during which I was often sorely tempted to ask Katie if she would care to come and act as nanny to our baby when the time came. But no it would not do. Katie must go on with her education and fulfil her dream.

In due course both girls learnt the basic stitches of plain and purl and knitted a trial strip such as children in England might fashion into a scarf for their dolls. Alas this was the sum total of their attainment, a far cry from the sartorial item desired.

It is doubtful if the girls were spurred on to higher things after our departure. And even less likely that Chief MweniMisuku ever got his patterned pullover.

CHAPTER 16

KNIGHT AND DAY

A Sabbath hush lay over Katobo. We slept on undisturbed by the work clanger or by labourers' voices far too near the bedroom window for comfort. The sick apparently had something better to do on Sundays, even the hornbills seemed subdued. We woke at last, screened by the red and white checked curtains which threw faintly tinted shadows across the bed, with the added privacy of the rest of the doors which had recently been delivered and installed by the Walrus and the Carpenter. From across the valley came the insistent beat of a drum. I got up and parted the curtains, cautiously in case some stray caller should be abroad. The morning splendour of the countryside caught at my throat yet again. I drank it in, registering as I did so a line of villagers on the opposing ridge threading their way to the church near the Court. Some of the women wore unaccustomed coloured nsaru, some carried wooden chairs on their heads - for them church going was an all day affair, a social as well as spiritual occasion, a hiatus in the drudgery of everyday life. Ken said,
"Come back to bed. No need to get up yet."
There followed a delightful interlude. We lay encapsulated in the big double bed, the airy cage of the mosquito net protecting us, not from malaria - that was hardly a threat in Misuku - but from the various creatures liable to drop on us from the thatch above. Briefly the worries and vexations of life were forgotten.
Hunger finally forced us to get up, William and Station arrived, on Sundays they too had the equivalent of a lie in.
We ate a leisurely breakfast, the open door giving on to the same panorama seen from the bedroom window. With a wave of his hand Ken said,
"Isn't it wonderful to have all this to ourselves? And no-one to get at us. It makes up for all the..."
"Listen!" I interrupted him in the manner that a castaway on a desert island sighting a puff of smoke on the horizon might cry "A ship!"
Distinctly from across the valley came a halloo in the unmistakable tones of Middle England.
"Oh no, groaned Ken, "Not on a Sunday."
"But who is it? It doesn't sound like Noel. Or the DC..."
Must be a stranger. A Bambo perhaps..."
"Bambo?"
"Roman Catholic priest. As I told you the Catholics bought up Lilford's place after he died. They send someone up to take the occasional service. Let's hope he won't stay long, whoever it is."
I did not in fact share Ken's reluctance at the prospect of a visitor. We had been in Misuku about six weeks and had seen no other Europeans, a new face and news of the outside world would not come amiss to me.

It proved to be neither a stranger nor a Bambo. It was Angus Day, well known to Ken, met briefly by me in Karonga. Angus was one half of the celebrated Knight and Day duo of PWD engineers who, between them were responsible for all the roads in the Northern Province. Henryk Knight lived in Mzimba and was but a formidable legend to me, Angus lived at Chisenga, not too far from Fort Hill.

Roads in the North were few and far between. The most important to us, I gathered, were so-called Great North Road and the Chendo Track, the latter never referred to without expletives, being lengthy and greedy of attention on account of the rough terrain and constant deterioration of its earth surface.

Roads were Angus's abiding passion. He spent his life on the move, repairing bridges and building new ones, replacing washed out culverts, improvising detours, chivvying up his workforce, and altogether spending little time at Chisenga. Travellers could, and invariably did, complain bitterly of the utterly impossible state of the roads, Angus defended them fiercely as a mother defending her young.

"How did you get here?" demanded Ken ungraciously, the first greetings over.

"In the jeep of course, replied Angus, "Well, most of the way. Across country. Had to walk the last bit though."

Although I did not know it at the time this simple sounding exercise had entailed driving from Chisenga on to a rough track to Kapoka on the edge of Misuku, thence blazing an upward trail through bush and brachystegia country, over rock and scree, avoiding anthills the while, until reaching the upper slopes of the Wilindi massif. When even he had been forced to get out and walk the intervening miles to Katobo

"What you need, he told us, his face, red with exertion, taking on a broody look, "Is a road up here. Oh, and I ran into Andrew at Kapoka. Offered to bring him along. He said yes at first, but changed his mind when I said we'd have to climb Wilindi on foot."

"What on earth was Andrew doing at Kapoka?" asked Ken none too pleased at the prospect of further invasion.

"Dunno. Don't worry though, you know he doesn't care for walking these days. I suppose he thought it would look good on his monthly report. You know - On ulendo to Misuku to inspect the coffee - and all that."

According to Ken it was in fact several years since Andrew has ventured into Misuku although when younger and somewhat fitter, he, and sometimes Jess and Tom as well, had made occasional visits. Jess' botanical Magnum Opus had been considerably enriched thereby.

"How are you getting on?" Angus continued, looking round at the sparse camping gear, the earth floor, the ant tunnels on the walls, and at the hole in the wall where the chimney had once been, now patched with mud and laths.

"Fine, I said defensibly, seeing it through his eyes, "It's a lot more comfortable than when we arrived. Glass in the windows you know, and doors. And curtains. And you should see our lovely double b...."

I stopped, confused, and sought to change the subject. Unfortunately all I could think of was the matter of lunch. What could we give him? And how would

William cook it? I knew with certainty that Angus's culinary standards would be a good deal higher than our own. There was nothing for it but to warn him in advance. I need not have worried.

"Sorlright, he said when I put it to him, "Always travel with provisions. Never know what you're going to find in rest-houses and, er, other places. Always take me own cook as well."

The cook was deaf and dumb but not at all put out by our primitive conditions. He cooked us the best meal we had so far enjoyed in Misuku and I very much hoped William was taking note. Before that however, despite a noticeable lack of enthusiasm on Angus's part, Ken insisted giving him a conducted tour of the coffee garden. Coffee it might be said, was in a fair way of becoming to Ken what roads were to Angus. But although the countryside was looking particularly beautiful that morning, there was no meeting of minds.

After lunch, the good food and Angus's beer having done its work, the men became expansive and I was able to ask for news of the District. Had anything interesting happened? Any new arrivals or visitors? Here I was on delicate ground since Jess in one of her letters, had indicated that Angus himself was the main subject of conversation. And for a most unfortunate reason. His South African wife, unable to cope with the isolation of Chisenga during Angus's almost constant absence, had decamped, leaving behind her two little girls aged five and three. They were now in the care of the Portuguese/African WENELA manager and his family at Fort Hill until other arrangements could be made. Angus alluded to the matter only briefly, then changed the subject.

"You know that Cotton Board fellow Steve Witting who's living in the Clover Leaf house in Karonga?"

"Only too well, said Ken bitterly, "Although we've never actually met him."

"Yes. Well he's a bit of a nutter. Leaves everything to his African staff. The other day he told one of them to fill up his jeep with petrol and top up the water. Well the chap got it the wrong way round. So now the engine's kaput and he's got no transport."

Being totally non-mechanical myself I thought this a perfectly reasonable mistake to make but did not say so. Ken's mind was still on the house.

"What? He's still in the Clover Leaf? We're definitely moving into it when we return. What about the new one he's building next door? That should be finished by now."

"Doesn't seem to be making much progress. He's usually away on the lake shore seeing about the cotton so nothing gets done."

"Well we'll be coming back in a few weeks. If you see him tell him for God's sake to get on with it."

Remembering the afternoon Jess and I had looked over it during my stay with her, and her comments about the builders, I doubted if this would have much effect. Angus must have thought the same for he said,

"Perhaps you could share the Clover leaf with him."

"Oh yes, replied Ken, "All three rooms of it."

I tried to visualise a menage á trois with this semi madman and it was probably just as well that at this point that the silent cook came to clear the lunch things. To create a diversion I asked Angus about him. He said he had been with him for years and they had solved the communication problem pretty well. As to his origins, it was thought he had been taken to Livingstonia Mission as a child when his disability became apparent. In the old days he might have been left to die in the bush. As it was he had grown up to be trained as a cook, and against all the odds, enabled to go out in the world and earn his living. This encouraging story lead to a discussion of missionaries in general, some of whom it must be said, were not held in high esteem by officers of Her Majesty's Government. The Scots were the earliest and most respected in the country. They had been followed by Anglican and Roman Catholic, but nowadays they were by no means the only ones. There were Jehovah's Witnesses, Seventh Day Adventists and other splinter groups, many of them American, such as the one to which the Udds adhered.

"Unfortunately, said Ken, "They all preach their own brand of Christianity, often contradictory to one another and the people don't know what to believe. Some sects are anti-Government because naturally they have different priorities. Another thing, unlike Livingstonia where the accent is on practical skills, some teach only academic subjects in their schools to youngsters hoping to become teachers or clerks. That's alright, but there aren't nearly enough of those jobs to go round. And that spells trouble."

"Yes, agreed Angus, Why don't they all teach something useful? Like mechanics, or road building for instance. And talking of trouble what about this Federation nobody wants?"

He was referring to the fledgling Federation of Northern and Southern Rhodesia and Nyasaland, about which I knew nothing, except that it was universally unpopular in the country at large. Being the smallest, weakest, poorest, lacking any natural resource but its labour, everyone feared Nyasaland would be swallowed up by the other two territories. This time there was no discussion, Angus and Ken agreed that with the people so deeply suspicious, it could not be a good idea.

When it was time for him to go, looking at the patched up wall, Angus said,
"I'll send up a few burnt bricks to rebuild that chimney. Mind you put a bend in it or it'll smoke. What's happened to your furniture? he added, "Haven't they sent it up yet?"

By 'they' he meant the PWD. Ken told him it was being stored at Fort Hill, that being our official posting."

"Only I've no intention of living there."

At which Angus, for whom officialdom existed to be flouted, replied,
"I'll look into it. It's a poor show if a pregnant girl can't have a proper chair to sit on."

He went to find his cook and they set off. Angus looked back to wave laconically before they disappeared down the path. Ken said,
"It'll be dark before they reach Wilindi. They'll have a rough ride back."

I reflected that such a man as Angus would have no qualms at crossing a mountain range on foot, then driving through uncharted bush in utter darkness before reaching any semblance of a road. Thought also that someone who turned up unexpectedly, bringing food not only for himself, but for his hosts as well, AND the means of cooking it, was quite the nicest sort of visitor to have.

We stood awhile as the sky darkened. Lengthening shadows on the ridge across the valley silhouetted the last of the villagers making their way back from church.

CHAPTER 17

'AND THEN THE LIGHTING OF THE LAMPS'

Angus was as good as his word. First he sent up a posse of carriers with burnt bricks for the chimney, and a note saying he had offloaded 'one or two things at Kapoka and left instructions there with the capitao there to get them sent up.'
Ken rebuilt the chimney. With a bend. Thereafter we were able to have fires again whenever we felt like it and sit in the evenings with the smoke curling smoothly upwards.
As to the furniture, we received four wooden dining chairs, rather hard to sit on but none the less welcome, and a day or two later, a battered but once handsome dining table. This last must surely have formed part of some administrative official's ulendo equipment, for it was sectional, could be carried in parts, easily assembled or dismantled, so that one could quite imagine a former District Commissioner sitting at it dispensing British justice in the bush. In the fullness of time with the aid of beeswax from a local swarm, and much elbow grease, this table was polished till it took on the sheen of a new conker. In the meantime we ate our meals at one end of it, the other end becoming Ken's office space, perpetually strewn with official letters and memos from Zomba, relentlessly forwarded by Andrew in Karonga.

We expected nothing more from Angus but we were wrong. One black, very wet night as we sat by the fire taking turns to read aloud, rain and the cacophony of rattling window panes almost drowning out our voices, there was a faint disturbance outside. Then came a tap on the door, barely audible. Ken strode across the room and flung the door open. Outside stood two dripping wet, near naked men; standing between them was a large upholstered armchair.
Even on such a night it was necessary to go through the customary courtesies, while I remained in the background staring in disbelief, imagining the appalling journey they must have had. From Kapoka they would have taken Angus's route, but on foot the whole way. In such weather and with such a load. In their place I would certainly have been tempted when at last reaching the summit of Wilindi, to hurl it down the mountain side, in the manner of Christian in Bunyan's Pilgrim's Progress casting off his burden of sin. As it was Ken helped the men to bring the monstrosity into the room. They stood blinking in lamplight as if uncertain even now, that they had come to the right place. The chair began to steam with the warmth of the fire. William and Station appeared, very excited. Ken told them to take the carriers to the kitchen, get them something to eat and arrange for them to dry out by the fire and spend the night there with Kalokhili the watchman.

The chair was even wetter than the men, the rain having soaked through the upholstery, it was also dirty and very smelly. Next morning when the rain had gone away I had it carried outside in the sun. William brought hot water and carbolic soap and I scrubbed it long and hard. Gradually the dirt came away and the semblance of a pattern emerged. It took several days to dry out completely, and even longer for the smell to disappear, but subsequently it saw sterling service, being soft and comfortable, an oasis of comfort in a Spartan setting. Appreciated the more for the manner of its arrival, and for Angus's kindness in sending it.

Needless to say these domestic incidents, so important to me, impinged on Ken hardly at all. His attention was on his work and that took up most of his time. Sometimes, as already mentioned, he went on day long ulendo to villages in the vicinity, leaving early and returning after nightfall. But other places were too distant for this, where, it was safe to assume, the villagers took advantage of their remoteness to flout the Agricultural Department's regulations. Without back-up the capitaos could do little about it. Accordingly Ken decided we would go on a week long ulendo to try and address the situation.
"You'll enjoy it, he told me, "The villages are only about five miles apart. Bit hilly though."
Another understatement as it turned out.

Partly due to my previous experience packing was not so traumatic as on the ulendo up from Karonga. Which was just as well for the villages were too poor to support either church or school and we must take Ken's (guaranteed lion-proof) canvas tent in addition to everything else. Fortunately there was no shortage of carriers, rather the reverse in fact, the local men regarding a change of scene as something of a holiday.
On the appointed morning Ken went off with Sutherland, intending to inspect gardens along the way and confer with village headmen and the elders. William went ahead with the carriers. I followed in more leisurely fashion with Station and a few hangers on, sharing with them the sense of novelty of walking the lovely land, through villages set among banana plantations, stands of pines and eucalypts, the scene shifting constantly with each undulation of the countryside. Once again came the excitement and friendliness of people who seldom saw Europeans, the initial shyness of the children swiftly turning to curiosity.
If fortune smiled, which is to say, if the rain held off, and the way not too arduous - for we were climbing all the time - we would arrive at the day's destination before dusk. William would have a fire going ready to make tea. Before he went off on more inspections Ken would already have picked out a suitable site to pitch the tent where, one hoped, it would not get washed down the hillside if it rained in the night, so that I merely needed to supervise its erection.
Ken always came in later; even then after a brief rest he would hold a meeting with the headmen and elders as the shadows lengthened. His fears over land usage were usually only too well founded. Often there were no bunds - ditches - no grass strips left necklace-like across the contours of the steep sided valleys. Sometimes there were signs of illegal slash and burn plantings; stream bank cultivation. If not checked, these practices would become the norm. In some places failure to observe these regulations laid down by the Agricultural Department, had already resulted

in severe erosion. Thus he must begin his address by castigating the people for this flouting of the rules which, he said, were for their own good. If they went on in this way the land would soon cease to support them. They and their families would have to abandon their homes and move on to other poor land and ever diminishing acres. He also told them that if matters did not improve the DC would come from Karonga and fine them. In point of fact a somewhat empty threat, it being unlikely the DC would have time to venture so far, or that his emissaries could squeeze fines out of people who had no money.

In the darkness the men sitting cross legged on the ground listened attentively, firelight leaping on grave faces. They became crest-fallen at the mention of the DC and discussion would break out among themselves. At last the village headman invariably said the people would mend their ways. Ken, well aware that they would revert after a few months if left to themselves, told them he would send his capitaos round to see if they had spoken truly, and these capitaos would report to him if they had not.

He would then go on to broach the topic dearest to his heart. Namely the coffee cooperative and the way it could transform their lives, inviting them to come to Katobo to inspect the coffee bushes growing there. At once the atmosphere lightened, everyone loved a good palaver and they interrupted him vigorously as he put forward the merits of the scheme. Indeed most of them embraced the idea enthusiastically, well knowing it to be a theoretical discussion committing them to nothing practical.

Surprisingly in spite of Ken's censure and threats, we were always treated with courtesy and customary ceremony and with gifts of food for the whole company according to the people's ability in such poor circumstances. Sometimes there was even moa - home brewed beer - for the carriers, in which case festivities went on far into the night.

Ken had not intended to make any other ulendo as the time of our departure drew near; certainly there was more than enough to keep him busy close at hand. But a few days after our return to Katobo he received a message from the capitao of the region on the far side of Wilindi, the direction whence Angus, and the carriers with the armchair, had come, asking him to go and settle some dispute there.

He thought about the matter, then said,

"It's too far for me to get there and back in a day. The complaint is bound to drag on, I'll have to spend a night away. Sorry you can't come with me this time, but if I go alone I can travel lighter and more quickly. You'll be alright here on your own won't you, just for one night?"

"But..."

I was far from sharing his confidence, but too cowardly to admit it, after a moment I replied lamely,

"But there won't be anybody here who speaks English. In an emergency I mean. Unless Sutherland comes back, he's on ulendo as well remember."

"Oh yes. But let's see, he consulted his diary, "It's alright, he's due back tomorrow, I'll go the day after. And I'll tell the district capitao to stay about here so you can call on him as well."

So far I had barely seen the district capitao.

"And Kalokhili will be sleeping in the kitchen."

I did not understand why we should have someone as old and deaf as Kalokhili for night watchman but when I had remarked on it Ken said he was a long term member of the workforce, and very reliable. It was true certainly, that he arrived faithfully every evening before William and Station left. Frequently we heard his cackling laugh in the kitchen as he exchanged ribaldries with them, but then to all intents and purposes he made himself comfortable by the fire and settled down for the night. He was of course meant to carry out regular patrols, but short of waking us up with the Chisukwa equivalent of 'Three of the clock and all's well,' there was no way of knowing.

"He's not supposed to be sleeping." I objected.

"No. But you know what I mean."

Ken left early on the appointed morning. As we parted (tenderly on his part, apprehensively on mine,) he said,

"Don't forget to light the lamps in good time. Outside preferably, just in case, you know."

When he was out of sight I went reluctantly to tackle the sick parade. Of the local capitao there was no sign, Sutherland had not arrived. So apart from treating straightforward cuts and sores I was forced to resort to mime. It was not very satisfactory. Comforting myself with the thought that a little aspirin or cough mixture could do harm to no-one, making excessive use of the one word all could understand - Dispensary - and waving my hand in the direction of the Court complex, I hoped the remaining patients would excuse my inadequacy.

Next I turned my attention to the kitchen. William had gone with Ken, which left me with Station and Trisom. The latter would fetch water and chop wood and make himself generally useful, the former looked apprehensive and doubtful as I struggled to relay my needs as to food. Later I made the usual scone bread and gave it to him to bake. Well, at least I would not starve.

In the afternoon I took a chair outside and sat in my favourite spot on the top terrace, the whole of Misuku spread out before me. Fountain pen poised I began writing a letter to a friend in England,

"Dear Mary,

The scenery here is wonderful. So is the weather,"

I paused, seeking words to convey the atmosphere, the ambience, the activity around, the life lived by the people, the whole situation in fact in which I now found myself. Failing entirely, my mind reverted to all that had happened in the months since Mary and I had last met. But the daydream was interrupted. The day's work was over, the labourers came noisily up from the coffee terraces below and began to make their various ways home, Station and Trisom also left for an hour or two and the place fell silent. I bent over my letter again, and was immediately transported to pre-marriage days in England when our sole aim in life, Mary's and mine, was to have a Good Time. Which, on the whole we did.

Once more there was a diversion, this time by fluting voices, and much giggling. It took me a moment to realise the knitting girls had come again. I never knew when they would appear with the results of their labours and it was pure luck they had come on a day when I was alone. I was certainly glad to have company. We exchanged greetings in Chisukwa for the benefit of the Chief's daughter then I thankfully reverted to English with Katie Chanya. Together we bent over the tangled mess that was the knitting, I resisting the urge to pull it all out and start again lest that should discourage them, and we struggled through what was left of the afternoon and eventually had it straight. We parted cheerfully.

Sounds at the back of the house indicated the return of Trisom, and realisation came that he was heating bath water in the debé on the kitchen fire. Therefore it would soon be dark; it was high time to light the lamps. I knew them to be well filled, for along with boiling the drinking water, this was a job I did myself. Lighting the Tilley lamp was not simple and I always left it to Ken if possible. Like the Primus stove it demanded methylated sprit by way of an aperitif. This must be heated to the exact temperature to tempt the mantle - a lacy affair of some flame proof material - grudgingly to glow and allow the paraffin stored in the base, to be pumped to ignite the mantle. If the meths was left a fraction too long it evaporated and nothing happened, if pumping began too soon the mantle drooped to a soggy mass. In which case there was nothing to be done but wait for it to dry out and start again. On this occasion I succeeded at the third attempt, but not without the flare-up hinted at by Ken. So it was just as well I had followed his advice.

Fortunately the kitchen lamp was altogether simpler to light, it was of the hurricane, or storm lantern type, used all over the world most likely, and an exact replica of the ones used to guard holes in the road at night, in the village of my youth. In the days before mechanical diggers, gangs of workmen would spend weeks, months even, with picks and shovels digging out trenches then filling them in again, becoming old friends, familiar to everyone in the process. Until war broke out leaving us all in darkness, these lanterns would supplement the lamp posts, giving a theatrical effect to the night sky. Not only that, there would be a real night watchman bearing absolutely no resemblance in character to Kalokhili, like as not sitting by the hole, beside a brazier of glowing coals. Hand in hand with my parents returning from visits to relatives by moonlight or starlight - as in Misuku almost everyone was related - we would sometimes come across the watchman cooking his supper of bacon and eggs, over the brazier, utilising a cleaned spade as a frying pan. I would stand silent as the grown-ups talked, an irresistible aroma filling the air.
For the second time that day I was transported. Reluctantly jerked back to the present as the lamp flared, I was left mourning the loss of childhood, the disappearance of gas light, fresh milk and dependable daily bread. But mourning the bacon and eggs most of all.

Later Station brought in a far less appetising supper. As I was eating it a tap on the door heralded Kalokhili reporting for duty. He stood in the outer doorway in his rusty black nsaru, armed with his spear, hard to make out in the darkness except when his face was lit up by a disarming gap toothed smile. He saluted, said something incomprehensible, then made his way to the kitchen. For a little the sound of his voice mingled with those of Station and Trisom. Then they were gone and the place was silent once more. Curled up in the great armchair I turned gratefully to Jane Austen and read late into the night. For once however the narrative failed fully to absorb. Sounds hardly noticed on ordinary nights with Ken at home, were magnified out of all proportion. The rattle of window panes in the night breeze, the hissing of the lamp and the sigh it gave every now and then to indicate it needed pumping. And above all, metaphorically and literally, the rustling and scratching in the bare thatch overhead of the creatures who lived there.

At last I made ready for bed, loath to put out the lamp, well knowing I would not be able to light it again in a hurry. On a box by the bed lay our useless hand torch, its battery long since flat, and the stump of candle and box of matches for emergencies. I prayed hard they would not be needed. The thought of Kalokhili sleeping in the kitchen was not particularly reassuring. Slightly more comforting was the mosquito net which would at least prevent bugs, beetles, hornets - one of which had bitten (stung?) me on the cheek one day as I worked in the garden - and other unknown insects dropping down from the thatch. Less terrifying because less likely, was the possibility of lion or leopard pushing the unlockable outer door open, but I wedged one of the dining chairs under the door knob all the same. I got into bed, tucked the net in securely and put my hands over my ears. Sleep came at last, and with it a dream. As if from a great height I saw Katobo and Misuku as infinitesimal particles of matter set in the immensity of Africa. The image was curiously comforting. I turned over and slept till the work clanger sounded in early morning.

Strangely enough I never spent another night entirely on my own at Katobo. Although Ken subsequently spent many nights away on ulendo I always had a child, or children, with me. And that of necessity makes one brave.

CHAPTER 18

NIGHT OF THE MANYEGA

Ken came back in the evening in good humour because of having settled the dispute amicably. He said with forced cheeriness,

"There, I told you you'd be alright on your own didn't I? It wasn't so bad was it?" Viewing my singed eyebrows, he added, "I see you managed to light the lamps." Then noticing my baleful stare went on, "Never mind, I quite like you like that, it makes you look, er, interesting. Perhaps it's just as well we haven't got a mirror though."

"Very droll, I retorted, "It wasn't funny. And it wasn't just the lamps. It was all that livestock in the thatch as well."

Indeed I was vindicated a few nights later, although on that occasion the attack did not come from above. We had gone to sleep as usual; after a while I woke up with what seemed like a bad dose of pins and needles. I lay in darkness wondering what manifestation of pregnancy this might be. Certainly one I had never heard of. Horror! Could it be the onset of labour? Thrombosis brought on by altitude? Perhaps if I lay still and kept calm it would go away. Just then however, to my relief, Ken woke up and gave a yell.

"What is it?" I asked stupidly.

He said nothing for a moment, threshing about in torment, only half awake, then, "Ants, he said tersely, "Don't move."

The admonition was quite unnecessary. I knew about ants. These were not the small white ones, annoying but innocuous, that marred whitewashed walls with their tunnels, or the termites responsible for boring into bamboo furniture, sometimes causing a chair leg to give way without warning, spilling the occupant on to the floor. No, these were the large red/brown carnivorous soldier ants - The Manyega.

Terrible tales were told of the manyega. Of babies being attacked in their cribs. Of the ears of sleeping adults invaded as they slept, although as I now knew, they would need to be in a drunken stupor not to notice.

I clawed at the attackers, wondering how they had got in under the mosquito net. Ken leapt out of bed, groped for the candle and lit it. Then he wrapped a towel round his waist and rushed out shouting for Kalokhili. Cautiously I raised my head. In the flickering light the bed was revealed as a seething solid mass. On the floor an unaccountable black column, straight as a Roman legion, stretched from beneath the sitting room door to the one leading to the bathroom/store, Diverging from it at intervals, were minor columns in the manner of scouting forays, including the one leading to the bed.

Ken came back with the kitchen lamp. He set it down, reached under the bed

for his mosquito boots, slapped them more or less free of ants, put them on and dashed out again. Kalokhili, obviously a sound sleeper, shuffled in, took one horrified look and backed out, stamping his feet as he went. Ken reappeared. He had a can of insecticide in one hand, with the other he dragged one of the dining chairs from the sitting room. Putting the latter down in a relatively ant free corner, he described a circle of insecticide round it, and said,
"Quickly! Cover yourself and go and stand on the chair"
I shook out the sheet as best I could, wrapped it round me and did as he said, picking my way carefully across the floor. Kalokhili returned with a flaming brand from the kitchen fire and began laying about him in a manner likely to add arson to the situation. Every now and then he collided with Ken crisscrossing the floor with the insecticide. From my vantage point on the chair the scene resembled the First Circle of Hell. The leaping figures, Ken naked but for his mosquito boots - the towel had fallen off - Kalokhili laying down his torch brand every now and then, turning to strip off his nsaru and shake it out. A neo Jackson Pollock covered half the earth floor as Ken continued to dribble the insecticide. Still the hordes came on, some maintaining their purposeful march in the main column, others scattering, as an army routed.
Impossible to say how long it went on.
At some stage Ken handed me my dress and somehow I managed to discard the sheet and put it on, noticing as I did so that the first streaks of dawn had appeared. By its light I saw that Man was at last gaining the upper hand. That is, the diminished troops were no longer heading for the bed but had regrouped to join the main column heading for the store room. Ken strode across the room and flung the door open.
"Don't move." he ordered, hastily shutting it again.
He went back to the sitting room and peered round.
"They don't seem to have come in this direction thank God, Come and sit down."
I got down from the chair and trod carefully over the debris. In the sitting room I drew back a curtain and examined the big armchair minutely. It was clear of ants and I sank down thankfully.
Presently Station brought in tea, shaking his head. Ken joined me and I said accusingly,
"You told me about leopards, and snakes and things. You didn't say anything about ants in the bed."
He was too preoccupied to take this up and instead said,
"Of course they were after the food in the back room. The bed just happened to be in the way. The thing is to find the nest and destroy it. As they came in from the sitting room to the bedroom it's safe to assume they came under the outer door, so that presupposes it's somewhere at the front of the house. I'll get the men to start looking for it."

By this time the work clanger had sounded and the labourers were assembled. All were excited, not to mention amused at the discomfiture of the Asungu yet again, Doubtless Kaolkhili's story lost nothing in the telling.

It was time to rouse myself. Reluctantly I went back to the bedroom; the bed, the canopy of the mosquito net above, were covered with ants, some of them still alive. The floor was a carnage of corpses, ash from Kalokhili's torch brand mixed with Ken's insecticidal art work on the floor.

I found my sandals and put them on, crossed to the door of the back room and opened it. Like Ken I took one look and shut it again quickly. One glimpse however was enough to stamp the scene indelibly on the mind. The floor, the food boxes, the sacks, the canvas bath, all possible surfaces, were black with ants still bent on plunder.

I leaned on my side of the door and wondered what to do next. Hideous as the sight undoubtedly was, the implication of damage to our already tenuous food supply was even more daunting. I put the thought behind me, the most pressing task was to get the place cleared.

Obviously fire and chemicals were out of the question here. I called Station and Trisom to come and make a start with their home-made besoms, then hurried out to find Ken. I encountered Sutherland instead. He too looked grave. He shook his head and said,

"These creatures are very bad Madam. Sometimes they attack pigs." (I had never seen pigs in Misuku.) "And sometimes they get into the noses and ears of little babies and kill them."

Seeing my stricken face he added,

"But it is alright because their mothers are always with them, so they are safe."

At any other time I would have paused to consider the merits of this bonding of mother and child, the baby living on the mother's back by day, and by night sleeping at her side on the mat, well within the reach of a comforting breast. As it was I said,

"But where do they come from? And how can we get rid of them?"

"Nobody knows where they come from. Or where they go to. The only way is to seek out the big one who lays the eggs and destroy the nest with fire."

As if to prove his point some of the labourers, armed with flaring torches, began enthusiastically to fire the grass all round the house, while I looked nervously on, hoping they would not get too close to the roof thatch.

When Station and Trisom had done their best in the store room, together we braved the arsonists outside and carried the foodstuff to the kitchen, which, fortunately had not been affected. After that we tackled the bedroom. We stripped off the bedding and the net, still crawling with ants, hung it over the improvised washing line in the garden and beat it soundly. Finally we swept out the house as best we could.

Ken and Sutherland meanwhile, had been conferring as to the best way to start looking for the nest. Would it be better to follow any stray column which had re-formed? Or to search at random at the front of the house? They decided on both. Indeed, with much stamping of feet some of the men were already casting about. When Ken announced that he would reward anyone finding the queen, with the huge sum of half a crown, they redoubled their efforts, fanning out over the garden and down on to the coffee terraces.

There was no shortage of trails. Many of the manyega had regrouped and could be seen progressing in haphazard lines that wound backwards and forwards, looping round on each other, as in a maze where only one path leads home. Whenever a column was disturbed by the trampling of feet, chaos ensued. Then the labourers must stand back and wait and watch.

After a while some sort of re-organisation was resumed among the manyega. Lesser columns were formed. Picking up stragglers as they went, they straightened out and began to march on purposefully once more. Soon it became apparent that all the minor columns were merging and heading in the same direction, That is to say they set off across the garden in front of the house, plunged briefly out of sight to the terrace below, then off down the valley path. Warily the men followed.

Presently a shout of jubilation went up. We all hurried on down. All the columns had converged on one spot and in orderly fashion were disappearing down a hole in the ground. In spite of the reward there was, understandably, no rush of volunteers to start digging for the queen. One and all were in favour of lighting a fire in the hope of smoking her out. Indeed some of the men had started back up the hill to get more fire brands, restrained only by Ken's ordering them back. They were bitterly disappointed when he ruled out the use of fire altogether. Although the lair was on the path rather than on one of the terraces, the coffee itself was close enough to be vulnerable. For the bushes, spaced out at intervals across the hillside, beautiful in full white blossom, had been mulched with grass which had long since dried. One spark could set the whole lot ablaze.

Once more Sutherland and Ken conferred. Only by digging could the queen be located. There was nothing for it but for Ken, having at least an advantage over the labourers in the form of shoes and socks, to begin the work. Sutherland also took up a spade. This had the desired effect. The labourers set to work, taking turns to dig, lest the half crown bounty be lost for ever.

At once there were ants everywhere, the onlookers including myself, scattered, stamped, squirmed. The diggers turned aside every few moments to strip off and shake out their nsaru, the rest of us clawed vainly at our clothes.

After a while Ken told the men to go carefully lest the 'big one' be dug out undetected and live to fight another day.

Suddenly a cry of triumph went up. One of the spades turned up something huge, bloated, loathsome, utterly un-ant-like. The queen. It was held up, and paraded. In all the excitement I did not see what became of it.

Once the excitement died down Ken ordered the nearby water furrow which ran parallel to the path and on down the hill, to be diverted on to what was left of the citadel.

The effect of the force of the water on up-turned soil was as of a nuclear attack. Earth, detritus, ants were sent whooshing down the hillside, there seemed little chance of any survivors regrouping to start another colony.

That night sounds of the half crown beer drink drifted across the valley with drumming and chanting, extolling the valour of those who had vanquished the enemy. That night also, Ken and I slept with the legs of the bed standing in tins half filled with paraffin, as we should have done from the first and were never again troubled by manyega. I pondered that, by and large, it was the small creatures of Africa one needed to watch out for rather than its big game.

CHAPTER 19

RETURN TO KARONGA

We salvaged what we could of the food stock. It might have been worse, supplies were even lower than usual because we were due to leave Misuku the following week and therefore had not replenished the staples. As it was, ants had penetrated the sugar container and indulged in a drunken orgy. They had also located the flour sack but as the content had long since needed rigorous sifting against weevils, a few more foreign bodies were neither here nor there. The diminished bag of rice had not been touched, clearly this and the remaining tinned goods, plus what we could buy locally, would have to make up our diet until we left.

Kalokhili was reprimanded for being less than wide awake. Thereafter he did actually make at least one nightly patrol and we would sometimes stir from sleep to catch the light of his hurricane lamp flickering past the bedroom window. Which in my case brought on dreams of street lights, electricity, bacon and eggs...

The days ran out. The baby was due in June, it was now the end of April and time to go. Ken had remarked with satisfaction how fortunate it was that the birth would take place in the dry season - already the rains were slackening - and not at the height of the coffee planting when he would have been far too busy to get away. He managed to give the impression of having engineered this, although that certainly had not been apparent at the time of conception in England a lifetime ago.

To my great relief he had engineered an alternative route for us to leave by.

During Allen Day's visit on that notable Sunday soon after our arrival Ken had said to him,

"I think it would be too much in May for Enid to walk back to Karonga the way we came, but she could walk out to Kapoka. If you could meet us there and drive us to Chisenga we could stay at the rest-house until Andrew can send up transport from Karonga."

"'Course I could , Angus replied, "And there's no need for you to go to the rest-house, you can stay with me. No need to trouble Andrew either, I'll drive you down myself, you know I'm always having to go up and down the Chendo."

I thanked him profusely but Ken, somewhat churlishly I thought, objected,

"Are you sure the Chendo will be passable? I wouldn't want to take any risks at that stage. We could still be getting rain you know. It might be better to go the long way round - via Livingstonia."

"Of course it'll be alright, said Angus leaping to the defence of his latest project, "I've had gangs working on it for weeks. I'm replacing the bridge over the Lufira. When that's done it'll be an all weather road."

This mastery of understatement did not become apparent till later. As it was, in bed that night I asked Ken why we had not come to Misuku by this simple

sounding route. He snorted and said,
"Because in spite of anything Angus says about it the Chendo is, and always
will be, an absolute shit. It's not even the semblance of a road, just a crazy track
dropping from about five thousand feet to lake level, through the sort of country
we walked over coming up here. Imagine trying to maintain a road over that terrain
with his limited resources. All those valleys, and stream crossings and steep hills.
It's virtually impossible to keep it open in the dry season even. Then there's the
Lufira, a sizeable river, Last year the bridge was washed away, obviously he's still
working on the replacement."
By this time I was sleepy and only just caught his last remark,
"Well, we'll go with him to Chisenga and take it from there."

For once packing presented little problem as almost everything was to be left for
Ken who intended to return to Misuku as soon as possible.
"Only for short periods, he assured me, "I can't hang around Karonga for weeks
now can I?"
So there remained only our personal belongings. Even so I found to my dismay
that as on board ship, after a mere three months in Misuku the detritus had
mushroomed. It consisted mainly of newspapers and magazines sent out by
families and friends, which as previously discovered, I was incapable of sorting
without reading through again. This time with a heroic effort I straightway handed
them over to William for lighting fires, not knowing then that any paper with
printing was far too highly regarded to be burnt or cast away as rubbish.
Thus it was that I came not only on Station and William, but the labourers
also, poring over pictures in the magazines when the day's work was finished.
Especially absorbing were the illustrations of women - fortunately decorously
clad for most part. Of course the words meant nothing since not one of them could
read, but numbers were familiar to one or two, who explained them to the others,
on account of the work chits Sutherland showed them on pay days. Nyasaland
currency of £s(pounds), shillings and pennies was as in England, these women
had prices on them, clearly they were for sale.
So this was how the Asungu arranged their marriages. On the whole, provided
one had the money of course, it seemed much simpler than their own system of
painfully acquiring the minimum of at least ten cattle as the lobola - bride-price.
When the misapprehension dawned on me - a reasonable enough mistake,
I realised belatedly for anyone unfamiliar with Western advertising - I sought
out Sutherland and asked him to explain that the sum referred to applied not to
the women themselves, but to the clothes they were wearing. This he did very
thoroughly; whether the men believed him was a different matter.

We got up very early on the morning of our departure. Kapoka was about 17miles
off, which Ken thought too much for me to tackle in one day at this stage of
the proceedings. For the journey would start with the walk across the enclave of
Misuku itself, some 7 miles, with its multiplicity of little hills and corresponding
valleys, followed by the climb to the top of Wilindi, hitherto but an outline on the
skyline to me, with luck reaching the summit before the sun grew too hot. Then

would come the scramble down the other flank, and after that another eight miles or so of hard walking before we reached Kapoka.

Therefore we were to camp for a night at a point roughly half way.

First however there were farewells to make. I parted from the people with real regret. From the sick women with their babies, from the gentle Trisom who had toiled faithfully, (albeit somewhat fruitlessly) in the garden, and helped me in the kitchen on the night Ken was away. From Simbeyé the messenger, from the gathered labourers, even from old Kalokhili the watchman. All must be saluted, all hands shaken. William and Station were to accompany us on this first stage of the journey.

As Ken chafed to be off a spokesman gave a speech God-speeding us, Ken responded in kind; others seemed set to take up the theme but desisted at a tactful word from Sutherland who was also coming with us.

The carriers hoisted up their loads and set off briskly. We followed them down the path bordering the coffee. Past the scene of the ant fortress of which nothing was left. The water furrow had quickly been restored to its former course and it now continued on its way down to the stream as if nothing had disturbed it.

At the nursery the butterfly bright girls were assembling, yawning as only adolescents can when woken too soon. On seeing Ken they began half-heartedly to fill their water pots and make their way slowly to the seedlings, the more awake among them pausing to wave.

We crossed the pole bridge and climbed up the hill.. To our right was the ridge on which stood the three or four houses for resident and visiting capitaos. In front of one stood Sutherland's wife, immobile, a baby on her back, a toddler at her side. Sutherland did not acknowledge her nor she him.

We came on homesteads wrapped in mist, the women already about their daily tasks, men shrouded in their sleeping blankets sitting under thatch eaves; all called out greetings..

And so on to my first sight of the Court complex as the sun rose. I had not seen Chief MweniMisuku since his visit to Katobo, now as we approached we found him waiting with the elders. The reason for our going was, naturally, common knowledge and the Chief embarked on a speech expressing his hope that God would bless our journey and give it a favourable outcome. By which he likely meant that it might result in the birth of a son. Probably the whole assembled company were privately wondering why the Asungu must go to the length of such a ulendo on account of the everyday occurrence of childbirth. They did not make it apparent however and we parted with yet more handshakes and mutual goodwill.

As we passed the nearby school the boys gathered outside; the older ones gave us the benefit of their English phrases. I looked for Katie Chanya whose father was the headmaster, but did not see her.

Not far off was the extensive homestead of Joseph Mkumbwa the early coffee grower, now very rich by Misuku standards. His was the last settlement in the locality, from now on there were merely occasional clusters of huts set in banana groves. Then these too gave out. As we came to the foothills of Wilindi we met no more people as we climbed, seeing only one or two boys on the slopes tending the belled cattle searching out tussocks of coarse grass which, apart from wild gladioli and mountain lilies, was the only vegetation. Unlike Mughessé, Wilindi had no crowning forest, its upper reaches were of barren rock. By now it was very hot, the way grew steeper, the rests became more frequent. Once we looked back to the way we had come and saw people small as ants going about their business. Our house was a white dot away in the distance, a Bruegel scene in a tropical setting. Ken urged me on constantly with promises of the splendour awaiting us at the summit.

We inched our way upward, the blazing sun, the rigorous climb, the altitude taking its toll of lungs, heart, legs, head. We reached the summit at last and I sank down on a rock. Once again Ken had not exaggerated. All around the land fell away sharply below us in full circle. At our backs lay the dream of Misuku, before and below was an unknown country of yet more tumbled hills and half hidden valleys stretching away to an infinity of violet shadow. The air was so clear, the sky so blue, it seemed only the limitation of the human eye prevented the vista going on for ever. Every slight turn of the head brought a different perspective, a new delight, fatigue was momentarily suspended. As with the prospect from our own house, the panorama from the heights of Wilindi never palled. On this and subsequent journeys we seldom failed to pause there for renewal of strength and spirits.

Ken's voice broke the silence,

"Look, you can just make out the lake. Over there."

He pointed, and there, amazingly, was Lake Nyasa, a silver streak of sunlight some seventy miles off. Even less believable was the faint line beyond it indicating the mountains on the shores of another country entirely, at a distance impossible to imagine. Oh to be by the lake this very instant without having to endure the tortuous miles between. To be lapped by limpid water, lie on golden sand...

Weariness returned soon enough as we made the steep descent. The need to get on was imperative. We came down from the heights in more senses than one, yet something of the vision lingered in the mind.

The path did not follow the contour or deviate on account of human weakness; the Asukwa, like the Romans in Britain, had followed a straight line when forging it out long ago, so that the stony track plunged inexorably down the mountain side. We left the slopes and the foothills behind at last and came gratefully to a gently undulating path on the watershed, the land falling sharply away on either hand. Thus we proceeded to Chato, the day's destination.

This isolated settlement could not be called a village. Rather it was a collection of huts below the path clinging to a slope marginally gentler than the rest. One could see at a glance it was a very poor place with meagre cultivation - and that little consisting of illicit slash and burn millet gardens. A place which would be abandoned when the scant soil gave out entirely.

It was touching therefore, not to say embarrassing, to receive the hospitality, obliged by custom, that must be accorded to any traveller whatever his race or circumstances. Nor were wayfarers rare as might be supposed. This was the only track leading out of Misuku to Kapoka and thence to Fort Hill, so most of the traffic consisted of young men footslogging their way en route for recruitment in the South African mines. And of course, the corresponding numbers of returnees. One could imagine the burden of this hospitality on the people of Chato, no wonder they were poor.

William and Station had preceded us with the carriers and arrived some time before. Already they had acquired firewood, and water from the stream in the valley below, now they brought welcome tea. I drank it gratefully. Ken's first task was to get the tent put up in the place least likely to get it washed away if we had rain in the night. But due to land pressure - every square foot it seemed was occupied - there was no place in the village, only the path on which we had walked was flat enough for the purpose.

Dusk came on swiftly. The tent erected and the beds made up, we sat outside, the village below dotted with cooking fires, the sky pin-pointed with stars. Surely it would not rain? Presently William accompanied by Station carrying a lamp, struggled up the hill with what passed for supper. Later the mingled voices of villagers and carriers floated up, soberly with no sounds of revelry.

"Ken, what's that noise?"

We had turned in early and sleep had overcome me at once. Impossible to tell how long it was before it was interrupted.

"Huh." grunted Ken,

"That noise. What is it?"

"Oh it's just the villagers and the carriers talking I expect. Go back to sleep."

"No no, it's nothing like that. It's an animal. Listen."

The sound was as cats yowling, but stronger, not far off. Groaning, still half asleep, Ken raised himself on one elbow. After a moment he said,

"It's a hyena."

"A hyena! Only one?"

"Well, probably not. They hunt in packs."

"Are you sure it's hyenas? And not lion?"

Certainly the deserted countryside round about made it seem only too likely.

"Lions don't sound like that."

"Or a leopard?"

"Leopards cough. Go to sleep."

"I can't."

Reluctantly he roused up, eased himself out of the tent (lion-proof?) and threw another log on the dying fire. The yowling faded, the night settled into silence.

In the morning ghostly light filtered through green canvas. Ken's bed inches from my own was empty; it was a slight movement outside that had woken me. There was a cough, a voice called 'Odi' and an extended hand appeared - Station's presumably - holding a cup of tea. I raised myself on one elbow to take it and looked out through the tent flap as I drank. To my surprise a mist had come down; the village below had vanished, sound as well as sight was diminished. I was startled when Ken appeared out of the gloom like an apparition.

"I've been inspecting gardens down there with Sutherland and Bodwin, the

District Capitao here. This is hill mist, he said waving a hand, "It's almost clear in the valley. What a place. Needless to say the headman tried to steer us away from the slash and burn gardens. They know they've breached regulations. But who can blame them?"

"So?"

"So I turned a blind eye for once and went off in the other direction. I gave them the usual spiel about leaving grass strips across the hillside, but they won't do anything about it. It would take years to check erosion like this. And time is something they haven't got."

There seemed no answer to this.

As we were eating breakfast the mist began to clear, light clouds drifted across the sky leaving the sun in command once more. There was little to hinder our early departure. The tent was struck, the bedding rolled up, cooking pots strung together and the whole divided into loads for the carriers to take back to Katobo. The returning ones shook hands all round, then with expressions of goodwill hoisted up their loads and started back for home.

Sutherland who was also returning, came to say goodbye. I thanked him sincerely for all the help he had given me, at which he looked embarrassed. Finally it was the turn of William and Station. Seldom had they been so far from home. At this parting my feelings surprised me. I had imagined the moment would be one of undiluted pleasure as I recalled all the miserable meals we had endured. And our almost total lack of communication. And yet...

They had stepped into the breach when we were desperate. They had never returned my bad temper or resented my irritable frustration. On the contrary they had remained good humoured and anxious to do their best in a situation not of their making. Moreover they had the endearing quality of assuming each failure to be their fault, which was not always the case. How churlish then to part from them without any feeling of gratitude. Through Sutherland I thanked them sincerely, They responded by saying they would pray God for my safe return, meanwhile they would look after the house and cook for Sir when he came back to Misuku. Ken, anxious to be off, looked underwhelmed at the prospect. We shook hands, then with more good wishes, they set off, with Sutherland, back up the winding track to Wilindi and were soon lost to sight

Accompanied by Bodwin, two carriers with our suitcases, two travellers glad not to be walking on their own, and the headman and elders, we ourselves took the other direction. After the half mile of courtesy the headman and his retinue, suitably recompensed, said goodbye with yet more hand shaking.

We met no-one, saw nothing to alarm us, the scene enlivened only once by a troupe of monkeys . The countryside was changing. From the hogs-back of the ridge the path led predominantly downward so that we now encountered in reverse, the terrain experienced on the ulendo up from Karonga, that is, of localised hills and valleys, and innumerable streams. This time we were losing altitude rather than climbing, so that despite a treacherous surface of shale and scree, the going was comparatively easy.

Ken had said that Kapoka was merely eight miles or so away with only the Kalengé river a possible impediment to progress, so I was anxious to reach it. Subsequently the Kalengé loomed large in our lives but on this occasion it presented no problem. We reached it at midday, it proved to be but a stream in a half dried up river bed running between high banks. Banks however hung with detritus, giving clear evidence of the level, the ferocity, of the river when, fed with run-off from the hills at the height of the rains, it came down in spate. Neither did the remains of a previous pole bridge washed away and carried further down stream leave much to the imagination. On that day however, it was a shady place to sit and dabble our feet and eat dry scone bread sandwiches.

After the Kalengé we walked a smooth, sandy track leading to Kapoka a few miles further on, where we hoped to find Angus Day waiting for us.

Kapoka had figured prominently in the scheme of things over the past few months, usually coupled with the Kalengé, and often with the Chendo Track as well. To me, never having been there, it was chiefly significant for being the place where Angus had dropped off our furniture, but I gathered it was important in its own right because of its tenuous connection with the road system proper. I had therefore assumed it to be a place of some size, a township with an African store, a church, a school perhaps. As it was one could have mistaken the few scattered huts set in a seemingly arbitrary spot in less than splendid isolation, for an outpost of the main concourse. Only later did I learn its history and its indirect link with my hero, Captain Lugard.

For Kapoka, now but a hamlet comprising the homestead of the Agricultural Department's local district capitao and his extended family, had in the late 19th century, been a staging post on the much vaunted Stevenson Road running northwards from Karonga. Named after a Scottish industrialist who had put up the money, the Stevenson Road was, itself, part of a grandiose scheme to rival Cecil Rhodes' mighty Cape to Cairo railway, "its purpose to (access and) "unite the Great lakes (of Africa,) as with a chain." Those are the words of a stalwart official of the African Lakes Company based in Karonga at the height of the slave trade - see L. Monteith Fotheringham, Adventures in Nyasaland, Sampson Low, 1891.

As the days of the internal combustion engine had not yet arrived, it now seems puzzling as to what overland type of transport was envisaged to form the links in the chain. Horses? Unlikely to flourish in this part because of African horse-sickness, Pack mules? An inexhaustible team of carriers on foot? Both were possibilities. Whatever the intention the scheme faltered and died. Perhaps through lack of funds, perhaps because the great era of Victorian expansionism was already in decline before the venture was accomplished.

Over the years the Stevenson Road fell into disrepair. By the 1950s, except for odd stretches between Kapoka and Karonga which Angus had utilised as part of the Chendo Track, it had degenerated into an overgrown, ill frequented, footpath.

As the tide of progress receded Kapoka, naturally, lost its importance and shrank accordingly. To me, and I had plenty of time to observe it for Angus was nowhere to be seen when we arrived, it had not so much the air of an abandoned gold rush town, but of another Victorian phenomenon. Namely the railway. Or rather, of Victorian cottages set down by the tracks, in the heart of the English countryside, that one sometimes glimpsed as the train rushed past. Rail workers and their wives and families must live in these isolated spots and fashion out their lives as best they could.

Not that anyone at Kapoka looked unhappy or discontented, rather the reverse in fact. The district capitao, either by coincidence or nepotism, was the brother of Bodwin who had accompanied us from the hills. He was tall, with the leanness of one used to walking long distances. He had lost one eye, the socket of which was neatly stitched over; his good eye twinkled. Unsurprisingly he was called Nelson. Surrounded by elders and a gaggle of children, he greeted us courteously. Ken responded then said,
"You got my note in good time?"
"Yes Sir, I received it three days ago. The messenger then went on to Chisenga. He has not yet returned."
Discreetly I asked Ken how far it was to Chisenga.
"Twenty miles or so, That's no distance for a messenger, he replied, reading my thoughts, "Don't worry, Angus will come."
I very much hoped he was right.
At a word from Nelson one of the women bystanders brought a wooden chair from the interior of a hut and placed it in front of Ken. Consternation set in when he told me to sit down on it. He and Nelson began discussing agricultural matters and moved off to inspect maize plots. I, not wholly reassured, sat down in shade wishing I could communicate with the women. I reasoned it would be sheer luck if Simbeyé found Angus at home. He was so often away and could easily have forgotten the casual arrangement made with Ken at Katobo months before.
What would we do if he did not come? Well, we would spend the night at Kapoka of course. Assuredly Nelson and his people would find us shelter and see that we did not go hungry. Indeed the women had already brought bananas and there was no mistaking their goodwill. But our camping gear had gone back to Katobo with the carriers, and we would have to sleep on the earth floor of a mud hut. I could cope with that. What I did find daunting however was the prospect of having to walk to Chisenga in the morning. Twenty miles eh? Was there a chance of getting a lift once we came to a road? I certainly hoped so.
The sun had gone round, I moved the chair to the shade of the thatch eaves of a hut, sharing the raised earth khondé - veranda - with a flopped out dog and several comatose chickens standing on one leg. It was very quiet, sleep was irresistible...

I woke with a raging thirst, longing for tea. Even in my ignorance of local habits I knew it would not be forthcoming. Even if these people enjoyed the luxury of tea, fires would be lit only for cooking the evening meal, the sparse bush country around made the scarcity of firewood abundantly clear. As I drank a little of the water remaining in our flask, I wondered how far the women must walk to find it.
Noticing the gathered children I spoke to them in English, which made them

giggle. Beyond the homestead the track bordered by tawny vegetation, wheel-tracks faintly visible between, wound away into the bush. Ken and Nelson came back. The strip of shade broadened; it would be dark within half an hour, surely Angus would not come now? Was Ken concerned?

Even as the thought occurred, above the chatter of the children, voices of the men, the orchestration of cicadas, came the faint but unmistakable throb of an engine. Presently the elephant grass along the path quivered and parted to reveal old Simbeyé leaning perilously out of Angus's jeep waving.

Angus slewed to a stop. He said,

"I'm a bit late. Got delayed by one of the road gangs along the way. Where's your katundu? That all you've got? Good. We can get off right away then."

We made hurried goodbyes and thanks to Nelson and his clan as Angus, not one to be kept waiting, turned the jeep.

It was not a sophisticated vehicle. Left over from the war most likely, it had no top, (which made for fresh air certainly, but for more dust as well,) no doors, so that one must climb over the side, and one hard bench seat designed for two. I was wedged in the middle, Ken was thin after our Spartan diet of the last few months, Angus was not. But oh the joy of being transported after months of footslogging. To reach the speed of 20mph when we reached the earth road that would take us to Chisenga was positively exhilarating.

By this time it was quite dark; our headlights stabbing the darkness revealed only the way winding before us. We reached Angus's house at last, lamplight streaming out a welcome.

"Got anywhere to live in Karonga?" asked Angus at supper.

"Yes, I replied, glancing at Ken who so far had been silent throughout the meal, "Steve Witting the Cotton Board fellow is moving out of the Clover Leaf house for us and is going to camp in the new one he's building next door. We heard just before we left Misuku. Isn't that good of him?"

"Oh, so he agreed then? Good."

I remembered then that Ken had asked Angus to put in a word with Steve if he got a chance.

We had arrived at Chisenga to the forgotten luxury of a house with floors, ceiling, a comfortable bedroom and, best of all at that point, a conventional bath with taps. Now we were enjoying a lavish meal put on by the deaf and dumb cook. Hence the silence as Ken did full justice to it. At length he said,

"How's the Chendo?"

"Very good." replied Angus automatically.

"No, I mean how is it really? I heard it was closed a few weeks ago. I don't want to take any risks just now you know."

"'Course it's alright, said Angus indignantly, " Bit bumpy in places. It was closed because the Lufira bridge got washed away. I've had a new one built. Permanent this time. I've recently been there, and left a gang there fixing the decking. That'll be done by now."

"Concrete?"

"No, timber. Tree-trunks from bank to bank, high across the gorge."

"You're sure it's OK then?"

"Of course I'm sure. Would you rather go the long way round? South on the main road then off on the Livingstonia Escarpment and back to Karonga by the lake shore road? Takes about ten times as long. Anything could happen on the way." he added shooting me a dark look.

It was easy to tell what he had in mind, and not without reason. Apart from the added miles, this route had its own hazards and hold ups. Indeed, having experienced the Livingstonia Escarpment with its twenty three hairpins, I was in no hurry to encounter it again. Ken must have felt the same for after a moment or two he said reluctantly,

"Alright then. The Chendo it is." A decision he was to question later.

The next day was one of relaxation. Chisenga, though isolated and not so spectacularly beautiful as Misuku, was in a very pleasant spot, at reasonable altitude, in countryside still green at this time of year. Angus's house stood on a slight rise against the backdrop of the Mafingé Hills, a short distance from the road which ran on to Fort Hill. By the road stood a rest-house and further off was a PWD depot, with Angus's office and ancillary houses for African staff and their families, similar to the capitaos' houses in Misuku.

Ken left after breakfast to inspect village gardens round about, although whether Chisenga fell within his area or was Andrew's responsibility was a moot point. Angus also went off, I sat on the khondé doing nothing, watching the passing scene.

A PWD lorry set off loaded with equipment for a road gang, a bit later a vehicle drove past in a cloud of dust. Once a traveller stopped off at the rest-house with engine trouble; Angus summoned from his office, was able to fix it, then he invited him in for coffee.

At tea that afternoon Angus said turned to me and said abruptly,

"Got a cot?"

"Er, no. Not yet."

In truth this was but one of the items I had not got.

"I hope to get one in Lilongwe when we get there."

"Well you can have the one we used for our kids."

He disappeared, I sat embarrassed at this indirect mention of the collapse of his marriage and loss of children. The two little girls plucked at tender age from parents, from the sunshine, the freedom of Chisenga, the only home they had ever known, had been flown to Angus's sister's home in England. Picturing them in the English Midlands, said by the poet to be 'sodden and unkind', I very much hoped their mother would soon reclaim them, even though it seemed unlikely she would ever return to Angus.

He came back carrying a long basket of the type that women further south used for tobacco picking. It was ideally suited to accommodate a baby or young child and I thanked him profusely. Over the years it served us well. With carrying poles, legs and a canopy against the sun added, it became a ulendo basket / cot.

We were to go to Karonga the following day and I knew instinctively that with

Angus an early start would mean just that. So it was next morning that we wedged ourselves in the jeep, as before, just as the sun was beginning to light up the Mafingé Hills. Angus, his hands on the steering wheel about to set off, paused thoughtfully, leapt out, ran back to the house and returned with a cushion which he thrust at me, saying,

"You might need this."

I sat on it gratefully, then we were off with as much speed as the twisting path would allow, back along the route we had covered in darkness two nights before. Away in the distance as the sun rose, Wilindi Ridge appeared as a faint smudge on the horizon. Presently we came to a deserted spot in the middle of nowhere designated PICCADILLY CIRCUS. A few yards further on at a turn-off, a finger-post said KARONGA JEEPS ONLY

"The DC made me put up that last bit." said Angus disgustedly as we swung off right.

So this was the Chendo Track. It was only marginally wider than the one from Kapoka and far rougher. The terrain meant we must swerve to avoid boulders, buckle crazily round rocky outcrops or large trees, make detours to find the best place for fording a stream. Sometimes for reasons best known to himself, Angus veered off into bush, inventing the route as we went along.

"How far is it to Karonga?" I ventured.

"Sixty seven miles." said Angus promptly.

I was impressed with this precision after all the indeterminate distances we had recently covered on foot. But when I mentioned it later to Ken he replied cynically that of course Angus would have long since registered it on the jeep's milometer.

We were back in remembered bush and brachystegia country, losing altitude all the time, as we would continue to do all the way to the lake shore. I prayed not to have another nose bleed.

Sometimes the track became a narrow ledge carved out of the hillside, sometimes the gradients were severe. Thus we went on our jaw clenching way, legs braced as we bumped from rock to rock and I was very thankful for the cushion.

At one point we stopped to drink coffee and dabble our feet in a stream, then on again through the limbo of the day. Our progress however, though slow, was unimpeded, the grating of cicadas the only sound above engine; the temperature soared. After a long time Ken said,

"We can't be too far from the Lufira now surely?"

"No, said Angus and added as if having pondered Ken's question of the previous day, "I didn't put in a concrete bridge because there wasn't enough money. And anyway any structure standing on the river bed is bound to get washed away in time if the rains are heavy enough. This one spans the gorge high enough to cope with anything short of Acts of God."

"Well, Ken replied, "So long as it's finished..."

"Oh it'll be finished alright. All the bearers are in place, I saw to that. I told you I was there last week, it only needed the decking and I left a good capitao in charge of that."

The Lufira was one of the two main rivers that went on to feed the flood plain on the lake shore before emptying itself in Lake Nyasa, leaving a muddy stain on the normally pellucid surface. This being the dry season we were unlikely to find the river in spate, nevertheless we heard it well before we reached the crossing point.

On arrival the new bridge looked impressive. As Angus had told us, it spanned a gorge, some 40feet wide, with three enormous tree-trunk bearers about 3feet apart. Alas, in spite of his earlier protestations, that was the extent of the progress. No decking was in place; once again it looked as though we might be spending the night in the bush.

Angus cut the engine, leapt out of the jeep with a roar and hit the ground running. There was no sign of the road gang, or indeed of any human life. The sound of our approach had been drowned by the rushing water, but Angus's anger would surely have wakened the dead. Nimbly for one so substantially built he made his way across on one of the tree-trunks, still cursing. For several moments nothing else stirred. Then as Ken and I watched from the jeep there was a slight movement near the further bank. A figure emerged, yawning, naked and very startled. Another minute and a laocoon of labourers, almost invisible in shade, disentangled itself from the bushes, the components pulling nsaru round themselves as they went. Lastly came a crumpled PWD capitao hastily buttoning up his bush shirt.

"You're fined a week's pay!" shouted Angus.

"But Sir..."

"This bridge should be finished. Why hasn't the decking been fixed as I ordered? You've had plenty of time!"

"But Sir, stammered the capitao, "The decking is not present. The PWD did not send decking. We could not fix it."

Angus checked himself in full flow of invective and looked round. To an impartial observer certainly, there were no planks, wood, or anything else around likely to be useful in finishing off a bridge. Perhaps Angus silently acknowledged this for he said in a more moderate tone,

"The decking should have come from Mzimba. You should have sent me a message."

"Sir I sent a messenger two days ago."

Always a man of action Angus wasted no more words but gave his attention to what seemed, to me at least, an impossible situation. He walked back to the bridge and stood for a moment immobile. We on our side were at a loss. At last Angus moved to the head of the bridge and squinted along the tree-trunks.

"Surely he's not thinking of driving across without decking? Just on the bearers? I said, "Surely that would spell disaster."

Although it was unlikely the jeep could actually fall through into the river, the tree-trunks were quite far enough apart for him to slip partly between them and damage the jeep in the process.

"I don't think even Angus would attempt that". Ken replied.

But Angus it seemed, had another plan,

"Get some bamboo poles cut, Angus told the capitao, "The longest and strongest ones you can find."

Of these there was no shortage for by now bush country had given way to the lush vegetation of the lake shore region and bamboos were dominant. The men, still yawning, took up their axes, the capitao between giving orders and justifying himself to Angus, ("Sir you said to fix the decking. You did not say to cut bamboo...") now worked with alacrity.

Soon the surrounding countryside was ringing with the sound of wood cutting and a pile of thick poles was shortly assembled. Then began one of the most skilful, not to mention intrepid, exploits I had ever witnessed.

Angus ordered the men to lay the poles close together across the tree-trunk bearers on our side of the river. There were enough to extend about one quarter of the distance to the opposite bank. When that was done to his satisfaction, he called Ken, the capitao and one or two labourers to him, explained his intention and their part in it. After that he came back to the jeep. When all the players were in position, and he was satisfied that everyone knew what they must do, Angus climbed back into the jeep, started the engine and eased on to the bamboos. I held my breath. As he reached the edge of the gorge the bamboos groaned as they took the weight - but they held in place. Inch by inch he began to cross. The poles behind were taken up when Angus had traversed them and the men passed them over the jeep to Ken and the capitao ready to re-lay them in front.

Stopping short Angus waited. Starting off again was possibly the most difficult part of the whole exercise. He achieved it however and moved slowly off again. The operation was repeated once, twice. He was half way across. Three quarters...

When he gained the further bank we all raised a cheer.

There remained the matter of my own crossing. Angus and Ken walked back across the bridge where I stood waiting nervously on the bank.

The bearers were stout certainly, but quite far enough apart for one false move to send a person falling between them into the water some thirty feet below. Nor would the rough, rounded sides of their trunks make for easy walking. With one on either side, arms extended to hold my hands, Ken and Angus led me to the bridge and on to the central bearer; the tree-trunk was rough beneath my feet, its surface was not reassuring. We paused, I held on desperately.

"Take your time, said Angus, "Watch where you're putting your feet, but don't look down at the river."

All too conscious of the water swirling below, its roar filling my head, I took a step. Then another and another...

After uncountable time we met the portion of decking remaining in place on the further bank. I stepped on to it, light headed with relief.

The rest of the journey was uneventful. The land sloped gently away to the plain, the track broadened out over smooth alluvial soil as we coasted down toward the lake shore road to Karonga.

When Ken and I had cause to come back up the Chendo some months later, the

bridge had long since been completed. The bearers were surmounted with decking of sawn planks, very sturdy and reassuring, So that, to misquote Eliot once more
-
'The river, from being a sullen, intractable barrier, was tamed / Ceased to be a problem, and so forgotten by men.'
But, this being Africa,
'Keeping its seasoned rages, unhonoured, un-propitiated, watching and waiting.'

CHAPTER 20

KARONGA DAYS AND NIGHTS

"Thank Goodness that's over, said Ken, "The journey I mean, and the Chendo in particular. Still It could have been worse."

I agreed. We were back in our old room at the rest-house. Bugles at dawn had disturbed us only briefly; for once Ken ignored them and we had slept our fill. Once awake I pondered the events of the last few days. The walk out of Misuku, hyenas in the night at Chato, the wait at Kapoka wondering if Angus would come. The potential for disaster at the Lufira and Angus's ingenuity and courage in preventing it. The heat, the dust, the general awfulness of the Chendo itself.
"I was glad of the cushion." I said, morning having brought out aches and pains from the jolting as well as a tendency to toothache due to all the teeth gritting..
In spite of everything I found myself very happy. Firstly at the prospect of seeing our friends again, secondly because of knowing we would shortly be leaving the rest-house for a house of our own.
I considered it very good of the Cotton Board chap to move out of the Cloverleaf house at Baka for us and camp in the new one he was building next door. When I mentioned it to Jess later, she said,
"Oh yes, Steve. A dear man." Which did not accord with Angus's opinion at all. "But of course he should have finished it months ago."

Ken left after breakfast to report to Andrew and also collect our truck which had been resting at Baka along with the big trunks. He would drive it back after work and we could move into the Cloverleaf in the afternoon.
I had a leisurely breakfast, after which I ventured out to Andanis to buy a bottle of whiskey for Angus, who had dropped us off at the rest-house and spent the night with one of the bachelors.
The heat and the forgotten humidity made any activity a major effort and I was glad to reach my objective. Inside the dark cavern of the store Mr Andani greeted me uneasily; obviously thinking of the near fainting fit of my last visit, the cause of which was now apparent. I made my purchase, got out as quickly as possible and made for the DC's residence. The houseboy told me the Dona DC was on the upstairs khondé with the children.
There was the remembered scene - the view of the lake, the children and their ayah listless in the heat - and Sue who had been so kind to me, dispensing iced coffee to visitors newly arrived on the plane. So unaltered was it, it seemed that the intervening months in Misuku had never been.
Yet change was in the air here too. When the visitors had gone Sue told me she and Joe were going on home leave and that when they returned it would be to a posting in the South.

"We don't yet know where." she said.

"Will you be sorry to leave Karonga?"

"Yes and no. We've been happy here on the whole, but the heat is very trying, especially for the children. Jane will be needing school soon, so something in the vicinity of Lilongwe would be handy. Or Zomba perhaps. In theory the powers that be are sympathetic to family needs but in practice, as with the army, basically we have to go where they send us."

Ken had returned when I got back to the rest-house; Angus and two of the bachelors were also there. Angus had spent an unsatisfactory morning at the Post Office vainly trying to contact the PWD at Mzimba by radio telephone to find out what had happened to the decking he had ordered for the bridge.

"Suppose I'll just have to drive a lorry down and bring it back myself." he said resignedly.

He brightened at the sight of the whiskey and would have opened it there and then, but the others protested it was too early in the day and too hot for spirits anyway, and settled for Castle lagers instead.

Of the three houses standing in line at Baka, counting the Cotton Board one under construction - which I noticed had proceeded apace since I last saw it - the Cloverleaf, as indicated previously, was the middle one. As Ken and I drove up to it that afternoon I wondered aloud as to why it had been built to such an unconventional design when all the other Government dwellings were severely rectangular. Ken did not know but said perhaps it had evolved out of three rondavels which had at some stage been linked together by a straight sided sitting/ dining room. At any event, as I now found, this room was flanked on two sides by bedrooms with curving walls, while the third leaf of the clover had become a front khondé. Windows and doors throughout were gloomily protected against mosquitos by rusting wire gauze. The walls, as in our Misuku house were decorated with ant tunnels and enlightened further by scurrying geckos; I discovered over the next few weeks that I did not mind the latter at all. Less welcome was a single scorpion which appeared over our bed one night. The house also boasted proper concrete floors and a matted ceiling throughout, which ensured that by and large, the intimate life of insects above could be conducted in privacy.

Tacked on at the back of the house was the bathroom. It had a wash-stand with a jug and basin as at the rest-house, and a full sized, freestanding bath with no taps; there was no running water in Karonga, not even at the DC's residence.

As a nod to modern plumbing however, the bath had a plug and plug hole with a pipe going through the outer wall, the waste water trickling on to the ground. In due course I manipulated the pipe to irrigate a short channel in which to grow marigolds. They grew at amazing speed.

Next to the bathroom was the type of lavatory known as a thunder box, a commode-like structure with a broad seat and a concealed bucket below. For sanitary purposes a second bucket by the side contained sand and a shovel, (for all the world like the ones placed in the corridors of my senior school in town during the 1939/45 war, with which we girls were supposed to smother fires caused by incendiary bombs.

A forlorn hope in my case.)

Sewage disposal in Karonga was surprising in its simplicity and efficiency. In the dark hours before dawn, occasionally heard but never seen, the night soil cart manned by trusties from the prison came trundling by. The thunder box bucket was removed , through a hatch in the outer wall, emptied and replaced, the cart creaked on its way. The sand bucket was re-filled as necessary.

I came to like the Cloverleaf house very much and fantasised on having a similar one built in England one day, with furniture expressly designed to fit the curved walls. As it was we now had the basics with which to start a home; the trunks were standing on the front khondé, I could not wait to unpack them. Before doing so however I was determined to go across and see Jess. Even as I formulated the thought she appeared in the doorway, great was my pleasure at the reunion.

"Well it doesn't look too bad does it? she said looking round shortsightedly, "Now that Steve's moved his stuff out and had the place cleared up a bit. He's still away on ulendo at the Khambwe. A dear man but not one of the tidiest."

To my relief she did not mention madness but went on,

"I'll send Umali over to lend you a hand. Come and have tea when you're ready. And you can have meals with us till you've settled in."

Oh the joy of having Jess' help and support once more.

The first task was to reorganise the sparse furniture to our requirements. The rectangular room had dining table and chairs plus two of the so-called easy chairs of wood and hide. The bedrooms either side each had a single iron-framed bed also like the ones at the rest-house, a locker and the customary wash-stand etc. Predictably we began by having the bed in the spare room brought into our own. Equally predictably we had not neglected to bring the double mosquito net back with us from Misuku. This done I opened up the trunks. For once there was no desire to read such wrappings as had escaped my attention before, the urge to transform the house into a home was stronger. I was delighted to see the wedding present dinner service once more - green dragons on a white background, with extra large plates made to Ken's specification, the lesser presents and souvenirs of our honeymoon which had suffered the risk of being left behind in the Chesham flat because Ken had deemed them inessential. Altogether, in spite of the heat I enjoyed myself.

We were about to go over to the Williamsons for tea when there was a discreet cough outside. It was Dan, cook to a departed bachelor whom Ken had known on his previous tour, now looking for work. To my relief Dan spoke English, Ken engaged him on the spot and took him out to the kitchen at the back of the house. It was of unburnt brick, with concrete floor and thatched roof, equipped with Dover stove, a table and chair, a vast improvement on conditions in Misuku.

Next morning Dan brought the tea very early. Ken got up at once when the equivalent of reveillé smote the quiet countryside. I went back to sleep but was woken again almost immediately by voices outside the window. For a moment it was as if we were back at Katobo with the labourers turning up for work.

Up and dressed I ventured out, knowing why these people had come. Not for medicine, but for work. Some were mere boys, some flourished work books, all clamoured to be taken on. Except one, the oldest among them who stood quietly to one side holding out a letter. It was from Sue,

"I'm shedding staff before we leave. The bearer of this note is Simeon, somewhat slow, but a trustworthy house-boy. I believe he would suit you."

After a few questions I gave him the job.

In spite of the enervating heat it was easy to slip back into the relaxed way of life in Karonga. Dan was an efficient cook, Simeon was indeed slow but good tempered and thorough. Fruit was abundant in the market, sometimes vendors came to the house. Meat was killed once or twice a week. Above all I had Jess' help and advice when I needed it.

Although there were only about a dozen Europeans in residence in Karonga at any one time, there were frequent visitors, mostly in the form of Government officials, or experts of some kind passing through. For a day or two they would swell our ranks on the tennis court and join the evening socialising.

One such visitor shortly after our return, was a doctor spending a week at the African hospital. His brief was to treat the local populace but he readily agreed to see me. Not long out from England, he was bluff and hearty. He examined me then said,

"Yes everything seems to be in order. When did you say the baby was due?"

I hadn't said, I was rather hoping he would corroborate the date given me months before by the doctor in Mzimba.. As that was not forthcoming I said firmly,

"Near the end of June."

"Right. You'll be flying down to Lilongwe I imagine?"

I explained that no, we would be going down by road because the airline had had too many narrow escapes to accept heavily pregnant women.

"Well don't leave it too long then, he told me, "It's quite a distance, I don't suppose you want to give birth on the side of the road?"

It was at this point that Ken announced he must go back to Misuku.

"But the doctor said..."

"Only for a fortnight or so."

"The doctor said the baby is due in the middle of June, I told him, stretching it a bit, "We must leave in three weeks."

"But this is only the middle of May! I can't hang about here all that time now can I? I'm not walking in this time. I shall drive up the Chendo, Angus says the Lufira bridge is finished now."

"He said that last time."

"Yes well, I'll drive to Kapoka and walk into Misuku the same day with luck. I've ordered a drum of petrol from Mzimba to be dropped off at Kapoka, so no trouble on that score. I'll be back in no time, you'll see. And there are plenty of people here to keep an eye on you, and see that you have company."

"It's not that." I protested, knowing now the difficult miles that would lie between us, the only too likely mishaps that could delay his return, "What if you were delayed on the way back? What if the Kalengé bridge..."

I knew it was no use; he left early next morning taking Dan the cook with him.

"For God's sake get him to show William how to make bread." I urged.

Ken had been right about one thing, I was not left on my own for long. Jess dropped over a bit later and around mid-day Angus, down for the weekend, came bearing a tin of chocolates.

"Heard it was your birthday." he said.

"Yes, but Ken has gone back to---"

"The Bishop's here." he put in quickly.

"The Bishop?"

"Yes, the Anglican bishop of Nyasaland. Touring the whole country or something. We're his last stop. Service at the Boma at ten tomorrow. Come and pick you up if you like."

I should of course have known that Nyasaland would have its own bishop given the religious zeal of the Victorians of 19th century England. They had made sure that the established church should not lag behind the Scots missionaries in claiming souls of the unenlightened. By contrast with the Scots however who had elected to live and work among warring tribes near Blantyre, the Anglicans, for reasons best known to themselves, had chosen Likoma Island far out in the lake for their headquarters and had built an impressive cathedral there.

My mind straying as it was only too apt to do, I recalled reading of a former bishop who had the misfortune to be shipwrecked in a storm when crossing to the mainland. His bones were washed up on shore some time later, picked clean by mpasa fish.

Angus meanwhile was ready to be about his business. He repeated the offer.

"Pick you up then, Tomorrow. Nine thirty."

"What? Oh, yes alright. Thank you."

Captain Lugard and his compatriots, of whom I thought as old friends, had begun each weekday with communal prayers, and on Sundays with guns at the ready in case of attack by the Arabs, held a service for all and sundry inside the stockade. Conversely the expatriate community in Karonga in the 1950s bore the almost total lack of religious provision with great equanimity. Yet here we were next day assembled in the open sided courthouse in front of the Boma, dressed with unaccustomed respectability. Sue, Jess and I were hatted and gloved, the men in tropical suits, their numbers swelled by others from outstations, anticipating a sociable weekend when the service was over.

The court-house was surrounded by a press of local people, the Bishop no doubt gave an uplifting address. It passed me by but my prayers were sincere enough. They were to the effect that God and daily Paludrine would keep us all from the predations of the several million mosquitos also in attendance.

Obviously my spiritual credence had run out for the DC went down with a dose of malaria a few days later.

After the Bishop's visit the days assumed a routine of sorts. Morning held chores which took a long time because of the heat, the lassitude of pregnancy and sometimes by visits of one or other of the bachelors. Each afternoon at three Andrew called me over to join him and Jess for tea. After that would come the usual swimming or tennis gatherings until we returned to the Cloverleaf at dusk. Nor were evenings without consolation. Dusk a few days later found me on the back khondé struggling to light the Tilley lamp without losing my eyebrows again. Suddenly, a pleasant Oxbridge voice outside said,

"Can I help?"

Flustered I looked up. A burly stranger stood at the wire-gauzed door.

"Steve Witting, he said stepping inside and holding out a hand.

Of course. This was the Cotton Board fellow who, until now, had been on such a prolonged ulendo as to be something of a myth as far as Ken and I were concerned. In the gloom I nervously scanned his face for signs of madness, then relinquished the lamp with relief. He soon had it burning nicely. By its light I could see his appearance somewhat supported his reputation, though eccentricity might have been a better word. For one thing, in this era of 'short back and sides', Steve's hair was decidedly shaggy. For another instead of the khaki drill worn for practicality by most of the men on the station, Steve's shirt was dull red rather washed out, and his shorts might once have been dark blue. He carried the lamp through to what was technically his own sitting room, placed it on the table, and sat down. I collected myself sufficiently to offer him a drink, and thank him for moving out for us.

"Are you comfortable next door?" I asked.

"Oh, yes, it's fine thank you. The roof's not finished yet but luckily the rains are almost over and it's pleasant to lie and look up at the stars."

Thereafter, seemingly having had enough of being on ulendo, Steve came over every night to light the lamp and usually stayed to supper. Fortunately, what with the comparative abundance of food in Karonga and the fact that his cook would come across to assist the elderly Simeon, entertaining was a pleasure rather than the worry it had been in Misuku.

Like Angus, Steve had fought in the 1939/45 war and that always sorted the men from the boys. Here the similarity ended however. Angus was practicality personified, Steve was an idealist, a romantic. Armed with new (to him that is,) strains of seeds with which to improve the lot of the impoverished people, he had made his own way to Nyasaland as a result of reading Laurence van der Post's book, Venture to the Interior. He spent some time wandering the high Nyika before coming to realise that the Government, in the form of the Department of Agriculture, had long been promoting the very thing he was trying to do. It was at this point that he joined the Cotton Board.

By now he knew a lot about the Africans and got on well with them. Knew for instance when the nightly drumming which formed a background to our conversation could be attributed to a routine beer drink, a wedding party, celebration of the slaying of a marauding lion or leopard, or to some other cause unlikely to meet with the approval of the DC. He once let slip that on his recent ulendo a local chief had offered him one of his daughters for the night, but did not divulge the outcome.

Steve was a great talker; best of all he loved to talk about his family. His mother, Olive, had visited Karonga the previous year. A martinet according to Andrew who was inclined to be uncharitable, strong minded according to Jess who was not. Olive had been the cause of almost all his staff giving notice. Everyone agreed that she ruled Steve with a rod of iron, the whole station, heaved a collective sigh of relief when she finally returned to England.

One of the stories Steve recounted during our nightly sessions concerned a cousin who, while on the Grand Tour of Europe early in the twentieth century, had disappeared and was presumed to have drowned when rowing on Lake Constance in a small boat. The whole family was devastated; the grieving mother consulted a medium who, with map and dowsing rod, claimed able to pin-point the exact spot where he had gone down. Although one was tempted to wonder what comfort the knowledge could bring her, the story made a great impression on me. It resonated years later when our own seventeen year old son flew over the same stretch of water with a dare-devil pilot not much older than himself. Mercifully un-eventfully. Thereafter I could never recall either incident without a shudder.

That Steve's family was impecunious to a man seemed not only inevitable but appropriate. His grandfather having made and lost several fortunes, had shuffled off this mortal coil when finances were at their lowest ebb.

A promising aunt had emigrated to Australia at the end of the 19th century, but little was heard from her until news of her death reached the relatives several years later. Under the terms of her will they inherited no money but instead received "My work-box and a bag of marbles for the kiddies."

True the box was beautifully carved but in no way was it likely to do much for the family coffers.

"But the marbles were beautiful, recalled Steve wistfully, "Not at all like the mass produced ones you get in the shops nowadays. These were cloudy, some pink and pale blue, some a bit misshapen. We played with them a lot. By the time the grown-ups realised that the work-box was Great Aunt's means of sending her opals to England, we kiddies, unfortunately, had lost most of them."

CHAPTER 21

'THE MOON WAS A GHOSTLY GALLEON...'

Unusually, Steve dropped in one day at lunchtime.
'The Ilala's in port, he said, "Would you like to come with me and have supper on board tonight?"
As usual in what I had come to regard as a new incarnation, my knowledge of the Ilala was historical rather than contemporary. I knew the original boat of that name had been shipped out from England around 1875 and was named after the place where David Livingstone died. Whence his body had been carried by devoted servants on a foot slogging journey of some weeks, so that he might be buried among his own people.
Replacements of the boat had followed over the years, their function then as now, one of transport and commerce. Traders and travellers embarked at Monkey Bay in the South, for part or all of the voyage, others joined or left it at every anchorage. The traders melted away into the interior with their wares, to re-embark on the boat's return several weeks later laden with anything the locals had to barter. A practice which had changed little since the 19th century.
In Karonga the arrival of the Ilala once a month was still eagerly anticipated as the means of obtaining bulky goods, some of them out from England, from furniture to supplement the spartan PWD issue, car spares, gramophones, the occasional piano modified it was said, especially for the tropics, to cases of whiskey for the more hardened drinkers.
Notable among the Ilala's recent commanders was Captain Flint, who apparently embodied his name, and around 1952 in conjunction with the Queen's Christmas speech, miraculously for the time, took part in a broadcast linking up far flung places of the British Empire.
All this I pondered as Steve repeated his invitation.
"Need you ask? I said, "Thank you very much."

The Ilala could not truthfully be said to be 'in port'. That term, surely, conjured up a scene of busy docks, wharfs, warehouses and ships of all shapes and sizes coming and going. We were headed for a solitary vessel moored offshore in the deep water of the Khambwe lagoon already mentioned, some three miles from Karonga.

Steve's Landrover was not appreciably more comfortable than Angus's jeep, but unlike the Chendo Track, the lake shore road was flat and smooth. Steve was very cheerful at being mobile again after the petrol and water tanks débacle, and when not talking, he whistled above the snorts and coughs of the engine and the rasping of cicadas.
The night was brilliant with stars and fireflies, with a full moon rising over the

lake. We passed through one or two villages with men seated round the remains of cooking fires, otherwise the track weaved its way between bango reeds that almost met over our heads. Once a pennant winged nightjar lurched across our path, its flight impeded by its long trailing plumes, once a warthog or some such creature hurriedly got out of our way.

At the Khambwe - its tragic history yet unknown to me - lake water was shot silk. The Ilala rode at anchor several hundred yards out; a dinghy was discernible pulling toward us, the light of its stern lantern splintering the water.

"They were on the look-out for us, said Steve, "And set off when they saw our headlights."

We splashed through warm shallows as the boat ran up the sandy beach, Steve helped me get in it and soon we were slipping easily through smooth water. I gave myself up to the moment.

But then a thought struck me. How did one get aboard the Ilala? Wondering why I had not considered this before, I found myself recalling Ken's fond accounts of evenings such as this in bachelor days during his tenure of Steve's job, and was almost sure he had said something about a rope ladder.

"Er, Steve, I ventured, "Is it very difficult getting on board?"

"Oh no. Well, the companionway up the side is a bit tricky perhaps. But don't worry, I'll hold on to you."

I sighed with relief, obviously things had moved on.

Even with Steve's help getting out of the bobbing dinghy was in fact the hardest part, the rest was easy. On reaching deck level one's eyes met a row of black, patent leather shoes, two more steps up and their owners in the form of officers in tropical white were revealed. They in turn were presented with a far less salubrious sight. Steve wore another of his dark red shirts with what might have been his old school tie, grey flannel trousers now damp at the bottoms, and a jacket of hunting pink which had seen better days. Nor had Jess' efforts (in spite of years of practice on Andrew,) to reduce Steve's hair to respectable proportions, been entirely successful. I wore my best maternity dress, but realised too late that I had kicked off my cherished high- heeled red shoes to wade out to the dinghy. Hurriedly I put them on.

Nothing registered by so much as the flicker of an eyebrow among our hosts; they would have come across all sorts, seen it all before in the course of their travels.

They welcomed us aboard, led us to the upper deck and introduced a group of people sitting in canvas chairs, sipping drinks. These were first class passengers, American mostly, indulging in an African Queen vacation; all needless to say, well dressed, well groomed, sophisticated. They too welcomed us warmly, disarming in their interest and cordiality, glad perhaps to see new faces. Steve, totally unaware of any incongruity in the situation, was soon well into his stride. Primed with questions, he talked of his work, of the local people and their customs. When it emerged that we were not married or rather, not married to each other and Steve not at all, one seemingly unattached girl was even more appreciative.

With the talk flowing freely I could give myself up to the beauty of the scene. The cloudless sky was an inverted bowl pierced by steadfast stars. The moon now fully risen, reflected perhaps its own Sea of Tranquillity. Time was suspended, my dream in Misuku on the night of Ken's absence returned, Earth was an insignificant speck in the infinity of the universe, mortals that peopled it 'merely players'.

The ship's bell cut across the image. Skilfully, without haste, the officers finished their drinks, wound up the threads of conversation and lead us aside to a polished table resplendent with silver and cut glass.

Steve sitting next to the semi-detached girl was enjoying himself hugely. I chatted to an American gentleman 'in oil', and rejoiced as course followed delicious course, that for once good food and the appetite to enjoy it, had coincided. The whole company was discretely amazed at how much we ate. But then, it was fairly safe to assume that none of them had recently been subjected to the equivalent of William's cooking in Misuku or, in Steve's case, a non-stop diet of rice on the flood plain of Mweniteté.

It grew late; all too soon it was time to leave, lest the stewards attending us turn into frog footmen, the dinghy into a pumpkin. We said goodbye with considerable reluctance.

Back on shore we climbed into the Landrover and cruised off erratically, Steve singing drunk, I intoxicated with beauty. Over the lake the long silver track of the moon held its course.

Ken was very angry when I recounted all this to him on his return a week later. "It was so beautiful, I said, "The lake, the moon. And the food was wonderful and ---"

"They all said that man was mad!" he exploded. (He had not yet met Steve.) "Anything could have happened. Suppose that clapped out old land-rover of his had broken down? Suppose a freak storm had washed down from the hills flooding the track and catching you on the wrong side - swept you away even?"

"But it's the dry season, I protested, "And Steve's not mad, just, well, different."

"Suppose you had gone into labour on the Ilala? Suppose the mwera (wind) had whipped up the water as it frequently does, and the dinghy overturned? You wouldn't have stood a chance!"

I was impressed by his vehemence. The more so because I knew he was right. Privately I thought those splendid officers would have taken childbirth in their stride, but was far less sure of Steve's land-rover, or of his ability to deal with any of the emergencies Ken had described. All the same I was not going to admit it. After consideration I said, firmly, if not entirely reasonably or grammatically,

"Well you should have come back sooner. Anyway it didn't did it? It couldn't have. Not on such a night."

Two days later we left for Lilongwe.

CHAPTER 22

'THERE WAS A BIRTH CERTAINLY'

The only thing we could be sure of on the 400mile or so journey south to Lilongwe, was that it would be hard going. Although we started off early that first morning, as we cruised past the Williamson's house next door, Jess was already at work in her garden. Ken pulled up and she came over to wish us well.

"It's not too hot yet, she said, "And once you get up past Livingstonia the air will be fresher."

We bade her goodbye; as we reached the track I looked back, suspecting that nothing would be quite the same on our return.

Once clear of Karonga we would be travelling in reverse, the route which had taken me there in the first place. That is, initially along the dusty lake shore road recently taken by Steve and me en route for the Ilala, and before that with Ken on our journey up country. Both times I had traversed it in darkness, this time villages in the clearings were revealed in early sunlight, friendly people waking to the day pausing to wave.

After about an hour we met the Livingstonia turnoff and began to climb. Too soon came the ordeal of the Livingstonia Escarpment; the pickup was hopelessly under powered, once again I got out and walked. As we reached the top at last the air was indeed fresher as Jess had said, but with the sun now high, the cab was still uncomfortably hot. Once on the main road south however, we were able to pick up speed and wind down the windows a little. Jolting over bumps and corrugations on the earth surface, dust flying, we eventually reached Rumphi, our first night's stopover.

Surrounded by hills and with a warm wind blowing incessantly, Rumphi was a smaller version of Karonga except that it was on a river rather than a lake, comprising merely a Boma and the usual cluster of offices and staff houses. The Last Post sounded as we checked in at the rest-house.

Our destination next morning was Mzimba - a comparatively short stretch with no complications, and Ken had time to report to the Provincial Agricultural Officer. To my great relief Robert and his wife had not returned to the North after home leave. In the event I never saw either of them again, but Ken unexpectedly met up with Robert in London many years later. Neither of them mentioned Fort Hill.

The new PAO John Sandys, was very friendly. Better still, as Ken had predicted, he knew nothing of Robert's erstwhile plan to send us to Fort Hill. Either the relevant document lay unread in some file, or else it had been scrapped. Either way our defection passed un-noticed.

John, newly arrived, invited us to stay the night with him. At supper he complimented Ken on what had already been achieved with the Misuku Coffee Co-operative, and expressed the intention of visiting us there as soon as he could get out and about the District. Gratified as I was at this appreciation of Ken's work, my heart sank at the thought of William's cooking, the general awfulness of our living conditions, and the impossibility of entertaining visitors adequately. Especially as John's own house evinced all the signs of gracious living appropriate to his position. As it happened he, and his wife Naomi who joined him later, were destined to become lifelong friends, but this we could not know at the time.

South of Mzimba as we continued our journey next day, the road showed no sign of improvement. Certainly there were more road gangs attending it than Angus had at his disposal, but there was more traffic too, which is to say we encountered perhaps two vehicles an hour, a lorry or two, a few private cars, a crowded bus, all throwing up their own cloud of dust. But the most dust of all was from a PWD grader ostensibly, but not noticeably, working to improve the surface.

Were corrugations in the form of ridges across the road at intervals, the cause of my intermittent back pains? Or were they, could they be, the onset of labour? The doctor in Karonga had said not to leave it too late before getting down to Lilongwe. Even though I knew we had allowed time for holdups on the way, I was seized with panic. In common with many girls of my generation my knowledge of childbirth was sketchy, I did know however, that the more frequent the pains, the more imminent the birth. But how to time them? My watch had long since broken, Ken never wore one, the truck did not have the refinement of a clock. I glued my eyes on the milometer in stead.

"How much further is it to Lilongwe?" I asked tentatively.

"Oh not far now, replied Ken, "Another fifty miles or so I should think."

The pains - contractions? - were about five miles apart. Fifty miles. A mile a minute? Ten more spasms perhaps. Should be alright then surely? There seemed no point in mentioning it. Better not think of it. Better to pray that the radiator would not boil dry, that no hidden rock would hit the sump, no other disaster be visited on us. This would not do. Think of something more agreeable.

Unwisely for it was still a sore subject between us, I said,

"If only we could have come south on the Ilala!"

Into my mind had come a vision of the boat slipping through placid waters, Ken and I reclining on deck under an awning sipping cool drinks, watching the hippos wallowing in the shallows, the life of lake-side villages unfolding before us. Nights spent under the stars, with good food, sparkling conversation among the officers ...

Ken hot, uncomfortable and tired as I was, said,

"And how would we have got inland from the Ilala to Lilongwe? There's no railway in case you hadn't noticed."

I muttered something about buses, knowing full well what they were like.

"Oh yes, you'd have loved that wouldn't you?"

This led on to an argument, reasoned and pragmatic on Ken's part, idealised and woolly on mine, as to why the roads were not tarred, why the buses were uncomfortable and over-crowded, etc. etc.

Inconclusive and half hearted as it was, the bickering served the purpose of taking our minds off ourselves. Presently we reached forgotten tarmac and came to Lilongwe at last.

Once more we were installed in the Lilongwe Hotel. If not in the same room, in one much like the one we had occupied months before during the journey North. The same bouganvillea trailed in at the window - apparently it bloomed all the year round - a replica of the rattlesnake hat-stand of my nightmare stood in the corner.

In the morning the swish of gardeners' palm frond brushes on the path outside was the first sound to wake us.

Just for once Ken had no pressing matters on hand and we lay in bed in no hurry to get up. The back pains of yesterday had gone after I had taken a bath and as far as one could tell there was nothing to stop us enjoying a spot of lotus eating once more. We ate an ample breakfast at a civilised hour then sat in the garden, the air deliciously cool and sparkling because of the chipperoni - so called 'small rains' which sometimes blessed the country out of season.

The day slipped pleasantly away. Evening sundowners in conversation with fellow travellers were followed by dinner in the dining room with its potted palms, under the attentive eye of John the majordomo. An imposing figure resplendent in white kanzu and red fez, with red cummerbund round his ample waist. He claimed to remember us, Ken was dubious.

On the second day he announced his intention of,

"Doing the rounds of the town to try and sell the truck and get something more suitable to the roads and gradients further north."

He left after breakfast. I sat in a conservatory suffused with green light which came partly from the exotic plants, some of which soared to the glass roof as they tried to escape, partly from the overcast sky heralding another shower. The effect was of being in an aquarium, with waiters gliding about like fish and guests swimming up to one other now and again to exchange a few words.

When the rain stopped I sat outside with a book among sparkling frangipani and hibiscus, birds fussing about them showering raindrops from the leaves on to my sewing.

Ken came back having had no luck with the pickup. No-one wanted to buy it and the garage dealer was not interested in part exchange.

"The trouble is, he said, "There are a lot of people going on home leave at this time of year. Most of them want to sell their vehicles and come back with something better. I'll ask around the hotel and tomorrow I'll follow up one or two other leads. I'll also call in at the Provincial Agric. H/Q, someone there might need something. If nothing turns up I'll have to go on down to Blantyre and see what I can do there."

I very much hoped it would not come to that.

After lunch we drove about a mile and a half to the hospital to check up on my booking. The hard pressed doctor was not there, the nursing sister in charge said he spent most of his time at the African hospital down the road; in fact I never did see him.

After consulting the records the sister said that, yes, I was booked in. She too questioned me as to a date and tut-tutted at my unsatisfactory reply. She gave me a cursory examination and reported,

"Any day now. Meanwhile get plenty of exercise. Go for walks round the golf course, it'll do you good."

Along with running water and electricity - Lilongwe had both - I had forgotten about golf courses. I should of course have known that any sizeable settlement where the British held sway would have one, along with a cricket pitch, tennis courts, club- house, dramatic society and the rest.

The sister had given me a list of things the baby and I would need. That evening I glanced at it casually. Then sat up in alarm. Ken had assured me that all a baby would need in the tropics was a few nappies. Knowing better than to take this literally I had sewn some little dresses readily adaptable into rompers, should we have a baby boy. Friends and family at home had been busy knitting matinée jackets and crocheting shawls, all of which, along with the napkins, were now packed neatly in the carry-cot kindly given me by Sue prior to their leaving Karonga. So all in all I felt satisfied with my preparations.

Not any more. The list was long. Baby bottles and teats - just in case - bottle brushes, sterilising solution, baby Paludrine tablets, creams, ointments, prickly heat powder to name but a few. Then there were the things I would need for myself...

Next day saw me hurrying off to the shops; mercifully one called simply The Pharmacy was able to supply everything.

Reassured I took the opportunity to look round the town. Like Blantyre it had a wide main street lined with trees and set with shops and African stalls. There was a Barclays Dominion, Colonial and Overseas bank, two hairdressers, one for men and one for ladies, the life saving servicing garage/petrol station, and a boutique displaying the latest fashions, at which I gazed longingly. A little way off was a handsome Anglican church.

Two more days slipped away. Infuriatingly the pains experienced on the last lap of our journey were now conspicuous by their absence. We walked the golf- course as instructed, it seemed very tame after the rigours of our Misuku ramblings. Lotus eating degenerated into an orgy of over-eating. Ken still had no takers for the truck and chafed to be off to Blantyre.

We paid another visit to the hospital; the baby was now well overdue by everyone's reckoning, the sister suggested that perhaps, in the circumstances, I should be admitted. Reluctantly I packed my bags. Next day Ken delivered me into her hands and we said goodbye. Thereafter I walked the golf course alone.

The hospital was a long low building consisting of two-bedded wards giving on to a common khondé, also a surgical theatre and a maternity unit. The whole stood slightly elevated on a hillside commanding a view of undulating countryside. I had a ward to myself, pleasant and airy, and told myself sternly that I was lucky to be there.

Apart from the ever absent doctor there were two nursing sisters, Sister Hunt, tall, calm, exuding an air of competence, was South African. The one who had admitted me, Sister Schnabel, Swiss, unsurprisingly had a sharp nose and an accent so thick, it was some time before I realised she was speaking English. Her starched white uniform rivalled those of the officers on the Ilala; I very much hoped she would not be the one on duty when the baby finally put in an appearance. There were also numerous African ward maids, but so far as I could tell only one other patient. This was an elderly alcoholic lady who, as we sat on the khondé regaled stories of her own agonising confinements in the bush during the early 1900s, with no medical assistance apart from her husband's clumsy efforts.

Two more days dragged boringly by. After breakfast on the third day Sister Schnabel rustled importantly into my room armed with a large bottle and a spoon. I eyed them warily, even I knew that castor oil was outdated as a method of inducing labour. On the other hand sitting around like an unexploded bomb was infuriating and if nothing else was on offer... In any case resistance was useless, Sister Schnabel fixed me with a glittering eye, I closed mine and opened my mouth.

The pains started almost at once, and went on a long time. To my vast relief however, Sister Schnabel having delivered the coup de grace, went off duty and, as another day dawned, it was left to Sister Hunt to deliver the baby. A girl, Wendy, tiny, red, wrinkled, with a cry out of all proportion to her size. I thought she was wonderful. When it was all over I went to sleep and dreamed a dream which had recurred frequently over the past few months, which had left me feeling cheated and forlorn on waking. It was that the birth had taken place, that I had a baby at last. This time, unbelievably, it was true! There lay the baby sleeping peacefully in a crib beside my bed as I swam back to consciousness. There too alas, stood Sister Schnabel, on duty again, looking very self satisfied.

"Ach so, she said, "Ze castor oil war sehr gut nicht war?"

I was forced to concede the point. I drifted off again, to another dream in which Ken was with me, better still he had his arms round me. Amazingly this too proved to be real.

"I was staying with the Khoulas in Blantyre, he said, "John and I were playing chess when I got word from the hospital. I left at once. But it was alright, he added " I was losing anyway. Just about caught the last ferry at Liwondé"

The feeble joke momentarily checked my tears. To cheer me further he told me of the deal he had done on the truck.

"I've got what's called a pickup. Part exchange. I'm very pleased with it."

He was quite pleased with the baby too.

Another parting. We spent the rest of the day together as a family, with Ken returning to the hotel in the evening, but when he came back next morning he told me he must be leaving later.

"I have to go, he said in answer to my protests. "My leave's up. Wouldn't do to overstay it. I must get back to work. Only to Karonga this time though, he added hastily, seeing my face, "Not to Misuku. Andrew will be only too happy to keep me busy. Anyway you'll be discharged in a few days, and we'll be together again."

He was wrong as it happened, but I knew it was no use to argue. I had learnt by now that the Colonial Service seemingly so generous in granting its officers six months leave at the end of a tour, was decidedly niggardly about local leave between times. Ken's annual allowance was 15 days and, as Saturday mornings counted as a working day there was no (official) possibility of the occasional long weekend. Exceeding the allowance without permission, fire, flood, earthquake or other Acts of God notwithstanding, was treated with military severity. Needless to say, in such a male orientated institution, childbirth was well down the list of perceived excuses.

It is possible, even probable, that with some women motherhood comes naturally. Some perhaps, give birth and resume their normal life without breaking stride, pausing only to feed the infant and clean it up occasionally. It was not so with me. I knew I was changed for ever. Old ideas, priorities, values were swept away in the face of immediate practicalities.

I had very little knowledge of babies and almost no experience. Did not know for instance that they could, and often did, cry for hours for no apparent reason. That they lacked awareness of day and night, did not know the latter was the time for sleeping. In fact only in the middle of a feed could they positively be relied on to go to sleep.

Neither had anyone warned me that newborn babies frequently lost weight during the first few days. Therefore when Wendy, already small enough in all conscience, began to shrink before my very eyes, I was seized with terror.

Every morning just as my child had dropped off to sleep after an energetically wakeful night, Sister Schnabel would stride in, scoop her up and lay her on the old-fashioned scales. Every morning to Wendy's loud protests and Sister Schnabel's tongue clicking, the scales registered a new low, while I looked on in horror, terrified lest the tiny spark of life go out for ever. For good measure the elderly alcoholic would sometimes wander into the room and relate how her own sickly infants had survived solely by her own heroic efforts. So it was fortunate indeed that Sister Hunt usually came on duty at this time to start her day shift.

"Don't take any notice of her, she said, "Her children all survived somehow. Big hefty sons, they come and see her sometimes."

As I knew no-one in Lilongwe apart from a few casual acquaintances at the hotel, I had not expected any visitors after Ken left, and was therefore surprised one day when Mollie, one of the ward maids, said there was a lady to see me. Improbably it was someone I did know. It was Mrs. Apthorpe, wife of the Chief of Police, with whom we had shared a table on the boat on the voyage out. I vaguely recalled her telling me on one of the few occasions that I had been able to brave the dining room, that she had been a nursing sister; no doubt hospital visiting in Lilongwe was one of her social duties. I was very pleased to see her, the more so as she was matter of fact about Wendy's progress or rather, lack of it. She was practiced in the art of saying the right thing, but even so may have been grateful on this occasion to have something unusual on which to comment,

"I hear she was born in a caul, she said, "Like David Copperfield. That's very lucky. In former times sailors believed a caul was a sure charm against drowning and would give good money for one."

I said I was glad to hear it, but thought to myself that it surely had not made things easier for Mrs Copperfield at the time, neither had she had much luck. As it was I packed the caul away carefully and kept it a long time, until at last it was lost in some upheaval.

In spite of the congratulatory cards, letters and telegrams which now began to arrive, it was not a happy time. Wendy steadfastly continued to refuse sustenance. Every morning she protested lustily as she lay spread-eagled on the scale, her tiny naked body on full view as Sister Schnabel removed one ounce weights relentlessly. For a full fortnight there was no let-up. So much for Ken's assertion that we would soon be re-united. Then one morning the scale quivered, hovered irresolutely as if deciding whether or not to achieve equilibrium. I held my breath. Next morning no change. But the following day the magnificent gain of half an ounce was recorded.

Eventually Wendy regained her birth weight, Sister Schnabel stopped tutting, my own health which, not unnaturally had been giving cause for concern, improved accordingly. It was time to go.

When the day came I was unexpectedly reluctant to leave the haven of the hospital. Realisation that from now on Wendy would be solely my responsibility, weighed heavily on my spirits. I would be without the reassuring presence of Sister Hunt - but was less reluctant to say goodbye to Sister Schnabel. Or to the elderly alcoholic.

The term 'airport' in relation to Lilongwe - for we were to fly back to Karonga - was about as apt as Steve's reference to the Ilala being 'in port' at the Khambwe Lagoon. For here was a single runway bordered by a shed or two and a wind-sock by way of high technology. [1]

Here it was that Wendy and I found ourselves one morning, quite alone, waiting to catch the five seater, single engined Beaver which, as already related, flew the length of the country twice weekly. I very thankful at not having to endure the arduous journey back by road, could visualise Ken waiting for us, with Jess alongside the runway waiting to refuel the plane. I could not wait to be there.

We sat on a bench in scant shade of one of the sheds, Wendy protesting at the wrappings Sister Schnabel had (rightly) insisted would be necessary once we were airborne. More or less on time the plane appeared and we were helped aboard.

Space in the tiny cabin was constrained to say the least. In the single front seat an

---

[1] Many years later when Nyasaland had become Malawi with Dr Hastings Banda as President, Lilongwe became the capital not only of the Central Province, but of the whole country. An international airport was established there, as well as an éliteist boarding school for girls as well as boys, run on the lines of Eton. The town expanded accordingly.

Indian business-man breathed gently down the pilot's neck, Wendy in her carry cot and I occupied the double seat close behind him, another man was at the rear. When the engine opened up to full throttle for take-off Wendy let loose the full power of her lungs. The Indian gentleman in front hunched his shoulders and seemed to be praying. Once in the air the engine subsided to a steady roar, as did Wendy's cries, At last, the odds being against her, sensibly she fell asleep.

Hedge-hopping, only there were no hedges, the plane headed northward following the road we had travelled down on. Seeing it again reminded me of that journey and all that had happened since. The false labour pains induced by the bumps - the ennui of the hotel - the walks round the golf course - Ken leaving me at the hospital - Sister Schnabel's castor oil. And, at last, the climacteric of motherhood.

The God's eye view of the countryside was comparable with the panoramic scene from the summit of Wilindi, but less beautiful. Here the land was not so hilly or diverse, but tawny bush for the most part, interspersed with clearings and scattered villages. People going about their daily lives were clearly visible at this height. The shadow of our small craft fell momentarily on them as we passed over, small children looked up and waved.

Presently we diverged from the road to cross some upland, the Vipya perhaps. The temperature inside the plane dropped. We lost height once more - and there was the lake below us, brazenly blue in sunlight, utterly different from my last sight of it under a full moon on the night of the Ilala, changed as I myself was changed...

Wendy stirred, the business man in front glanced round perhaps fearing more protests, or perhaps struck, as I was, by our total dependence on the single engine of our tiny plane which, should it falter and fail would send us all plunging into the water below. It had been known to happen. However, due no doubt to good maintenance and Wendy's caul, all was well, the engine hummed steadily on.

Some time later the northern tip of the lake came into sight, then Karonga. itself. The bumpy runway loomed up. At the end of it, a lone figure, Ken stood waiting for us.

CHAPTER 23

'AND WE THE BRIDAL PATH WILL TRAVEL WITH RUBIES STREWN AS THICK AS GRAVEL' [1]

The reception as we stepped out of the Beaver was most satisfactory since virtually the whole station had turned out to welcome us. Reluctantly I freed myself from Ken's arms to unravel Wendy from the swaddling clothes before the blanketing heat of Karonga overwhelmed her. She emerged red and angry, to be admired by Jess, though not by Andrew who loathed babies, by Angus down from Chisenga, and by the bachelors who did not know what to say.

When at last the congratulations were over and the Beaver on its way again Ken led me to the new pickup and we drove back to the Cloverleaf.

The next few days passed in a blur of three hourly feeds and nappy changing. Sister Schnabel had said firmly that babies must be fed only at regular times and not topped up between; on no account must they be picked up when they cried. Sister Hunt, more moderate, had advocated flexibility as Wendy was so small. Either way I could not help thinking wistfully of African babies who lived on their mothers' backs and were merely transferred to the front for sustenance when they cried, thus allowing the women to carry on with what they were doing. In practice, given Wendy's propensity for dropping off to sleep immediately her first needs were satisfied, each feed took over an hour and there was precious little time for topping up between. Or for anything else.

Jess, a tower of strength, dropped in every day.

"Dehydration and malaria are the great hazards for babies here, she said, " It's imperative that they're kept out of the sun at all times. They need plenty of water. Boiled of course. And they're must be kept under a net. Day and night while they're little. And always after dark of course when they're bigger. And Wendy must have baby Paludrine tablets every day against malaria."

Shuddering, I recalled the miniscule graves behind the Boma, of European babies who had succumbed while their missionary parents laboured, some sixty years before, to save unenlightened people from eternal damnation.

And what of the present-day African babies one saw all around? I could not conceive their being any less dear to their mothers than Wendy was to me. They had no mosquito nets, no prophylactics, their only protection was the fetish of the witch doctor, a string of small (unidentifiable) objects worn round the necks of little girls, round the groin of the boys. Or, as a last resort the mankwala - medicine - of the Asungu - Europeans. By which time it was often too late.

---

[1] From 'Lines written in the Tower the night before he was beheaded', by Sir Walter Raleigh. With apologies.

Certainly all the babies one saw were fat and healthy looking, as they should be given the abundance of food in Karonga, but that did not necessarily rule out a high, hidden mortality rate. Did the prevailing immune systems, and/or blood group, different from our own, give them a measure of protection? I fervently hoped so.

By the end of the second week Wendy and I reached a compromise on feeding, and very occasionally on sleeping, so that I was at last able to raise my head above the parapet.
"Did anything interesting happen while I was away?" I asked Ken one evening.
We were sitting on the single beds pushed together, under the double mosquito net. Wendy as usual was dozing instead of feeding, lamplight forming a halo round her head and casting soft shadows on the gently curving wall. Ken preoccupied, thought for a moment,
"Well the PAO came up from Mzimba. Sent his congratulations by the way. He brought an improved strain of maize seed for trial. I might take some back to Misuku with me. Of course, maize doesn't do too well there, it's too high and cold, but on sheltered slopes..."
I sighed. He tried again,
"The shock absorbers on the pickup aren't too good. Or, rather, the roads are too bad."
Later I was to become only too dismally familiar with the state of these shock absorbers, but at that moment that was not what I wanted to hear either.
"I said anything interesting."
"Er... Oh yes, the new DC's arrived. Seems very decent. His wife's joining him shortly."
"I already knew that. Jess told me when I first got back."
"Oh, and Steve's got engaged. I only heard this morning. From Andrew."
I sat bolt upright causing Wendy to wake up and splutter indignantly.
"What? Steve engaged! Are you sure? Are you sure Andrew didn't mean one of the other bachelors?"
Such a thing seemed utterly unlikely, not least because so far as I knew there were no eligible females within a radius of fifty miles.
"Of course I'm sure. Steve came into the office as Andrew and I were talking about it and I congratulated him."
Here it should be said that Ken had revised his opinion of Steve after meeting him during my absence. Indeed few could resist his charm and inner logic when they were actually within his orbit.
"But who to? Where does she come from? What's her name?"
Suddenly, into my mind came remembrance of the unattached girl on the Ilala. She and Steve had got on very well. She must have given him her address and they had been corresponding. Undoubtedly she was the one, no question. I started to say so but Ken cut in,
"I'll tell you if you'll let me. It's to a girl he met during the war. He was wounded and she and her family sheltered him and nursed him back to health."
"Oh. How romantic! I said, interrupting again as my thoughts rapidly rerouted

themselves.

"But where?"

"In the leg I think." Then relenting he went on, "Oh alright. It was somewhere in the desert. Libya I think. No, not Libya, Syria. Yes, that's right, she's Syrian. Seems he had a blinding revelation on the road to Damascus."

Geography was yet another subject of which I was woefully ignorant, but my knowledge of the Bible was not - though at this distance in time from Sunday School days some of the stories were apt to get muddled.

But Damascus! I could see it all. Steve had staggered to an oasis and there was this young girl drawing water from the well. She had given him a drink then helped him to her house and nursed him and saved his life. This time I was certain, could almost hear the camel bells.

Another thing was also certain. This was one story which had not figured in our Scheheradzada evenings while Ken was away.

Needless to say I hurried over to discuss it with Jess at the very first opportunity.

"Yes, it's quite true, she said, "We are as surprised as you are. Her name is Suad, she comes from a small town near Damascus. Steve showed us a photograph but said it was an old one taken in 1944. She was about sixteen then."

"But that was about ten years ago. Has she been to England? Or has he been back there to visit her?"

"Apparently they haven't met since. But Steve says she's a very good correspondent."

This silenced me utterly. I recalled how different Ken had seemed when he returned to England at the end of his first tour of duty. And that was after a mere four years.

"It could be a bit awkward though," Jess continued.

"I should think so if they haven't met for all that time."

"Not just that. I mean--"

But at this point Andrew came back from the office for morning coffee. He did not like to be kept waiting so our conversation was interrupted.

Steve himself however was very forth coming when we all met up that afternoon. He wanted to get married as soon as possible. He told us a good deal about Suad and her family. Of their kindness to him when he was hors de combat and showed us the old photograph. We saw a slim young girl, dark eyed, dark haired, wearing a nondescript dark garment. Andrew, not an advocate of marriage at any time as 'It gets in the way of a chap's work', said bluntly,

"But do you think she'll fit in here Steve? A lot of women find it hard to settle down. And coming from a different culture..."

I personally thought that, with the exception of the Williamsons themselves, culture in Karonga was notable mainly by its absence. But Steve had no such misgivings.

"Oh no. She speaks good English. And she is very adaptable. I'm sure she'll soon feel at home here."

It was not clear how he knew this. As Ken said later she would need adaptability

and a lot more beside if she married Steve, especially if he expected her to accompany him to the lake shore mud flats when he was buying the cotton.
"I hope she's a good walker, I told Steve, but added hastily, "Well, she'll have a nice house won't she? The best in Karonga. When it's finished that is."
He shot me a grateful look and got up to leave, saying,
"Yes, that's quite true. I'd better go and get on with it."
"And not before time." Ken put in brutally.

Jess also continued to have doubts. The following day as she and I were chatting on the khondé, Wendy asleep under a net in her crib alongside, she said,
"Of course if it actually comes off we'll all do everything we can to welcome her and make her feel at home. But the obstacles are formidable."
I must have looked puzzled for she continued,
"Well, first of all Steve must get permission from Zomba to leave the country in the middle of a tour if he intends to get married in Syria. That's only given on compassionate grounds and I doubt if marriage would count as such. Then there are the difficulties over Suad's nationality. She might not be allowed in the country."
Until that moment the problems had appeared to me to be purely emotional and psychological, now it seemed there was more to it than that. Certainly I knew that H.M. Government regarded the wives of their toilers in the field as unnecessary appendages, and they certainly received little support once the unfortunate event had taken place. But it appeared that this particular union would be less popular than most. Ken enlightened me later.
"Certain countries are 'proscribed' by Britain. Which means, among other things, that British Colonial Servants aren't permitted to marry their nationals. I've no idea if Syria is in that category."
"What! I cried, Are you saying Steve might have to choose between Suad and his job?"
"Something like that."
"But it's so unfair! She and her family saved his life."
"Yes. But since when has life been fair?"

Ten days or a fortnight passed during which we saw little of Steve. He spent his days standing over the men working on his house and his evenings, according to Jess, in correspondence. I hoped this meant he was writing love letters to Suad, tactfully preparing her for her new life among us. But Jess said it was much more likely he was grappling with officialdom, British and Syrian, and with immigration and emigration departments in particular.
Then one day as we were once more forgathered, Steve breezed in looking very pleased with himself.
"It's all fixed, he announced, "All arranged. Suad is flying in to Mbeya at the end of next week and I'm meeting her there. Then we'll fly back here and be married right away."
There was a stunned silence. The jumbled thoughts crowding my mind were -
'Getting married here? And so soon! And where exactly? And who by? And

who will be Best Man? And who give her away? And what about the wedding breakfast?'

Jess, as she told me afterwards, was thinking -

'Can it be possible that Steve has got permission to marry? Has he got ALL the right documentation? If not he'll surely be in trouble later.'

As it was, after not too long a pause, we hastened to offer him our congratulations and Jess asked faintly,

"What kind of a wedding is it to be Steve? I mean, er, of what religious persuasion is Suad?"

We all knew Steve to be a staunch Anglican and unlike most of the rest of those on the station, took his religion seriously.

"Christian of course. The ceremony will be at the Scots Mission church along the lake shore. Its all fixed." he repeated.

"But will a religious ceremony be sufficient? asked Andrew, "The DC is the official registrar of Births, Marriages and Deaths you know. It must be done properly."

"We shall be married in the sight of God." said Steve loftily.

"That might not be sufficient for Suad. Or for Government".

"Oh alright then, I'll go and see the DC as well."

We were destined never to know what took place at this meeting, but for once Steve must have got something right. Undoubtedly a civil ceremony did take place prior to the religious one, but none of us were privy to it.

Meanwhile Steve was still talking,

"Now, after the ceremony we must have a party. At my house. It's almost finished. I intend to ask all my friends."

"All?" queried Jess, well knowing Steve's propensity for friendship with all and sundry.

"All." he said firmly.

"You mean - everyone on the station, including Mr Andani and his family? And all the Chiefs and villagers you stay with on ulendo? And your capitaos, and the workforce, and the rest..."

"That's exactly what I mean, he beamed. "No, no more tea thank you. Must get on. Got a lot to do."

At the door he paused thoughtfully,

"Oh yes. Of course there must be a wedding cake. White you know, with decorations. Two tiers at least. Three would be even better. Oh, and jellies. We always had jellies at parties at home. Red ones."

"He can't." said Andrew when Steve had gone.

Whether he was referring to the wedding in general, or to the red jellies in particular, was not clear, but In either case the rest of us agreed with him, albeit for different reasons. Jess said,

"Well he's going ahead regardless, so we must all rally round. But so many people! There wouldn't be room for them even if the house were finished. Which it isn't. And they'd all need different food - "

"And drink." put in Ken. "

- And so little time to organise it. Oh dear."

Steve himself was quite unmoved when the logistics of space were pointed out to him.

"Well, it can be a garden party as well. How lucky it's the dry season."

"Some people might feel affronted if they're left outside. Especially as the so-called garden is nothing but a building site covered with debris."

At this Andrew and Ken said they would gladly stay outside if that would help. Andrew indeed went further and said he had just remembered he had arranged to go on ulendo to Mpata at that time, so would not be taking up any space at all.

Clearly we were getting nowhere. Then I remembered the wedding of Bathsheba and Gabriel Oak and said,

"Instead of having one free for all in the afternoon, why not have a beer drink in the evening for the Chiefs and the villagers and anyone else who cares to stay on?"

Fortunately Steve agreed to this enthusiastically. Moreover he said he would organise it.

"I'll tell my capitao to see about it. Get meat killed you know. And a mega brew of moa." (Local beer)

So that part of the matter was settled at least.

"I hope he remembers to buy a ring." I said to Ken a week later.

We had just seen Steve leave his house en route for the airfield to take the Beaver to Mbeya.

"Never mind the ring, Ken replied, "Let's just hope they recognise one another. It's been a long time. Still, I don't suppose there will be many unattached girls waiting about at Mbeya airport."

This was only too likely, Mbeya was in the neighbouring territory of Tanganyika, and although a considerable township by Nyasaland standards, still suffered the complaint common to most, if not all, the countries that made up British Africa, namely, a chronic shortage of unmarried women.

In two days time the whole station would be at the airfield to welcome the happy couple back to Karonga.

Meanwhile, although several of us had already worked hard on Steve's behalf, there was still much to be done.

Mr Andani's store did not boast much in the way of wedding refinements but he was happy to supply cases of bottled beer, and tinned goods which had languished at the back of his shelves for many a long day. He also promised to provide Indian delicacies for the feast.

Jess in her capacity as Central African Airways Agent, was able to put in an order for goods from Lilongwe, some of which had already come up on the Beaver. Icing sugar, red jellies and other forgotten items to name but a few. The bachelors were dragooned into getting their cooks to bake extra bread at the appropriate time, likewise their garden boys to gather flowers from the jungles they called gardens. They were also given to understand that the odd bottle or two would not come amiss. An unexpected boost in the proceedings came from Joan, the newly arrived wife of the DC, who won instant popularity by offering to make the wedding cake. Thus, by and large, it looked as though there would be a respectable feast.

In addition to organising food and drink, the habitable part of Steve's house must be made ready. Angus Day had undertaken to get the 'garden' cleared so that it looked marginally less like a bomb site. He had also delivered an extra bed for our spare room at the Cloverleaf as Ken and I had offered to accommodate Suad the short time till the wedding. (Steve;- "Well she can't stay with me until we're married, can she? It wouldn't be right.")

On the fateful morning of the Beaver's return everyone gathered on the airfield, Jess and I nervously prepared to give Suad a reassuringly warm welcome. The Beaver circled over the lake, descended on the runway, made its customary erratic landing and lurched to a halt. Its door opened, Steve jumped down. But who was this stepping out confidently after him, tall, buxom, impressive? Certainly not the sylph-like young girl of the photograph. Could there have been some mix-up at Mbeya after all? Jess echoed my own incredulous "Oh!" Hastily we re-adjusted our expressions and went forward to greet her.

Early on the wedding morning, with Suad still sleeping and Wendy left in Ken's care, I went across to Steve's house to help Jess with the arrangements. She of course, had preceded me and had already persuaded Steve to make himself scarce. With the assistance of our combined domestics we set about transforming the place. At the far end of the large lounge was a trestle table covered by a white sheet in lieu of a cloth. The DC and his wife had generously lent prestigious silver ware and crockery. We laid them out prominently, relegating the less impressive array supplied by the rest of us, to the back of the table, where they would be hidden by the food which would not be put out until the last moment. For this I was thankful as I had rashly agreed to be responsible for the red jellies and they had shown a distinct reluctance to set. Ken said kindly that it was because of the heat, but spoilt it by adding that we could always drink them if necessary.
This being the dry season flowers were hard to come by. Jess' well watered gerbera and one or two roses had been sacrificed, I could manage only a few marigolds from the bath water furrow at the back of the Cloverleaf. The choicest blooms came from the DC's garden which was constantly tended by the convicts - or rather, by their wives, who toiled back and forth from the lake with water pots on their heads. We placed these in tall vases or jugs, and trailed the window ledges with bouganvillea from the bachelors' gardens. Altogether the room looked surprisingly elegant. We left it all in the care of Jess' Umali and old Simeon and went to make our own preparations for the ceremony.

Andrew having fulfilled his intention of going on ulendo, Jess, Wendy and I were driven to the Scots Mission church by one of the bachelors. I had the impression of a rectangular, brick building. Unfortunately, instead of thatch it had a corrugated iron roof which held out no hope of a cool dim interior usually associated with churches; already the day was hot.

'AND WE THE BRIDAL PATH WILL TRAVEL
WITH RUBIES STREWN AS THICK AS GRAVEL'

A large crowd had gathered outside, the African pastor in snowy surplice was trying to keep a path cleared for the invited guests. He greeted us cordially and ushered us inside; the heat met us like an oven. An acolyte showed us to a wooden bench near the front, at the back was a press of local people.

The interior of the church was familiar to me from our having slept in its humbler mud and thatch counterparts on ulendo in Misuku. On the end wall with its low dais, was a wooden cross, before it stood Steve looking passably presentable in a suit. Only he and I knew, because I had mended it, that rats had chewed the collar. At his side was Ken as Best Man - such had their relationship advanced - looking distinguished in the suit last worn at our own wedding. The DC was in full dress uniform; his wife, Jess and I, hatted and gloved, wore our best frocks, Wendy had on a new dress. Behind us the bachelors sweated quietly in tropical jackets; across the aisle were Mr Andani and his women folk, the latter veiled and clad in gorgeous saris. Even they however were upstaged by the local chiefs in full regalia of feather head dresses and ceremonial leopard skins.

In scanty idle moments Jess and I had speculated as to what Suad would be wearing. I betted on a long diaphanous creation of some sort, with a beaded head- dress low across her forehead. Jess thought this unlikely, especially as Suad had been wearing western clothes ever since her arrival. Now we were about to find out.

A momentary hush and there she was, floating down the aisle in a cloud of white on the arm of Angus Day. Jess was nearer the mark. The conventional wedding dress of the West was surmounted by a misty veil. Behind her came two little girls, grand-daughters of Mr Andani, pretty in gauzy pink dresses, carrying posies of marigolds. The whole scene was one of enchantment.

If Suad was nervous behind her veil she did not show it but made her vows clearly and firmly. If either she or Steve were saddened by the absence of their families, loved ones, that was not apparent either. Remembering our own wedding, a much more modest affair, but with all those most dear to us present, I felt duty bound to shed a few tears on their behalf. As the ceremony proceeded Wendy grew restive, as well she might in such heat. I took her outside and looked round in vain for shade.

Local women pressed round to get a sight of her. Besotted as I was with my child, it was impossible not to compare her looks adversely with the beautiful fat and glossy African babies slung contentedly on their mothers' backs and it was probably just as well that I could not understand the flying comments.

At last the pastor came through the open doorway. Steve, and Suad with veil thrown back, emerged into the sunlight. A collective gasp of admiration went up from the crowd, followed at once by the ululation of the women. The congregation spilled out. With difficulty the guests grouped themselves for photographs. Brownie box cameras clicked as the bride and bridegroom, flanked by the pastor and Angus and Ken, gave their best smiles. After that came the group photographs. The Chiefs perhaps a shade warily, knowing that, along with strands of hair and nail parings falling into the hands of an enemy, image taking could cause nfiti - bad magic.

However there was no escape, there we all were, Chiefs, the Andani family, Europeans, fixed in sepia for posterity. In a daze of heat I hoped Suad's relatives back home in Damascus would be impressed.

Jess and I were the first to break away and head back to Steve's house to make everything ready for the guests. The food was assembled according to instructions, it was merely a question of arranging it to advantage on the table. The result was an impressive banquet designed to cater for all tastes. Piles of sandwiches already curling at the edges, jostled with mountains of rice, fiery curry puffs from Mr Andani, quails eggs, cold meats, African delicacies. Inconspicuously to one side the once voluptuous curves of the red jellies sagged into old age.

Surmounting everything the two tier wedding cake rose up magnificently. To the surprise of no-one the cake decorations ordered from Lilongwe had failed to materialise. But the ones crafted by Joan from silver foil, tiny pearl beads and one or two real rose buds, exceeded all expectations.

Below the table stood crates of bottled beer, a bottle of whiskey or two, and a plentiful supply of Mazoe orange juice. Moa would come later.

It was a noisy, cheerful party. As usual at such functions with drink flowing freely, the speeches seemed witty and pertinent. Angus's especially, considering his own marital experience. Toasts were proposed and drunk with enthusiasm, more photographs were taken. At some stage the happy couple cut the cake with that most useful of accessories, the DC's ceremonial sword.

At last, in gathering dusk, guests began to drift away.

"It doesn't seem possible Steve actually got married without major disaster does it?" I said to Ken as we lay in bed that night absorbing the heartbeat of the drums, next door, the resonance of deep voices raised in complex harmony as the beer flowed. There seemed little possibility of sleep. Ken yawned, tossed restlessly in the heat and said,

"Well it only took the combined efforts of the whole station didn't it?"

Next day Steve and Suad left to sample the delights of a honeymoon on the flood plain of Mweniteté where millions of mosquitos made merry. Where he, and Ken before him, had spent weeks of servitude buying the cotton. Where their predecessor had gone mad and shot himself in the foot...

Disaster struck soon enough. Steve returned to Karonga to find an official letter notifying him of his transfer to the (figurative) penal settlement of the Lower River.

A posting to the lower reaches of the Shiré river was regarded as a sentence dreaded by one and all. Not only because of the implied black mark on one's career, but also because the area was even hotter, less healthy, more humid than Karonga, with positively no redeeming features, such as the lake to swim in.

"But they can't do this, I protested to Ken, "Just as Suad has arrived and getting to know us all, and with a fair chance of settling down here."

They could and did, objections to the VIPs in Zomba from Andrew and the DC not withstanding. Barely ten days later the whole station was forgathered once more, but in very different mood. Steve, unusually subdued, made sorrowful goodbyes, then, he helped Suad into the battered old Landrover piled high with their worldly goods. In a cloud of dust they drove off to a chorus of good wishes, leaving us all with a sense of loss.

"The trouble with Steve, said Andrew, "Is that he has his own logic. But who's to say he's not right?"

But there was some kind of coda. Twenty-five years later when Nyasaland had become Malawi, Wendy and her husband, a doctor, returned to the land of her birth. He as a Medical Officer, she to teach at Rumhi Boys Secondary School.

On one of their vacations they toured Zimbabwe and visited Harari. (Formerly Southern Rhodesia and Salisbury respectively.) At the latter they visited the cathedral and fell into conversation with an elderly European who appeared to be some sort of guide. He asked where they came from, they said they were English, working in Malawi. Wendy also told him she had started life in Karonga in the 1950s when Malawi was still Nyasaland. He said he too had been in Karonga at that time. Said his name was Steve Witting.

CHAPTER 24

'MARY, MARY...'

"Oh! I exclaimed, "Oh good. Mary's coming to stay."

One of the advantages of living in Karonga was the twice weekly arrival of mail on the Beaver. In theory at least, letters from England could reach us in a mere ten days. In practice they were often held up somewhere along the line. Not least at the post office hard by the Boma, in Karonga itself.

There was however no system of home delivery, each Department sent a messenger to collect and distribute its own mail. On relevant days Ken would bring our letters from Andrew's office when he came back for breakfast and it was on such an occasion, a few weeks after Steve and Suad's departure, that I made my announcement.

Mary Clargo was the friend from pre-marriage days with whom I worked at the town library. One morning as we were shuffling books about on the shelves, ostensibly putting them in alphabetical order, Mary yawned and said,

"There must be something more to life than this, don't you think?"

"Well, yes, I suppose so. But last night wasn't too bad was it?"

We had in fact enjoyed a good night out after work, which might have accounted for her discontent.

"Oh last night. That was different. It's the days I'm talking about, I mean, they're all the same aren't they"

Cautiously I agreed. Certainly the days held their share of boring routine. But what with staff gossip, conversations with the readers - both activities frowned on by our superiors - not to mention our ongoing preoccupation with dating the (far too few) eligible males who came in, for me the days passed pleasantly enough. All the same I knew what she meant. I said,

"Well never mind. If I marry Ken and go off to the wilds of Africa, you can come and visit us."

Mary yawned again and said,

"Not sure I can wait that long."

At this point the senior assistant loomed up and demanded indignantly to know what we thought we were doing. So that, naturally, once she was out of earshot our talk turned to the topic of elderly librarians of thirty-five or so, whose main pleasure in life was to torment juniors such as ourselves. It all seemed a long time ago.

I scanned the letter again, noticed the date, recalled the vagaries of the postal service and said in alarm,

"Good Gracious! She must actually be on her way! This was posted from the Canary Islands."

Ken looked over my shoulder at the letter and replied,

"Why the panic? She can't possibly be here for three weeks at least. Probably longer. You can wire her at Durban, the boat will pick up mail there. And I'll write to the Peripatetic Pole in Blantyre telling him when she's likely to arrive there, and ask him to meet her off the train at Limbé."

The said Pole was an acquaintance with a somewhat ill-defined job, whom we had met at Karonga rest-house during our initial stay there, when I happened to mention that we hoped to have a girl friend coming on a visit. He had immediately offered, not only to meet her off the train, but accommodate her as well until she was ready to travel up country.

"Do not worry Kenneth, he added in response to Ken's dubious glance, "I am a married man."

What he did not tell us was that he had left his wife behind somewhere in Eastern Europe, a common enough occurrence in those days when many Communist countries sealed their borders against anyone wishing to get in or out.

News of the impending visit of one of that endangered species Eligible Young Female spread through the station like wildfire. To a man the bachelors buttonholed Ken for details of her age, appearance, and most important of all, the exact date of her arrival. His replies were probably vague and less than satisfactory, especially as to the last. Be that as it may, that they all found reasons for re-scheduling their ulendos to make sure of being in Karonga over the next few weeks, was only to be expected. I fully sympathised. Indeed to mis-quote one of my favourite writers, "It is a truth universally acknowledged that a single woman in possession of youth and good looks, must be in want of a husband."

And in my opinion Mary having attained her twenties, had been single long enough, a matter I intended to rectify as soon as possible. The fact that, as Ken pointed out, Mary herself might have other ideas, deterred me not at all.

Magnanimously I cast the net wide, from the bachelors at hand to the unmarried (albeit not in the first flush of youth,) Governor down in Zomba. I wasted no time in discussing it with Jess when she and Andrew came over to tea, "

"But would she make a suitable First Lady to the Governor? I mean, is she off the top shelf?" asked Andrew who was inclined to get his metaphors mixed.

"Certainly she is, I replied huffily, "She went to a very good school. She has a private income from her father and doesn't need to go to work. She only takes a job when a life of leisure gets too much for her."

"But wouldn't His Excellency be a bit old for Mary? said Jess, "And anyway how would you get them together? He hardly ever ventures this far north."

She certainly had a point.

The men soon lost interest in the subject and began to talk of other things, but Jess and I pursued it, discussing the relatives merits of all the eligible men within a fifty mile radius and beyond. Suddenly she said,

"What about Tycho? He's a bachelor. And still quite young, in mid thirties I would say."

Tycho Hassett. Of course, the very man. He had escaped my attention only because I had never met him. Had in fact, merely glimpsed the back of him in Mzimba, when Ken pointed him out to me on our stopover on my first journey upcountry. I could not help knowing all about him though. Universally spoken of as a 'jolly good chap', Tycho, ex Guards officer in the war, was Provisional Commissioner for the Northern Province. Which is to say, he was her Britannic Majesty's senior administrator of the area, technically responsible for all that went on there. More to the point as far as I was concerned, he was tall - that much I knew - reputedly good-looking, and above all, unbelievably single.

At the mention of his name the men broke off their talk.

"But why should Tycho want to get married? said Andrew, "He's got everything he needs as it is. Money, position, excellent staff. Why on earth should he want a wife to complicate matters?"

Jess and I looked at each other and turned up our eyes.

"Never mind all that, I said, "The question is, that as he never comes here either, how will we ever bring them together?"

"He does come up occasionally, put in Ken, "He tours the whole district every so often."

"Perhaps you could suggest to Mary that she spends a few day in Mzimba before coming on here." This from Jess, "They would be bound to come across each other then. Unless he was on ulendo of course."

Very grudgingly Andrew, whose view of marriage was clear to me by now, said, "As a matter of fact he is coming here. In a few weeks. It's Karonga's turn to host the Conclave of the Chiefs, a really big barazza. Tycho will be presiding."

"That's it then. I exclaimed triumphantly, "Fate."

Andrew looked disgusted and did not reply. In any case it was time for them to leave, Jess to supervise the evening watering of her garden, Andrew to listen to the BBC World Service news in his bath.

The estimated time of Mary's arrival in the country narrowed to certainty and the anticipation of certain members of the station grew accordingly. Disappointment and frustration therefore were palpable when she wrote from Blantyre to say she intended to stay there for a bit and catch a plane a week later. Obviously she was having a good time with the Peripatetic Pole. Which was not what I had in mind for her at all.

Once a definite day of arrival was firmly established, there was a technique in Karonga for meeting visitors flying in. As the Beaver was often late everyone waited till the drone of an engine was heard, then set off at speed for the airfield. On this occasion it was late indeed, so much so that Ken and I out at Baka thought we had failed to hear it. At last we decided to set off anyway, which was just as well for it appeared as a speck over the lake as we drove. We arrived just in time to register the presence, not only of Jess standing near the petrol drum, but of Joan, of Angus who had come down from Chisenga in the hope of meeting Mary, ("Just down to check over the Lufira crossing,") of the bachelors to a man, the DC, the ADC, both in uniform, and for good measure a squad of Askari smartly lined up at attention.

"Good Gracious! I exclaimed, highly gratified, "What a welcome! I hope she'll be impressed."

"Oh, didn't I tell you..." Ken began innocently.

But here his voice was drowned out as the Beaver touched down, lurched the length of the rough runway and jerked to its usual abrupt halt. The door opened and the pilot jumped down. Mary was not the first passenger to emerge. Instead, to my surprise the stout, dapper figure of Col Apthorpe, Chief of Police Northern Province, Nyasaland, last seen by Ken and me - slightly spotty from chickenpox - on board the SS Rhodesia Castle on the memorable voyage out.

Furious, I turned to Ken, but there was no time to harangue him for deceiving me. Even as I began, the Colonel, after saluting the DC, turned back to the plane to hand down Mary, tall, cool, elegant, exactly as she always had been. But wait, who was the tall, handsome stranger behind her, the last passenger to get out?. Certainly it was not the Pole with whom she had been staying.

"Who is it?" I hissed at Ken.

Tycho." he replied briefly. This silenced me utterly.

Tycho and the Colonel inspected the Guard of honour. Mary watched with detached amusement.

The ceremony over Colonel Apthorpe presented Mary to the DC as if she were part of the official party. So preoccupied was he with her that as the Askari marched off and the DC prepared to escort him and Tycho to the Residence for lunch, Mary was in danger of being carried off as well. It was a tricky moment.

Fortunately Noel the ADC sized up the situation, stepped forward, coughed discretely and whispered a few words. The Colonel looked decidedly put out. He let go of Mary's arm reluctantly. After a pause he shook her hand lingeringly and, with Tycho looking on dispassionately, was heard to say he hoped very much that they would meet again soon.

While this was going on Ken belatedly informed me that the two VIPs were merely breaking their journey at Karonga en route for a conference in Mbeya. They left at last, we were free to greet our guest and merry was the meeting.

The unofficial welcome was, in its way, quite as satisfactory as the official. Mary was introduced to Wendy who scowled, being distinctly bad tempered from the heat, to Jess and to everyone else assembled. Before we left the airfield her entire week was booked up with invitations.

Back at the Clover Leaf Mary gave us an account - edited most likely - of her voyage and her stay in Blantyre. So it was some time before I could allude to Tycho, whose presence on the plane I took to be a sure sign of divine intervention. Not wishing to divulge my plan however, I asked casually,

"What did you think of him? The man on the plane?"

"Oh, Colonel Apthorpe. Yes, he's a real sweetie. The plane broke down you know, that's why we were so late. One of the tyres had a blowout. It was at some place on the lake."

"Nkhata Bay probably." put in Ken.

"Yes that was it. Well we walked down to the shore while it was being fixed, and there were some of these home made-canoes -"

"Dugouts."

"And the Colonel paid one of the fishermen to take us out. It was very tippy, but a wonderful experience."

So happy was she at the recollection it seemed cruel to recall her to the present. Nevertheless I persisted,

"I didn't mean Colonel Apthorpe, I meant the other man. The tall one."

"Oh him. He didn't come with us in the canoe. There wouldn't have been room even if he'd wanted to. He sat behind me on the plane so I didn't notice him much. Except that he was big and heavy, you know how small and squashy the Beaver is."

I did indeed, I could picture the scene, the pilot and the Colonel in front, Tycho aft and Mary cosily amid-ships.

"Now Colonel Apthorpe, she went on, "He really is..."

"Yes, yes, so you said. We know him anyway. And his wife. We shared a table with them coming out on the boat. And she visited me at Lilongwe hospital when I had Wendy."

I forbore to point out that apart from being married already, the Colonel was old, at least fifty, and moreover had the reputation of being decidedly peppery. So we left the subject, and I comforted myself with the thought that Tycho's next visit to Karonga would be longer and it would be impossible for her to ignore him then.

The spare room, so recently occupied by Suad prior to her wedding, was sparsely furnished with the single PWD bed supplied by Angus, and with one of our big trunks doing duty as bedside table. I had added local grass mats for the floor and a vase of marigolds from the bath water soak-away near the back door. It looked habitable enough. But my heart sank as I thought of the bathroom and the thunder-box loo adjoining it. I was relieved therefore at Mary's nonchalant acceptance of the primitive conditions. Perhaps, like me, she would have been disappointed to have come so far, only to find it much the same as Watford, say, but hotter.

She quickly made friends with Jess, with Joan the DC's wife, was cordially impartial toward the bachelors, and entered 100% in the social life of the station. Ken, the only male apart from the DC and Andrew, who did not consider his presence in Karonga to be absolutely vital, took advantage of my having company to go off for a prolonged spell in Misuku. All the other men felt it their bounden duty to entertain Mary non-stop. Apart from the usual tennis or swimming afternoons, they organised picnics to picturesque spots nearby and visits to the more interesting villages. To all night parties on the beach, swimming at midnight, the water silky and warm. With breakfast on the shore at sunrise, of fresh fish grilled over a driftwood fire, caught by the counterpart of the fishermen in dugout canoes featured on the stamps. In some of these activities Wendy and I participated, in others not.

One memorable weekend Mary was carried off on the gruelling road to Mzimba for a dance at the Club. Did she encounter Tycho there? If she did she did not mention it.

Meanwhile the occasion of the Conclave of the Chiefs was building up. Already colourful members of their retinues had arrived in Karonga on foot, by lorry or crowded truck. Mary, without knowledge of my secret agenda, was as interested as I. She asked,

"What exactly is it all about?"

"Oh, it's very important. It's about er, - " I paused.

Truth to tell, what with my preoccupation with motherhood, Steve's wedding, and prior to that, the remote months spent in Misuku, I was woefully ignorant of African politics and knew little more than she did.

"We'd better go and see Jess." I said.

Jess told us,

"As you know, for all practical purposes Nyasaland is administered by Provincial Commissioners, District Commissioners and their aides. They are based in the townships and regions and hold courts there. But they spend much of their time going round the villages, keeping in touch by conferring with chiefs and village headmen, holding meetings etc, so that ordinary people can meet them and put their problems and air grievances. DCs report back to the PCs, who in turn keep the Legislative Council - LEGCO, - in Zomba informed. LEGCO is responsible for ruling the country under the jurisdiction of the British Government in England, so that Members of Parliament know what's going on here. In theory at least.

As you know, Tycho is PC for the North that's why he's coming here to preside over the Conclave. Conclaves are held periodically, in different places, and Chiefs come from far and wide with their advisers. This is the first time Karonga has hosted it, it's considered a great privilege. Formerly it was most likely little more than a jamboree, an excuse for the Chiefs to get together, with much feasting and jollification. Federation has changed all that, now it's a much more serious business. Shall I go on?"

"Please do." We said.

The newly formed Federation of Northern Rhodesia, Southern Rhodesia, and Nyasaland which Angus had touched on in Misuku, was virtually but a name to me. As it had not made banner headlines in the national newspapers in Britain Mary, quite understandably, had never heard of it. Jess continued,

"Well some years ago the idea was conceived that the three territories would benefit from closer alliance. A good idea in principle, especially for Nyasaland which, as you know, is the smallest and poorest, with no natural resources - apart from its labour force that is. Whereas the other two are rich in minerals, and agriculture, and have flourishing economies.

A lot of time and energy was spent on explaining the federal idea to the people here. But it was a difficult concept to get across, and it is doubtful whether many of them understood it. At any rate in Nyasaland Africans viewed the scheme with great suspicion from the start. People feared that their land would be under threat. Eventually a referendum was conducted - another unknown concept - and Federation was rejected out of hand.

However, in spite of warnings from administrators on the spot, for reasons best known to itself, the British Government went ahead with it. It is deeply unpopular throughout the country, so you see there are some thorny problems to be thrashed out.

"But of course, she added, "None of this will affect us. We are just part of the general scene, invited to the opening ceremony, and to a reception or two afterwards."

Which just went to show that even Jess was not infallible. Federation would cast a long shadow, eventually change many lives including our own. However Jess had not quite finished, she went on,

"It will be at the boma of Paramount Chief Kyungu, a few miles out of Karonga. Quite appropriate really, Karonga being one of the oldest settlements, and important even in pre-Colonial days."

Here I was on firmer ground and could have held forth on the subject of Captain Lugard and his men, and the pioneers of the African Lakes Company, but Wendy was getting restive, and anyway those far off days seemed to have little relevance to the here and now. It was time to leave.

To talk of Chief Kyungu (or Chungu) was something of a tautology since Kyungu was itself a title meaning chief. In former times to be elevated to this exalted position was to be the recipient of a poisoned chalice. Certainly, as with the Pharaohs of ancient Egypt, the chief was all powerful, with unlimited privileges, with all the land, cattle, wives, concubines, slaves, goods and chattels he could desire. A god in fact. And there was the rub. For privilege brought responsibility and a chief was solely responsible for his people's welfare and prosperity. He must settle disputes wisely. He must be victorious over his enemies - or else die in battle. In time of drought he must be a rain-maker by sacrificing a black cockerel to the spirits of the ancestors and crave their blessing.

Not only that, because of his supposed divinity he must be seen to be above human frailty, therefore signs of illness or infirmity must at all costs be concealed. When this was no longer possible he, and possibly his household, were discreetly despatched by the nobles and another kyungu chosen. So the line continued ostensibly unbroken. [1]

The practice however, had been put down by the British well before the 1950s. The Kyungu and lesser chiefs were regulated by Government, although old customs such as the rain making, undoubtedly survived.

'Boma' was another word which had evolved over the years. Formerly it denoted the stronghold of a chief, enclosing by means of a stockade of pointed staves, the warriors, wives, children, relatives and hangers-on, as well as the cattle and livestock. Captain Lugard wrote of Kopakopa's boma near Karonga as

"Having an added broad bank of mud round it, which made it more difficult and dangerous to attack."

Over the years when these strongholds were no longer necessary, a boma could refer to a village of some importance, or merely to a cattle kraal. By far and away

---

[1] See:- Kalinga, Owen J M, 'A history of the Ngondé (Nkondé) kingdom of Malawi.' Berlin, 1985. ISBN 0899250416 v.

however, its most common current usage was to denote the DCs' headquarters in the townships, comprising the courthouse and complex of offices and staff houses. Everyone in the vicinity went to the Boma with their disputes and problems, as did strangers and travellers in need of help or advice.

It appeared that in the case of Paramount Chief Kyungu the word had retained much of its old meaning, although one hoped, without the stockade, as it was to his Boma that Jess, Mary, Wendy and I, in Ken's absence, were driven by Andrew early on the day of the great Conclave.

This was a rare social occasion approved by Andrew and he was unaccustomedly well turned out. Jess, Wendy and I looked much as we had looked at Steve's wedding; Mary's smart new clothes left me very envious.

We jolted along the track. Already it was choked with people making their way on foot hoping to get a good view of the proceedings, their excitement palpable; as we drew nearer the size and importance of the place became apparent.

We found ourselves approaching a large village where, very soon the winding ways between huts became too narrow for vehicles and we must get out and walk. At last we came to the hub of the place - the customary space of beaten earth - far larger than any I had so far encountered - and were conducted to one side, mercifully shaded by tall blue-gums, with wooden chairs set in a semicircle. Some of them were already occupied by visiting chiefs in ceremonial robes. Behind each of them stood a bodyguard armed with long spear and a shield of stiffened leopard skin decorated with strips of hide in different tribal patterns.

Chief Kyungu sat out in front in a great carved chair, the most splendid of all, the plumes of his feather head-dress dipping and nodding as he greeted his guests. When it was our turn to be presented a strange thing happened. In this male orientated society, where babies and young children of all races and creeds were virtually ignored by their fathers and other male relatives until they were old enough to be interesting or useful, as I approached with Wendy, Chief Kyungu held out his arms and took her from me. Smiling broadly he laid her across his knees, where she remained quite still, looking up at him with unwinking blue eyes. Nonplussed I made for the nearest empty chair, praying she would not disgrace me by crying.

By this time most of the European contingent was assembled and seated. The hubbub from the surrounding throng was considerable. There was a pause of some minutes, then came a stir at the edge of the crowd. A hush fell as a squad of Askari cleared a way for the Provincial Commissioner's cavalcade, comprising Tycho, the DC Karonga, the ADC and several African officials. All except the last were immaculate in tropical uniforms, Tycho's especially eye searingly white. His height also was accentuated by feathers in the form of a cockaded hat surmounted by ostrich plumes, the whole ensemble completed by that accessory so useful for cutting wedding cakes, a ceremonial sword. Fleetingly I glanced across to Mary who sat absorbed in the proceedings, and reflected that she could hardly fail to notice Tycho this time. So taken was I with this thought, for a moment I failed to notice that Chief Kyungu had risen and was looking round. Hastily I moved across to reclaim Wendy.

There followed an elaborate exchange of greetings. The PC presented the DC and the others to the Chief, who then presented the visiting Chiefs to Tycho. The most senior of them made an effusive speech of welcome, to which Tycho responded fluently in Chitumbukwa, a tongue only Jess among us could follow. Chief Kyungu acknowledged it in similar fashion. More speeches followed. It was very hot. The voices droned on, sleep must be resisted at all costs. Fortunately only Wendy succumbed.

When everyone had had their say it was time for non-participants like ourselves to leave. There were more handshakes and expressions of goodwill as we made our goodbyes, leaving the principle players to sweat it out in the midday sun.

"Well, what did you think of it?" I asked Mary when we had regained the comparative cool of the Cloverleaf house.

"Very impressive. I'll probably never see the like again."

"And Tycho?"

"He certainly handled it very well."

Gratifying as this was it sounded more like an objective observation on the general proceedings than an enthusiastic endorsement of the man himself. Had he noticed her? Reluctantly I was obliged to concede it to be unlikely. I sighed, this was heavy going. No matter. The morning ceremonial had been but the prelude to days of private discussions with the chiefs and Tycho would be in Karonga for the whole week. Moreover In the evenings he would be meeting all the ex-patriots informally for drinks at the rest-house commandeered for the purpose. (Did bugles at dawn wake Tycho as they had woken Ken and me during our time there? But no, such a one would be awake already. Up and about as well most likely.) It was on one of these confined meetings I now relied to keep my matrimonial plans for Mary alive.

The rest-house being small and the official party large, we residents were invited in groups. In Ken's continued absence in Misuku, Mary and I were once again escorted by Andrew and Jess. The rest-house had been transformed, was almost un- recognisable. Even so its moderate size meant that it retained its intimate character and dictated that conversation was general in the central lounge in which we were gathered.

Jess was naturally reticent in unfamiliar company, Mary flanked by two aides happy to have her attention, responded easily to conversation. For myself, the conviction that my machinations were writ large across my forehead plain for all to see, held me silent. Which left only Andrew of our party to talk to the VIPs until the atmosphere thawed out.

Was there an electric charge of attraction between Mary and Tycho as their eyes met across a crowded room? Sadly I could detect none. In fact, so far as I could tell only the barest exchanges demanded by polite society passed between them the whole evening.

Presently Tycho asked Jess of the progress of 'Useful Plants of Nyasaland', saying he had heard of it from the PAO in Mzimba, and declaring it a worthwhile project. Then I was startled to find myself addressed by him. He said he had also heard of the good work Ken was doing in Misuku, and was sorry he was not here to tell him more about it. I glowed with pleasure, and when he expressed the hope of visiting the area himself if he had time, momentarily forgetting the many reasons why official visitors to Misuku should be discouraged at all costs, to my horror I heard myself saying I hoped he would come and see us at Katobo if he did. He said he would very much like to.

So carried away was I by the implications of my rash invitation, it was only later as we were driving back and Andrew remarked that Tycho was unlikely to return to the North for some time, that I realised my plans for Mary were in fact no further forward.

"What did Tycho say to you?" I asked her.

"Oh, he said "Did you actually mean to come to Karonga?" As if I'd been washed up on the lake shore or something. He made it sound like the end of the world."

"So it is for some people." said Jess.

The official party flew out at the end of the week. The tumult and the metaphorical shouting died, the captains and the kings departed, life in Karonga resumed its even tenor. Mary continued to play the field among the bachelors and my matrimonial plans withered on the vine.

Tycho did indeed visit us in Misuku, but that was after Mary's departure. Some time later he went on home leave and did not return to the North. He subsequently had a brilliant career, ending up as Governor of the Falkland Islands. Somewhere along the line he got married. But not, alas, to Mary.

CHAPTER 25

RETURN TO THE HILLS

It was now October and the rains were but a memory, Karonga was dry, dusty, brown, and hotter than ever. Wendy was three months old, so it was no surprise that the next time Ken came back he said it was time for us to return to Misuku.

I was both pleased and daunted by the prospect. Pleased, for I had grown to love Misuku in the short time I was there; pleased also at the prospect of resuming 'normal family life' - a phrase lodged in the mind in inverted commas in view of the circumstances. Daunted at the idea of taking a baby to so remote and primitive a place, so much had my perspective changed since becoming a mother.

"But what if Wendy should get ill? I asked fearfully, "There's no doctor within a hundred miles. No telephone, no other Europeans. No road. Nothing."

"There's no doctor here either." he pointed out.

"No, but there are people here to give advice and help, Jess especially. And anyway, from here we could drive down to Mzimba and see the doctor if necessary. Or even fly to Lilongwe on the Beaver."

"Well, it's not true about the road. From Misuku we could drive to Fort Hill and from there fly to Mbeya. There's a hospital there as well."

He made it sound quite easy but by now I knew better. At best, that is in the dry season, we must walk out of Misuku, up and over Wilindi and down to Chisi, the pick-up point where the truck rested. But for most of the year it must be left on the other side of the Kalengé river, which would mean walking miles further on to Kapoka - a ulendo of some seventeen miles or so in total.

And even after Kapoka would come the drive to Fort Hill - and the possibility of having to wait days for the plane to arrive. By which time Wendy would either be better or... But I could not allow myself to envisage the alternative, and Ken was still talking,

"I've got a road gang out. The track is being improved all the time. Soon I'll be able to leave the truck at Chisi all the year round, because I'm going to put in a new bridge over the Kalengé. I intend to make it an all weather road and bring it right to the house. Eventually."

"Eventually, I echoed with heavy sarcasm. "Just how long will that be?"

"And anyway, he added, "Why should she get ill? Misuku is far healthier than Karonga. It's a wonderful environment for a child."

He was very persuasive, and indeed in my pre-motherhood days I had agreed with him. Had gone with him and had not regretted it. Now I was not so sure. I tried again,

"But that awful kitchen! It's impossible to keep it clean and hygienic. And then there's William's cooking. That alone will kill us if we're not careful."

"Oh I forgot to tell you. Angus sent up a Dover stove - like the one we've got here - and I've had a new kitchen built. The old one fell down in a storm."

This in no way surprised me. But I was cheered by the stove, even though it was doubtful of William would know how to use it.

"And I've been working on the house. The sitting room floor is concreted now. And I've fixed a ceiling there. So you see, things are improving."

"But William - "

"Well I've been thinking about that as well. I'm going to get Dan and Simeon to come with us. So you'll still have proper staff and it won't be nearly as difficult for you."

The thought of the elderly Simeon changing his tribal way of life in easy going Karonga for the rigours of the mountains, among alien people, was too much for credibility. I said so and later had the dubious pleasure of being proved right.

I was also concerned on Mary's behalf. I put it to Ken,

"Where will she sleep? There's only one bedroom in case you've forgotten"

"You're wrong, he replied airily, "I told you, I've had a rondavel built to one side of the house. Brick and thatch. I got the bricks from Angus, and it looks pretty good. It's almost finished, and she can have it all to herself."

This was encouraging, though one suspected that 'almost finished' might well approximate to Steve's assertion that the Cotton Board house was in a similar state prior to Suad's arrival. However, practical details aside, what I really feared for Mary was that she might find Misuku not only difficult, but dull as well. At the moment, what with all the attention from the bachelors, gracing the DC's dinner parties for visiting VIPs, and the occasional appearance of the Ilala with all that it implied, she was passing the time very agreeably.

On the other hand, to my regret, though not apparently to hers, the Peripatetic Pole had also re-appeared at the rest-house, engaged on some unspecified research. So that even though my matrimonial plans were in abeyance, it might be no bad thing at all to get her out of the way for a bit.

At the same time I felt bound to warn her what to expect.

"About going to Misuku, I began cautiously as the time grew near,

"Yes, I'm really looking forward to it.' said Mary.

"Yes, well, it's very beautiful. Wonderful for a short visit. But, er, it's primitive. And remote as you know. And there's not much social life." Then steeling myself, "Well, none at all really. You might be bored after a week or two."

"Oh I don't think so, it will all be new and different. And people do come and see you from time to time you say? So if I wanted to leave I could always hitch a lift back to Karonga couldn't I?"

I heaved a sigh of relief. But even though we were not to repeat the marathon of walking into Misuku as on my first incursion, I knew I should also warn her about the journey.

"We'll be driving up the Chendo Track, I told her, "Luckily the Lufira bridge is in place now, but it's a gruelling ride whatever Angus says about it. The Misuku track is just as bad. It stops short of Wilindi - the mountain range that forms one boundary of Misuku. The truck has to be left in the foothills and we do the rest on foot. It's quite a climb to the summit. Then there's another five miles or so across country to reach our house at Katobo."

She listened carefully, then said,

"Well I promise not to wear high heels."

Truth to tell, it was now apparent to me that despite her sophistication, Mary had the pioneering spirit. Regretfully I reflected once more what a splendid wife she would have made Tycho, and mourned anew the fact that it looked less and less likely.

In Karonga consternation raged among the bachelors when Ken's intention became known. Their attitude to him had run a fair gamut of feeling ever since his return from leave. Initial envy at his having come back with a wife, quickly dissipated it must be said, at the sight of the sickly creature presented to them. Doubts of his sanity at his intention of starting married life with a pregnant woman in such a lonely place as Misuku. Grudging admiration when we returned to Karonga unscathed. Instant popularity on Mary's arrival, incredulity and bitterness at his present intention of carrying off this desirable female to outer darkness.

I hastened to assure them that any or all of them would be welcome at Katobo at any time, but this was poor comfort, access being so difficult. Nevertheless they once again began consulting their working diaries and re-scheduling their ulendos, stretching the boundaries of their duties to include places in Misuku not visited by them or their predecessors for many a long day. If ever.

It was noticeable that as the day of our departure drew near Ken became less reassuring about the state of what he euphemistically termed the 'Misuku Road', and even less so about the Kalengé river crossing. After some thought he decided that we would not attempt the whole journey in one day, but to spend a night en route at Chisenga with Angus who was "Only too happy to oblige old boy."

This however would be the only concession to female frailty.

The necessity of the early start was stressed once more, as was the need to cut down on the katundu - luggage.

"Remember, bare necessities only, otherwise the truck will be over-loaded and we'll never get up the Chendo. Let alone into Misuku itself."

For once I did not waste time arguing, but did point out that Wendy's bare necessities alone would take up most of the space. At which I was firmly admonished to "Cut it down."

The departure date fixed, Mary spent the last few days and nights in a whirl of even greater social activity so that we barely saw her. I packed the two large trunks, which would be transported by lorry to Kapoka via Livingstonia and the Great North Road and eventually be brought up to Katobo by carriers on foot. I very much hoped that would not take too long.

Even with severe self discipline there remained a fair amount of overflow which Ken threatened to leave behind. Fortunately crisis was averted by the (unmarried) Forestry Officer having a sudden urge to inspect the various strains of the blue-gums in which Misuku abounded, and offering to bring up all excess luggage the following week. At which the Veterinary Officer said he would go along too, to check that cattle there were being dipped regularly. An unlikely, not to mention unheard of, state of affairs according to Ken.

On the last night the whole station gathered for a farewell party, which Ken and I left early to make final preparations for the morning start.

Came the dawn, Mary, fresh and alert in spite of her late night, I bleary eyed and morose after a disturbed one with Wendy, who had just been vaccinated against smallpox, by a visiting doctor. With yellow fever and polio inoculations thrown in for good measure.

She was still crying angrily when Jess came across to bid us a last goodbye. She picked her up and said soothingly,

"How lucky you all are to be getting out of this heat."

She was right of course. From dawn to dusk Karonga quivered in brazen sun. The evening breeze off the lake was a thing of the past, torrid nights under the mosquito net in a stuffy bedroom were a punishment. So I agreed with her, but at that moment could only feel in my heart how much I would miss her and her common sense and support, and did not feel lucky at all.

Outside Andrew's office the workforce was beginning to assemble. Men drifted across to call out their farewells, wives with babies and children looking on. Old Simeon, not coming with us, was also there looking very cheerful, in marked contrast to Dan who was. Andrew about to open up the office, strolled over to give Ken advice on how to load the truck properly. He was too late for it was already crammed with cases, boxes of food, bags and odd looking bundles. Ken took the driving seat, I sat between him and Mary with Wendy in my arms.

We waved our goodbyes and cruised off down the dusty drive to the equally dusty road leading to the lake shore, in the direction taken by Steve and myself on the night of the Ilala.

Soon however we came to the Chendo turn-off, the land remaining flat and sandy. Until we came to a dambo that is - a small grassy plain, damp from some underground water source, brilliantly green in contrast with the tawny bush surrounding it. After that we began the climb on the stonier ground which would continue for many miles and several gruelling hours, until we met up with the road which would take us to Chisenga.

Long before that however came the Lufira river. As on the momentous journey down with Angus, we heard it well before we saw it. Vainly I strove to describe to Mary the seemingly insuperable barrier it had presented then. But it was no use, the drama was lost, impossible to convey in the telling, So I concentrated on the bridge itself as we swept across, grateful to Angus for the stout superstructure which had superceded the makeshift bamboo decking. Grateful too for all that had happened since, above all for the safe arrival of Wendy, who at last was sleeping peacefully in my arms.

From the Lufira we began the slow tortuous ascent to the hills, seeing no-one. The only sound was that of the labouring engine, the grind of gears, except during frequent stops at streams to top up the boiling radiator, when the rasp of cicadas filled our consciousness.

The heat intensified; due to defective shock absorbers the truck was even less comfortable than Angus's jeep and because of the gradients and lack of power, a good deal slower. Only after several hours did the streams, mere trickles at this time of year, become more frequent. With them came the first intimation of a cool breeze and realisation that we had left the simmering humidity of the lake shore behind.

At one stream we dabbled our feet and ate dry sandwiches, but only Ken was hungry. On again all day, at last reaching the T junction in the middle of nowhere known as Piccadilly Circus, and a finger post pointing to Chisenga. The road was deserted, we met no other traffic. The certainty of Angus's welcome within an hour went some way to off-set our fatigue.

Nor were we disappointed. Angus on his khondé, drink in hand, the epitome of hospitality, immediately offered us the choice between tea and sundowners. Having arrived at dusk, Ken had a beer but Mary and I opted for the former.

Angus said as a statement of fact,

"The Chendo's pretty good now isn't it? As you know I've put a lot of work into it lately."

We did know. That and Mary's presence had accounted for Angus's many weekend appearances in Karonga. Ken made no comment except to say that he must go and get the katundu unloaded and find somewhere for Dan to sleep, but I said by way of compensation,

"It's a lot better. A bit bumpy in places perhaps. But the new bridge is wonderful."

Mary, less inhibited, said,

"Call that a road? I've never been so thrown about in my life!"

To my surprise Angus merely laughed and did not seem to mind.

We had baths, then a good supper; later there were bedrooms with cool night air gently stirring curtains at the ungauzed windows.

In the morning, miraculously, there was also a leisurely breakfast, Ken having surprisingly agreed with Angus's suggestion of the night before that we stay an extra day with him -

"So the girls can rest up a bit in comfort."

The real reason for compliance became clear as we ate when Ken announced that he must check over the truck.

"Must have shaken a good few nuts and bolts loose on the Chendo, he said, "Lost some as well I shouldn't wonder. I'll put it over the car pit at the rest-house."

The men left but Mary and I lingered over our pawpaw and toast, attended by the deaf and dumb cook, whose many accomplishments included producing excellent bread. I said,

"It's a nice house isn't it?"

Mary agreed, but added,

"A bit spartan though don't you think?"

I looked round and realised belatedly that all signs of wife and children were lacking. I knew that the former had returned to her native South Africa. The two little girls, parted from both parents, plucked from day long sunshine and freedom to play outside whenever they felt like it, had been transported to the English Midlands - said by the poet to be sodden and unkind - to be cared for by Angus's relatives.

Suddenly I felt depressed.

"It's beautiful here, and certainly a lot cooler than Karonga, Mary continued, "But Chisenga isn't exactly the hub of the universe is it? No other Europeans except travellers passing through, and with Angus away so much it's no wonder the wife left. I mean, what would she do here all day?"

"But to leave her children!"

I glanced down at Wendy, from whom I hated to be parted even for an hour, who to my vast relief, seemed to have shaken off the effects of the doctor's hypodermic and was trying to eat her toes as she lay on the polished floor.

Ken's suspicions about the truck were well-founded but fortunately or not according to one's viewpoint - for Mary and I would not have been averse to another day of idling - the matter was soon put right with spares from the PWD store/depot and some help from Angus.

Consequently there was nothing to hinder our getting off early next day. That night at supper Angus tried hard to persuade Mary to stay on till the weekend.

"Then I could drive you right into Misuku in the jeep. Well, almost anyway. Save you that long trek over Wilindi."

She declined the offer and we parted from him in the morning with grateful thanks which he shrugged off, saying he would come and see us anyway, as soon as he could.

The morning was fresh and cool, the road wound among the foothills of the Mafingé mountains, the profile of the Wilindi massif rose up faintly in the distance. We retraced our route to the Chendo turn-off, ignored it and kept straight on till we came to the track leading to Kapoka. It was just as narrow and pot-holed as before and our speed was reduced accordingly.

At Kapoka in spite of our being a day late Nelson the capitao, surely one of nature's gentlemen, was there to greet us. So too were the wives who had been so kind to me on another memorable occasion, and the usual attendance of elders and children. I was very pleased to see them again. The women exclaimed over the pink baby with blue eyes and almost invisible fair hair. But although Wendy smiled obligingly, as at Steve's wedding, she did not compare favourably with their own thriving infants with their well rounded limbs oiled to glossy perfection, and their general air, not only of health, but also of being at one with the environment.

Understandably the men were more interested in Mary. They knew that Europeans were not allowed to have more than one wife, but pulled Ken's leg about it anyway. Ken told Nelson to expect the arrival in the next few days of the PWD lorry with our trunks and Nelson said he would hire carriers to bring them up to Misuku. He said also that he had sent men up early the previous day to await our coming "where the road dies" - Chisi - and that they would be waiting there still. After a little we said cordial goodbyes and went on our way.

In the rainy season the track was defined by borders of tall grasses but at this time with everything dry and tawny coloured, it was barely discernible. Only the brachystegia trees and low scrub seemed to renew themselves all the year round. In practical terms it mattered little to us, it was merely a matter of Ken fixing the direction then picking out the most tolerable route over the stony surface, avoiding anthills, rocky outcrops and other minor obstacles as we went. In fact as I had warned Mary, in many places it was the Chendo Track all over again - but not quite so hot thank God.

We reached the Kalengé river and found it reasonably low, waiting for the rains and the run-off from the hills to restore its self importance.

Getting the truck over the rickety pole bridge however, was quite a different matter. The bank on the further side was very steep, with a wicked bend at the top.

Mary, Dan still subdued, I with Wendy in my arms, got out of the truck to lighten the load.

Ken drove on to the creaking poles and cruised slowly across to the other side, So far so good. He revved up the engine for the incline of the further bank. Halfway up the wheels spun, the truck slipped backwards almost off the bridge and into the water. Mary and I held our breath. The second attempt ended in similar fashion.

Somehow at the third attempt he succeeded in getting to the top. Sharply he slewed the truck round the bend and disappeared from sight. The rest of us crossed over the bridge and trudged after him, I with spirits sinking under the certain knowledge that if the Kalengé could cause this much trouble in the dry season, in the wet we would be imprisoned in Misuku as surely as in a moated castle with the drawbridge up. What price then of getting out to Fort Hill in an emergency?

At the top Ken, having knocked the cap off the boiling radiator, stood waiting for us.

"I know I know, he said reading my deadly look, "Getting that bank cut back and ironing out the bend at the top will be absolutely my top priority. And rebuilding the bridge. As soon as we meet up with Bodwin, (the capitao of the adjoining region,) I'll tell him to get a road gang on it, and I'll come back in a day or two to supervise it myself."

After the Kalengé the going was comparatively easy. Though still rock strewn and bumpy it led gently upwards until, approaching the foothills of Wilindi it became steeper. The countryside was deserted until we came to the impoverished village of Chato where Ken and I had camped on the first night of our exodus some six months before. Now it lay abandoned below us. Only a few small boys herding scrawny cattle below the ridge gave signs of life.

On again, the mountain looming above us until we reached the high saddle of land 'where the road dies'. Ken cut the engine. There was a moment of complete silence before the disturbed cicadas struck up again. On the near side the rock face rose up sharply to a height of some twenty feet, on the other the land fell away to a steep sided valley of rocky outcrops interspersed with coarse grass.

As at the Lufira with Angus, there was no evidence of the men supposedly waiting for us. Ken got out of the truck cursing, and set off up the winding path, once more we were left alone. We too got out, Mary looked round at the countryside appreciatively.

"Wait till we get to the summit, I told her, "It's even more impressive."

Dan on the other hand was eyeing with distaste the cataclysmic tumble of empty hills and valleys stretching away to infinity.

A slight sound recalled us to the immediate, a few stones from the top of the rock-face clattered at our feet. Leopard? Lion even? Instinctively I clutched Wendy more tightly and looked up. A head appeared. Mercifully it was human. One of the carriers of course. Another head joined it, obviously the men had not heard us coming. It was

It was hard to tell whether they or we were the more startled. Then the faces broke into smiles, called out greetings and withdrew, presumably to find a way down. At the same time others came walking down the path, Ken bringing up the rear. Briefly I wondered where, due to our dalliance at Chisenga, they had been forced unexpectedly to spend the night. In spite of this there were such expressions of goodwill, (why should it be so?) that it was impossible not to be affected. Ken said later that Bodwin, capitao of that region, would have taken them to the nearest village where they would be given hospitality and shelter.

The truck was unloaded, Mary changed into tennis shoes, Ken arranged the head loads. Angus's tobacco basket with its adaptation of carrying poles and improvised awning, was ready for Wendy's first ulendo. The two carriers assigned to it were given strict instructions to take extra care not to tip her out on the steep, narrow path to the summit. Finally, when all was ready Ken slewed the truck over on to a flat piece of land where the rock face gave out, so that Angus and other lucky jeep owners could pass when they fulfilled their promises of early visits. Finally he put rocks behind the wheels to prevent the truck backsliding.

As is the way of mountains on clear days the summit looked easily attainable; predictably it receded like a rainbow as we climbed towards it. Although tortuous in places, for the most part, the path led inexorably upwards, eschewing bends and detours, straight as a Roman road. Which meant that Mary and I must have frequent rests, taking the chance to admire the grandeur all round us. The carriers, except for the ones with Wendy, pulled away.

When we reached the highest point at last we sank down on a rock, the full circle vista at hand, Mary's appreciation gratifying as though we were personally responsible for it. We sat enjoying sandwiches supplied by Angus's cook. In one direction unknown hills and valleys were revealed, stretching as far as eye could see, in another lay Misuku, all of it new to Mary. Nearer at hand below us was the tree-line with the stands of pines and eucalyptus trees, then the banana groves, and a little further off, villages and homesteads with people going about the measured activities of daily life. Faintly on the hills came the sound of cow bells. On the opposing horizon was the violet smudge of Mughessé. Somewhere among its foothills was our house, hidden in heat haze.

There was no time to be lost if we were to reach it by dusk. The descent, steep at first, became more gradual, less taxing. After a while we came on the boys tending the belled cattle. On again to the villages, by this time wrapped in afternoon torpor. From dark interiors of huts came muted greetings as we passed, otherwise all was quiet. Dogs flopped out under thatch eaves ignored us or raised a limp tail, chickens sharing scant shade did not bother to open their eyes.

We proceeded as the afternoon wore on and the scene changed again. The way was more populous, the villages were coming to life once more. Women came running to exclaim over Wendy, the men looked at Mary with surprise. At one place a familiar figure - Sutherland. I was very glad to see him.

Ken introduced him to Mary, but it was clear Sutherland was not at ease. As on a previous occasion he apologised for not having been on hand to welcome us as he thought fit.

"Sir, he said," I came yesterday to that place called Chisi, but when you did not come I went to another village. Today I started off early but many people stopped me along the way."

This was only too likely, for who would miss the opportunity of waylaying such an important person as the head capitao and off-loading their problems on him? Indeed many of them were still grouped about him as he turned to accompany us, and joined in to swell the entourage we had already acquired.

At the Court a few elders had gathered to greet us but Chief MweniMisuku was not among them. At the nearby school lessons were over for the day but on a bit of flat land, too small for a football pitch but graced with goal posts, a few boys kicked a home-made ball about. Momentarily they stopped their game to call out and air their sparse English, delighted to be understood and acknowledged.

Soon I was able to assure Mary that we had not much farther to go. In another mile or so we reached the stream bordering the coffee nursery, deserted at this hour but for the night watchman guarding the precious seedlings. We crossed the spindly pole bridge to the very last hill of the journey, and climbed the path at the edge of the terraces, the dark, glossy leaves of the coffee bushes glimmering in the gloaming. Halfway up I recalled the erstwhile citadel of the manyega, but was too tired to tell Mary about it.

At the top we erupted on the lower lawn of our own garden. And there was the house; a solitary lamp in one window spilled its light across the grass.

CHAPTER 26

MARY'S MISUKU DAYS

"How are you feeling now?" I asked Mary next morning as we sat outside on the top terrace, the splendour of Misuku spread out before us.

So absorbed was she in the scene that at first she did not answer. Then rousing herself, she said,

"Oh, reeling a bit. The house was a shock. But Misuku itself, well, you were right about that."

Remembering my first arrival at Katobo I did not wonder at her reaction. Indeed a certain amount of reeling over the house, was not only inevitable but entirely called for, notwithstanding the improvements Ken had made in my absence. Not all of them successful. The one most obvious, an attempt at a sitting room ceiling, had failed dismally. In an effort to prevent bits of thatch and various forms of wildlife dropping on all and sundry, he had tacked strips of tarred paper to the underside of the bare rafters. Unaccountably these had stretched, sagged, and now hung down in a series of loops, giving one a distinct sense of seasickness. Other things had no doubt changed for the better, but there was too much to be done immediately before one could even begin to notice them.

We had been met the night before by William and Trisom the garden boy, both so delighted to see us, so interested in Wendy, that the memory of former disasters temporarily faded from the mind. In any case we now had Dan to cook for us. He it was who had brought us life restoring tea on our arrival, having gone on ahead with the carriers from Chisi - and later produced a creditable supper. Before that however there was bedding to unpack, baths to organise, Wendy to attend to. Ken disappeared to pay off the carriers from Kapoka and find them somewhere to sleep, while listening to the most urgent of Sutherland's queries. So it was late before we finished eating and made ready for bed.

It was not a peaceful night. Mary's 'virtually finished' rondavel had no glass in the window and no door. Therefore she must sleep on a camp bed in the sitting room with the loopy ceiling. No particular hardship, except for the fact that in common with the rest of the house, the wall separating the sitting room from our bedroom reached only to the eaves, giving visual, but not audio privacy. Every sound made in one room could be heard in the next. Even this would not have mattered too much, for we were all tired out, had not Wendy who had slept away the whole journey, chosen the night to become lively and vociferous. Not until the small hours did any of us sleep - only to be wakened, far too soon, by the morning work clanger.

We were a ragged bunch next morning.

Ken got up and went out at once. When he returned at breakfast he told Mary,

"I've sent for the carpenter to bring the door for the rondavel. I ordered it last time

175

I was here and it will come today. Or tomorrow. I'll fix the glass in the window myself, so you'll be able to move in."

Remembering the tardiness of the carpenter on a previous occasion I thought it likely Mary would be spending several nights in the sitting room, and ventured to say so. To which she replied firmly,

"I shall sleep in it tonight, door or no door."

I had in fact been encouraged at sight of the rondavel; having forgotten what Ken had said about Angus's bricks, I feared it would be just another wattle and daub hut. So was agreeably surprised at the stout structure sited to one side of the house, close by the tall tree in which the hornbills roosted, about 15feet in diameter, with a roof of deep thatch. Its window commanded a fine view of the countryside. Mary went inside, looked round, then said,

"This will do nicely."

Such was the position as she and I sat outside admiring the scenery, Wendy in the ulendo basket along side, sleeping peacefully at last, I stitching a curtain from the roll of red checked gingham left over from our own windows. Every now and then we glanced across at Ken cutting panes for the rondavel window with customary blood, sweat, toil and swearing. The glass cutter was very blunt by this time.

It was sometime before he finished and, due to numerous interruptions, almost dusk before he succeeded in getting them puttied in.

Before that however, to my amazement a tall figure in a large hat appeared over the rim of the lower terrace - the carpenter - closely followed by his mate, carrying between them a rough hewn door. Not only that, the usual courtesies over, they were anxious to start work, and at once set about hanging it. Probably they were hoping to return to their village before nightfall. At any rate at the end of three hours or so they had it swinging nicely. Only the appurtenances were lacking.

"Don't worry about the latch and doorknobs, Ken told Mary, "I'll look them out of the store and fix them tomorrow. Tonight I'll nail you in from the outside."

"Like an anchorite, I put in encouragingly, since Mary looked less than delighted at being thus immured.

"Then you'll be quite safe from marauding leopard or whatever."

At which Ken gave a cynical laugh and said he thought the greatest danger Mary would have to face in Misuku would be from marauding Europeans of the male variety. He was in high good humour at having actually finished something practical for once. Well, almost.

So Mary moved in. We brought the camp bed from the sitting room, one of the dining chairs for a bedside table, and fashioned a wash-stand from two ulendo boxes covered with a scrap of vivid material she had picked up on her travels. The curtain at the window, a grass mat on the floor and a few mementos arranged with her customary flair, completed the furnishings. The more so when I remembered Keen Hammersen's dark red roses. Would they be blooming still? They were.

Next morning after the work clanger had sounded, the hornbills roused to their cacophony, Ken judged Mary to be awake and hastened to release her; after breakfast he fixed the latch and the doorknobs and the place was secure against all comers.

Another of the improvements not noticed on arrival, was that putty had replaced nails on the windows of the house itself. Which meant that the former orchestration of rattles and whistles whenever the wind got up, was reduced to a mere lullaby. Also, the beaten earth floors throughout all three rooms had been concreted, the neo Jackson Pollock created in our bedroom by Ken on the night of the manyega gone for ever.

In due course the floors would be stained red, the sitting room one polished to a high finish, its beauty marred once only. A full three years later the concrete in the middle of the room fractured. A bump appeared, erupted and delivered itself of a germinated coffee bean. I nursed the resultant seedling tenderly and made everyone walk round it in salutation to its tenacity of life.

A significant change had also taken place in the small back room we used as a food store and bathroom. It still fulfilled these functions, but a partition now separated one from the other. On one side there was now a rack to stand bulk stores on, and shelves above. On the bathroom side stood a full-size, free standing bath complete with vestigial taps; the latter useless of course as we had no running water, but a great advance none the less. Showing the transformation to Mary I tried to convey the torture of bathing in the canvas monstrosity, (collapsible,) with its 5inches of water and low sides, set on a cold earth floor, while the wind whistled in at the at the wind-hole. Once again it was no use. As at the Lufira bridge crossing, one needed to have experienced it to appreciate the change.

Mary however was impressed with the new hot water system however, even though she had not known the previous arrangement. In place of two debés of water heated on the fire on the old kitchen floor, at a short distance from the back door there now stood a brick construction, circa three feet cubed, housing a 44 gallon, ex petrol, drum with a hole in the top and a tap fitted near the bottom. It was raised off the ground a little with a fire-place arrangement beneath so that a fire could be lit under it. True the drum must be filled manually from the water furrow - one of Trisom's tasks - and hauled into the bathroom in buckets, but provided it had sufficient water in when the fire was lit, the system was practically foolproof.

Undoubtedly however, to my mind the biggest improvement was the new kitchen. In truth it was but a replica of the old one, that is another mud hut, but bigger, more robust and less likely to fall down in the first gale. The aforementioned Dover stove was in place complete with stove-pipe going out through the roof thatch, ensuring that no longer would the place be filled with smoke. There was also a window letting in much needed light. The walls had been whitewashed inside as well as out, and the floor concreted. Altogether, though it might not have passed any Health and Safely regulations, the potential for cleanliness and hygiene was greatly increased. That William was delighted with it was obvious. Perhaps it recalled to him the days of his youth spent in Mr Lilford's kitchen long ago. Equally obvious was that he had no idea how to operate the various knobs and dampers on the stove. But that did not matter as he would in future be acting merely as Dan's assistant.

Angus arrived at the weekend as promised. He said to Ken,

"I see you're working on the Kalengé crossing."

True to his word Ken had gone back there the second day after our return, had organised a work force and demonstrated to the capitao exactly what he wanted done.

"That bridge will never be any good, Angus continued, "It'll get washed out with the first good rain storm. And that won't be long now."

"I know it won't be permanent, Ken was defensive, "But it'll have to do for now. I'm looking for a better crossing before rebuilding it. I hope to get Ragnor Udd to help, his road comes in there so he has to use it too. His truck is much bigger than mine so his need is greater. And he has more resources."

"Hm. Well I can't help you this time, I'd never get away with it as it's unofficial. You'll just have to go on leaving your jalopy at Kapoka."

This was not at all what I wanted to hear, especially as I knew he was right. I pushed the thought to the back of my mind and sought to change the subject.

"We're very grateful for the stuff you sent up, I told him, "The bricks for the rondavel. And the bath. And especially for the stove."

As usual he was embarrassed at being thanked. We knew he was scornful not merely of the bridge, but of the road, the house, the coffee, of the whole Misuku project in fact. Unexpectedly however he gave qualified approval of the rondavel. Less one felt, because he had had a hand in it, but rather because of its association with Mary.

As he prepared to leave in late afternoon he tried hard to get her to go back with him and stay for a few days. Once again she refused.

We had not expected further visitors until the bachelors arrived from Karonga with our excess baggage. However a few days later as we sat at lunch, the door open as usual giving a panoramic view of the countryside, we were surprised, and none too pleased, by the arrival of the Peripatetic Pole. Unlike Angus who was wont to blaze a trail as far as possible into Misuku in his jeep, the PP had been obliged to leave his unorthodox vehicle along-side ours at Chisi and walk the difficult miles between. It was patently obvious that walking was not his favourite form of exercise and he came in hot and sweaty. Nevertheless he eyed Mary cheerfully and said,

"I have heard how beautiful is this Misuku. So I come."

We gave him lunch and as he clearly had every intention of staying, there was nothing for it but to pitch Ken's small tent for him in the garden. Not too near Mary's rondavel.

What his job was, or how he came to have so much leisure we never discovered. Possibly he was taking his long leave in odd weeks, because of being unable to return to Poland due to the political situation prevailing in that country at that time. Or rather that, once re-entry had been noted, he would not have been allowed to leave again. This of course aroused our sympathy, for who could fail to feel sorry for one cut off from family and loved ones in such a way?

He alternately exasperated and amused us, but although we did what we could for him he did not at all fit in with my plans for Mary. For her part, in the ensuing days she appeared to be treading a fine line between acknowledging thanks for the good time he had given her in Blantyre, but of not wishing to encourage him further.

When finally he prepared to leave to 'see other nice places' he implored Mary to go with him.

"Then I bring you back here safely."

But by this time Mary was quite good at saying no.

Ken went off on ulendo. Apart from the Kalengé bridge there were many matters to be settled in distant villages before the rains set in and he intended to be away for several days.

The bachelors arrived a few days after he had gone and we were very pleased to see them. Alas neither of them were likely to change Mary's name. The Veterinary Officer revealed a newly acquired fiancée back home in New Zealand, and the Forestry officer, somewhat older, had as we already knew, a wife and children in England all set to join him in Karonga. In spite of this however their visit was a great success, the more so as they, like Angus, knew of our difficult circumstances and came prepared. They told us they were about to give a party for Angus in Karonga the following weekend.

"It's his birthday, they said, "As you know he's been through a bad patch, so it'll cheer him up. Why don't you join us? Do come!."

The invitation included both of us but clearly it was directed at Mary. They were very persuasive, presenting it as her bounden duty to be there. This time she said yes.

CHAPTER 27

ADVENT OF ENOS

In spite of having urged Mary to go with the others I knew I would miss her. Yet in truth there was another whose absence I would feel even more keenly. Dan the cook was not happy in Misuku, Like James before him, and for the same reasons, he had become more and more dejected as the days passed. I suspected, but would not acknowledge to myself, that he would leave at the first opportunity, and this was too good a chance to miss.

True, in the meantime he had been giving William what could only be described as a crash course in the workings of the stove and the mysteries of European cooking, but the full extent of the situation did not come home to me until next morning when everyone had left. There was no morning tea for a start, for William had gone on ulendo with Ken. More seriously there was no boiled water to make up the formula for Wendy's milk. With sinking heart I got up and hurried to the kitchen. It was empty, the stove cold and dead.

We had not seen Station since our return and no-one seemed to know where he was. It was the old situation, but worse now with a young baby to care for. Moreover, I now knew it unlikely that any trained outsider would choose to stay in Misuku.

Could I do more myself now that we had a stove? Could I train William to become a proficient cook? But he was he was too old to learn very much, a few simple recipes at most. Obviously we could not rely solely on William...

Well, first things first. I sent for the gentle Trisom, already at work in the vegetable garden up-rooting weeds and vegetable seedlings alike, and managed to convey the idea that until William returned he must give up gardening and not only bring water and chop wood and light the stove, but help me in the kitchen as well. He looked nervous at the prospect, his Arab nose twitching. Next I set water to boil on the Primus stove then sent one of the men with a note to Sutherland, who, thank goodness was at hand, asking him to come as soon as possible.

When Wendy had been fed and safely sleeping once more, I went outside again. There was the inevitable sick line-up, lately swollen to new proportions by women and girls who were not sick at all, but had heard of Ken's return with two wives, and came out of curiosity. Without even Dan to give an approximation of a translation - being native to the lake shore he understood Chisukwa only marginally better than I - there was little I could do for the genuinely sick except deal with the obvious, and was therefore relieved when Sutherland appeared. As usual he quickly took command, diagnosing coughs, colds, fevers, assessing the most needy and admonishing the time wasters. When all had been dealt with and were gone, wringing my hands almost literally, I expatiated on my woes at length to him and waited for sympathy.

To my surprise it was not forthcoming. Instead Sutherland gave a slight cough and began hesitantly,

"Madam, the brother of my wife has returned from South Africa."

Wrenching attention from my own concerns with utmost difficulty, I assumed this man also to be in need of medicine and asked what was wrong with him. But Sutherland was continuing,

"Yes, Madam, this man is the full brother of my wife. Same father, same mother."

Feeling this rather uncommon relationship might somehow be worthy of congratulation but not knowing how to express it, I ventured cautiously to hope that he had been successful in his travels.

"Oh yes Madam. He went to work in the mines, and sent back much money."

Still no enlightenment. But I knew Sutherland never talked without purpose, so contained my impatience as best I could and waited. Just as well, for his next statement had me riveted.

"And as he was digging for the gold the master of the mine saw that he was educated and spoke English. So that man said he must come into his house and learn to be a cook. So the master's wife..."

"A cook!" I put in breathlessly, almost incoherent with excitement, "Spoke English?"

"Yes Madam. And he worked in that man's house for three years and the madam taught him all things. Now he has returned to his village and that madam was sad too much when he left that house."

I took a deep breath and was about to say, "Do you mean this cook is actually looking for a job?" but paused less the directness and lack of circumspection should lead me to an unfortunate turn of phrase. Tentatively I asked,

"And where does this man live?"

Sutherland pointed,

"It is that village over the hill. It is also the village of his father and grandfather, and he has a wife and two children but one is a girl."

An established family background. Better and better.

"Well then, he may wish to stay and work in Misuku?"

"That is so Madam."

"In that case, I replied, "Tell him to come and see me."

I went indoors telling myself to keep calm and not expect too much. But the day which had started so badly was suddenly full of hope. The possibility of there being a fully trained cook who spoke English actually here in Misuku, seemed the stuff that dreams are made on. Perhaps Sutherland had unintentionally exaggerated? On the other hand the claim could be well-founded for I knew the standards of domestic help in South Africa to be considerably higher than those of Nyasaland. In any case any change in our present arrangements would be an improvement. Oh how wonderful if it were all true! But then another thought cast me down again, Would such a paragon put up with our primitive conditions, even with the new kitchen and stove?. Not to mention my own inadequacies as a housekeeper. My mind ran on, I could settle to nothing.

In the dead time of the afternoon when the labourers and Trisom had gone home, the place deserted, the silence palpable, as I sat restlessly encouraging Wendy in her efforts at crawling, a shadow fell across the open doorway.

What can one say of that first meeting with Enos Kitha, when years of close association and the passing of time have made inroads on that first impression? He was taller than average, looked about the same age as Ken, well built and dressed in neat khaki shirt and shorts.

We greeted each other politely, I made some comment on his having recently returned from South Africa.

"Yes Madam, that is so. I remained for three years in that place." he said in good English.

He repeated more fully what Sutherland had already told me; the conversation proceeded somewhat obliquely, I trying to conceal my eagerness, he elaborating on the great regret of his employers at his leaving.. Skilfully he managed to give the impression of great condescension at his deigning to consider coming to work for us. I was becoming dispirited. Nevertheless I pressed on and eventually, in trepidation, put the ultimate question -

"Can you make bread?"

At this he looked so affronted that for one awful moment I feared he might walk away. Then he drew himself up and said,

"Madam I can do everything."

This sweeping statement had a familiar ring, in this instance however it might have more credence. In South Africa many of the houses were modern and had modern appliances, so that these days white women did many of the chores themselves - using a washing machine instead of hiring a dhobi for instance. Therefore fewer servants were needed, but higher wages were paid to those willing and able to turn his or her hand to anything. This arrangement was quite unknown in Nyasaland where household amenities were few to nonexistent, and labour costs a good deal lower. Even a bachelor living on his own would have a cook, kitchen boy, houseboy, gardener, and a dhobi as well, all working along strict demarcation lines.

I knew instinctively this man would expect to work in the South African way and be paid accordingly. Should he do us the favour of coming to work for us that is. Whether he would 'do everything' in a household where modern amenities were conspicuous by their absence, was quite another matter. Never mind, this was no time to quibble. Restraining my overwhelming urge to engage him on the spot, I temporised, held back by the thought that in this paternalistic society such a weighty matter should be conducted by the man of the house. Therefore I told the cook what he, and everybody else knew, that my husband was away on ulendo. When he returned he would send for him. We parted with the customary courtesies.

When he had gone my feelings were as of having sat an important examination and attempted to answer the wrong questions. Why oh why had I not taken him on there and then at whatever cost? Ken would not have minded, knowing the urgency of the matter as well as I did. Should I call the man back in the morning?

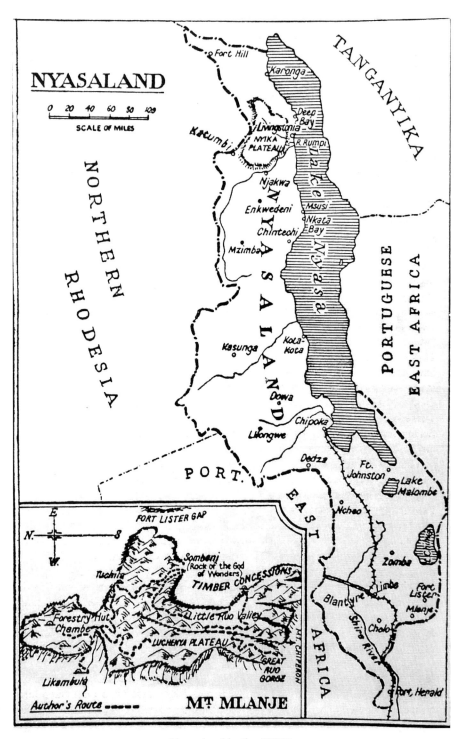

Nyasaland in the 1880's

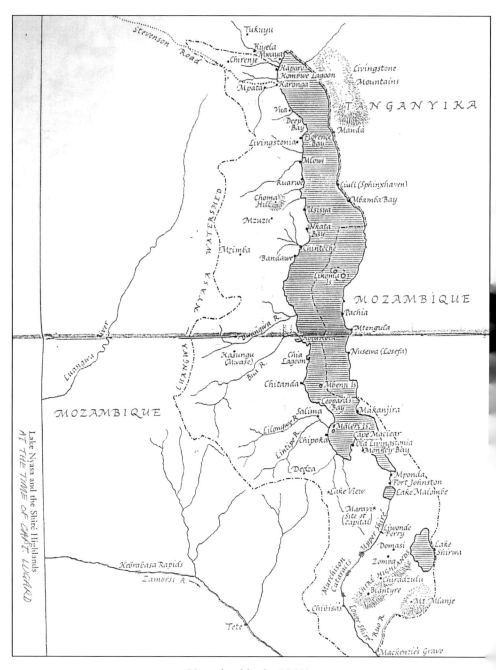

Nyasaland in the 1950's
The Times 1959

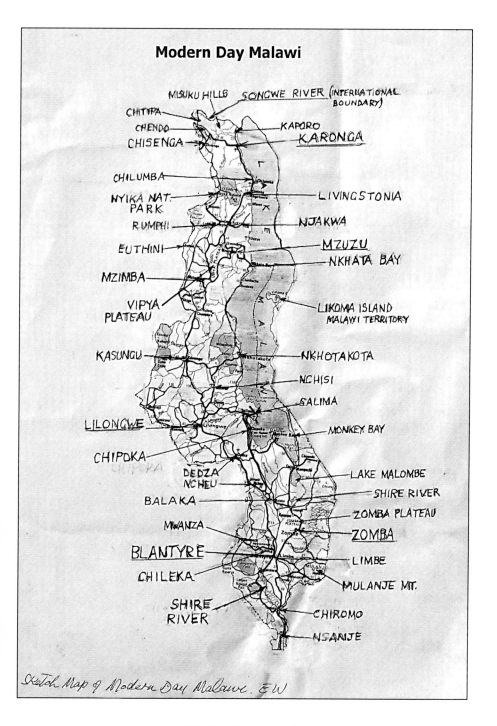

Modern Day Malawi

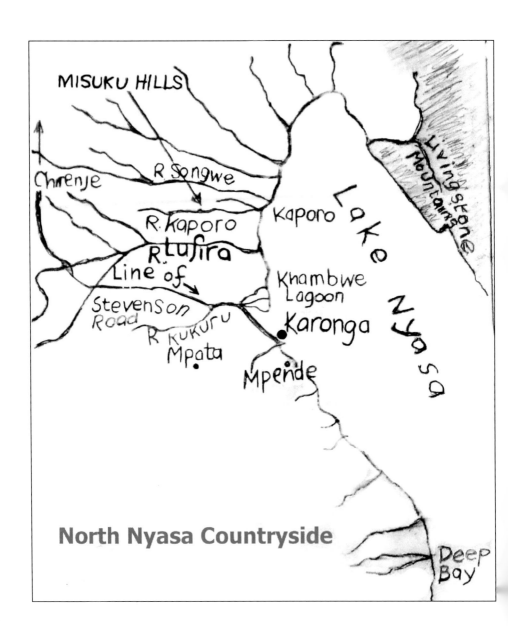

North Nyasa Countryside

Bugles at Dawn, Karonga, 1951
Chapter 7

Mandala House near Blantyre, 1880's. It could have been captioned
'The DC's House in Karonga in the 1950's, such being the similarity.

An African adventure

INTREPID botanist and dietician Jessie Williamson, who lived in Bridport for 30 years, has died at the age of 86.

In 1938, she became part of a team sent by the Colonial Office to Nyasaland — now Malawi — to study the nutrition and health of the local people in the context of their traditional culture.

Poisonous

Camping in villages, she gained the confidence of the women who told her about the diverse uses of the indigenous plants.

As well as cooking and eating the various fruits, leaves, roots, bark and fungi, the villagers told her how they could also be used to treat venereal and other diseases, madness, as contraceptives, insecticides, remedies for snake bite and even in cases of suspected infertility.

Her son, Tom, who was born in Malawi and now lives in Weymouth, said: "For instance, they told her that if a husband suspected that his wife had become pregnant by another man, a poisonous infusion prepared from a certain bark would be fed to a cock, representing the husband, and a hen, representing the wife.

"If the hen died, the husband's suspicions would be confirmed, but the cock's death would demonstrate the wife's innocence."

Surviving the attentions of marauding lions, she became popular with the villagers whose nickname for her was Mwadyachiani — "what have you eaten?", a question she invariably asked them.

Her son said her book, *Useful Plants of Malawi*, had proved an increasingly valuable resource for Malawians and others in an age when traditional cultures were rapidly being eroded by Western influences.

OBITUARY

The youngest daughter of Dr Chesman Barker — a London doctor — she enjoyed childhood holidays in West Dorset, staying with her uncle, the Rev. James Lethbridge Templer, Rector of Burton Bradstock in the early 1900s and Maiden Newton from 1911-1929.

After obtaining a degree in botany at Newnham College, Cambridge, she took up a series of teaching posts, first in County Durham and then in the more exotic locations of Hyderabad, India, and New South Wales, Australia.

Returning to England in the mid-1930s, she decided to embark on a new career as a dietician and took a post-graduate course in dietetics at the University of London.

She met her future husband, Andrew Williamson, in Malawi. He was an agricultural official working with the Colonial Office team. They married in 1943.

On his retirement from the Colonial Civil Service, the couple spent several years in Tanzania where, with the help

☐ MWADYACHIANI: Jessie Williamson's Malawian nickname meant "what have you eaten?"

of his wife, Mr Williamson set up business as a professional water dowser.

Mr and Mrs Williamson's adventures in Africa are recounted in two books published this year.

The Nyasaland Survey Papers, 1938-1943, edited by Veronica Berry and Celia Petty, gives a full account of the Colonial Office's nutritional survey and Jessie Williamson's role in it.

Tom Williamson's *Dowsing — New Light on an Ancient Art*, published by Robert Hale, tells the story of Andrew Williamson's dowsing exploits in Tanzania.

Jess Williamson, 1920's. Bridport news. Photo: Tom Williamson

RICHARD KETTLEWELL

Richard Kettlewell, CMG, former Director of Agriculture and Member of the Legislative and Executive Councils of Nyasaland, died on November 8 aged 84. He was born on February 12, 1910.

THE senior agriculturalist in Nyasaland (now Malawi) during much of the 1950s, Richard Kettlewell orchestrated a determined campaign to conserve the country's natural resources which were in danger of being overwhelmed by an alarming rise in population and the consequent threat of serious soil erosion. He coupled this with the enforcement by planting legislation to avoid repetition of a near-disastrous famine.

The measures placed upon African cultivators much arduous labour and was gravely unpopular and a cause for political attack. There were, however, two major lasting results of Kettlewell's leadership. First, soil erosion was slowed down and in many places stopped — an invaluable legacy to later cultivators. Second, the increased individual and national incomes derived from greatly improved production and improved marketing, demonstrated — for those who wished to see it — Nyasaland's capacity to support itself and to do so in a relatively short period.

When the time came, Nyasaland survived the withdrawal of Federal support and relatively soon after independence was able to manage without British financial support on recurrent account.

Dick Kettlewell was educated at the Dragon School, Oxford, and Clifton College. His early intention was to join the Royal Navy, but vacancies were few and instead he read Agriculture at Reading University. He was then appointed to the Colonial Agricultural Service and, following postgraduate study, arrived in Nyasaland in July 1934. It was in this Protectorate that he was to spend the whole of his colonial service career and to which he was to make an outstanding and lasting contribution.

His early years in Nyasaland were spent as the only Agricultural Officer in the Northern Province, touring in remote areas, encouraging better cultivation of staple food crops and the limited range of commercial crops: an "endlessly interesting and infinitely valuable" experience. During this prewar period he acquired a deep knowledge of the people and the value of working closely with the District Commissioners as well as of the soils and vegetation.

Early in 1939 Kettlewell was commissioned in the King's African Rifles Reserve and served in Kenya,

Somaliland, Aden, Abyssinia and Ceylon, as intelligence officer and later adjutant and brigade major. By mid-1943, however, the imperial need for increased food production was such that he was recalled to Nyasaland and was shortly promoted Senior Agricultural Officer.

By 1949 the Colonial Office had recognised Kettlewell's potential, and believed that he would benefit from experience in another territory before being further promoted. At this point fate, in the form of the new Governor, Sir Geoffrey Colby, intervened. Faced with a serious famine, Colby refused to allow any officer connected with food supply to leave the country, so Kettlewell remained.

Colby then asked for Kettlewell — whose worth he had immediately recognised — to be promoted and left in Nyasaland. The Colonial Office countered with the offer of a Professorship in Trinidad, which Kettlewell declined. The incumbent Director in Nyasaland was transferred to the Gambia, and after his successor stayed only six months, the Governor had had enough changes at the top of his Agricultural Department and successfully demanded that Kettlewell be made Director in April 1951.

Colby, the most progressive development Governor Nyasaland ever had, a man determined rapidly to raise living standards primarily through improved African agriculture, could have had no more loyal, gifted and dynamic colleague with whom to implement his policies than his new Director of Agriculture. Under Kettlewell, the field staff and experimental work of the Department expanded rapidly, and the production of food crops and a widening range of cash crops in-

creased many-fold. Such was the development foundation laid by Colby and Kettlewell in the years 1951 to 1956. It was a crucial period: the last chance to make major agricultural progress before rising nationalism made such progress impossible until after independence.

During the subsequent period of political agitation, Kettlewell — with his military experience, his profound knowledge of the country and his close working relationships with District Commissioners — was appointed to the Nyasaland Operations Committee when the March 1959 state of emergency was declared. He played a vital role, planning activities in a way which quickly brought the violence under control.

Later in 1959 he was appointed Secretary for Natural Resources, a post which was short lived. With the end of the emergency and rapid steps towards self-government, Kettlewell became the first of Nyasaland's "constitutional casualties", being compulsorily retired in 1962.

He returned to Britain, and spent 16 years as a consultant specialising in tropical agriculture, travelling extensively, especially in South-East Asia. He finally retired in 1979.

In 1935 he married Margaret Palmer who had studied with him at Reading and died in 1990. He is survived by a son and a daughter.

Richard Kettlewell, Director of Agriculture, Nyasaland, 1950's. The Times

The attack on KopaKopa's Stockade, 1888
From Lugard: 'The Rise of Our East African Empire'
Chapter 7

Captain Lugard's Cannon, circa 1889

Buying Cotton on the Lake Shore - Crocodiles and Tilapia Fish
Chapter 32

Coffee Nursery, Katobo Agricultural Station, Misuku, 1950's

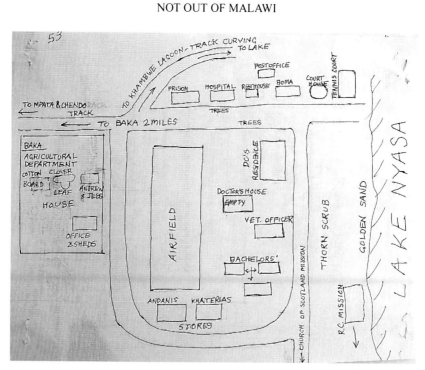

Karonga, 1950's

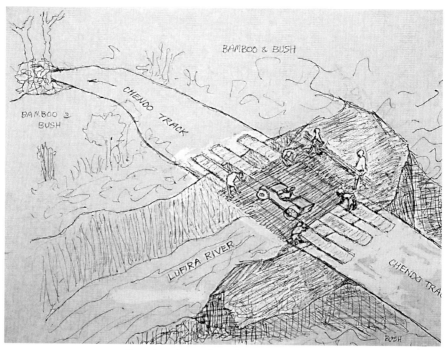

Crossing the Lufira River early 1950's
Chapter 19

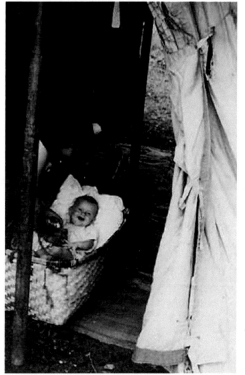

Wendy aged 6 months, in lion proof tent, on ulendo. Misuku 1956

Wendy at 10 months with Enos our cook. Katobo, Misuku 1956

The Agricultural Station at Katobo, Misuku in the 1950's. Capitaos' Houses in foreground, our house and Coffee Terraces in Background

Wendy on Ulendo in Misuku in the 1950's

Liness and Wendy outside the original Misuku house in the 1950's

Clover Leaf House, Karonga, 1950's

Christening at Karonga 1950's

Liwondé ferry on the Shire River,
October 1951

The author with son Ben, Misuku 1958

Enos' homestead at Chisenga, 1982

Gordon Burridge's Landrover & KAR troops on the Misuku road near Katobo, after we had left.   These photo's courtesy of Gordon Burridge, with thanks.
Chapter 36

KAR troops at the Kalengé, 1959, after Ragnor Udd's bridge was destroyed. Had this happened prior to our leaving, we would never have got out.

Brachystegia Country, Misuku Foothills
Oil painting by Ken Waterfield

Something at the back of my mind told me it would be unwise. No, there was nothing for it but to wait.

Once again I could settle to nothing. I picked up Wendy and took a turn round the garden. Mary would be away for a week, Ken's ulendo had three more days to run. Suddenly the inactivity of waiting for his return seemed unendurable. Then it struck me that I need not stay here alone. Why should Wendy and I not join Ken for these last days? I knew the direction he had taken, Sutherland would know his precise whereabouts, he would tell me if the idea were feasible or not.

Indoors again I quickly scribbled a note, then gathering up Wendy once more, in fading light, set off on the path to the capitaos' houses on the ridge.

Sutherland's wife was outside bent over the evening cooking fire. Unlike her full brother the cook, she had not been educated, neither did she speak English. Holding out the note I tried, and failed, to indicate that I wished her to give it to Sutherland when he returned. Oh the frustration of not being understood. Fortunately at this point there was a stirring in the house and Sutherland himself came out at the sound of my voice, having no doubt just finished work. I told him what I wanted. Was it possible? He paused and looked thoughtful. He told me Ken was about eight miles away, he himself would get Simbeyé the messenger to carry a letter to him in the morning at first light. If all went well I would have an answer at midday. He said also that I would need carriers, he would appoint some among the labourers. I thanked him profusely. By this time it was quite dark.

In Misuku nothing happened quickly, but just for once things went according to plan. The work clanger woke me next day after a somewhat disturbed night. Nervously Trisom brought in morning tea, the labourers chattered outside in close proximity to the closed curtains, it was time to get up to attend to Wendy and do something about breakfast. Sutherland came a bit later and translated as I was struggling to hand out appropriate medicines, for the sick were always with us, when to my amazement Simbeyé appeared, beaming.

Ken's reply was all I had hoped and more, he urged me to come without delay.

I packed Wendy's things and made the tobacco basket ready for carrying her, made up my own bedding roll, stuffing it with bare necessities, and we were ready to go. I felt no qualms about going off in this way. Trisom would keep an eye on the house, the journey would be straightforward for the carriers knew the way, if there were any problems en route the villagers would certainly help us.

To my surprise however Sutherland returned just as we were leaving, clearly intent on accompanying us. Surely as a matter of etiquette rather than need? Obviously, to him the prospect of our undertaking the journey escorted by carriers only, was scandalously out of the question.

Our destination was one of the villages on the other side of Mughessé, the massif on the foothills of which our house nestled. Climbing the stony track behind the house, always upward, we eventually left villages and homesteads behind and came to the bare slopes that would one day be transformed into terraced gardens supporting flourishing coffee bushes if Ken had his way. At present there were only a few scrawny cattle foraging coarse grass, tossing their heads against flies to the intermittent sound of their bells as they moved from one tuft to another They were tended by equally scrawny boys looking woefully inadequate to deal with any lion or leopard liable to stray down from the forest above.

The primaeval remnant crowning the ridge with age old trees loomed up before us all day, as usual seemingly so near in the translucent air, in actuality taking a long time to reach. Recalling the time we had traversed the forest, in reverse, on leaving the Udd's place on my first arrival in Misuku, I looked forward to its moist coolness, the dappled shade, the still pools with butterflies hovering over. Alas. As we drew nearer the carriers sheared off on a tortuous path on the contour just below the line of scrub. I opened my mouth to protest, but remembered in time, on that occasion the men had been distinctly uneasy during our passage through it. Only later, as stated, was I told of the true cause. (Namely that the forest was the burial place of Chiefs and the home of their spirits.) Therefore it was shunned by the Asukwa, a detour of several miles notwithstanding; even Sutherland acknowledged it without comment. So we worked our way round the end of the ridge and in late afternoon came in sight of the designated village perched high on one of the slopes. In remote homesteads along the way the people saw few Europeans; Ken went there at intervals, also the ADC from Karonga. White women were rare, white babies even rarer, and Wendy was an object of interest accordingly.

We arrived at our objective at dusk; a village elder greeted us on the outskirts. He told Sutherland that Ken had been out all day inspecting gardens - by which he meant the eroded plots on which the lives of the people depended - but that he was now holding a meeting with the headman and his advisers. He led us to the mud and thatch church where Ken had set up camp and there we found William who, cheerful and willing as ever, presently brought much needed tea.

Ken returned after dark, decidedly pleased to see us but too tired to talk much. This obviously was proving to be a tough ulendo, my own affairs would have to wait.

A strong whiskey helped and even the collapsible bath contributed to his revival. When Wendy had been fed, bathed and put down to sleep, we sat outside the church to wait for supper, the sky shot with stars, village sounds all about us. Was this a good time to tell him my news? But Ken's mind was still on the last few days.

"It's the same wherever I go in these parts, he said, "The land is exhausted and getting poorer. So the people are poor, and frequently hungry.."

I remembered the village of Chato on the far side of Wilindi, where we had stayed, and the impoverished ones in which we had camped on the journey up from Karonga. All had the same air rural squalor.

"Of course they know the Department's regulations, he said, "But take advantage of their remoteness to flout them. They haven't left grass strips across the slopes to check the erosion, they've been cultivating the stream banks, and who can blame them? They would starve otherwise. But that's only a temporary solution. They don't believe in conservation because it's long term, and their need is now.

This year it was another bad harvest even by their standards and some won't have enough food left till the rains come again. Then they'll be frantically replanting, and the whole cycle will repeat it self. I could report them to the DC, but what good would that do? He would fine them, but they have no money."
He was very discouraged.
"But what can you do then?" I asked.
"I can only try to persuade them to grow coffee. That way they would have a small cash crop. If they wished they could then walk down to Karonga to buy a bag of rice so they would at least have something to eat in the hungry season. Or they might buy salt to trade with, start up a small business even. So I've been pushing it hard in every place I've been to. I'll be holding another meeting before we move off tomorrow. I was too late to say much this evening after going round those depressing gardens. Of course they were ashamed of having broken the rules. They promised to mend their ways. But they won't. Or only for a few weeks at least. Then they'll revert to the same old ways."
At this point William announced supper. Soup - or rather hot water in which a stringy chicken had been boiled - followed by the leathery old bird itself, accompanied by plantain bananas and a tin of baked beans. No worse really than most of William's offerings. Even though I knew Ken would be paying for it I ate it guiltily, well knowing of incipient hunger all around.
When we had finished eating and were both feeling better I judged it right to divulge my own stupendous news.
"This man's a real cook, I told him, "Trained in South Africa. Also he's Sutherland's brother-in-law and he recommends him."
He listened in silence, still preoccupied, and by now sleepy as well.
"We'll talk about it tomorrow." he said.

We woke early next day. The village sounds of the morning were subtly different from those at Katobo. Ken got up at once and went out, William brought in tea as I was feeding Wendy. She had slept well in the tobacco basket between our camp beds and on waking had lain for some time watching the wavering pattern of bamboo leaves at the bright square of the unglazed window.
There was no need to hurry because of Ken's meeting. Already the elders and villagers were beginning to assemble outside under one of the few straggly trees. Ken came back for a hasty breakfast then went out to them. Presently the hum of voices subsided as he addressed them. I knew very well that he would be extolling the advantages of coffee growing, and could guess their response. Without understanding a word of their rejoinders it was clear to me that although they saw the need for change, were enthusiastic even, they had many doubts and objections. It went on a long time and I hoped there would be no ill feeling after all their goodwill in providing for us all out of their meagre store.
It was over at last, to my surprise everyone seemed in good spirits, the more so when Ken over-paid them for the chicken and the men's provisions of the previous evening.
Had anything been achieved? Unlikely. Friendly and well meaning as they undoubtedly were, good intentions and action seldom matched up. And yet... The

idea had been floated, a new concept broached.

We made our goodbyes. With customary courtesy the headman and his retinue accompanied us the first half mile and we parted with more expressions of goodwill.
Here we also parted from Sutherland who was returning directly to Katobo. I thanked him again for his help. Ken went ahead with the capitao of the region, Wendy and I, with William and one of the carriers, were left to follow in more leisurely manner. Once more the ravaged hillsides, their gauntness softened slightly by sunlight, the scattered homesteads with children playing in the dust among scavenging chickens, women outside their huts pounding millet two by two. In one place an empty hut, its doorway blocked with crossed sticks. A sure sign of sickness or death. Smallpox? Measles? Both could be a killer among such malnourished people. Kufi tick? Whatever the cause, for me the crossed sticks stood as a symbol for all the hidden menace that could strike at any time, with no redress, no possibility of medical aid or deliverance of any kind. I identified with these people as never before.

That night, the last of the ulendo, another church, another village, another headman. In the morning at breakfast we ate the last of Dan's bread which I had brought with me. It was stale and dry by now and contemplation of my own woes returned. Hunger adding to my cause I said forcibly to Ken,
"You won't let this cook get away will you? Cost what it may we must take him on."
"Of course I won't , Ken replied, "I know the need as well as you do. But it wouldn't do to let him think we're made of money."
"But we wouldn't need anyone else. He will do everything.!"
He was sceptical,
"Don't worry, he went on, "We'll arrange something. But now it's time to pack up, I'd like to get home as soon as possible."
It was a long trek. Luckily Ken turned off frequently to inspect gardens on the way, so my contingent was able to rest each time. We arrived at Katobo after dark.

Next day was Sunday, the one day of the week we could sleep on undisturbed by the work clanger. Even the hornbills in the tree by the rondavel seemed to appreciate the quiet and delayed setting off with raucous cries to their unknown haunts on the far side of Wilindi.
Finally we got up and had a leisurely breakfast, even William could make millet porridge by now; it was the staple of the people, had been so since time immemorial, filling rather than appetising.
Insistently across the valley the church drum began to throb. People appeared on the ridge on their way to the day long devotions and socialising.
When we had eaten, Ken began to sort through mail that had accumulated in his absence, separating the official from the personal. He gave the latter to me and we both settled down to read, I eagerly, he resignedly.
It was at this moment the cook who could do everything reappeared. Ken

went out to him, I hovered nervously in the doorway while the obligatory polite exchanges were made The man called Enos introduced himself to Ken and once more set out his accomplishments and experience. Ken asked leading questions, seemingly doubtful. The cook countered them and stated the conditions under which he would be willing to work for us, Ken raised certain objections. I became more and more anxious. This man could get a job anywhere he chose, we were about to let him slip through our fingers, once more we would be left to William's tender mercies.

After a while however each began to get the measure of the other. General agreement was established, only the details remained to be sorted out. At last these too were agreed on. Now however came the most contentious matter of all, the question of wages. Enos named an astronomical sum, Ken responded with one he considered reasonable. Between the two a great gulf yawned, I turned away to hide my agitation. Slowly, slowly, the gap narrowed; only when they finally reached a compromise did I breathe freely again.

But the haggling was by no means over, Enos stipulated that for such a paltry sum he must have a dhobi to wash the clothes. Ken hesitated - he had disbelieved in the "I will do everything" concept from the start - then gave in. Making a speech on the necessity of punctuality and reliability, he agreed to give Enos a month's trial. Honour upheld, Enos declared himself willing to start next day.

Next day morning tea arrived promptly. By the time I got up the sitting/dining room had been cleaned as never before, just as it would have been in Jess' house in Karonga, at the DC's residence, and in countless European households throughout the country.. Best of all however was the excellent bread which accompanied breakfast. I was rapturous and listened only half-heartedly to Ken's strictures that, naturally, all servants started off well but usually began to lapse after a few weeks.

In this case he was wrong. Enos WAS punctual, reliable too and always put in a good day's work. He improved the kitchen further with small contrivances. Outside there soon stood a rustic bamboo table, such as people further south sometimes made for themselves to drain pots and pans on, thus giving them an extra, unsolicited, wash in the rainy season.

Ken furthered things by getting Angus to send up regulation PWD appurtenances in the form of kitchen table and chair. Another wooden chair appeared from somewhere which, after a few weeks was always occupied by cronies gossiping as they peeled potatoes or performed some other chore in the hope of future favours.

All in all we had never been so well fed since coming to Misuku, never approximated to such a standard of cleanliness and hygiene since leaving Karonga.

And there was another advantage. Enos with his good English and local knowledge, could translate and determine ailments at the sick parade so that I was no longer dependent on Sutherland's intermittent presence.

The trial month passed smoothly, the result a foregone conclusion.

To me the fact of Enos' return to Misuku at the precise moment when my need was greatest, was nothing short of a miracle. That in some indefinable way he was superior to his peers was acknowledged by them as a matter of course, his status only slightly less than that of Sutherland himself.

How to account for it? By his own admission he had not benefited much from his schooling. Therefore to understand it one needed to know, as I came to know later, something of his background and upbringing. His father, Joseph, clever as a boy, had gone to a local village school, been picked out by a visiting Scots missionary and sent on to Livingstonia Mission for further education; eventually he trained to be a teacher. He also became a devout Christian, marrying only one wife, hence Enos' full blooded relationship to Sutherland's wife.

There was nothing devout about Enos himself however. Perhaps he was a throwback to his grandfather old Amos Kitha who lived in some style in the village over the hill. According to Enos, Amos had seventeen wives, and his children living or dead, numbered seventy-eight, which presupposes that he must have been very rich and very active. Enos also told me that Grandfather was however, unlikely to have more offspring now as he had fat legs (elephantiasis) and could not get about much any more. On the plus side this condition apparently gave him exemption from paying poll tax when the DC and his henchmen came round.

Listening to Enos' account of all this it occurred to me that Amos must be in his seventies, therefore born some time in the 1880s when Arab slavers were still wreaking havoc on the country. It was even possible that he had come across Captain Lugard...

Inevitably every silver lining has a cloud. Although as well as being hard working and conscientious and possessed of the qualities mentioned above, Enos knew the meaning of scarcity value and was temperamental as a prima donna. In the early days I was as putty in his hands for he was expert in aspects of housekeeping quite unknown to me, and certainly a much better cook.

He was also single minded as a child in getting his own way. In addition to the dhobi, and itinerant help from his cronies, it was not long before a succession of boys appeared in the kitchen for 'training'. Mostly they were failed schoolboys with a little English, or rather, boys forced to leave school because their fathers could no longer pay the fees. Possibly Enos was being recompensed in some way. Occasionally Ken remonstrated, well knowing if he did not, that sooner or later the boys' presence would be taken for granted and they would expect to be paid. Then the practice would stop for a while, only to start up again a few weeks later. In actual fact Ken's protests were less than forceful. He knew it was not good to be solely reliant on one person. If a kitchen boy who spoke a bit of English could be trained to help me when he took Enos on ulendo, so much the better.

In the early days skirmishes between Enos and myself were many and varied. He would preface every grievance with,

"Madam, you are my Mother."

Which irritated me considerably, not only because we were about the same age, but because his real mother who lived with his father in the family enclave, sometimes came hobbling over the hill for medicine. Or perhaps just to see her son. Nevertheless we soon achieved a working relationship, each only too aware of our dependence on the other to allow any dispute to get out of hand. My debt to him was undoubtedly the greater, indeed it is unlikely I could have survived in Misuku without him. He in turn had the advantage of living at home among his own people and the security of a regular income.

Enos served us faithfully all the years we were in Nyasaland. The association persisted long after we had left the country, with a tenuous connection surviving even into the 21st Century.

Long after our departure, often on a dark, dismal day of the English winter, an air-letter emblazoned with the familiar exotic stamps would drop on the doormat. Probably they were written by Winford, Enos' eldest son. The very sight of them would give a lurch to the stomach, bringing back memories of sunny days lit with the idealism of youth, the colour, the exuberance of life all round us among people we had grown to know and respect. All remembrance of their poverty, the disease, the difficulties they faced, not to mention our own failures, frustration and hardships, miraculously ironed out.

By dint of hard work he and his family - families rather, for he emulated old Amos rather than his father Joseph in this respect - Enos prospered. When, as already mentioned, Wendy returned to the land of her birth - by that time Malawi - with her husband, they visited Misuku hoping to see him. Katobo was still an Agricultural Station but our house had become a training centre for capitaos. Enos was not there but one labourer who remembered her as a child, told her he was in charge of the rest-house at Chisenga and that they would find him there. This they did, they took photographs, sent us one of Enos with his third wife and several young children. He looked barely a day older than when we had last seen him. Which, considering the undeniable changes in ourselves, seemed rather unfair.

CHAPTER 28

SHOPPING AT MBEYA

Mary returned with Nigel the Forestry Officer, a few days later. I was very pleased to see her, but less enthusiastic about Nigel whose intentions were clearly dishonourable since he was the one with the wife and children all set to join him. Not only that, without the companion of his previous visit he had the distinct air of a dependent, with which we could well do without. Fortunately he only stayed one night and left next morning looking apprehensive at the thought of having to tackle Wilindi and the Chendo on his own. Mary's visit to Karonga had been a great success.

"Angus was really touched, she said, "It was the first birthday he'd had since his wife left, so he would have had a pretty dismal time of it alone at Chisenga. It was a really good party. Everyone was there. Almost. We ended up swimming in the lake at midnight. The water was so warm. And the lake so beautiful in moonlight"

"I know all about that." I put in wistfully, recalling the night on the Ilala with Steve.

"We were still there when the sun came up, she went on, "So the fishermen sold us their catch and we made a fire of driftwood and had fish for breakfast like we did before."

That too I could imagine.

She also gave us the gossip of Karonga, and was well placed to do so as since the DC and Joan had been her hosts and she was at the centre of things.

"Oh, and Jess sends her love. She and Andrew are off on local leave next week. Joan is taking on the job of refuelling the Beaver while she's away. They're driving to Tanganyika and Kenya, the Williamsons that is, looking for some delectable place to retire to."

This was not at all what I wanted to hear. Karonga without Jess and Andrew would be unthinkable. So I put away the thought and changed the subject.

"Anything else?"

"Well some chap has moved into the new Cotton Board house next to the Cloverleaf. He's under some sort of cloud apparently. But he came to the party and seemed quite decent."

This had a familiar ring.

"They said that about Steve." remarked Ken.

"Well Steve was decent." I put in, remembering our Scheheradzada evenings, and hoping with more fervour than conviction, that he and Suad were making a go of things down on the Lower River.

Although the advent of Enos was obviously of less import to Mary than to Ken and me, she was nevertheless very pleased.

"Oh good. I was beginning to fear for my digestion. What about William though?

Has he been cast off without a shilling?"

"Oh no."

I explained that William had happily gone back to labouring, after giving us an assurance that he would always step into the breach again at any time it should prove necessary. At which I had thanked him, repressing a shudder.

It was in fact, a long time before I came to appreciate William's good qualities, and realise that but for him and Station I might not have been able to tolerate those early months in Misuku.

The dry season was nearly over. Every day rain clouds massed over Wilindi; they promised but did not deliver. Possibly no-one scanned the sky more anxiously than Chief MweniMisuku who in time of drought, must brave the forest on Mughessé and sacrifice a black cockerel there to appease the spirits of the ancestors.

In the villages food stocks were running low. People were inspecting the contents of their nkokwe - grain stores - hoping supplies would last out till the next harvest.

It was also a time of great activity, existing gardens must be tilled ready for planting at the first sign of rain, new ones must be opened up. Even the men took part and there was absenteeism among Ken's labour force. The sick line-up also diminished, only women and children with genuine complaints appeared and these, alas, were largely beyond my competence.

Though Mary had fulfilled a list of items I had given her for Mr Andani's store, though Jess had sent up more than just her love, our own supplies were also running low. Given the circumstances the villagers clearly had nothing to sell us, dried or fresh. Our only meagre source of the latter was our own vegetable plot. I had put Mary in charge of this soon after our arrival on the strength of her having once taken a Constance Spry floristry course in London. Every morning she and Trisom bent over the earth, she trying to identify weeds, he struggling to identify seedlings. The results however were encouraging and we soon we had lettuce and tomatoes, with New Zealand spinach coming on.

In no way however, could these make up for our shrinking stock of staples, flour and rice foremost among them. Clearly it was time to go shopping. The more so as Christmas was coming on, and we were woefully unprepared.

"We'll go to Mbeya, said Ken when I put the matter to him, "They have everything there."

Mbeya was in Tanganyika, about 160miles off on the circuitous route we must take. Ken had fond memories of carefree weekends there as a bachelor when he was stationed at Chinunka, near Fort Hill.

"Mbeya is a proper town. A bit like Blantyre but not so big, he told us, "We shall have to start off really early though, because it's a long way. We'll go next Friday and come back the following Monday. That way we can have two full days there. Oh, and we must take passports because the borders straggle about a bit in some places. It's not always easy to tell whether you are in Nyasaland, or Northern Rhodesia. Or Southern Rhodesia for that matter, and Mbeya itself is in Tanganyika. They're all British territories but they all have borders with custom posts for some reason."

On the night before the appointed day, Enos who was going with us, slept in the kitchen armed with the fat, round, alarm clock which had once graced our Chesham flat. He had strict instructions to wake us next day at 4AM. When Mary and I protested it would hardly be worth while going to bed, Ken said,
"Well you two can stay up all night if you want to. But I assure you it won't be worth going at all if we're not away before dawn. We can eat breakfast going along once we have reached the truck."

Thus morning found us struggling from sleep in eerie, pre-dawn light before even the hornbills were stirring, the only sound the subdued voices of the carriers coming with us as far as Chisi.
With Wendy in the tobacco basket as usual, we set off on the path down the valley in a zombie-like state, still hardly awake. Coffee bushes on the terraces were invisible but a rising mist was discernible as we approached the nursery by the stream. No-one was there, not even the night watchman supposedly guarding the coffee seedlings. No doubt Ken made a mental note. We crossed the rickety pole bridge; on the further bank two forms loomed out of the gloom. They materialised as young men, neatly dressed, one of them carrying a spear.
Enos, who had almost certainly connived at the meeting and stood to gain from it, said,
"Sir, these men wish to go to Fort Hill for work in the mines. They wish for a ride in the galimoto."
Thereafter whenever we left Misuku, provided we had space enough we picked up fellow travellers - who sometimes got more than they bargained for by having to help haul the truck out of mud, push if the engine failed, go for water when the radiator boiled, or assist with other Acts of God only too common in those parts.

We walked quietly through sleeping villages with the chickens cooped up in their own nkokwe, even the dogs silent. The Court complex was deserted. Perhaps the Chief dreamt uneasily of rain, of black cockerels. On past the dark rectangle of the school, the air still fresh and cool, threading our way through banana groves and stands of bluegums. Then these too were left behind, the light broadening, the sky slashed with bars of saffron as we neared the foothills of Wilindi.
The sun rose dramatically as we came to the summit, cloud shadows throwing the myriad small hills below us into sharp relief. There was no time to stop and admire the view however. At the highest point we paused only long enough to get our breath back, then started the steep descent. Enos and the two youths led the way, followed by Ken and the carriers with Wendy. Knees buckling with the effort, Mary and I sought to keep up.
Some time later we reached the truck. The baggage was loaded, Ken instructed the carriers to meet us on this spot in three days time. Enos and his companions climbed up in the back, Mary and I with Wendy in my arms, got in the cab. Ken made brief farewells, climbed in after us and slipped the gears; that the engine fired first time was not a matter of luck, he had been out the previous day to check it over. We cruised off on the watershed.

At one place we came across the road gang, the men working assiduously having heard our approach. In spite of their efforts improvements to the stony track were apparent only to Ken. In unconscious emulation of Angus's defence of the Chendo, he expressed satisfaction at consolidation of the surface, repairs to troublesome culverts etc. and Mary and I had the sense to keep our mouths shut. In fact nothing held us up and we reached the Kalengé in good time. Here the improvement was perceptible. The intended new bridge was as yet a figment of imagination but the old one had been reinforced with stouter poles, the bend at the top of the steep bank ironed out by removal of a tree and several boulders, and the bank itself cut back to a reasonable gradient. We crossed without difficulty.

There was no sign of Nelson at Kapoka, only a few boys who came running and women who looked up from early chores to wave. Reciprocating we passed without stopping and some miles beyond Kapoka left the track for the recognised road leading to Fort Hill.

Fort Hill at last. So far it had been merely a name to me, etched on the mind since the memorable night at dinner with the PAO and his wife at Mzimba on our journey upcountry, when it was decreed that Ken be based there. Was it as bad as he had painted? Now I was about to find out.

A pall of smoke was visible well before we reached it, evidence of many cooking fires. Only when we drew near did the dry, dusty compound become apparent. It was crowded with men squatting on the ground or swarming about booths selling food or beer. These were the new recruits who, surely, could have no conception of how their lives were about to change or what the work in South African mines would entail. Ken did not attempt to remonstrate with the youths who had come with us - it was none of his business - did not repeat what he had told James. That the plane would swallow them up and before they knew it their days would be spent deep in the bowels of the earth, shut off from daylight and the scenes of home, their nights passed in single sex compounds, contact with loved ones virtually nil.

Nor did it take much imagination to picture their return after three gruelling years. They were leaving home completely ignorant of the ways of the world, they would come back changed, initiates, in their own eyes at least. At Fort Hill the beer stalls, the booths selling worthless finery would relieve them of money even before they got home. The prostitutes would move in...

The noise, the hub-bub apparent even from the road, would one suspected, be continuous throughout the day and half the night. Mary said,
"Well you certainly couldn't have lived anywhere near this hellhole."
I agreed. The more so when Ken pointed out our intended house which stood less than 100yards from the perimeter fence. It looked very basic, contrasting adversely with the big WENELA house at the edge of the compound, where the Portuguese/African recruiting manager lived with his family.

We dropped off the two young Asukwa and wished them well. They seemed excited, rather than appalled as we were. I hoped Enos had told them what to expect. He, after all, had survived it though his own experience was by no means typical.

Fort Hill was the border point, manned rather casually by two Askari. We were waved through without having to show our passports and were happy to get away from such a miserable spot. We passed into a kind of no-man's-land which might have been part of Northern Rhodesia, or Tanganyika, or perhaps neither. Certainly the road had received little or no attention recently, the surface deteriorated at once and our speed was reduced; fine dust was more troublesome and the only option was of keeping the windows open and risk being suffocated, or shutting them and being overcome by heat. As usual we compromised and wound them down a couple of inches. Riding corrugations, negotiating a slalom between pot-holes, the truck's defective shock absorbers ensured a journey about as comfortable as a toboggan ride on hard packed ice, as we traversed a landscape of indeterminate bush with very few villages and virtually no traffic. So on through the day, not talking much, stopping once in scant shade to eat curling sandwiches. Time lost its meaning until Ken said,
"We'll be coming to the customs post at Mbozi soon, better have passports handy."
As if to bear this out the area became slightly more populous, villages more frequent, some of them boasting 'hotelis' - crude shacks selling bottled beer and Fanta. At one place a tailor under a baobab tree sat working a treddle sewing machine.

All this time our progress, though slow, had been unimpeded, this changed when we came to Mbosi at last. There the border was zealously guarded, the barrier down. Why this should be so was not clear. Regardless of which territory we were leaving, or entering, all were British, like much of Africa and indeed one fifth of the world at this time.
At the barrier stood a Sikh notorious for obstruction and bad temper. Reputedly he could and did, hold up travellers for hours on a whim, or simply by non-appearance. This was easy to believe when we saw him. Even in our weariness it was impossible not to acknowledge his magnificence. At least 6feet tall in his turban, his uniform immaculate, his piercing eyes missing nothing, one felt he would have been quite at home defending the Khyber Pass single-handed against all comers.
On the opposite side of the barrier waiting to come through, were two trucks, a private car and a bus loaded with passengers and assorted livestock. We on our side, were preceded by only one vehicle. The Sikh waved it through with lordly hand, we moved to follow. To our dismay the barrier came down, the Sikh turned on his heel ignoring the passports Ken held out to him, and made to cross the road to deal with the queue on the other side.
Clearly he was within his rights to do so - on the other hand checking our documents would have been a matter of seconds. Now we would have to wait at least an hour - more if everyone on the bus needed to be checked individually. We were in no mood to be impartial, in the heat of full sun we sat and fumed.

Incredibly it was Wendy who saved the day. She had survived the journey better than any of us by sleeping through most of it. Even awake she was happy enough provided there was perpetual motion. Once we stopped however, the heat in the cab became insufferable and she had had enough. She set up a cry of such intensity that the Sikh checked in mid stride, looked back, disbelieving that so small a creature could command such decibels. Not only that, as he stood undecided, before his very eyes she proceeded to turn from pale pink to puce in the manner of a chameleon on a tartan rug.

The Sikh recognised superior strength when he saw it. He came back, scrutinised the rest of us briefly, Wendy turned up the volume even higher. He grabbed the passports from Ken, stamped them, raised a hand, limp now rather than lordly. The Askari raised the barrier. We were through before we knew it and went on our way; Wendy went back to sleep.

After a while we joined a major road which carried more traffic. Not metalled alas, the earth surface corrugated, carved up. People trudging along the verge ignored us or merely stared. No-one waved a greeting, vehicles were too common here, too troublesome. All the same we missed the charm of this friendly custom which in Nyasaland never failed to enlighten the most tedious journey.

Perhaps history also played a part in the detachment of these people.

Tanganyika had formerly been a German colony with quite a different kind of rule. The country had natural resources, and the labour to access them, but not without coercion. [1]

Of course nothing of this concerned us at the time. We were all far too tired, our sole aim to reach Mbeya as soon as possible. Even a sign saying 'Meteorite', leading off on another dusty track, which normally would have claimed the attention of Mary and me, failed to raise much interest. Ken who had seen it, said it looked much like any other old chunk of rock to him. But that might have been to deter us from insisting on going to inspect it on our return journey. In any case, though the sun hung overhead as it had done throughout the day, Mary's watch indicated that there was but half an hour or so of daylight left - and the prospect of being benighted in this alien land was decidedly unattractive.

The road streamed endlessly ahead. Until that is, it vanished abruptly. Or appeared to; Ken familiar with the route, stopped the truck. We seemed to be on the edge of a precipice. In gathering dusk myriad pin-points of light below us suggested small boats, but the sea was hundreds of miles away.

Much has been written of that geological fault formed millions of years ago, known as the Great Rift Valley, which runs North/South through much of East

---

[1] At the outbreak of the 1914/18 war the German overlords had attempted to invade Nyasaland from the North and had actually mounted an attack on Karonga. That it failed was due partly to the force getting lost in the bush, but mainly because of stout resistance of local people, assisted by the small British garrison who had been apprised of the attack. There was also some gunboat skirmishing on Lake Nyasa. But with the end of hostilities Tanganyika was ceded to the British and had remained so ever since.

and Central Africa, of which the plain below us was a tiny part.

Of course there was a way down. An inland cliff with a narrow road blasted out of rock face snaked down before us. Sheer drops at its edges rendered 'Polé Polé' - slowly slowly - notices quite superfluous.

It was dark when we reached the bottom, the lights of the cooking fires we had glimpsed from the heights were more numerous, more distinct. Somewhere across the plain lay Mbeya.

The rest of the journey was less arduous, the track though dusty, was flat and direct. Sometime later the lights of the fires merged into one bright glow indicating the town and we realised we had reached our destination.

A few days before we started our journey Ken had despatched Simbeyé to Fort Hill with a telegram booking rooms for us at the Mbeya Hotel. Mary and I had watched him set out, barefoot, armed with his spear and battered satchel She had said,

"It takes quite a leap of faith to believe the telegram will actually get through, don't you think? How many miles must he walk to reach Fort Hill?"

I was not sure about the mileage but thought Simbeyé would get there in a couple of days. I added, for I too had doubts,

"Surprisingly though, most of our mail does get through. Eventually."

It must be admitted however, that during the last stage of our journey, with the need for baths, food and clean beds so urgent, my confidence in the ability of our aged messenger to fulfil his mission on time, if at all, had dwindled somewhat. So much so that as the lights of the town loomed up like a mirage, I ventured to ask,

"Supposing Simbeyé didn't get through on time? Suppose the hotel is full?"

Ken who may have been reflecting on the difference between setting off on the jaunt of a carefree weekend as a bachelor, and tackling it with a baby and two dependent females in tow, replied shortly,

"It won't be. It never is." adding, "I only gave Simbeyé that telegram because I was sending him to Fort Hill with mail anyway."

Now Mary and I sat anxiously in the truck on the hotel forecourt while Ken went inside. He came back almost at once.

"Plenty of room. I told you so. Come on."

We stumbled stiffly out of the cab, an African porter appeared and took our luggage. Ken asked him to show Enos where he could sleep.

Then the mirage became reality. Comfortably furnished rooms, beds, baths with running water, electricity, materialised as if by magic.

In the excitement I forgot to ask Ken whether his telegram had arrived.

Next morning Wendy and I had another bath for the pleasure of turning on the taps. (In the evening when it was dark again I took her tiny finger and initiated her into the miracle of turning darkness into day at the flick of a switch.)

When we went down to breakfast, Ken who had preceded us, was just leaving, saying he must get the truck serviced, without delay; there was a reasonably

reliable garage he knew of. When he had gone Mary said,
"I hope to goodness he gets those shock absorbers fixed. The road wasn't
as bad as the Chendo, but all the same I feel I've had enough shocks to last
a lifetime."
We lingered over exotic fruit, long forgotten cereals, bacon, eggs, toast,
marmalade, coffee, and planned our morning. My priority perforce was the
boring household shopping.
"I've got a list a mile long." I told her.
"I shall go sight-seeing." she replied.
By which she meant she hoped to sight a dress shop or two, and a hairdressing
salon.

Leaving Wendy sleeping in our room in a proper cot, in the care of Enos whom
she loved, Mary and I started off. The noise, the colour, the forgotten bustle,
struck us like a blow. At once we were surrounded by vendors peddling goods
of every description, we pushed our way through with difficulty.
On either side of the broad street Indian stores similar to Mr Andani's, but
bigger, were interspersed with European glass fronted shops and many African
stalls and booths. A few cars cruised the tarmac, well spaced out
Ken had told me to go to the Indian store he had patronised in single days,
describing its location as best he could, and saying he would join me there as
soon as he was free.
But how to find it? All looked exactly alike. All afforded glimpses of cavernous
interiors, not one displayed a name. Instead, in front of each stood the Indian
proprietor urging, exhorting, imploring passers by to go inside their own
emporium. Even to pause in perplexity was to risk being ushered inside.
To my great relief, as I cast about hesitantly, I saw Ken across the road. Mary
drifted off saying she would see us at lunch.
Outside the favoured store the owner greeted Ken like the Prodigal Son
returned rich, obviously remembering large orders placed previously. He
shook hands with both of us and led us inside. I was given a chair, an underling
was told to bring tea. These niceties over, as soon as my eyes had become
accustomed to the gloom I got out my list. Rather than crates of bottled beer
which, I suspected, had come high on Ken's list in bachelor days, mine was
headed Baby Milk.
Since returning to Misuku, ensuring sufficiency of this commodity so vital
to Wendy's welfare, had dogged my waking and sleeping hours. For I feared,
with good cause, that the tenuous 600mile line of supply we depended on -
from Blantyre to the Ilala by road, thence by lake to the Khambwe lagoon, off
loaded for Karonga, thence to Misuku on foot - might one day be disrupted,
and Wendy go hungry.
The inclusion of feeding bottles and accessories on the list of post-natal
necessities given to me at Lilongwe hospital 'Just in case', had unfortunately
proved only too necessary on account of my getting malaria when Wendy was
a month old, with resultant failure of breast milk. Not only had this made life
more difficult, but it left me with a feeling of guilt, slight, as it was not of my

making, but unsettling all the same.[2]
The store was hot but crammed with all manner of interesting things. So it was pleasant to sit sipping (sweet) tea, murmuring my requirements, which the owner would relay to an underling who hurried off to murky recesses and returned with them in very short order.
In this way the list of essentials was soon satisfied, leaving me to gaze round at long forgotten items such as shampoo, scented soap, silk stockings - admittedly not much call for those in Misuku but I did not let that deter me - and many other things impossible to resist. Nor did I try very hard, Christmas was coming and our austere regime had lasted long enough.
Soon a mountain of goods had accumulated. The proprietor and I were delighted, Ken less so as he eyed the bill, likewise mountainous.
Leaving him to haggle over it, anxious to get back to Wendy in the unlikely event of her being awake and fretting, I hurried back to the hotel. She was awake, but playing contentedly with the toys in her cot and keeping an eye on Enos asleep on a chair.

The character of Mbeya was unique to my experience, being very different from that of Blantyre, perhaps on account of the way each had evolved. Blantyre had a settled, even staid air about it. Which may have been due partly to the early Scots missionaries who had founded it, and partly because most of the Europeans who followed on were British Government officers. Mbeya on the other hand gave clear evidence of the discovery of gold in the area. Finds which had not been substantiated in sufficient quantity to warrant large scale investment as in South Africa. This however had not deterred diggers and panners of many nations flocking there to try their luck. Most had been unsuccessful and left empty-handed, but others had stayed on and prospered in other directions, shop keepers, artisans, farmers. Hence the cosmopolitan feel to the place.
Correspondingly the Mbeya Hotel was quite different from Ryalls. It was a two storey building and something of the style of a conventional European establishment, but more racy. One thing it did have in common with Ryalls however, was a shady garden, and it was here I sat with Wendy to wait for the others to return. Ken came back first, hot and thirsty, having been less than a match for the practised store owner in the art of bargaining. Mary arrived laden with packages and with her dark hair newly cropped and styled. She looked very chic. She said,

---

[2] I knew that some African women witnessing Europeans rearing their babies in this fashion, from necessity or choice, assumed it must be the best and tried to do likewise. A retrograde step on several counts. Firstly it was an expense they could ill afford, secondly they sometimes mixed it with un-boiled water. Thirdly it was difficult to keep bottles etc clean and hygienic. Added to which some women diluted the milk powder excessively to make it go further and babies did not flourish. A tragic situation, the more so as most of these women had plentiful breast milk of their own. OXFAM and other charities were trying hard to prevent the manufactures of baby milk promoting their product in the third world. With what success was unclear.

"There are some quite decent shops here. I've bought some new dresses. Oh, and there's a wonderful bakery. German I think, with all different kinds of bread, and gateaux, and torte and things. Later I shall buy some to take back with us."

As we sat relaxing over cool drinks Ken, slightly restored, told us of an old Nyasaland acquaintance he had bumped into in the bank.

"Yes, only met him once or twice before, in Mzimba. Decent chap, his name is Gerry Williams, he works on a Government tung station down there. He's staying at the other hotel, Queens."

"What is he doing here then? I said, "Wrong territory surely?"

"He's been on home leave. Came back by sea to Mombasa and drove over-land from there. He'll go on to Mzimba via Fort Hill, then down the Great North Road."

Restraining Wendy who was crawling on the grass and trying to eat some unidentified weed, I sat up, my matrimonial plans for Mary rekindled. Only just in time did I stop myself from saying,

"Is he married?"

Better proceed cautiously, I decided as a plan formed in my mind. The matter could wait, and I had something even more pressing on my mind. I asked Mary, "Whereabouts, exactly, is that dress shop?"

Later in the afternoon as Ken, Wendy and I were having a brief siesta, I reverted to my scheme.

"Gerry? Married? No I don't think so, said Ken, "I seem to recall he had something of the reputation of being a confirmed bachelor."

"How old is he then?"

"Oh, I don't know. Mid thirties I should think."

Thirty something seemed a bit young for confirmed bachelorhood, so I went on, "Why don't we ask him over to supper tonight?"

We put the suggestion to Mary as we all sat in the garden once more. She thought it a good idea and Ken, rather pleased at the prospect of having a bit of masculine company for a change, said he would send Enos over to Queens with a note.

"Why don't you just phone him? asked Mary, "Surely there's a telephone at the reception desk?"

I gazed at her with admiration, this means of communication having long since faded from my consciousness.

She was right of course. The invitation was made and accepted and the evening hour fixed.

"Good, I said, and to Mary, "You and I can wear our new dresses."

Naturally, when the time came I made sure that Ken and I went down to the lounge five minutes late so that Mary was obliged to receive Gerry on her own and, with luck, get to know him a bit. By the time we put in an appearance they had introduced each other and were chatting amiably.

Gerry had a lived in sort of face, very attractive, he also proved to be good company. By strange coincidence it transpired he had been born in Karonga, his father having been DC there in the 1920s. I immediately wanted to know what it was like in those days. Was the hospital there then? (unlikely,) Or the prison? Did Captain Lugard's cannon stand outside the Boma as it did today? And had Gerry actually been born in one of the old two storey Residences? Unfortunately he could not enlighten me on any of these topics. Not only because his father had been transferred shortly after his, Gerry's, birth, but also because the lake level had risen a few years later, swallowing up whole villages, submerging most of the European buildings, so that by now, they were under several feet of water offshore.

There was something inherently romantic about this. I could see the drowned house of his birth quite clearly, still intact, the wet walls hung with faded prints, windows curtained with swaying water weed, mpasa and chambo fish nosing the abandoned cot in the nursery. I resolved to look very hard for evidence of it when next we swam at Karonga. Did so in fact. But the lake kept its secrets.

Gerry also told us that his father had been mauled by a lion while out hunting one day, but had survived. Whereat Ken told him about Mr Lilford in Misuku, who had not, remarking that being attacked by lion appeared to have been an occupational hazard in those days. So much so that victims could have formed a club and been lionised in London when they went on leave. Provided they lived long enough of course.

I privately thought however, that brave as her husband undoubtedly was, given the primitive natal conditions almost certainly prevailing in Karonga at the time, Gerry's mother had survived quite a hazardous ordeal of her own.

Before he said goodnight Gerry asked us if we had seen the film showing at the cinema, to which Mary and I replied that we had not even seen the cinema, much less the film. So it was arranged we should all go as his guest the following evening. I was very excited and briefly considered whether, in the interests of true love, I should suggest to Ken that he and I stay behind so that Mary and Gerry could have the night to themselves. But dismissed the thought at once, the prospect of entertainment was too tempting, and it must be admitted, the odds too great. In the event Ken opted to stay behind with Wendy.

The cinema was not, alas, of the open air variety so popular in South Africa. Against the night sky its bulk loomed up like a warehouse or aeroplane hangar. As we entered the heat of the womb-like auditorium met us like a wall, The place was packed with a seething, claustrophobic mass of bodies. We fought our way to seats at the back with difficulty.

In spite of having turned up at the advertised time we found the film already in full blast. Billed as Spartacus the Gladiator, this particular version was so old it might have been a silent movie, but this was impossible to tell due to audience participation in the many tongues of the multi-racial audience. Nor was the on-screen action easy to follow when one was sufficiently composed to give attention to it. Perhaps the reels had got muddled. Suffice it to say that most of the film comprised energetic fighting bouts between scantily clad males with enormous biceps, scenes which were received enthusiastically by all and sundry.

It seemed an eternity to the interval. When at last the lights went up there was a brief hush. Then pandemonium broke out anew, everyone discussing it all excitedly, shouting, stamping, calling to friends several seats away.

To Mary and me it seemed a good time to leave, but in whispered consultation we reluctantly decided against it, in consideration to our host. Indeed Gerry was obviously enjoying himself, he did not appear to feel the heat, perhaps because of having been born to it.

Darkness again. Clearly continuity had played little part in the training of the projectionist. The audience did not care, enthusiasm undimmed they kept up their running commentary, voices dropping at the (very few) tender moments, cries and shouts rising to crescendo during the battle scenes.

It was over at last, the screen went blank, the lights went up. This time the silence was prolonged. Then came a long, collective sigh, full of yearning...

Outside a cool velvet night embraced us, the audience spilled out reliving it all, silent at last.

"Did you enjoy it?" asked Gerry heartily as he drove us back to the hotel.

"Well I wouldn't have missed it for anything." replied Mary. I added,

"It was an unforgettable experience."

We thanked him profusely and made friendly goodbyes. In the morning we would be going our separate ways. Gerry said,

"Perhaps we'll meet up again soon? In Mzimba maybe"

As it happened Ken and I did come across him some years later, in a place called Mzuzu. He was accompanied by a wife and fine baby boy - so much for the confirmed bachelor - in circumstances far from entertaining.

Monday morning and the prospect of another bone-shaking ride. For once Mary and I were ready for the obligatory early morning start. Dawn found us shivering on the hotel forecourt, our katundu - luggage - assembled about us. Including boxes of groceries which the Indian storekeeper had sent up to our room directly after Ken had settled the bill, so that the place took on the aspect of a depot for foreign aid.

Now we were waiting for Ken to come from the servicing garage where the pickup had languished ever since our arrival. The proprietor had promised to have it ready by Sunday afternoon, a fruitless hope. Now there was nothing for it but wait. I fervently hoped the delayed start would not mean our spending the night in God- forsaken bush country.

By the time Ken returned, after paying another astronomical bill, thoughts of getting back to Misuku by nightfall had already diminished.

"Fellow said he'd been working on it all night, he told us, "Some story. Now there's no time for me to try it out or anything. We'll just have to hope for the best."

He and Enos quickly loaded up. The latter also had a lot more baggage than he started out with, much of it doubtless in fulfilment of commissions for friends back home.

The first part of the return journey was as a film run backwards. Films were on our minds, Mary and I still suffering a Spartacus hangover as we cruised across the plain. Climbing the escarpment in daylight gave a different, but no less terrifying perspective. As we reached the top it started to rain.

I had forgotten and Mary having arrived in the dry season, had not experienced the savagery of an African downpour. Once more the assault on the truck, the streaming windows, rain pounding the roof like high blood pressure, the road surface transformed in an instant from all embracing dust to mud the colour of milk chocolate. We ground to a halt, once again it became very hot in the cab. Leaks appeared from unlikely sources, With ineffectual handkerchief I utilised them to mop up Wendy. We sat it out for perhaps half an hour, then the sky lightened, the rain slackened and stopped. Cautiously we moved off, holding to the crown of the road, uncomfortably aware that help, should it be needed, would not be so readily forthcoming as in Nyasaland,

At one point we passed a bus lying on its side in the ditch bordering the road. The passengers had scrambled out through up-turned windows and were now sitting passively for someone - the PWD presumably - to rescue them. There was nothing we could do for them beyond reporting the matter to authority if the opportunity should occur.

The rain returned sporadically throughout the morning but with less force, our progress though slow was unimpeded. In an unexpected way conditions favoured us for at the Mbosi customs post the Sikh was nowhere to be seen. Two dispirited Askari checked our passports, lifted the barrier to let us through, then hurried back to the shelter of their guard-post.

In this connection, at the hotel we had been enlightened by seasoned travellers of the route that the customs post could be by-passed altogether simply by detouring into the bush. It was easy to find the track, said our informants, but only if you were on the look-out for it. Ken determined to be vigilant on our next shopping expedition, found it and in fact we were never held up at Mbozi again.

The rain finally petered out, the road steamed in sunlight. For a few blessed miles the surface was in that state between mud and dust conducive to a less back breaking, less suffocating ride, we wound the windows right down.

We came to Fort Hill in late afternoon and passed by without stopping. The scene had not changed.

The possibility of reaching Misuku had receded as the day wore on, now we were headed for Chisenga. If Angus were at home he would gladly take us in, if not we would stay at the rest-house. It proved to be the latter, Angus was away, probably in Karonga, and his house on the rise dark against the sky.

The rest-house a sturdy, functional building just off the road, had been built by the redoubtable Henryk Knight, other half of the aforementioned Knight and Day duo, and used by him and the no less celebrated wife who always accompanied him on his pioneer work. The enormous built-in concrete bath, of which we took full advantage - there were no other travellers - did indeed bear out rumours of their legendary girth.

Next morning with the air still fresh and cool, we drove back to Kapoka, to the Kalengé, and on to Chisi where the carriers waited in spite of our once more being a day late. There we left the truck as usual to climb on foot to the summit of Wilindi and down to the lovely land, the friendly people. For once the eight mile trek was a pleasure rather than a penance.

Misuku had had rain as well and everyone was happy.

In our own double bed that night I said,

"I'm so glad you chose to come to Nyasaland. And not to Tanganyika, or Rhodesia. Or Uganda."

"Well, it was on account of the stamps wasn't it? Ken replied sleepily, "They weren't nearly as good."

CHAPTER 29

'LIGHT THE CANDLE / DECK THE TREE...'

Christmas was fast approaching and to our great pleasure, rains permitting, Andrew and Jess were to spend it with us. Indeed they too were happy at the prospect of escaping the steamy heat of Karonga for a few days.

"It doesn't seem much like Christmas though does it?" sighed Mary one morning as we sat on the top terrace drinking coffee, the whole of Misuku laid out before us fresh after a shower, Wilindi startlingly close in the washed air. I shared her thoughts of how it would be at home in England at this time. A real Christmas with frost and snow, Christmas trees, coloured lights, friends and relatives foregathering, the churches full for once.

Watching Wendy clutching at the coarse grass at our feet with a view to eating it, I also recalled in shuddering fashion the travesty of last year's Christmas offshore at Beira. The stupor induced by humid heat, the oven of our cabin, the dry swimming pool, the ennui of the few fellow passengers. And my own personal misery of pregnancy sickness. I started to tell Mary about it but stopped short, by now knowing reportage could not compete with reality.

"We've got to conjure up a bit of festivity somehow." she added.

"We've got plenty of drink, I said, " Ken made sure of that in Mbeya."

"Yes, well that's a start. But we need a bit more than that. A few streamers and things - perhaps we could make some. And get a bit of greenery."

"Oh, I remember, there's a stand of pine trees up the hill. We can get some boughs and make a Christmas tree. And luckily I couldn't resist those coloured baubles at the Indian store at Mbeya. I almost bought coloured lights as well but remembered just in time that they'd need electricity."

"What about Christmas dinner? No chance of a turkey I suppose?"

I said that as far as I knew there were no turkeys in the whole of Nyasaland.

"We sometimes get these huge wild birds called turkey bustards. I've only heard them, never seen one. We call them DumDum birds because of the sound they make. Ken says they're big and ungainly. I've no idea if they're edible, even if we could catch one, which is doubtful."

A good deal later I came to know that these creatures were bad nfeté, that is, birds of ill omen like the Ancient Mariner's albatross, perhaps because its call was akin to the two beats of the funeral drum heard intermittently throughout our years in Misuku. Perhaps three or four times a year the call of the dum-dum birds resonated from the terraces on the hillside below the house, Possibly they needed the steep slope to get airborne again because of their size. Be that as it may, it helped explain why the Chief and elders were quite happy to lease the land at Katobo to the British Government. Not only was its rocky soil too barren to grow crops, but it was known to harbour the manyega, the soldier ants. And for good measure, the unlucky turkey bustard en passant.

As for that mad Asungu, Waterfield, well, no good would ever come to him there, that much was certain.

"...So I suppose it's got to be the old athletic hen as usual then?" sighed Mary.
"What? Oh, sorry, my mind had wandered a bit. Afraid it rather looks like it."
We continued the discussion that night at supper. Surprisingly Ken, who normally never gave a thought to food until he was hungry, had his own ideas.
"What about the pudding? We've got to have Christmas pudding. A black one with lots of fruit in, and silver threepenny bits. We always had silver threepenny bits at home. And mince pies. We must have mince pies or it won't be any sort of Christmas. Can't you make them?
It was my turn to sigh, knowing full well that conjuring up Christmas puddings and mince pies would be quite as troublesome as red jellies and two tier cake for Steve's wedding feast.
Next morning I got out my Good Housekeeping cookery book and Mary read out the recipe.
"Flour? sugar?"
"Yes, plenty of both."
"Fat, and breadcrumbs?"
"Fat yes, and I'll get Enos to make an extra loaf and we can crumble it up."
"Spices?"
"Yes, I said feelingly. "I brought some out from home, Ken said they'd come in useful for curries and that. But somehow one of the containers was faulty and the smell pervaded the whole trunk. When I was unpacking some of our things in the rest-house at Karonga it made me feel even more nauseous than usual."
She ignored this,
"Dried fruit?"
"Ah." I said, well knowing this vital ingredient to be lacking. "Well, we'll just have to make our own. Shouldn't be difficult, we've got bananas of course, and local lemons and oranges which are seasonal, - a bit small and hard but still. Oh and I went really wild in Mbeya and bought a box of dates. We always had..."
"Yes, yes. Well that'll have to do I suppose."
So we chopped up the fruit, including orange and lemon peel, and soaked it all in the juice, then laid it all on a baking tray and put it outside to dry in the dependable sun. The result was surprisingly successful.
Of the other ingredients eggs were the hardest to come by but I asked Sutherland to publicise our need and soon we had plenty.
"Only about half will be any good, I told Mary, "We must test them in a bowl of water. If they float they are old and addled." (A method not infallible, more than once I had come across an embryo chick using this method.)
The next afternoon when Enos had gone home and we had the place to ourselves Mary and I went out to the kitchen to start work. She stirred as I, cookery book in hand, read out the instructions. When all the ingredients were assembled she said,
eyeing the khaki morass in the bowl dubiously,
"It doesn't look much like Christmas pudding."

"No, I agreed, adding a generous slug of cherry brandy in lieu of rum, "It's nothing like my Mother's. Not even like the one she made just before the war in 1939 and kept to celebrate the victory in 1945."

"Suppose we had lost?" asked Mary absently, licking her fingers.

"Oh, I don't think that ever occurred to her. But we were sorely tempted to eat it many times. All that food rationing you know. When we did eat it at last though it was wonderful! Rich and black." The very thought caused me to slaver at the jaws.

"Perhaps it'll go darker when it's cooked." said Mary.

With that she threw in a handful of tikkis - Nyasaland threepenny bits of doubtful silver - bad me have a stir and not forget to wish. I wished that the result might prove edible.

We ladled it all into a basin and tied it in a cloth according to the instructions in the recipe, then we put it in a saucepan of boiling water on the stove.

When Enos came back in the evening I instructed him to keep the water boiling all the time and on no account let the saucepan run dry. Several times I went back to check up. Finally, just before we went to bed, Enos having gone off duty and only old Khalokili the watchman in the kitchen, Mary and I went back to the kitchen to investigate. We lifted the basin from the saucepan, and cautiously untied the cloth. The pudding was no longer khaki, brown rather than black, but undeniably smelling like Christmas pudding.

Encouraged, next day we set about making mince pies, using the rest of the dried fruit kept back for the purpose.

So far so good. But there was still the vexed question of meat for Christmas dinner.

Ken had long since been in sporadic consultation with Chief MweniMisuku about an occasional killing of cattle for general sale, so that we might have beef for supper occasionally. So far with total lack of success. Now I urged him to try again so that by some miracle we might have some for Christmas.

"Not a chance." he said, "In Karonga as you know they slaughter regularly and sell meat in the market. Here the concept is still entirely alien to the people. Their cattle constitute their wealth and they won't part even with the scrawniest beast. He paused, "However, he went on seemingly casually, "When I did that ulendo round the back of Mughessé I came to a village where a man kept a few sheep. God knows where he got them from. Over the Songwe border I should think..."

"Sheep!" I interjected. Mary and I looked at each other and held our breath.

"...I asked him if he would be willing to sell one. Thought it would make a change at Christmas."

"Oh Darling, I cried jumping up. "And did he say yes? Shall we really be getting one? And how will we get it? And who will kill it? And skin it? And who will cut it up and..."

"I'll tell you if you stop throttling me. Yes, he was willing to sell. At a price, sixteen shillings!."

"Never mind, it's Christmas."

"The man himself will bring it over and kill it and cut it up, no doubt he's had

plenty of practice. Enos can give him a hand. He can do everything remember."
Mary remarked that she had never thought to get so excited at the prospect of
mutton for Christmas dinner.

Over the next few days, with the flair we had come to expect, she improvised
paper chains out of coloured paper from presents guiltily opened early, and stuck
them together with flour and water paste. Ken had one of the labourers bring in
boughs from the pine trees up the hill planted by the Forestry Department some
years before. We fashioned them into some kind of Christmas tree, decorated it
with the baubles bought in Mbeya, silver foil and any other bright objects we
could find. Wendy found it irresistible and grabbed at the lowest boughs. Enos
made an iced sponge cake and a quantity of biscuits; old Simbeyé returned from
Karonga with his battered satchel bulging and an extra bag of mail from England.
It began to feel more festive.

One morning a few days later, above the cries of the hornbills and the voices of
the labourers, came the long forgotten sound of bleating. Enos bringing in the
morning tea said, un-necessarily,
"Sir, the man has come with the ram."
By which he meant lamb, l,s and r,s being interchangeable among the Chisukwa.
No matter what its sex, Christmas dinner had arrived.
We lost no time in going out to view the rarity. The animal, attached to the
shepherd by a length of bark string, bore no resemblance to the clean woolly
creatures cavorting the springtime fields of home. It was far less attractive, its
grubby coat so sparse as to make it seem almost bald; altogether it looked more
like a goat than a sheep, I eyed it suspiciously. Fortunately Sutherland was among
the interested bystanders. He said firmly,
"Oh yes, Madam. This animal is indeed a ram lamb."
We settled for that. Mary and I in fact agreed it was probably just as well the
creature was not more appealing or, given one's double standards, we might have
felt regret at eating it. As it was I got Enos to tell the owner to lead the animal to a
shady place behind the house, where it could at least live out its last few hours of
life enjoying the tender young grass which had sprouted with the rain.
On the day preceding Christmas Eve the scapegoat, sacrificial lamb, call it what you
will, was lead early from its pasture and slaughtered well off stage. The shepherd
and Enos set about cutting it up. Ken picked out the meat for the Christmas Day
roast, and as much beside as we could cram into our newly acquired paraffin
refrigerator; the rest was given to the men for a communal feast.

All that day the rain held off, it boded well for the morrow. Our visitors would be
starting out from Chisenga, where they had spent a few days. We began to look for
them at lunch time but the day wore on. The labourers, very happy at the thought
of a night's carousing and prospect of two days holiday, finished the day's work
and began making their various ways home. Suddenly from one group a shout
went up, Andrew and Jess had been sighted.
Happily we went to meet them. They were no strangers to Misuku for they had

visited it several times in their early days in the District. Now with advancing years and increasing girth, Andrew was only too happy to leave the area to Ken, unofficial though the situation might be. Judging by the cavalcade they had acquired on the trek from Chisi, they were remembered with affection.

The greetings over, Jess said,

"I had forgotten how beautiful Misuku is, adding, "And how Wendy has grown!"

Andrew, breathing heavily with the unaccustomed exercise, remarked,

"I see Joseph Mkumbwa's coffee is flourishing. Glad I got him to go in for it when I did."

Which may, or may not have been true. But that was virtually all he did say until we were all back at the house and restored by tea.

Unlike Angus the Williamsons were both impressed by the house. ("Well, you've really got everything you need haven't you?") and Jess was generous in her praise of Mary's efforts in the garden. In the evening we lit the fire for cheer and the novelty of it for our visitors. Sounds of feasting drifted across the valley, deep voices resonating to the beat of the drums, the nasal tones of women breaking in with the recitative.

The drum beat, subtly different from the night before, started up again early on Christmas morning. Andrew and Jess had spent the night in the tent on the lower terrace, they appeared at breakfast rejoicing at the freshness of the morning.

We sat over a leisurely meal, the door open as usual, and watched the people, in Sunday like procession, make their way to the church. Some of the men wore khaki shirts and shorts in place of their rusty black cloths, a few of the women even had colourful nsaru.

Breakfast over at last we opened our presents. The ones from the visitors were largely edible. Dried fish from the lake shore, sweet mangos and guavas - they never ripened in Misuku - a fruit cake and, unheard of luxury, a packet of cornflakes ordered by Jess and flown in on the Beaver.

Our own giving included a pair of gloves knitted by Mary and me (the fingers some- what askew as we had no pattern,) for Jess who was shortly going on a visit to England. For Andrew there was a honeycomb from local bees, collected by villagers in hives made from hollowed out logs placed in tall trees. Ken's contribution, apart from the lamb, was a bottle of Van der Hum bought in Mbeya.

Wendy, naturally, had more presents than anyone. For her Jess had made a proper looking lamb from white terry toweling. Then there were the parcels from home, with little dresses, sun hats, soft toys, wind up toys, squeaky toys. On the whole however she still preferred the rattle Enos made her from an empty baked bean tin containing a few pebbles.

By common consent Christmas Dinner was to be a late lunch so that Enos and his latest acolyte Lamek, Umali the Williamson's faithful retainer, and the usual hangers on, could have the rest of the day off, Umali would, undoubtedly, later enjoy the unfailing hospitality of the Asukwa in the form of Enos' extended family.

Beforehand Ken took Andrew to look at the coffee on the terraces, followed by a tour of the station. While I was attending to Wendy - by tacit understanding there was no sick parade for once - Jess and Mary drifted off, ostensibly to go for a walk but in reality to concoct (cherry) brandy butter to go with the pudding.

Soon the delicious, long forgotten, aroma of roast lamb began to drift across from the kitchen. As we fore-gathered once more, with breakfast but a distant memory and pre lunch drinks threatening to get out of hand, Enos pronounced lunch ready.

The lamb had not yielded up its life in vain. It had spent most of its days foraging the sparse grass on the further slopes of Mughessé, so had little of the fat associated with its rich pastured relatives in England; the flavour of the lean flesh was superb. It was accompanied by rather small potatoes from Trisom's vegetable patch, courtesy of the returning rains, green beans, and more exotic vegetables brought by Jess from Karonga.

And the pudding? Admittedly by this time no-one was in any mood to be critical, but surmounted by a sprig of real holly included in one of the parcels from England, and laced with the brandy butter, it was very good. As Mary commented later, one of life's major triumphs. When we finally finished eating the gargantuan meal everyone was in need of a pooma - rest.

Things became very convivial in the evening sitting round the fire, with mince pies, runny chocolate, ground-nuts and an array of bottles. Not surprisingly we fell to recalling Christmases past, then moved on to more general reminiscences. Of which Andrew and Jess had, in the course of their rich and varied lives, acquired quite a store.

Mary asked them how they had met in the first place. Jess said she had arrived in Nyasaland in the 1930s to take part in a Colonial Office nutrition survey.[1] Based on an outstation called Mwera Hill. It was here she had acquired the African name 'Mwadyachiani' - 'What have you eaten today?' Here too she met Andrew who had been in the country some time, working for the Agricultural Department. Then as now single women were rare. Engrossed in her work Jess did not notice him unduly until the advent of a rabid dog, which necessitated a course of twelve daily anti rabies injections for everyone on the station. Needles were scarce, Andrew and Jess were obliged to share. It would be tempting to say that romance blossomed over the hypodermic, but that was not quite so. At the end of it all, the needle very blunt, Andrew, another so-called confirmed bachelor, went off on a short holiday to Salisbury, Rhodesia where he had leisure to reflect that fortitude and courage such as Jess' was not met with every day. Great was her surprise when she received a telegram from him proposing marriage. After some consideration she accepted.

As the night wore on we began to sing Christmas carols. Andrew, not noted for his musical ability, desisted, but finally made several attempts at a rendering of 'A Donkey Stood in a Field of Hay', a carol known only to him and destined to

---

[1] See Nyasaland Papers 1938/49; a dietary survey carried out under Professor B.S. Platt. edited by Veronica Berry and Celia Petty.

remain so, as he invariably dissolved into mirth after the first line. He was very happy by the time he and Jess retired to the lion proof tent.

On Boxing Day we packed a picnic and mounted an expedition up the slopes of Mughessé, where with the rain, a profusion of plants and flowers had appeared virtually over-night, delighting Jess the botanist. We hoped to reach the primaeval forest on the summit, but what with a late start due to the previous night's festivities, Jess' absorption in plants along the way, and the inclination of Andrew and Ken to turn aside to inspect millet gardens, progress was slow. No matter. The day was radiant, the scenery spectacular, the villagers friendly. Vlei lilies, wild gladioli, small, exquisite, and many other flowers abounded.

"Oh look! I exclaimed at one point, "Red Hot Pokers."

"Kniphofia." said Mary knowledgeably.

"Kaluateté in the vernacular." added Jess.

We did not attain the forest, but collected several specimens to be considered for inclusion in 'Useful Plants of Nyasaland', Jess' magnum opus. She also gave it out to people encountered along the way that she would be interested in anything unusual they could bring her.

The remaining few days of the visit passed all too quickly. Ken and Andrew went off on more tours of inspection of gardens, held meetings with village headmen and elders, and paid a courtesy call on Chief MweniMisuku at the Court. Jess, for whom days were always too short, began with contemplation of the of the splendour of the countryside, before coming to help me with the sick line-up, which caused the quality of treatment to improve considerably. She made further forays into the hills, and with Enos translating - for not even Jess had mastered Chisukwa -interrogated the people who came bearing droopy plants. Frequently there were animated discussions, and sometimes rewards.

Animated too were our discussions in the evenings, many and varied the subjects freely aired, as is possible only with old friends.

In Misuku Ken and I were acutely aware of the world passing us by. Virtually our only contacts with it were the fortnightly, overseas adapted, airmail edition of The Times, which arrived from London about a month late, and the vagaries of our 'wet' battery radio which occasionally allowed us to hear BBC World Service.

The Williamsons on the other hand, were very well informed. What with their subscriptions to several international magazines and newspapers, Jess' prolific, world-wide correspondence, and contact with travellers passing through Karonga, they did not feel cut off at all. They were especially informed about Africa, having travelled it widely, and followed public and political events over many years. Recently, as Mary had informed us, they had just spent local leave touring Tanganyika and Kenya with a view to retiring, far too soon for my liking, somewhere in the region. Kenya was at this time still suffering the effects of the terrorist activity of the MauMau, a secret society whose members carried out hideous atrocities, not only on Europeans, but on their fellow countrymen, the majority who did not support them.[2] Jess, whose preference was for retiring to

---

[2] See Nine faces of Kenya, Elspeth Huxley, pub Collins, 1990. And the history books.

England, said,
"But of course the whole of Africa is in the melting pot."
It was true. All over the continent it seemed, the 'Wind of Change', the idea of
Independence was gaining ground, the British Empire was unravelling.
On this sombre note our talk naturally led on to a discussion of the Federation
of Northern and Southern Rhodesia and Nyasaland. On which Jess had sought
to enlighten Mary and me in Karonga, prior to the Convocation of Chiefs and
the British Government in the form of Tycho and his cohorts. As yet Nyasaland
seemed little touched by it, Ken said it was doubtful if the Asukwa here in Misuku,
had in general, even heard of it.

Enjoyable as this time was, it was also tinged with sadness. For when our guests
left, Mary would go too, this time for good.
What can one say on the matter of friendship? Although I had not participated
in all her junketings in Karonga, she and I had been constant companions from
the time of her arrival some five months before. Her common sense, her wit and
humour, had prevented many a drama turning to crisis, I had come to rely on it and
now wondered dully how I would manage without her. Knew too that time and
distance would erode the relationship, making it unlikely we would ever achieve
such a closeness again.
Not only that. My failure to find her a rich and influential husband weighed heavily
on me as dereliction of duty.

The day of departure came and with it the customary early start. In spite of the
hour many locals gathered round the house to wish the travellers Godspeed. The
women no doubt lamenting the loss of Jess' superior medical knowledge, others
sorry that the lively discussions of, and sometime recompense for plants, were at
an end. Yet more, including Sutherland and ourselves, waited to accompany the
cavalcade as far as the Court.
The last goodbyes said, the carriers adjusted their head-rings, hoisted up their
loads and started off. The rest of us followed in single file down the steep path
bordering the coffee terraces. As usual in homesteads along the way early rising
women paused in their millet pounding to wave and call good wishes, children
tagged along in our wake.
At the Court the Chief, and a few elders wrapped in blankets against the morning
chill, were waiting. Through his interpreter MweniMisuku made Andrew a fulsome
speech, to which he responded in kind. Then came the ceremonial hand shaking
and expressions of good will on both sides. When this was over Jess, Mary and I
parted sorrowfully, the former promising that she and Andrew would come again
in August, with their son Tom, during the long English school summer holiday.
For her part Mary promised to write often; she said her stay in Nyasaland would
be unforgettable. Which rather caused me to recall her diplomatic reply to Gerry
Williams in Mbeya after the Spartacus film.
They left us, turning now and then to wave. We in turn waved till they were out of
sight, then retraced our steps to Katobo, not talking much.
Jess and Andrew did indeed come again in the summer, not only with Tom, but also

with Jess' sister, another, older, Mary. This made possible due to the completion of the new road, thus enabling them to come by Landrover.
This meeting was our last in Nyasaland. Andrew's retirement was imminent and to our great regret he - they - must leave the country. They headed for East Africa.

True to her word Mary was a good correspondent. Her progress south was leisurely. She spent a week in Karonga, where the bachelors to a man kept up their attentions, collectively and individually, until the very last moment, then perforce, bid her a fond farewell. During a few days in Mzimba she attended another fancy dress ball at the Club, but did not reveal whether she met Tycho there.
In Lilongwe she gladdened the eye of Colonel Apthorpe the Chief of Police, by staying with him and his kindly wife. In Blantyre she was met by the Persistent Pole, who persisted until the moment of seeing her off on the plane to England.
After which there was a break in communication while she was catching up with family and friends and sampling the social delights of an English winter.
When letters resumed we received long and interesting accounts of her activities but surprisingly, they contained no mention of marital intent.

CHAPTER 30

PAY-DAY

I missed Mary sorely, the more so as the rain which over the Christmas period had obligingly confined itself to refreshing early morning showers, now intensified dramatically. Young boys tending cattle went about the hills holding banana leaf umbrellas aloft, small defence against downpours from clouds which until now had brooded watchfully over Wilindi, biding their time. Now they advanced across the valley disgorging their contents as they came. The countryside was blotted out, our house islanded as a ship at sea. Rain cascaded down the window panes and punished the roof thatch, Enos and I must hurry from room to room with bowls, tins, saucepans, anything that would catch the drips. Frequently without warning, storms erupted and I would cower in a corner, clutching Wendy in my arms as the world crashed about us.

The commotion would die away abruptly as it had started. The sun returned, the land steamed, labourers emerged from the shelter of outhouses and sheds with mud squelching between their toes, delighted at the prospect of a good harvest. Enos requested, and at our expense managed to acquire, a real umbrella, big and black, "To keep the soup dry Madam when I bring it from the kitchen for supper." and a minion to hold it aloft. Which caused Ken to remark that even a good rainy season had its drawbacks.

This indeed was, seriously, only too true. Inevitably villagers got wet going about their work by day. Babies on their mother's backs would be soaked through and chilled, not even the proximity of her body could warm them till the sun returned to dry them out. Nor could sleeping on the earth floor of the hut with their mothers, with little or no covering, during cold nights, do anything to help the matter.

No wonder colds, coughs and fevers were rife, the young especially vulnerable; no wonder the sick line-up lengthened every day. Since becoming a mother myself my awareness had increased, and with it the sense of my own inadequacy, both as to knowledge, and lack of any effective means of alleviating the situation.

We had no visitors at this time, not even Angus Day. Either, with Mary's departure he lacked the incentive to make the difficult journey, or else he was preoccupied with his precious roads, grinding through mud from one damaged bridge, one washed out culvert to another, like a demented Dutch boy plugging holes in the dyke.

Thus our lives were bounded by the close confines of the station, virtually our only link with the outside world old Simbeyé when he returned from Karonga every ten days or so with the mail. One day was much like another. Ken made only daytime ulendos, the outlying villages must be left to their own devices till the weather improved. A state of affairs which assuredly troubled the villagers very little.

He did of necessity undertake one journey. This was to Chisi, to drive the truck down to Kapoka. To my dismay but not surprise, he announced that even with reinforcement, the Kalengé bridge could not be relied on to withstand likely floods. Therefore he must leave the truck with Nelson until the worst was over. So much for the all weather road.

There was however, one day in the month which stood out from all the others. An occasion fraught with trouble, dreaded by Ken in direct proportion with which it was anticipated by the work force. This was pay-day, a time not only of recompense but of entertainment as well, from which the labourers squeezed the last drop of metaphorical blood.

That it occurred monthly was greatly deplored. Without exception the men thought they should be paid daily the moment they downed tools, or failing that, once a week at least. Over time they had learned that Government in the form of Ken, was not to be moved on the subject, but they never failed to wrangle over it.

Predictably their earnings were bespoken well beforehand. Requests for advances were many and various, the reasons for most of them absurd enough to be dismissed out of hand. But how to turn down the plea of a labourer needing to buy medicine (ostensibly free,) from the Dispensary near the Court, for a sick child? Or to deny another in arrears with his poll tax when the DC's henchmen were due?

If Ken were convinced a case was genuine he made the advance. But always regretted it on pay-day. As did Sutherland, whose unenviable task it was to note it all down and make it accord with the amended amount due.

The monthly wages bill was calculated by Ken and Sutherland, and the DC in Karonga notified well in advance. The cash was brought thence by the DC's messenger escorted by two Askari; they followed the route regularly taken by Simbeyé, (and by ourselves on my introductory foot ulendo to Misuku,) and stayed in the same impoverished villages. Sometimes during the rains they were delayed by swollen rivers, sometimes they started off late if the DC had not managed to gather in enough revenues to pay out all the various Departments at once. If they were even one day overdue there were sullen faces at Katobo, and dark muttering. On the whole though, this part of the operation worked well enough.

On arrival at Katobo, the Askari saluted Ken and Sutherland, the messenger handed over the weighty leather bag and watched as the contents were tipped on to our large dining table and counted out.

There were a few £1 notes, some silver, and a considerable quantity of copper. When it was found to be correct, which is to say, that it tallied with the accompanying docket, Ken signed the receipt. The messenger secreted it securely in a button down pocket of his uniform, the Askari saluted once more. Then not wishing to spend any more time than necessary in this cold high place, all three made off on the return journey to the civilisation of the lake shore.

The routine of pay-day was always the same, only the aggravation level varied from moderate, to gale force.

At lunch Ken and I ate our food cramped up at one end of the table, Enos, (paid privately by us,) taking care to avoid, and not look at, the glistening pile of shillings, sixpences, tikkis - threepenny bits - pennies and halfpennies at the other. For once the outer door was closed, outside there was an exited buzz of conversation, the words nbombo - work, ndarama - money, frequently breaking surface.

As soon as we had finished eating Ken opened the door and called Sutherland in; he also was paid privately as befitted his exalted status as Head Capitao.

After Sutherland the District Capitaos, ten or twelve of them, trooped in together; they came from all parts of the district. From Chisenga and Fort Hill in one direction, from the Songwe area in another, from the barren villages on the far side of Wilindi. They wore khaki drill shirts and shorts which, mostly, had seen better days, and they went barefoot. All were educated to a certain standard, had a good working knowledge of English, and according to Government policy, were seldom native to the area they served.

This meant they could be transferred or moved around as the need arose. If for some reason their families chose not to accompany them to a new posting, they often took second wives there. This had happened to the local capitao, a somewhat shadowy and rather unsatisfactory figure, who chose to live in a village nearby, rather than at Katobo in one of the purpose-built houses on the ridge.

I saw most of these men on pay- day only, or if Wendy and I went on ulendo with Ken to their areas. The ones I knew best were the Mwandofi brothers, Bodwin and Nelson, whose adjoining districts took in the Misuku Road from Chisi down to Kapoka, and we saw them whenever we travelled.

Bodwin, tall and good natured, covered the high land including Wilindi Ridge and the erstwhile village of Chato. Nelson, truly one of nature's gentlemen, served the Kapoka region. Unsurprisingly he had only one eye. Older than most of the others but also tall, and rangey from walking his territory, Nelson had fought with the King's African Rifles in the 1939/45 war. His good eye twinkled; over the socket of the other the skin was neatly stitched. In what obscure skirmish had he lost half his sight? Had his service been recognised? A medal? A pension? Perhaps.

Payment of the capitaos presented little difficulty. Their salaries were fixed, moreover they understood the system. The only grounds for gentle dispute were subsistence claims, or for occasional use of a bicycle in the less hilly parts.

When all the capitaos had been paid and the £1 notes used up, the door was thrown open. It was time for the real business to begin.

First came old Kalokhili the night watchman. He was probably in his sixties but I could not tell, pay-day being the only time I ever saw him in daylight. Certainly he had nipped about smartly enough on the night of the manyega, but he was deaf as well as elderly and in no way inspired confidence. He came every evening at dusk and installed himself in the kitchen after Enos had gone home. Most likely he made himself comfortable there and settled down to sleep. Although after the night of the manyega, at Ken's insistence, he did make at least one patrol during the hours of darkness.

We had grown used to stirring momentarily to the light of his flickering firebrand, but for the first week or so of Mary's stay, she was unable to account for her dreams of hell fire and was most indignant when we enlightened her.

"He's not safe, she told us, "He'll set the place on fire one of these days. Nights, I mean. Why on earth don't you get rid of him?"

I had wondered this myself, but Ken replied that Kalokhili had been on the payroll for years, and was very reliable in attendance.

"Besides, he went on, "There really is nothing to be afraid of is there?"

"Except Kalokhili himself." retorted Mary.

"And ants and things." I added.

Simbeyé the messenger who came next, genial, scrawny, really was old. Unusually for Misuku he had lost several teeth, those remaining were scattered about his mouth like leaning tombstones. Armed with a leather satchel, old, battered, but prestigious, and a spear like an iron railing, it was his task constantly to tramp the obscure paths between Misuku and Karonga, on the move for three or four days, resting for a couple, then starting back again. Why he should choose to spend his declining years in this fashion was hard to tell. Ken said perhaps he had a girl in every port. It seemed unlikely. A more probable reason was that, being trusted by the people in the poor, scattered villages along the way, he undertook small commissions for a few pennies, such as bringing back a bag of rice, or salt for the people, which would supplement his income nicely.

When Simbeyé's legs finally gave out he was replaced by Akim, a jaunty young man with a soft insidious voice and a rare talent for teasing out new and ingenious ways of claiming poso - food money. Although of average height only, Akim had legs like beer bottles and, while in sight of the house at least, his feet fairly twinkled over the ground. If so minded he could, and very occasionally did, accomplish the return journey to Karonga in half the time taken by Simbeyé. With the expansion of Ken's work in the region, he also carried messages to the capitaos or village headmen in outlying areas, and sometimes went as far as Fort Hill. In slack periods he hung about the kitchen getting in Enos' way, or more usefully, keeping an eye on Wendy as I was tending the sick, when she began first to crawl, then stagger about the garden where everything was new and interesting.

Last in this group was Trisom the garden boy. 'Boy' only in the parlance of the day, he was perhaps thirty or so, his status fractionally higher than that of the labourers. In common with them, he was related to almost everyone else about the place, yet he was utterly unlike them in appearance.

For Trisom was light skinned and had a decidedly hawkish nose which quivered slightly when he was nervous. What village girl on the lake shore at the turn of the 19th century, had been raped by what Arab slaver to become Trisom's progenitor? And how had she escaped the chain-gang, the enforced march to the coast, deportation to America or the West Indies, the fate of so many of her countrymen?

In imagination I saw her eluding crocodiles and immolation in the fired bango reeds fringing the shore of the Khambwe lagoon, and fleeing to the hills where the good people of some village took her in, cared for her and helped her bring up her baby...

Not that Trisom displayed any of the qualities associated with the Arabs of those times. On the contrary he was the most gentle person on the station, much given to leaning on his shovel and communing with nature. That he could not at first distinguish our fledgling vegetables from weeds was hardly his fault, but this, alas, did not prevent my getting angry with him from time to time, for much was at stake. With Mary's training and Jess' brief sojourn, he improved. Strangely enough however, for the concept was alien to the Asukwa, from the first he loved growing flowers. So that the seeds bought by me by mistake in Blantyre on my arrival there, which I gave him to plant around the house, soon blossomed magnificently into cannas, passion flowers, morning glories etc under his care.

Kalokhili, Simbeyé and Trisom were never troublesome over their pay, the first two perhaps sensing their days were numbered, Trisom because it would have been entirely foreign to his nature to cause trouble.
It was a different story with the labourers whose turn it now was. All this time they had been grouped in a semicircle on the upper terrace, sitting or squatting, their eyes fixed on the open doorway.
Sutherland now began to call out their names. These were seldom the ones by which Ken and everyone else knew them but those they had adopted to distinguish them from their many relatives. Sutherland must now work hard to recollect what they were.
"Chabinga." called Sutherland consulting his notebook.
"Which Chabinga is that? queried Ken going down the list, "I've got three listed here."
The relevant Chabinga identified, came forward. He took his money and retreated to one side of the garden to count it.
"Chisumela."
"Chisumela? said Ken, "I haven't got any Chisumelas down."
"Yes Sir, that is right. There is no Chisumela written, but that man Chisumela has come in place of his mother's brother's son. The son cannot come himself because -" Ken swore softly.
"Yes, alright, let's get on with it."
The man, Chisumela or not, stepped forward nervously, took the money then turned and made off. Probably a complicated debt was involved.
"I can't read this one. Looks like Joshuwiré..."

In the rainy season the sitting room floor between door and table was soon patterned with the print of bare feet. It was not long before there was another interruption.
"Sir, said Sutherland, "This man says he worked for twelve days but he has been paid for nine days only."
There was further discussion, then Sutherland again,
"Sir, it is true. This man worked for nine days and his wife worked for three days. He says therefore that he must be paid for twelve days."
To a man the labourers knew very well that according to the inscrutable ways of the Asungu, women were paid separately. To a man they deplored the custom

and never failed to dispute it. Their reasoning was that wives belonged to their husbands, bought with the libola - bride price - ergo, a wife's wages belonged to her husband. Of course the outcome was the same, the wife would hand over her earnings as a matter of course, the man had only to wait, but it was a matter of principle. Yet again Sutherland must launch into the familiar argument.

The husband in question returned to his place, glaring balefully at his wife sitting quietly to one side with her companions, as if it were her fault. Not one of these women would think to question this state of affairs, it was all part of the unalterable pattern of life. Men did what they pleased. If they chose they could sit all day in the shade gossiping with their cronies or playing their complicated game of chequers. [1]*

She on the other hand would be busy from dawn till dusk. Beginning with the family's need for water. This meant going down the steep hill to draw water from the stream, trudge back up again, heavy water pot on her head, a baby on her back and, like as not, a toddler tugging at her nsaru. Should she by ill chance come on a man tripping down the hill unencumbered, she must be the one to stand aside with a civil greeting, and let him pass. Unless that is, he should by some unlucky coincidence be her son-in-law, in which case she must on no account address him within one year of the marriage.

Drawing water was but the prelude to the day. All her work was heavy, some of it back-breaking. Unaccountably however, although the women most certainly aged prematurely, unless trouble were visited on them, they did not look unhappy. On the contrary they were cheerful in their daily lives. The sound of their mingled voices interspersed with laughter, floated frequently across the valley as they went about their work. Two women pounding millet in a hollowed out log mortar invariably sang rhythmically in time to the alternate strokes of their pestle poles with a camaraderie I envied. It was all very puzzling.

The afternoon wore on, almost every transaction carried some confrontation. With the pile of coins on the table dwindling, those still waiting their turn eyed it nervously from the doorway lest it should run out before their turn came. The men already paid were counting their earnings and voicing their complaints. Ken exasperated by the noise, but not yet at boiling point, called for silence. "Sutherland, tell them I'll deal with their queries later."

When all the regulars had been paid, the part timers, for whom the term 'casual labourers' might have been expressly coined, must be contended with. They were hired, not just at Katobo but out in the districts as well as the work warranted. Because of its irregular nature both as to time and place, it was difficult to supervise and keep accurate records. The fact that clocks and watches were conspicuous by their absence, did nothing to help matters when the number of hours, or even half hours, must be calculated to a nicety, and the notional earnings noted down to the last halfpenny.

Needless to say those lucky enough to undertake this work under- stood the

---

[1] This game was played with smooth stones set in a square of hollows on a flat piece of wood and was said by some Europeans to be a precursor of draughts, or chess.

system very well and milked it for all they were worth. It follows therefore that discrepancies between their claims and what had been written down by the capitaos involved - to whom a degree in higher mathematics, and another in behavioural studies, would not have come amiss - were considerable.
It all took a lot of time and temper to sort out.

Eventually it was the turn of the older women. They were hired occasionally to carry out tasks traditionally assigned to them, such as mud puddling for new houses and the aforementioned plastering etc. They had been sitting passively in a group on the lower terrace, missing nothing, now they came forward one by one as they were called, eyes downcast. They never made trouble but held out cupped hands as if for the Sacrament. Then, fists clenched, they edged out of the door and resumed their places on the grass. The men closed in.

Last of all to be paid were the half dozen girls who fluttered like butterflies in the coffee nursery down by the stream pandering to the needs of the tender seedlings. Not for them old black nsarus. Languidly they moved between stream and plants in colourful cloths, gracefully they filled water pots and hoisted them on their heads, well aware of the admiring glances of the men working on the terraces above.
Here there were no disputes over money, but no lack of confusion either. It too was about names, but for a different reason. Dissatisfied with the boring old tribal ones given them at birth, they devised themselves more glamourous ones. Lyness, (Lioness?) Winessé, Alisi - after Alice Udd perhaps - which they now failed to recognise until nudged by their giggling companions. Then they came forward boldly Not yet locked into the system there was a fair chance these girls would persuade their fathers to return some of their earnings to them in the form of a bangle, or bead necklace which as they all knew, would do nothing to hinder their chances in the marriage market.

With everyone finally paid it was time for the real entertainment to begin in the form of complaints and allowances. Foremost among them, apart from the plea for medicine money, the less orthodox advances so vitally urgent at the time, now conveniently forgotten, were wrangled over at length, and with such intensity that Ken declared he would refuse ALL advances unless they were paid back promptly and without argument.
Allowances were of a different order. They too were noted down by Sutherland or the relevant capitao, they too were difficult to regulate. Men were paid extra if they worked away from home, on the road gang for instance, or acted as carriers. In Misuku there was never any shortage of volunteers for the latter. They would in most cases be virtually on home ground, and it made a nice change from the routine of everyday life. An allowance was also made if a labourer used his own tools - hoes, axes, grass knives, spades - always in short supply at Katobo. That they invariably claimed to have used these implements simultaneously, all day, every day, may not have been surprising, but in spite of the well known fact that they would be paid only for one, they never failed to try it.

By this time, the amounts being paid out being small, there was often a scarcity of change left to meet individual needs. Then Ken, Sutherland, the other capitaos, and even Enos, who enjoyed the proceedings hugely although he was not involved, went through their pockets, while I hunted in my purse for coppers. If our combined efforts failed it followed sometimes, that two men must share a tikki - threepenny bit - or even a sixpence, a concept quite alien, and viewed with deep suspicion. It needed all Sutherland's tact and mathematical skill to explain it, by which time even he was beginning to wilt.

One might suppose that with settlement of the above, plus one or two other minor matters arising, the proceedings would be at an end, but worse was to come. There yet remained the vexed question of poso.
Poso! A word to cause the hearts of administrators all over the country to plummet. Its meaning originally was the food freely given to all travellers, - the carriers in this case - by villagers according to their ancient tradition of hospitality.
Latterly however, if the people were poor, which was often the case in Misuku, Government officers on ulendo would make discreet payment to the village headman for food provided. In the unlikely event of food not being forthcoming, the carriers were given money in lieu with which to buy it for themselves. As with the exaggerated claims over tools, the men always tried to claim money even if hospitality had already been extended. If Ken or a capitao had been present on the occasion the matter was summarily dealt with, if not the argument went on and on. Poso claims were never settled to everyone's satisfaction.

The proceedings were officially over at last but some of the men still lingered, complaining they had been short changed, pointing to the few remaining coins on the table and claiming they were rightly theirs. Patiently, routinely, Sutherland explained that this money was to pay those unavoidably absent.
Ken refused to enter into it further. He shook hands with all the capitaos, they would spend the night in the houses on the ridge. Probably some of the labourers' wives would cook for them.
The knot of labourers continued to argue among themselves, but half-heartedly, well knowing they were the lucky ones, the privileged few to have paid employment, that there were many who envied them and would be glad to take their place. They too dispersed eventually, weaving their ways along the vague paths to their homesteads with dusk coming on.
Ken came inside, shut the door firmly and slumped down in the big armchair. Unprompted Enos came in with a tray of drinks, Ken poured himself a stiff whiskey.

CHAPTER 31

COFFEE BREAK

The coffee bushes on the terraced hillside below the house were now in full bloom, their white blossom felicitously set off by dark glossy leaves. Altogether a beautiful sight, fully justifying Ken's eulogies that coffee was a fine crop to grow.

Not that beauty at large had too much consideration at this time. The purpose was to demonstrate to all and sundry, what could be achieved with hard work and persistence, on such poor stony land.

Soon the blossom would be succeeded by the so-called cherry, the red casing containing twin coffee beans

The seedlings down by the stream, in the nursery on which the whole future of the Cooperative depended, were likewise flourishing as well they might be. Cosseted like babies from the moment of germination, they had been mulched, shaded and watered continuously. Not only did Ken inspect them every morning, but often in the afternoon as well. When everyone had finished work and gone home he and I would take a walk down to the nursery, taking turns to carry Wendy. Usually this was an enjoyable exercise. But let one seedling show signs of being sickly he would look very thoughtful and we would climb back up the hill in silence as he pondered the cause.

Disaster struck when the seedlings were shortly to be sold off to the villagers. Enos bringing in the morning tea reported that Sutherland was waiting outside wishing to see Ken urgently. Ken groaned, but drank his tea hastily, got up, dressed, and went out, muttering that surely the matter could have waited till work time. I called Enos back to ask what it might be about.

"Madam, there is trouble." he said with satisfaction.

"Yes of course." Trouble was endemic to our lives in Misuku. "But what kind of trouble is this?"

"It is the small coffee down by the stream. It is not alright."

It sounded serious and it was. In the night, or perhaps at dawn, some sizeable animal appeared to have watered at the stream, breaking its bank and flooding the nursery. Much was now under water, with erstwhile healthy seedlings floating on the surface or trampled in the mud. Ken furious, immediately mounted a damage limitation exercise. Blame as to the cause could wait.

Labourers now arriving were set to mend the bank and send the stream flowing once more in its accustomed course. The seedlings were rounded up. When the water level fell sufficiently the nursery was reconstructed, the beds re-formed and the seedlings re-planted in their accustomed rows. The rich moist soil of the valley bottom welcomed them back hospitably.

Amazingly, after a week or two all was well again, with irredeemable casualties replaced by seedlings previously planted on higher ground as a contingency plot

221

designed to gap up any failures.

As to the cause of the trouble, Sutherland tactfully suggested it was due to a warthog. Ken thought it more likely that a villager going early to lead his cattle to new pasture, had allowed a beast to stray too near the stream and stumble in. Damage to stream banks, and indeed any infringement of water rights, were serious offences notifiable to the DC in Karonga via Chief MweniMisuku. Ken did not go that far. He let it be known that the culprit, when caught, would be reported. Needless to say he never was. A conspiracy of silence ensued, a night watchman was appointed to prevent further tragedies.

All through the preceding months Ken and the district capitaos had been holding meetings throughout the region extolling the merits of coffee growing.

"This would cost you very little money, they told their audience. "But only the work of your hands. If it is done in the right way coffee can be grown on poor land no good for anything else. If you do not believe us, you can go to the coffee garden at Katobo and see for yourselves."

A telling argument this since everyone in Misuku knew that only the very poorest land had been leased to the mad Asungu - Europeans. Village headmen and elders from outlying villages took up the offer in fact, but at this point of the meetings they would protest that even the poorest slopes were needed to graze cattle. It was then pointed out to them that if they continued in this way the land would become more eroded every year until the higher slopes would become bare rock, like Wilindi, and support no cattle at all. This mantra was reiterated at all gatherings, Ken especially extolling the advantages of such a scheme. He told the villagers, "Coffee grown on terraces improves the land. If you prepare terraces, Government will sell you coffee seedlings cheaply. And when the bushes grow and start to bear, Government will buy your coffee at a fair price."

The men would listen gravely. The thought of a cash crop was attractive of course, the thought of all the labour involved was less so. The capitaos followed up this message, reinforced the gospel, spelled out details, putting in the metaphorical spadework..

Of course the great stumbling block to all this was the hard graft that must precede any reward. First of all the terraces must be hacked out of hillsides hard as concrete. Next scarce soil must be garnered to make beds on them ready to receive the seedlings. As at Katobo the young plants must be watered assiduously in the dry season, they must be mulched, and in some cases shaded. At times they must even be bribed to grow by offerings of cattle dung which, according to the mad Asungu held nfité -magic properties. And on top of all this, they must wait for at least three seasons for the bushes to grow and bear coffee.

No wonder they hesitated, no surprise that their response was invariably the same,

"Sir, this work is too much for our wives. They have no time to do this."

Ken's assertion that they should undertake the work themselves was always received with shocked silence.

It was not that the men were inherently idle. Indeed at certain times they worked very hard. On breaking ground for a new garden for instance, or communally building a hut which traditionally must be finished in one day, to accommodate a new wife, or relative. Rather it was that the role of men forged out by need in the mists of antiquity had largely disappeared. There was very little hunting for food these days, and no fighting at all. As they saw it this was not their fault. Neither was the fact that the role of women was pretty much the same as it always had been.

In any case everyone knew men were superior to women. Women could not discuss weighty matters, make important decisions, these undoubtedly were male functions.

In the weeks after the meetings the men would hold their own palavers, thrash out the intention of growing coffee, or not, with the village headmen and elders.

In time the capitaos reported back to Ken that opinion on the whole was favourable, but then, they knew that that was what he wanted to hear.

He himself was doubtful if the project would, literally, get off the ground. And this not only because of the people's natural reluctance. He was also fighting on another front.

He had written to a new PAO in Mzimba, who knew the Northern Province very little and Misuku not at all, asking that if, in view of the severe poverty in the region, as a goodwill gesture in this first year, the seedlings could be given, rather than sold, to villagers who had prepared terraces to the required standard. Back came the reply to the effect that if the plants were once given away no-one would be willing to pay for them in future years. Moreover, that on the whole, people did not fully appreciate something freely given. The coffee enterprise was a Cooperative, money had been already been spent on it, now it must be self supporting.

Perhaps he was right, certainly the people of Great Britain whose taxes helped to prop up this expensive Territory, would have agreed with him. But it did not make Ken's work any easier. Especially as the PAO stipulated that the price was to be fixed at two pence per seedling, rather than at one penny as Ken had visualised.

"If only he would come up here and see for himself, he said gloomily, "Then he'd see just how things are. Some of these people virtually don't handle money from one year's end to the other. We shall never sell at that price."

Indeed it was difficult to see where the money could come from. However the die was cast, there was nothing for it but for the sell-off to go ahead.

In order to have the least chance of success the sale must be widely publicised and well organised. The wet season ran approximately from December to April, we were now well into January, and the scheme running late because of the ravages of the unknown beast that had flooded the nursery. Clearly a day must be fixed without delay. Ken and Sutherland consulted and a date in mid February was agreed. At that time it could reasonably be expected that the soil would still be moist, but less likely to be deluged by storms. If the rains held out as they should, the newly planted seedlings would become established in favourable conditions. The capitaos were instructed to publicise the date verbally to all and sundry and redouble their proselytising efforts over the whole region. Ken told them he would be sending them kalatas - forms - which must be given to each would-be buyer. An act of faith since few of them could read, but records must be kept for officialdom.

To this end, over the next few evenings he and I, with rather smudgy carbon paper, replicated a form indicating the date, time and place of sale. It had a space for the buyer's name, the number of plants he required, and the cost. At the bottom of the form was a space for the capitao to sign that the person named had prepared terraces to the standard laid down by the Agricultural Department.

When he estimated there were enough copies, Ken called the capitaos together to explain the procedure.

"Here are the forms for you to distribute, he said, " You must make sure it is filled in correctly. But on no account must you sign the bottom until you have seen the terraces for yourself and are satisfied the conditions have been met. Only when you have done this can you sign the kalata. Then you must give it to the buyer and tell him to keep it safe and not lose it, because he must bring it to Katobo on the day of the sale."

The final injunction was hardly necessary. Such was the rarity of, the awe in which paper with writing on was held, the people would automatically take great care of it.

"Be sure to tell them, he reiterated, "That only if they bring the kalata signed by you, and the money, will they be able to buy the seedlings."

The capitaos listened attentively then once more assured Ken things were going well, Which if anything, left him feeling even more pessimistic.

A feeling not helped by a story which had begun to circulate among the labourers.

As a matter of courtesy Ken had, earlier on, paid a visit to Chief MweniMisuku to tell him what was going on, promising to keep him informed of the proceedings throughout. Now the rumour ran that the Chief had said two pennies was a price too high for one seedling. The price should be one penny for one plant. It was true that the Chief had no ultimate authority in the matter but his words carried a good deal of weight nevertheless.

As we lay in bed on the eve of the sell-off Ken fell to wondering what would happen if no-one came to buy. The Coffee Cooperative, the key to his unofficial toe-hold in Misuku, would fail. Would the Department lose patience and cancel the whole enterprise? If so he would almost certainly be posted somewhere else. "To the Lower river probably."

On that troubled note we fell asleep.

Daylight again. I would have overslept, but Ken was already awake when Enos came in with the morning tea. We drank it in silence.

But what was this? What were the unaccustomed shadows flickering across the curtained windows? It was too early for the labourers, the work clanger had not yet sounded, the hornbills were still silent. Was it...? Could it possibly be...? Already...? But no, it must be women coming for medicine earlier than usual, anxious not to miss any excitement later. Yes, that was certainly it.

Ken got up, washed, dressed and went out. I too got up to attend to Wendy. When she and I were presentable I drew back the curtain. And saw a steady trickle of strangers making their way across the garden to the path leading down to the nursery. I drew my breath.

Ken came back and made a hasty breakfast, remarking as he hurried off again,

"Of course they won't all be buying. Most of them will have come out of curiosity."

By the time I was free to follow him down, a considerable crowd had gathered, with men milling about in the confines of the valley. So much so that the nursery was in danger of being invaded and the seedlings trampled underfoot.

"Stop!" shouted Ken. "Sutherland, tell everyone to go to the other side of the stream. I'm not going to start selling until everything is orderly and quiet. Tell the capitaos to make sure buyers have their kalatas ready. And the money."

"Good naturedly, for the scene clearly had a sense of holiday about it, buyers allowed the assembled district capitaos to shepherd them through the shallows. In a short time all were assembled on the opposite bank, it looked as if business could begin.

But no. It was unthinkable that an event of such magnitude could go ahead without due ceremony. A spokesman came forward and made a speech thanking God for giving them land on which to grow coffee. (Sutherland supplementing Ken's shaky Chisukwa made it sound rather a dubious privilege,) and for Mr Waterfield's part in the matter. He went on a long time. Ken with one eye on the rain clouds hovering over Wilindi, concealed his impatience and scepticism as best he could. At the first opportunity he cut in,

"Yes, this is a great opportunity for the people of Misuku. If you work hard, for a modest price..."

He got no further. The spokesman, for whom the foregoing had clearly been but a preamble, interrupted,

"Sir, two pennies for one seedling is too strong. Chief MweniMisuku has said the price must be penny penny."

A chorus of assent followed, it was a delicate situation. Above the buzz Ken said firmly,

"It is true that MweniMisuku is your Chief. But it is Government who brought this good thing among you. So it is Government who sets the price. And Government has said the price must be two pennies."

More muttering. Ken pushed on,

"Do you wish to see these plants dug up because you will not pay this small price? And carried to the South to add to the gardens of men who are already rich with coffee growing?"

It was a telling argument, a hush fell on the crowd, I held my breath. Ken seizing the moment, called,

"Bodwin, call the first man over the bridge. One at a time now or the bridge will collapse."

Another pause. For an instant it looked as if the bluff had failed. Then, slowly, carefully, with the air of one crossing the Rubicon, a man shuffled on to the pole bridge amid the half hearted cheers of his friends. On the nursery side he was received by two more capitaos, one to collect the note, the other to take the money. Ken told them to make sure the money and the number of seedlings tallied.

The ice broken other people moved forward, the pace quickened. Soon there was an eager press.

The money. Where had it come from? The immediate source was, of course, evident. Some produced it from a knotted corner of their nsaru, others wore the holed pennies strung on chingwe - bark twine - round their necks. But how in the wider context of their economy had they come by it?

Admittedly the amounts were small. Most were able to afford only a dozen plants or so. But that added up to 24 pence - two shillings - the equivalent of 2 day's pay for those lucky enough to have jobs.

It follows therefore that the labourers at Katobo were foremost among the buyers, the fortunate few, on whom the message was not lost because they had worked on the scheme from the start and seen the results. Several had asked for advances on their pay, not just for themselves but to help members of their families also wishing to buy. For once Ken had agreed, knowing there would be more aggravation on pay-day, but worth it for once.

Secondly there were a few itinerant traders who laboriously carried up sacks of rice or salt on their heads, from Karonga, selling it in the villages, making a small profit on each small transaction.

Undoubtedly however such being the nature of international economics, ethical or not, the bulk of the money came from South Africa in the form of remittances made by husbands or sons working in the mines.

At any rate, from whatever source, the cash though handed over with reluctance, was eventually forthcoming.

Parting with the kalata was likewise painful. Perhaps some had the idea that with a bit of clever manoeuvring, it might be of use again at some later date, but mainly they wished to keep them for intrinsic value alone.

Be that as it may the routine, once established, went smoothly enough, though once they had attained the nursery, some men tried to pick out the biggest, strongest looking plants and others demanded that weedier specimens should be thrown in for nothing.

When at last they were persuaded to leave they re-crossed the stream still protesting, wrapped their booty in banana leaves and tied the bundle round with chingwe. Then they sat down to wait for their friends, with the air of farmers at a market prepared to make a day of it.

Except, that is, for a small group of older men, prominent from the start, who perhaps spent as much as five whole shillings. Each of them had brought their several wives along, colourfully dressed, partly to carry the plants but mainly for prestige and to show off the wealth of their husbands. These men talked gravely to one another for a while, then their purchases completed to the astonished admiration of the crowd, they re-assembled their retinues and in dignified fashion set off back to their villages.

So the sale proceeded. Distant thunder rumbled but the rain held off. At one point it seemed that demand might outstrip supply. But no, an insignificant number of plants remained as the last man re-crossed the stream.

Gradually the crowd thinned, the place became quiet; the nursery was a scene of desolation.

As already mentioned coffee growing was not entirely new to Misuku. Mr Lilford had started up a plantation in the 1930s. Perhaps with Lilford's encouragement, and seed supplied by him, one or two villagers had followed suit but only Joseph Mkumbwa appeared to have bean successful. Old now, he was very rich by Misuku standards, with a large homestead near the Court to accommodate his wives and children.

The present Cooperative was the first attempt to grow it in the area on a wider scale. Why had the sale succeeded? What had tipped the balance? Ken said it was solely to do with the efforts he and the capitaos had put in in the districts over time, plus all the publicity and organisation of the sale itself. My thoughts were quite different. On ulendo with Ken I had observed the women who, though not allowed to attend meetings or take part in the village moot, remained in the shadows, fully aware of what was going on.

The advantages of having a cash crop would not be lost on them. True the burden of the work would fall on them, but if the men could be persuaded to play their part as the Nsungu (Ken) had suggested, who knew what might become of it?

There might be money for a son's schooling so that he would go on to be a capitao, or even a teacher and not have to go away to the mines. Or he might become a coffee farmer here in Misuku and grow very rich. Why, it was not outside the realms of possibility that she herself might one day have a coloured nsaru to wear to church on Sundays.

Whatever the reason the Cooperative was now established. Most of the tiny coffee gardens survived and even flourished. Most people increased their holdings every year and the sale of seedlings at Katobo became an annual event. Until at Ken's suggestion, unofficially at first, later with the Department's blessing, villagers were encouraged to start up their own nurseries. In the first instance they were given seed berries from the bearing bushes at Katobo, subsequently they saved their own. The resultant seedlings were distributed among those with terraces made ready as before.

By the time we left Misuku several years later a few hundred tons of coffee found its way annually to Kapoka, thence to be carried south by Government lorry.

That the promised fair price fluctuated according to world markets, though inevitable, was a concept not easy for the villagers to grasp or accept. If it fell, there was suspicion and discontent all round. If one year it was unexpectedly high, well, that was only as it should be. The cream on the coffee one might say.

CHAPTER 3 2

BUYING COTTON ON THE LAKE SHORE

That night Ken found a tadpole in his soup. There was nothing surprising in this, or even rare, for with the onset of the rains the furrow carrying our water supply abounded with them, and as the season went on that part of the garden was soon alive with baby frogs. Fortunately, restored by drink and a bath, and above all by having brought the seedlings sell-off to a successful conclusion, he was in high good humour.

"Actually, he said, "It was nothing compared with buying the cotton on the lake shore when I was with the Cotton Board."

"I would have thought buying anything would be easier than selling, I replied, "Provided one had the money of course."

"Yes, you would think so. But that job went on so long - about two months at a stretch - and in conditions so dire, it was hell all the way."

Unlike coffee growing in Misuku, growing cotton on the flood plain of the lake shore required little effort. Cotton seed saved from the previous season was sown at the appropriate time, rainfall and the rich alluvial soil did the rest. Except, that is, for unseasonable drought, occasional flash floods which washed everything away, and the depredations of hippos who sometimes came ashore at night to graze.

There was nothing to be done about any of these, but by and large, the cotton survived somehow, and the people prospered. The only real labour involved was the planting, and the picking, Both tasks needless to say, carried out by the women, the men merely collecting the money at the sell-off.

"I was based in Karonga, Ken continued, "That's when I was living in the Cloverleaf house, but away for weeks at a time."

"Like Steve, " I put in.

"Yes that's right. Anyway, apart from the market near Karonga itself - that was OK because I could get back at night - there were two others. One at Mweniteté, the other at the Khambwe. Mweniteté was the worst of all, hot as hell, well they all were really, with millions of mosquitoes, highly malarial, But I never got it luckily.

"No other Europeans around of course. I lived in a hut on the edge of the mud flats at Mweniteté. That's where the previous chap went mad."

"I remember Mweniteté , I said, "We were dropped off there by the launch when we walked up from Karonga the first time I came to Misuku."

"Oh yes, so we were. I'd forgotten. So you can picture the scene."

I could indeed picture it, a more desolate place would be hard to imagine. Steve had inherited this delectable task, which was why he had been absent from Karonga so much during our sojourn at the Cloverleaf.

"Steve took Suad there for their honeymoon." I put in.

"What? Oh, well that's just the sort of thing he would do isn't it? Anyway, as I was saying, numerous streams come out to the lake there, as well as the Lufira river. They all join up in the rains to form the flood plain. Of course it's un-bridgeable because the river mouth gets silted up and the river forges a new channel every few years. So I was often cut off. If the water was not too deep I would wade across carrying a push bike aloft, then pedal the twelve miles or so to Karonga for weekends, which just about saved my sanity. Didn't cross alone of course, that would have been suicidal because of the crocodiles. But there were always locals waiting to get from one side to the other and we would cross together, all yelling like mad to scare off the beasts.

There wasn't much one could do about the bilharzia snails though, which also infect river mouths. But I didn't get that either thank God"

"Too thick skinned?" I suggested. He ignored this and went on,

"The first hurdle with opening up the markets was to make sure the money was in place on time. It had to come from Zomba of course, By water, on the Ilala, from Chipoka at the southern end of the lake to the Khambwe. About £25,000 pounds in £1 notes, silver and lots of copper, all nailed up in wooden boxes. I had to go on board the Ilala at the Khambwe to receipt it. That was the only bright spot, having a drink on board with the officers."

This too I could picture.

"But then it all had to be off loaded into the dinghy which bobbed about like mad, especially if the mwera - wind off the lake - was blowing. And it was very small, the boat that is, so I had to make several trips to get it all ashore and there was virtually no freeboard once the heavy boxes were on board. God knows what would have happened if any had gone over the side. Instant dismissal for Waterfield most likely, jail too for embezzlements probably. Questions in LEGCO for sure."

"LEGCO?"

"The Legislative Council in Zomba. The ultimate authority of Government in the country, directly responsible to Parliament in London. Fortunately I didn't have that kind of trouble though, and somehow it all got ashore safely.

Then it had to be transported to Karonga to be counted, by lorry where possible, by head loads across the swamp if the water was too high. Then I would withdraw what I needed for each market and get it lugged back again. At Mweniteté there was a big iron safe in the middle of the floor of the hut to store it in. It doubled as my table."

Here my attention slipped once more. I recalled that during my time in Karonga which coincided with Steve's tenure of this unenviable task, while Ken was away in Misuku, thieves had broken into the Boma one night. They had eluded the guard who had probably fallen asleep, and made off with two of the heaviest boxes, the ones containing coppers as likely to be most valuable. The incident could not have done much to enhance Steve's career prospects.

"....And once a market was open, Ken was saying as I returned to the present, "It was sheer sloggery. We started before dawn and even then it was hot and humid.

Already there queues of people waiting. We had one of those big old fashioned scales with a low platform, and a dial at the top. Each load of cotton weighed about 30 to 50 lbs (pounds,) depending on what the women could carry, all stuffed into home made wickerwork baskets. Longish, with a hole at one end.

The price was fixed by the government at 4d (pence) a lb. I had two or three capitaos with me, one of them did the weighing, the others controlled the crowd and stuffed the cotton into sacks once it had been weighed. There was also a clerk to issue receipts in duplicate from a notebook, hundreds of small transactions, and I paid out the money accordingly. You can imagine the fluff. It got everywhere, in our noses, eyes, ears.

"At first we worked under an open sided shed with a bit of shade but as the sun rose there wasn't any shade at all. After the first week the shed space, the Dutch barn you saw, was all taken up with sacks of cotton, We couldn't work in full sun so we had to get shelters made of bamboo poles and banana leaf thatch. Fluff was flying about all the time, and the air getting thicker. Except when it rained that is, but that brought its own problems.

So that was the routine. Simple enough in theory, a world of difference in practice."

"Like pay-day here, I put in, "Like most things in fact."

"Exactly. There were constant disputes. The men stood over the wives as they unloaded the baskets, then watched the scales eagle eyed. You got to know the trouble makers, they would argue over every ounce and always protested at what they were paid.

A further complication was that the quality of the cotton varied, due to poor growth when the rains failed at any stage, or perhaps because of bad picking, with bolls or twigs left in. Then it was down graded and the price reduced. That caused a rumpus I can tell you and was an ongoing source of grievance. This went on all day every day apart from a short lunch break."

"Not very lively in the evenings then were you?" I said, feeling a fair bit of sympathy was called for. He gave a mirthless laugh,

"You could say that. Sometimes I had a quick dip in the lake before going back to the hut when we stopped at last. Had to have someone on the lookout for crocodiles because it would be dusk dark by then.

After supper - I had a good cook with me thank God - I mostly fell asleep. If I could summon up the energy I cast an eye over the receipt books to make sure the entries were legible and made sense. Eventually when all the markets were over for the season, and everything wound up till next time, I had to go through all those blasted books thoroughly to make sure all the entries, hundreds of them, all in small transactions as I say, tallied with the sums paid out. But fortunately I did that in Karonga and had the clerk to help me. We bought about 400hundred tons altogether and I got pretty agile at mental arithmetic I can tell you."

Here my attention wandered again. I imagined the scene and began to grapple with figures. There were 2240lbs in a ton, that much I knew. With the price set at 4pence per lb weight, and the average load say, 40lbs per person, each would receive 160pence. Or, to put it another way, with 12pence to the shilling,

13shillings and 4pence. This presumably must be multiplied by the number of days of the procedure...But wait, there was also the question of the down graded cotton which fetched less. What percentage did that make up? And how to work it out? Arithmetic had never been my strong point and in any case Ken was still talking -

"But wherever I was I had to guard those blasted receipt books with my life, because finally they all had to go down to Zomba with the balance of the cash, to be edited. And if any money had gone missing, or if the sums didn't add up I'd probably have been sacked for fraud. All very well those for those jokers in the Secretariat sitting on their backsides haggling over every halfpenny, they should get out and try doing it themselves for a change."

We sat silent over this for a while, each busy with our thoughts, then Ken resumed,

"The market at the Khambwe wasn't as bad. It's nearer to Karonga for a start, well you've been there too, haven't you? Only about three miles along the shore. The Rukuru comes out there, quite a sizeable river, and when it comes down in spate with runoff from the hills you can hear the roar in Karonga itself. And there again it's impossible to bridge or build a causeway because the course is constantly changing as one channel after another gets silted up.

"In the dry season it's shallow enough to wade, but treacherous because of deep holes in places. And again the crocs lurk there.

There was no hut at the Khambwe, nothing in fact but the buying shed similar to the one at Mweniteté and the market set up in a clearing a little way back from the shore.

I had a tent at the water's edge if it was too wet to get back to Karonga. It was beautiful there. There were hippos wallowing offshore. And lots of birds. Bateleur, fish eagles, lily trotters treading the water weed, kingfishers, butcher birds and others. And there was a tiny island nearby covered with reeds and thorn scrub where ibises, spoonbills and different kinds of crane came to roost at dusk. They made a terrific racket till they all settled down as you can imagine.

"One evening there was a most extraordinary sight, one I'll never forget. I was sitting outside the tent with a beer just before sundown, when suddenly there was a disturbance in the lake. I got up to take a closer look, the whole surface of the water was heaving with fish - and innumerable crocodiles were rearing up off shore to feast on them. The lake was a cauldron of fiendish activity. The noise was considerable, the fish flashing silver, the snapping jaws of the crocs. And on the skyline continuous sheet lightning from a storm far out beyond the lagoon."

"Perhaps that was what had brought the fish in?"

"Could be. They were tilapia, the so-called lake salmon, very good to eat and some of them quite big. They were making their way up the Rukuru to their spawning grounds. The odds were seriously against them because, apart from everything else, far too close to the crocs, strung out across the river mouth was a line of fishermen with flashing spears. They were so skilful. Practised too I suppose, so it may have been a regular occurrence. The light was fading but I could see that each man had his catch of fish slung on a cord round his waist, and was adding to it all the time. What a harvest.

After the initial feasting the women would cut up the rest and dry it in the sun to eat later, or they would take some of it to Karonga to sell in the market.

Behind the fishermen was a line of stakes across the river holding basket work fish traps in place. So one way and another the fish had a poor time of it getting past all the obstacles and it was a wonder that any got through. Some made it as far as the strand where they flapped about miserably for a while, but others undoubtedly did go on to reach the spawning grounds.

"I had proof of this on quite a different occasion. One day weeks later when I was on ulendo miles inland, I came across a boy of twelve or so, carrying a tilapia almost as big as himself. He had caught it in one of the small tributary streams of the Rukuru."

So vivid were these reminiscences as Ken described them, that I could see the scene clearly. The turbid water of the lake, the snapping jaws of the crocodiles, their tussles with one another as they fought for the prey, the agile fishermen, the fish traps beyond. In imagination saw too the boy trudging home exultantly, rejoicing in anticipation of the praise of his parents and the prospect of a good supper...

By this time it was getting late. Enos had bidden us goodnight, Kalokhili had reported for duty. I had not quite finished with the subject however.

"What happened to the cotton when you'd finished all the buying?"

"Oh, it went down the lake on barges to a cotton ginnery at a place called Ngara. That's a processing plant for sorting and grading. It belonged to an old time Scottish planter who had managed to acquire land there before the Protectorate was set up. I used to go there and see him occasionally, tall and impressive he was. He hated Andrew, even though he was a fellow Scot. But it was Andrew's job to enforce the Government cotton scheme, see that the people got a fair price and weren't exploited, and all that. From Ngara the cotton was reloaded and transported south. I believe most of it was exported under the same Government scheme. But none of that concerned me thank God."

The subject was exhausted at last. In view of all that Ken had told me as we made our way to bed, I reflected sleepily that, yes, compared with cotton buying on the lake shore, selling off a few hundred coffee seedlings at Katobo, was but a summer's day picnic.

CHAPTER 33

SPEAKING IN TONGUES

A week or two after the seedlings sell off we were surprised by a visit from Angus Day whom we had not seen since Mary's departure. As usual he had fought his way up and over Wilindi in his jeep and driven as far as possible across Misuku itself. As well as the deaf and dumb cook he was accompanied by old Simbeyé the mail messenger, on what was to be one of his last assignments, who had begged a lift from Kapoka.

Angus as usual was well supplied with the gossip of the area. When he had finished regaling it he told us with a smirk,

"Going down to Zomba next week to see the medics. Got an ingrowing toe nail."

"Long way to go for that isn't it? queried Ken, "Can't you get it done in Mzimba? Or even in Karonga, the medical orderly there is very good."

"Oh no. Zomba's the place. Been there before."

"It sounds like a bit of a jolly to me." said Ken cynically after he had said his goodbyes and left.

"An expensive one surely? I replied, "The round trip must be over a thousand miles."

"Something like that."

In the event it proved to be anything but a jolly. For reasons best known to themselves the doctors did not stop at one ingrowing toe nail, but removed the tops of two toe joints as well.

"For want of a nail---"

In this case it was not the horse that was lost, or even a horseshoe, but one good foot. For a time at least Angus was reduced to a painful hobble. Admittedly the loss of two toes might have been more serious in someone less wedded to wheels, but it did not improve his temper. And he got out of his jeep even less.

Thereafter to our regret, we saw little of him. A bit later we heard with regret that he had applied for a transfer to the South where roads, even roads with tarmac, were regarded as essential, rather than mere daydreams, as they were in the North.

Given the absence of telephones or any other means of instant communication, and the reluctance of most of us to put pen to paper, it was inevitable that he, like Steve, gradually dropped out of our life. We never heard what happened to him - or to his motherless little girls.

We missed him and his unscheduled visits, Ken for his unfailing advice and practical help, I for his kindness and sociability. We also felt the loss of being able to turn up at Chisenga unexpectedly and be sure of a welcome at any time of day or night, As it was his house stood empty for many a long day, dark and lonely on the hillside.

The morning after the aforesaid visit Ken, having much to do, got up early to attend to the mail brought by Simbeyé. I heard him empty the contents of the old battered satchel on to the dining table in the adjoining room and knew from experience he was sorting the personal letters - a meagre portion - from the official buff envelopes marked OHMS which bred like flies from Mzimba, Zomba, and even from London.

After a few moments I got up, collected my share and returned to bed with it.

By now I knew very well that the temptation to open all the letters straightaway and devour the contents all at once, should be resisted at all costs, anticipation after all, being part of the pleasure. But as Wendy slept on I paid no heed and settled down happily to read.

From the next room came snorts of exasperation intermingled with scrunching of paper and the occasional ping of a missile missing the waste paper bin. For Ken too had settled down, not happily but with resignation, needing positively no self discipline to resist opening his communications. Indeed it must be admitted that he sometimes put off the task for days, and even then threw out a good deal after a cursory glance, marking just one or two URGENT to be dealt with later. Sometimes a good bit later.

Suddenly there was an eruption and a more than usually violent expletive. I sighed, suspecting I was about to be dragged from scenes of home half a world away, back to the immediate and obviously troublesome present. Silently I speculated on what it might be.

Were we to be transferred to the Lower River? A daunting prospect - but surely an unlikely one now that the Coffee Cooperative had got off to a good start? But then Steve had put in good work on the cotton on the lake shore, but that had not saved him. Could it be that some VIP in the Secretariat had just heard of Ken's unofficial status in Misuku and was about to seal our fate? I dismissed the idea firmly. What then? Had World War Three broken out un-noticed by us in our isolation? Or, even worse, could it be a dreaded tax demand? Gloomily I reflected that the last was the most likely.

Here it should be explained that in the Colonial Service of the 1950s nothing so sophisticated as 'Pay (tax) as You Earn' was in operation. Salaries were paid in full except for deductions for health costs, pension contributions and a few minor matters, and income tax was clawed back once a year in the form of a huge bill.

It goes without saying that most people failed fully to make provision for this, living up to their income, and that the demand invariably arrived without warning just when finances were at their lowest ebb. Not only that, it was accompanied by a dire warning of what would happen if one did not pay up immediately.

This had happened to us once already in the course of our married life. On my first arrival in Karonga, on Ken's first day back at work after home leave, he had been met by such a bill. Worse still, due to our travels, payment was already overdue. True an explanatory letter might have gained him a few weeks grace, but what with the wedding, the honeymoon - how long ago all that seemed now - and everything that had happened since, the Waterfield coffers were empty. Andrew Williamson had stepped into the breach and not only lent us the required sum with minimum fuss and no security, but had fore-borne to remind us of it, even though repayment was somewhat tardy. Such friends are rare, their kindness never forgotten.

I had just decided that, yes, it must be the tax, guiltily remembering the substantial cheque I had just sent off for books reviewed in the fortnightly airmail edition of The Times, when Ken came through to the bedroom. "Typical! he raged, "Just like those imbeciles down in Zomba. What sort of a world do they live in? They should..."

"Yes yes, I put in breathlessly, "Never mind all that now. WHAT IS IT?"

He paused. When the explanation came not one of my conjectures was even in the running, for the actuality was something I had never heard of.

"They say I've got to take my language exam!"

"Language exam?" I echoed stupidly.

"Yes. And if I don't take it, and pass of course, I shan't get the increment on my pay."

It sounded ominous.

"Did you know about this?"

"Oh yes, of course I knew. But there's never any time, there's always something more pressing on hand. Everyone in the Service has to take it sooner or later. Everyone puts it off, well most people anyway. Of course it's easier for the ones using Chinyanja every day in their work."

"So you have to take it in Chinyanja?"

"Yes. Or Chitumbukwa. Those are the two main languages."

"But it's so unfair, I protested, "We never hear either in Misuku. The people speak only Chisukwa, they don't understand anything else."

This was indeed true, as poor James our very first cook, had found out to his cost. His mother tongue was Chinyanja the 'language of the lake', and it was his grievance that he had no means of communicating with the locals.

A few examples will serve to point up differences.

CHINYANJA			CHISUKWA
Greetings -			Greetings -
Moni			Ndaga
Moni. Muli buino?"	-	Is it well with you? -	Eh Makora?
Indé. Ali buino.	-	Yes it is well -	
Aya, makora.			
Thanks -			Thanks -
Si como.	-	-	- Ndaga, Ndaga mawomba.
Potatoes -	-	-	- Potatoes -
Mpatata -	-	-	- Kartoffé. (Probably indirectly from German occupation of the North)

The two main languages of Nyasaland were however, by no means exclusive even to their own strongholds. Probably stemming from the days when tribes were nomadic, there was a plethora of minor tongues and much has been written on the subject since. As near to Misuku as the Khambwe region the people spoke Chikondé and, no doubt with a fair bit of overlapping, the same obtained all over the country. Unlike the Swahili of Tanganyika and several other east African countries, there was no lingua-franca except for the minority of people who spoke English.

In this connection however, one word, 'Kaya" , meaning "I don't know", appears to have been an exception. When early Europeans were mapping the country and asked what a place was called, the people often as not being tribal nomads, replied reasonably "I don't know." Consequently there was a sprinkling of places called "Kaya" on the early maps.

Ken, having worked over most of Karonga District, had come across several different languages or dialects, but unfortunately for him neither Chinyanja or Chitumbuwa were among them. Of course he was not alone in this, indeed most officers on out- stations had the same problem, though perhaps most of them faced up to it sooner. Nor was the thinking behind it as unreasonable as it may sound, the theory being, according to those responsible for the matter in the Colonial Department in London, that as staff were liable to be moved around the country, knowledge of the two major tongues would come in useful sooner or later. British people abroad had at this time the reputation of not bothering to learn indigenous languages, arrogantly expecting everyone to speak English. Yet there is no reason to suppose that Her Majesty's Colonial Service had imposed the language examination on Nyasaland alone, but on the rest of British Africa as well.

And if in Africa, presumably in the rest of the British Empire comprising one fifth of the world's land mass, on which 'The Sun Never Set.' As a contemporary poet put it:-

"And should the sea with stealthy care/ Throw up an island anywhere/ An Englishman was always there.."

So it is reasonable to suppose that in all these place there were hard pressed British Colonial Service officers sweating over the 'local patois of some three hundred words.'

Nothing of this concerned me however on the morning that Ken thrust the letter angrily under my nose. Knowing that by now he had a reasonable working relationship with the local people, I ventured hopefully,

"I suppose they wouldn't let you take it in Chisukwa?"

"Not a chance. No, I've just got to get to grips with Chinyanja. Or Chitumbukwa. That at least is understood in Karonga."

In the end he opted for the latter and in due course obtained a battered grammar from Zomba, over which he toiled for many an evening.

The examination was scheduled to be held in Mzimba in a few weeks time.

"We'll all go, Ken decided, "The rain should be almost over by then. We can combine it with a shopping trip instead of going to Mbeya. And I can claim expenses as it'll be an official journey."

I did not like this idea at all. The stores at Mzimba were nowhere near as well stocked as those in Mbeya, nor was the rest-house there as comfortable as the Mbeya hotel. Moreover I considered the whole thing a farce, a lot of trouble for nothing. It could not be avoided however, and the appointed day found us following the ritual of walking out of Misuku with carriers, down to Kapoka, negotiating the pole bridge at the Kalengé en route, the water frighteningly high after recent storms.

Ken, as he told me later, was concerned lest the truck would not start after its long sojourn at Nelson's homestead, for he had not had the opportunity of getting down to check it over beforehand. Inevitably it was so. Nelson's women gathered round me kind as ever, as I hovered nervously with Wendy in my arms. While Ken worked on the engine, I recalled a previous occasion and wondered what we would do if he failed to get it going, well knowing there would be no kind Angus Day to rescue us this time.

Reluctantly, after a sweaty hour or so under the bonnet Ken swung the crank handle and was rewarded with a spark of life. Hastily he leapt into the cab and revved the engine. We gave thanks to our hosts for their hospitality and said our goodbyes.

Late in the day we reached Chisenga and spent the night in the rest-house. Next day we made an uneventful journey to Mzimba.

Another rest-house, for we now had no friends in Mzimba with whom to stay. Ken left early in the morning to make himself known to the new PAO - the one who had been obstructive over the coffee seedlings. After that he went on to the Boma to grapple with the examination. I still bad tempered, went to stock up on provisions at the town's Spartan stores, seeing no-one I knew. At lunch Ken said his ordeal "hadn't been too bad." In the evening we went to the Club where Ken met one or two convivial acquaintances; I looked for Tycho Hassett or Gerry Williams, but saw neither of them.

Fortune did not favour us on the return journey. The rain which had held off so far, attacked us forcefully an hour out of Mzimba. Soon we were slipping and slithering on all too familiar mud. During a relative lull in the downpour Ken got out to fit newly acquired wheel chains of the type usually used in the Northern Hemisphere to combat snow. He got wet and dirty, his efforts abortive as the chains clogged up with mud immediately. We pressed on, veering from side to side, praying not to meet any oncoming traffic. We crept into Chisenga in darkness.
Next day the carriers were waiting for us at Kapoka. The rain had disappeared, now all that remained was the footslogging trek back to Misuku...

The expedition left both of us tired and dispirited. Only in retrospect did it seem remotely worth while when, a few weeks later, a letter arrived from Zomba telling Ken he had passed the exam, was now officially proficient in Chitumbwa, and that his salary would be enhanced accordingly.

CHAPTER 34

UNWILLINGLY TO SCHOOL

The boma of Chief MweniMisuku, the official hub of Misuku life, was about a mile and a half from Katobo. It consisted of the open sided court where Chief MweniMisuku handed down his own brand of justice on cases not deemed desirable to be brought to the attention of the DC in Karonga. Also a Dispensary in the charge of an African medical orderly. The Scots Mission church and school stood a short way off. Added to these the clustered the huts of the extended families of the Chief, the elders and the teacher, the whole enclave formed a sizeable village.

Many tracks led to the complex, including the one directly on our path whenever we walked out of Misuku en route for the wider world.

How it was that everyone was aware of our precise comings and goings was never clear to me, but unless we made an excessively early start there were always people waiting to buttonhole Ken with pleas or complaints. If MweniMisuku himself was already present he and Ken would confer on the issues of the day and I, an interested bystander surrounded by women, was free to admire their babies and in turn receive their qualified admiration of Wendy. From the schoolhouse would come the sonorous voices of children learning their lessons by rote. Until that is, our presence became known when they would spill out, the older ones anxious to try out their English phrases, always delighted to find themselves understood.

It was on one of these occasions that I was roused from my pleasant preoccupation by the approach of Sutherland and a well dressed stranger. Sutherland said, "Madam, this is Mr Chanya. He is the headmaster of the school."

Why did the name have a familiar ring to it? Silently I speculated during the polite exchanges that followed, then remembered the knitting girls sent by the Chief in my early days in Misuku before Wendy's birth, exclaimed,

"Ah, you must be Katie Chanya's father." He looked surprised, but in excellent English acknowledged it to be so. Then he said,

"Madam, Chief MweniMisuku and I wish to ask if you would come and give a talk to the school children."

It was my turn to be surprised, though shocked would have been a better word.

"But what about?" I asked feebly to gain time.

"They wish to know about schools in England." he said gently as if to one of his less bright pupils.

"Well, er I..."

He and Sutherland waited expectantly. Never had I opened my mouth in public, never had I felt the slightest wish to do so. Yet how to refuse? Faintly, and with sinking heart I heard myself assenting.

239

The commission bothered me considerably, even to the point of losing sleep. The thought of all those keen young minds waiting for pearls of wisdom to fall from my lips, and the certain knowledge they would be disappointed, depressed me sorely. How could one begin to describe the schools of post war Britain to these children?, The current preponderance of glass for instance, to those whose experience of that commodity was limited to sight of the small panes in the windows of our own house? And that was just the start. How explain that education in England was not only free to both boys and girls to the age of fourteen, but that it was largely unappreciated, even to the point of truancy? The concept, the very word, would have no meaning for them.

Desperately I cast my mind back to my own school days, beginning with the Church of England village school in the 1930s. A Victorian Gothic structure, with windows set high up to stop us looking out, which though small in the scheme of things, had seemed enormous to a four year old.

Centre stage in the classroom was a shiny black coal burning stove round which, in winter, a much loved teacher stood our diminutive bottles of milk to thaw out and in summer placed jam-jars on the top, of the wilting dog daisies we picked for her along the way.

In a noisy playground boys played marbles, cowboys and Indians, and the girls skipped in long ropes or played 'Sevenses' with a tennis ball against a wall. Occasionally boys and girls joined together for mad chasing games of 'It' or Stuck in the Mud. Somewhere along the line we all learnt to read and write and do sums.

"There's no need to get worked up about it, said Ken, "They won't be critical."
I was not so sure.

Revisiting this long forgotten part of my education it occurred to me that perhaps this first school experience might have more in common with Misuku children than previously thought. I recalled visits of well meaning strangers, friends of the squire or the vicar most likely, who spoke with funny - that is educated - voices. Their talks were largely incomprehensible to us, not only because of the way they talked, but also because the words they used, the things they talked about, were well beyond our experience. I resolved to keep things simple.

Having once started to look back, my mind followed a natural course on to the senior school in the town. My time there had corresponded with the 1939/45 war, with classes frequently disrupted by the air-raid siren, which necessitated hurried evacuation to underground shelters nearby. Here, due to the tunnel-like construction and the impossibility of supervision by our teachers, we read novels covered with plain brown paper when we should have been studying Shakespeare or conning French verbs, or covertly played noughts and crosses instead of working out the long division sums set for us.

Clearly that experience would be of little use to me now.

"Just do your best."
advised Ken as I prepared to set out on the appointed morning, armed with a long text describing contemporary schools in England, as well as I could in the light of the children's understanding. Unlike me, my companions, Enos carrying the big

black umbrella against sun or rain, and Wendy in the tenga-tenga basket with its two carriers, showed every sign of enjoying themselves.

Never had the distance between Katobo and the school seemed so insignificant. On arrival we found not only Mr Chanya and his assistant waiting for us, but the whole school, with shining morning faces lined up outside expectantly. This was worse than anticipated. Enos in the lead approached with lordly air, I followed more reluctantly, and was saluted by the assembly with,

"Good Morning Madam."

Then at a word of command all turned and filed inside quietly and in orderly fashion.

While this was going on the headmaster conducted me round the school garden, A moderate plot planted up to finger millet, maize and beans to supplement the pupils' diet, indistinguishable from other gardens nearby but for a small patch of flowers. The unexpected sight cheered me and I praised them inordinately.

I asked Mr Chanya to tell me a bit about the school itself. He said there were approximately forty pupils, mostly boys, whose ages ranged from 8 to16 years, or even more, the age limit depending on the ability to progress through the various Standards. Passing Standard 4 was the summit of attainment, the magic key to Government posts, opening up the possibility of becoming clerks, capitaos, even teachers, with all the wages, status and respect such careers commanded. In Misuku, only Sutherland - and Mr Chanya himself presumably - had to my knowledge achieved this eminence.

He then went on to tell me what I already knew, that most students walked miles every day to school, whiles others living further away must stay with relatives or others living nearby, thus adding to the financial burden on the parents.

As well as the core subjects of English, reading, writing and maths, they studied practical matters such as good crop husbandry and hygiene, the need to boil drinking water, the necessity of washing one's hands before eating etc, A forlorn hope, one felt, when the concept of microbes was not demonstrable and water had to be carried so far.

Once in a while a Scots missionary from Livingstonia came on a tour of inspection. If a pupil were really outstanding there was a chance of his going on to the school at Livingstonia for further education and training. Perhaps this was how Enos' father had become a teacher.

I would gladly have prolonged this part of the visit, but at last there was no putting off the ordeal. Leaving Wendy outside in Enos' care I followed the headmaster into the school.

Another world. Bolts of sunlight fell shortly from the open door and from two small unglazed windows on one wall. Otherwise near darkness. When my eyes had adjusted I found myself on a dais overlooking an undivided rectangle - the usual design of church or school in which Ken and I had often stayed on ulendo. Except that the platform on which I stood was against a side wall opposite the one with the wind-holes, rather than at one end, presumably to give teachers a better view of the whole proceedings. The other difference was that we had always had those places to ourselves, this one was crammed with bodies of various sizes. It came to me then that although a good many lessons may have taken place outside, in the rains this one classroom must serve all ages and grades. As the day wore on it would become even hotter, more airless.

The sound of Mr Chanya's voice making an introduction brought me up with a start. I focused my attention on the sea of faces, upturned expectantly, of the children sitting on the earth floor below me and realised with horror, that in the gloom I would not be able to read my notes. With a dry mouth I started to speak. After a few moments I became aware that another voice in the background - the headmaster was giving a brief translation of my words. Fool! Why had I not realised that few of these children would understand English? Indeed how could they be expected to when they so seldom heard it spoken? I went on more slowly, trying to enunciate clearly.

Nothing of what I said remained with me afterwards, nor had I any idea how long my talk lasted, but suddenly as if from afar, heard a boring voice droning on. With dismay I recognised it as my own; I stopped abruptly. In the silence that followed I peered round the room desperately seeking inspiration. On the end wall I dimly made out a diagrammatic poster of the human body with the principle organs and the blood circulatory system picked out in lurid colours. Next to it was a framed picture of the Queen in full coronation regalia.

No help there then. Turning to the children again I resorted to that refuge of dried up speakers and asked if they had any questions. At once a forest of hands shot up. I picked one out at random.

"Madam. what crops do people in England grow in their gardens?"

Here was a dilemma. Easy enough to say that in England most people had small gardens where they just grew flowers for pleasure. But that would be woefully inadequate, the gulf between their idea of a garden and my own being well nigh unbridgeable. Remembering my resolve to keep things simple, after consideration I said with truth that my father grew peas, beans and tomatoes in his garden when the weather was warm, and was about to add parsnips and carrots to the list, but caught myself in time, knowing these vegetables would be quite unknown to them. Instead I added rashly,

"But in England very few people grow their own food. Food is grown either by big farmers, or brought across the sea in ships. Then people go to the shops and buy it."

Once again I stopped short. Misuku did not boast so much as a shack selling damp salt from a sack. How then could these children visualise the size and complexity of English shops? And if that were not difficult enough to imagine, given that most of them had not even seen Lake Nyasa with its dugout canoes, how much more so would be the concept of vast seas trafficked with vessels of all shapes, sizes and complexity?

To my relief, before I was called on to explain the entire structure of global economy, technology, commerce and distribution, another hand went up, "If gardens in England are so small, where do the people graze their cattle?"

This was relatively simple. I said that few people kept cattle, the big farmers already mentioned had much land and were the only ones to keep cattle. This was received with shocked silence and I braced myself for the question that would inevitably follow. It came,

"How then do men pay the libola (bride price)?"

I explained the English mating system as best I could and hoped the worst was over. But one boy persisted on reverting to the wider issues,

"If the people do not grow crops, if they have no cattle, how do they get this money to go to the shops to buy their food?"

This opened up another can of worms.

"They have jobs to go to, I said, "They must work to get the money to buy food and everything else they need. That is how they get their money."

Predictably this was followed this up by another query,

"What sort of work is this Madam?"

I paused, trying to think of occupations meaningful to them.

"Some are teachers, I said at last, "Some work for the Government." This at least was safe enough. I hesitated again, "Some are er - "

Train drivers? Lorry drivers? Factory workers?

There were no trains within hundreds of miles, or lorries, there being no roads. And certainly no factories. Neither could one be sure they would even have seen pictures of them.

"- Carpenters, I went on firmly. Then with a flash of inspiration added,

"Some men go to work in the mines."

Craftily I did not specify what kind of mines these were, well knowing a description of coal and its uses to be well beyond me. But as the children digested this it came to me they would be left with the impression that gold was found in England, as in the South African mines which swallowed up their fathers and brothers.

I opened my mouth to redress the matter but even as I did so one of the very few girls - Katie Chanya was not among them as far as I could see - nervously put up her hand. She wished to know if the Queen kept her crown on her head when she lay down on her sleeping mat at night. This at least I could answer with reasonable assurance. Carefully so as not to destroy any ideas she might have about royalty, I said I thought not.

At this point I became aware of the headmaster at my elbow and turned eagerly to ask him to correct the false impression I had given over the mines. Alas he forestalled me and was already proposing a vote of thanks and holding out his hand.

Somehow or other I found myself once more outside in the glare of the sun, and managed to collect my wits sufficiently to tell him how impressed I was with the school, meaning it.

I made my way over to Wendy. She apparently, having long since tired of the confines of the tobacco basket had tried unsuccessfully to join in the activities of bigger children playing in the dust. Now she was resting in Enos' lap under a shade tree.

"How did it go?" asked Ken at lunch time.

"Not very well, I replied, not wanting to talk about it, "I'd never make a teacher. I learnt a lot though."

The next afternoon two girls came to the house, one of whom I recognised as having asked the question about the Queen. On her head she carried a gourd of marigolds and zinnias from the school garden. The gesture pleased me very much.

All the same the feeling of having failed the children lingered at the back of the mind, intermittently as a vague toothache, obtruding itself whenever we passed by the school. Not for many years later long after we had left Africa, would there come some sort of vindication, and that through no merit of mine.

As already mentioned, Wendy, grown up and married, returned to the land of her birth accompanied by her doctor husband. She became a teacher at Rumphi Boys Secondary School, the only woman and the only European on the staff. Coincidentally during her time there the school attained the highest grades in the country in History and English.

The headmaster was subsequently awarded an educational visit to England and came to see us. A happy occasion, when my only regret was that he had too little time to give a talk at our own village school, which was similar in size to the one in Misuku - but oh so different in every other respect.

CHAPTER 35

VISITATIONS

After Angus's departure from the North, with the rains at full strength we often passed several weeks without seeing any other Europeans, thrown very much on our own resources, our lives revolving around the microscopic world of Katobo Agricultural Station and its environs. This would be the yearly pattern of life throughout our time in Misuku. A pattern disturbed only by echoes of the outside world in the form of letters when the mail arrived, or by the unexpected appearance of the few stalwarts not deterred by the elements. One of these was our friend Noel Harvey the ADC in Karonga, who walked the District whatever the weather and was always welcome.

Another was Ragnor Udd, who being almost local, could choose his day to walk over to see us.

The Udds, the American missionaries in whose rest-house we had spent a lifesaving night on our trek up from Karonga though they themselves were away at the time, were our nearest neighbours by far. Their mission at Mubula on the edge of Misuku was but 7 or 8 miles off by the narrow footpath which wound its way up toward Mughessé, forking just below the heights, as I have mentioned, to give one the choice, according to one's beliefs, either of taking the direct route up through the crowning forest with its spirits, or walking the lower, longer path which skirted the tree line following the contour. Like ourselves, Ragnor, sometimes accompanied by his teenage son Rodney, invariably chose the former.

Another occasional weekend visitor was Oda Cerek, a sad silent Czech, very tough. He was a veterinary assistant living alone at Chinunka not far from Fort Hill. Ken who had himself been stationed there for a while, said living alone at Chinunka would make anyone sad, mad as well most likely. The very name meant 'bad smell' and it was shunned by the locals. Possibly there were sulphur springs nearby.

In Oda's case there was more to it than that. In Czechoslovakia in 1940 during the 1939/45 war, going out one afternoon on a trivial errand, saying he would be back for tea, he had been picked up by the secret police, torn from home and family and transported to hard labour in the Russian salt mines.

When finally released after the war, his body bloated with salt, he found himself persona non grata in his own country due to the political situation, and stateless to the rest of the world.

Somehow or other, within the accommodating realms of the far flung British Empire he had managed to gain the toe-hold of a Government job in Nyasaland, and had predictably, been posted to a God forsaken outpost, putting up with conditions no-one else would tolerate.

Why he should choose to make the lengthy and arduous journey to Misuku in his old jeep to spend weekends with us, was a mystery. Perhaps he hungered for family life. Or there again, perhaps anything was better than staying on his own at Chinunka.

At intervals we were as well visited by Father Butzelaar, a Roman Catholic priest of the Order of the White Fathers, known colloquially as the Bambos, who was based near Fort Hill. There were those who said he took the 'Father' part of his title a shade too literally, but we never saw evidence of it in Misuku.
Father Butzelaar always arrived unannounced, the first intimation of his coming the putt-putt of his motorbike as he blazed a trail down the path as far as the Court. Like Sister Schnabel at Lilongwe hospital, his accent was thick to the point of incomprehensibility, but he was good-natured and practical, always willing to give advice or lend a hand, so welcome wherever he went. He it was who surprised us soon after our return to Misuku, with Mary, when he picked up a brush to assist in a bit of whitewashing that was going on.
He seldom stayed longer than to have lunch however, his destination being the former estate of Mr Lilford some miles off, which after that man's death by lion, had been sold to his Order. The White Fathers had established a small settlement there with a school/church, under an African pastor.
After a while Father Butzelaar's visits ceased and we assumed that he, like Angus, had been transferred. We heard later however that his motorbike had burst into flames under him one day. He was not badly hurt but his motorbike was a write-off, was not replaced and we never saw him again.

When the rains slackened and finally stopped it was open season for all kinds of Government experts - agronomists, geologists, biologists, ecologists, sociologists, to name but a few - to lift up their eyes unto the hills and head for Misuku. Although often somewhat impractical, by and large they were interesting people committed to their subject, and we were usually pleased to see them.
Less welcome were their desk bound colleagues from the Secretariat in Zomba, accountants statisticians and the like, whose wheels never normally left the tarmac, but who either felt the need of a change of scene, or else had been told to broaden their horizons. At any rate they too would arrive unheralded, ill prepared and exhausted after the trek over Wilindi. With their last remaining energy, they would proceed to complain bitterly of the lack of hotel, rest-house , or even rough shack selling drinks along the way. We would give them coffee or tea as appropriate to the time of day, and sometimes followed that up with the offer of the small tent pitched on the lower terrace. Beyond that we did not feel obliged to go for there was seldom any meeting of minds. Fortunately they never stayed long. But if we were foolish enough to hope that, after their return to civilisation, they might appreciate our own difficulties, be less zealous in chasing up every odd halfpenny, be swifter in responding to Ken's reasonable pleas for vital funding, we were doomed to disappointment.

As opposed to official visitors unofficial ones were rare. One of the most unusual among the latter was not only elderly, but female as well. Given Government policy of zero white settlement which required officers to leave the country on retirement, in a locality where Andrew was the oldest person around, and he not yet sixty, where older women were even scarcer than young ones, she seemed positively ancient.

She appeared without warning over the rim of the lower terrace one afternoon during Ken's absence on ulendo, as Wendy and I were taking tea on the upper terrace which by then was smooth and respectably grassed over.

If the sight of this domestic scene so far off the beaten track, was surprising to her, it was as nothing compared with my admiration of her hardihood at tackling the long walk in. She began to explain that she was a botanist wishing to explore the region for a few days, but got no further before being interrupted by the appearance of a droopy looking youth in his late teens or early twenties. Their relationship was never made clear, Grandson? Nephew? Paid hanger on? No matter. I gave them tea, and told them of the red hot pokers and the delicate, beautiful wild gladioli growing in profusion on the slopes of Mughessé. I went on to describe the primaeval forest that crowned the summit, but said nothing of the ancestral spirits ostensibly inhabiting it, though I knew they would have trouble hiring guides to take them there.

I also asked if they had met Jess Williamson in the course of their travels, or heard of her activities. They had not. Furthermore with the disdain only too common alas, for research not actually carried out by themselves, they were very dismissive. I put

Mary's rondavel at the old lady's disposal however, but left the youth to fend for himself. Later I saw he had pitched a flimsy looking tent higher up in the back garden in a prime spot for it to get blown away if the wind got up, or washed away should we have an untimely downpour.

Thereafter the whole station was treated to the daily spectacle of the old lady issuing from the rondavel soon after the work clanger sounded and making her way up the path, sketch book in hand, peering about her as she went.

Her companion on the other hand, deaf to the labourers as they assembled for work, to the squawking of hornbills the mothers of wailing of infants en route for the sick parade, did not surface for another hour. Then he would crawl out of the tent looking very rumpled, yawn, stretch, and shamble off, oblivious of the beauty of his surroundings and of everything going on around him.

After their breakfast (which I did not enquire into,) the two of them started out again, having hired local guides. We saw nothing more of them till early afternoon when they returned, the young man still yawning, and settled down to drink tea and examine their specimens. Only once did the elderly lady venture criticism in my hearing,

"...After all I'm seventy two. Why should you be tired?"

Needless to say, because of Jess' visit, the locals all knew of the mad Asungus' obsession with useless greenery and soon we were once more inundated with people bearing wilting weeds. They were not disappointed. Intrepid and energetic as this aged Dona undoubtedly was, she was not familiar with the local flora and bought indiscriminately. Nor was she accustomed to bargaining; the asking price shot up to heights which would have horrified Jess. Needless to say the vendors were very sorry to see her go.

In our second year in Misuku the Udds invited us to spend Christmas with them, an invitation we were only too happy to accept.
Ragnor was large and ebullient, more of a pioneer farmer than a missionary, popular
with the people because of his geniality, his practicality and his communication skills. Alice was small and spiritual, but also practical of necessity, greatly trusted, loved one might say, by the women who brought their children to her for medicine. Alice had already suffered in her life as a missionary by contracting blackwater fever in the Congo, their former posting, and had nearly died. Hence their transfer to the healthier climate of Misuku.
I knew nothing of this as we set out on Christmas Eve to walk the seven or eight miles to their mission at Mubula. Ken had managed to buy another unsuspecting lamb which we took as a present, Enos leading it on a length of chingwe.
The Udd's was the only homely house I had encountered since leaving England, though so far I had seen only the rest-house in their absence, as already related.
Now I looked forward to seeing the rest of the place. I was not disappointed. By contrast with the austere bungalows built by the PWD for Government officers, all much of a muchness, all supplied with uncomfortable single beds, hard wooden chairs and minimum appurtenances, the Udds' house was spacious, furnished - over furnished even - with soft beds and upholstered furniture of their own choice, selected from the Sears Roebuck catalogue and shipped out from the USA. There was also a profusion of rugs, cushions, pictures and other forgotten items formerly taken for granted in England.
What impressed me most of all however was the integral kitchen with its wood burning stove and the biggest refrigerator I had ever seen. Later the Udd's house became a marvel to all, though we never witnessed it ourselves, for the electricity Ragnor installed with a petrol driven generator.

The Udds were kindness itself. All their children were home for Christmas, Rodney 16, who spent most of his time out and about with his new air rifle, Jewel, a pretty girl of 14, and a younger boy Timmy. On Christmas Day we were showered with gifts from missionary parcels from the faithful back home who, assuredly were not only affluent but generous as well. Wendy, a toddler by this time, hugely enjoyed the excitement, and especially the attention lavished on her by Jewel.
In spite of its being Christmas, though surely in keeping with the spirit of things, Alice had no respite from the sick line-up. Her ministrations were, needless to say, far more competent, more comprehensive than mine at Katobo. Even with this demand on her time however, helped by the faithful Samueli, she cooked us a wonderful, American style Christmas dinner. Altogether the day passed most agreeably.

At night Ken, Wendy and I retired to the remembered rest-house with its text.

On Boxing Day Ragnor gave us a conducted tour of the mission. It comprised a church, a brick built school with an African teacher, workshops where Ragnor produced most of the artifacts he needed, watched by several students in training to become carpenters or artisans in their own right. There were also several garden plots cultivated with indigenous crops, supplemented by others common in the USA.

He showed us the big American truck he had bought to negotiate 'Udd's Road' and told us that he and Alice never ventured on a journey without first saying a prayer. Having encountered the road ourselves on foot, I recalled the Hill called Difficulty and could understand why.

In the afternoon the men went further afield among the villages, Ken combining business with pleasure, the area being part of his district. Alice and I stayed behind chatting and drinking tea; Jewel played on the floor with Wendy. Presently a storm struck, rain lashed the windows, lightning danced on the hills, thunder rumbled. Suddenly lightning forked the sky immediately before us. Simultaneously a thunderbolt sent Wendy flying into to my arms.

We were anxious for the men but they returned a little later, wet through but unharmed. They told us the school fifty yards below us had been struck and its roof damaged.

I felt both envy and pity for Alice. Envy of the house which really was a home, pity, not only because of her impaired health, but for the faint air of sadness that she wore like an aura. Alice's sorrow was that her children must spend three quarters of each year hundreds of miles away in Uganda at a boarding school attached to the parent mission of their sect. Every parting was agony to her, every reunion an exhausting effort to restore the family bond. This had been her experience with the two older children for several years, now she was about to part with Tim as well. A high price to pay for her faith.

CHAPTER 36

"GENESIS OF A ROAD"

Perhaps the most unexpected visitor of all was a man who appeared about six months after Angus's departure. He was nasty, brutish, and short of breath due to unaccustomed walking. All the way from Chisi in this case. To our surprise he proved to be a PWD road engineer from Mzimba. Said his name was Jubb.

"I've heard about you, he said accusingly when we had revived him with a beer.

"Came across Angus Day down South, He said you wanted a road brought in."

"Er, not exactly a road..." began Ken cautiously.

In truth a full scale road was the last thing we wanted.

"...More of a single line track really. With passing places..."

The man paid no heed but went on to pour scorn on the very idea. In vain did Ken protest that all he wanted was a bit of finance and back-up. He could do the rest himself with a road gang, had already made a start in fact. Jubb did not even hear him but went on,

"Have you any idea what it would cost?"

His indignation at having expended so much time and energy in coming to such an impossible place on what was patently a wild goose chase, was matched only by his contempt at having to deal with such imbeciles when he got there. Then answering his own question, he said,

"Thousands. Millions in the long run most likely. And for what? Just to get a few hundred tons of coffee out. And that not guaranteed even."

There was a good deal more in this vein. Like Angus, Jubb seemed to have little conception of anything short of three lane highways gobbling up the countryside. An idea perhaps common in road engineers; probably their dreams were tenanted by such visions.

"Well I can tell you here and now, he finished at last, "The PWD hasn't got that sort of money. Forget it."

We were happy to do so. We gave him lunch but his temper did not improve. The prospect of the unnatural foot slogging trek to be endured before he regained the sanctuary of his truck could not have done much to aid his digestion. At any rate he did not linger. We saw him off without regret and to our relief never heard from him again.

Would Misuku have benefited from a proper road? Would the embryo coffee enterprise have expanded to justify it? Would the lives of the people have improved accordingly, or would the fragile ecology, the social balance of the area, have been destroyed for ever? Fortunately the decision was not ours to make.

All the same the matter of a track into Misuku for our own use, preoccupied us throughout our early years there. Always at the back of my mind was the terrifying prospect of illness or accident - with Wendy especially vulnerable - when we would need to get out in a hurry. True we had all so far enjoyed near perfect health, with no desperate disasters, but no-one had the right to expect that sort of luck to continue indefinitely.

Ken's attitude was slightly ambiguous. On the one hand he recognised the need as well as I, which was why he had already made a start, setting a road gang to work whenever (unofficial) funds permitted. On the other hand, almost subconsciously he wished to maintain the status quo, fearing that a real road would encourage entrepreneurs to exploit the region for their own enrichment, shattering lives in the process.

I did not share his misgivings. But perhaps that was because I did not want to.

"If there were resources to exploit, I said firmly, "The Arabs would have discovered them long ago."

I kept up pressure on the subject to the point of nagging whenever his attention, usually taken up with more immediate matters, was actually focused on what I was saying.

"Before we came back here to live you promised me we would have an all weather road, I reminded him, "That's the only reason I agreed to come with you. As it is, after all this time we have only the beginnings of a dry weather track. In the rains we still have to walk right out to Kapoka. Just how long is 'Eventually'?"

I knew this to be unfair, that I was preaching to the converted. For by this time with the Jubb-Jubb bird a distant memory, due to the success of the seedlings sell-off and the ongoing development of the Coffee Cooperative his presence in Misuku had been officially sanctioned and he had constantly badgered the Department for funds. Not only to maintain the existing track, but to extend it as a permanent all weather route, up and over Wilindi, and down into Misuku itself.

But my tirades were compulsive, necessary to keep up my own spirits, and to ensure his resolve to persist in what we both knew would be a long and difficult task.

Labouring the point, I repeated that during the rainy season, every journey undertaken to the outside world involved the long and arduous, time consuming walk out of Misuku down to Kapoka and all that it involved. Notably scaling Wilindi - the descent as arduous as the ascent, on the footpath trodden by the Asukwa for generations. They had made no concession to human frailty, the way led inexorably downwards, straight as a Roman road, regardless of gradient, deviating only where rock falls made the way impassable. In more than one place there was a sheer drop at the outer edge.

Only in the dry season was it relatively safe for Ken to drive the truck in as far as the flat saddle of land known as Chisi. During the rains the Kalengé river lower down, gorged with runoff from the hills, could be transformed from a rippling stream to a raging torrent in an instant. The bridge, even with Ken's modification and reinforcement stood no chance against such force.

Obviously having the truck stranded on the wrong side of the river would spell disaster; therefore it must languish at Kapoka until the dry season returned and we must continue to walk the whole way. A journey of some fifteen miles which took all day. Then would come the laborious drive to comparative civilisation...

This remained the situation for several years until one blessed day, returning from one journey we were amazed to find the Kalengé spanned by a CONCRETE bridge, stout, strong and high enough above the water to withstand all eventualities short of a spiteful Act of God.

Had we the PWD to thank for it? We had not. It was Ragnor Udd who had done such a workmanlike job. He needed such a bridge to take his big American truck, and as 'Udd's Road' road coincided here with our track, we ourselves were incidental beneficiaries. But none the less thankful for it. On such matters, insignificant in the great scheme of things, massively important to those involved, do our lives turn. At last we could drive in to Chisi all the year round and the possibility of an all weather track from Kapoka to Misuku was feasible.

Of course the new bridge lay unforeseen in the future at the time of my harangue. Meanwhile another surprise was in store. Not long after Ken's position in Misuku had been ratified, unexpectedly, funds for an improved track were approved. Road building proper could now begin.

Clearly, for reasons given above, the footpath down from Wilindi could form no basis for a motorised route. The real work of hacking out a track up and down the bare mountain side would be the most difficult, the most hazardous of the whole enterprise. It was this that Ken was determined to tackle first, reasoning that the rest would be easy by comparison.

Surveying is an abstract art not easily understood by the uninitiated who, in this case consisted of Bodwin the capitao of that region, myself, and even Sutherland. Ken on the other hand had a good grasp of it due to his time as a Sapper with the Royal Engineers. Which was fortunate, for now that it had come to it, to me at least the conquest of Wilindi seemed daunting as an assault on the south col of Everest. So much so that for the very first time I had misgivings about the whole project.

Not so Ken however, he had got the bit between his teeth and was anxious to get on with it. He borrowed chains and a level from the PWD depot at Chisenga which still functioned in Angus's absence, in the charge of an African capitao . Then as soon as the weather allowed, he set out with Bodwin to reconnoitre. Any time thereafter that could be spared from day to day Departmental work they spent tramping the foothills and upper reaches of the massif, peering round rock faces, following contours, assessing gradients, prodding surfaces and making calculations. Days lengthened into weeks before even a tentative line was decided on. Then markers were laid down and followed up by stake posts driven into the stony ground. By which time the rains were on us once more and work was halted.

The posts were regarded with great respect by the few people living in the vicinity and itinerant travellers alike, which rendered Bodwin's injunction that they must not on any account be damaged or removed for firewood, quite superfluous.

That however did not protect them from further rock-falls, or from being used as

GENESIS OF A ROAD"

scratching-posts by cattle, or being tossed aside by animals of the wilder kind. So that when the weather improved and work resumed, much of it had to be done again. A tedious business, but a salutary one as the need for some realignment became obvious.

It goes without saying that hacking a track out of solid rock is not the work of a moment. Progress was painfully slow even when Ken or Bodwin were present. It dwindled to imperceptibility when they were not. Delays were inevitable.

Nevertheless, snaking round outcrops, hair-pinning on itself to gain height, undulating in dips and hollows, the trail inched towards the summit. A summit seemingly so near in the translucent air, so distant in terms of slogging groundwork.

Witnessing it from time to time as we continued to walk out, I noted the places where it clung precariously to the rock face, no more than a narrow ledge in some places, with sheer drops at the outer edge, and reflected that it would not be a ride for the faint hearted. Indeed it seemed to me that once word had got around, Ken's fears of invading hordes from Zomba and elsewhere would be quite unfounded.

In due course Wilindi, if not conquered exactly, was circumnavigated on the contour just below the highest point. It was an occasion of great excitement and celebration in the nearest village, in the form of a beer drink at Ken's expense, which lasted all night and drew in people over a wide area.

Inevitably work on the steep descent on the Misuku side was anti-climax and effort declined accordingly. But once the homeward slopes were reached and the going easier, the men proceeded to work steadily at their own pace, first reaching as far as Joseph Mkumbwa's homestead, then on to the Court. At that point Ken decided on a trial run and nearly killed himself. One fine day he drove up toward Wilindi from Chisi, with Bodwin and several of the road gang following in close attendance, armed with rocks to chock the wheels if the truck should slip back.

Up and round he went, the radiator boiling after the first half mile. Incredibly the ageing pickup kept going. At the very highest point Ken cut the engine. The men raised a cheer as they struggled after him. He got out and knocked off the radiator cap with a stick. When the engine had cooled he topped up with water and started off down again on the homeward run.

Alas the brakes could not cope with the gradient. They failed on a sharp bend with a steep drop to one side. He avoided plunging over the edge only by adroit steering and the fact that the track had been cambered inwards to prevent just such a disaster. Naturally this episode caused our spirits to plummet, for what use would the road be to us if we could not use it?

The project must be completed however.

Thereafter we had the galling experience of witnessing fortunate jeep owners, the DC and others, driving in as far as the Court, while we, for the foreseeable future, must continue to walk. Too late I realised that from the very start, I should have stipulated not only an all weather road, but for a vehicle capable of negotiating it as well.

In the event this did not happen for some time. Only when we went on home leave to England were we able at last to buy a land-rover. Brand new, with bodywork modified to Ken's specification. Even this was not straightforward. As with our involuntary stay at Beira over Christmas on my first voyage out when the dockers had gone on strike, so the British car workers downed tools over some dispute. A common enough occurrence we were told. We feared our pride and joy would not be ready before we must set out for Africa again. It was, but only by dint of Ken travelling to Solihull to take personal possession of it.

After leaving England and disembarking at Mombasa we drove through Kenya and Tanganyika to approach Nyasaland from the North, - a journey described in more detail later - to Fort Hill, Chisenga, Kapoka, and on to the Kalengé. There we swept smoothly across Ragnor's bridge and followed the undulating track to Chisi. Then, for the very first time we DROVE up and over Wilindi, down the other side to the Misuku heartland, waving to all and sundry as we went. On again, past the school, the Court and so to the bottom of the home valley, where Ken parked the land-rover in the shade of a tall tree. Here we must get out and complete the remaining distance on foot. We crossed the rickety pole bridge over the stream by the coffee nursery, up the familiar path at the edge of the terraces with their mature coffee bushes. And so to our own house at last.

Next morning Ngomba a new District Capitao who, with the rest of the staff, had been on hand to welcome us, said to Ken,
"Sir, it is not good to leave the galimoto - vehicle - in that place. That tree is in a place to get taken by lightning."
Ken remonstrated that the tree being mature, had stood there many years without coming to harm, but for the sake of good relations moved the land-rover anyway. The lightning struck a fortnight later, the tree rendered skeletal. Thereafter it was always referred to by us as Ngomba's blasted bluegum.

As to the rest of the road building, the last chapter came when the track was brought from the Court to Katobo, winding its way along the valley bottom then up the hill on which the capitaos' houses stood. From there it was but a hundred yards or so along the contoured track to the house itself. 'Eventually' had become reality at last.

As a final touch, about one year before we left Misuku for good when, incredibly, we had achieved a new house as well, enough bricks were left over to build Ken an office with adjoining lean-to garage, where the land-rover rested snugly. "Pray God it doesn't get struck by lightning." said Ken.

CHAPTER 37

"THURSDAY'S CHILD HAS FAR TO GO"

One of the requirements of Ken's employment as an Agricultural Supervisor was that he must spend 14 nights of every month away on ulendo in the District. Sometimes he compromised on this by setting out before dawn and returning late at night, at other times Wendy and I would go with him, camping in churches or schools as before. But this necessarily complicated matters and was not always possible. He would go off by himself therefore, for two or three days at a time, taking Enos with him, and we were left on our own at Katobo.

My day started, as always, with the sick parade, which since becoming a mother myself, I had begun to take more seriously. Although in all honesty, not much more expertly. Moreover, if Enos and Sutherland were both away I had to rely on the current kitchen boy with little knowledge of English, to translate for me.

The number of people attending varied according to the season. Less at the time of planting up new gardens when the rains were due, as everyone, men as well as women, were busy throughout the daylight hours, More during the rains, when illness and ailments proliferated as in a northern winter.

My policy was to deal first with those whose needs were obvious. Namely burns - little children were only too prone to stumble into cooking fires on the floors of dark smoky huts - and cuts, and running sores caused largely by sharp bladed grass or thorns, to bare legs and feet. If neglected they turned ulcerous but with care and elementary hygiene usually responded well to treatment.

Next, my heart sinking under the knowledge of how little I could do for them, I tackled the babies drooping at their mothers' breasts and the toddlers sitting listlessly by on the ground. Moto - fever - it also meant fire. Kakora - coughs, pakati - stomach ache. were rife at this time of year.

Obviously a high temperature could be caused by many things. Probably the most common among babies was due to their getting drenched on their mother's back when she was caught in a sudden downpour as she tended her garden. There was no possibility of their getting dry till the sun came through again, not even the proximity of her body would do much to help in such a circumstance. Nor would the baby's sleeping at night by her side on the bare earth floor of the hut with little or no covering, do much to help matters. Heart-breakingly all I could do was administer a little crushed aspirin dissolved in boiled water, and urge the mother to take the child to the Dispensary at the Court.

Coughs were easier to diagnose, but not unfortunately to treat, the prevalence of tuberculosis being only too likely. Doses of cough mixture from a large bottle sent up from the chipitala - hospital in Karonga could only give a measure of temporary relief and a certain amount of psychological reassurance to the mother.

Stomach troubles usually meant constipation or diarrhoea, for which I had

two more bottles known as stoppers and starters, obtained from the same source. Diarrhoea,
a form of dysentery perhaps, was only too common, indeed how could it not be, given the multiplicity of parasites, ticks and other microbes around? As for constipation, the local staples of finger millet and plantain bananas made it almost inevitable. Once again children were the most vulnerable, especially at the dangerous time of weaning. Having until that time subsisted solely on the rich nourishment of their mother's milk, they must now learn to digest this tasteless, unpalatable stodge in the form of a stiff porridge. Moreover, often as not, this time coincided with banishment from their mother's back due to the arrival of a new baby, so that for the infant 'finding its feet' was a literal necessity.
Finally among the children's complaints were intestinal worms, graphically described by Enos as 'snakes in the belly'. A condition brought home to me one day when Wendy, by then a toddler about the place, passed what looked like a perfectly ordinary earthworm, but was not.

In all cases where the cause was not apparent, or when my treatment was patently inadequate, I reiterated to the mothers that my medicine had not sufficient nfité and that they should go on to the Dispensary. Whether they did so was anybody's guess.

Self effacing women who came on their own behalf invariably placed themselves at the back of the queue. Their commonest complaint was of headache. How could they not have headache considering the loads they must carry every day of their lives? Going down to the stream to fetch water and carrying it up in a pot on her head, was but the prelude to the many daily tasks. Later they must go to gather firewood on the hills, carry it home in the same manner, then chop it up. They must wash the family's scant clothing at the stream by pounding it on a rock, all the while attending to babies and children who seldom, if ever, went to school.
They must hunt out fresh, edible plants known as relish, to accompany food they themselves had grown. This must be pounded, ground, or otherwise prepared, in preparation for the evening meal - the main and sometimes the only meal of the day - which they would partake themselves, with the girls and the younger boys, only after the men and youths had eaten their fill.
In addition to this daily round in due season they helped the men to break the ground for new gardens and plant the crops which must sustain the family throughout the coming year. At harvest time they must set about drying, preserving and storing the precious horde, inspecting it periodically for mildew or decay and/ or the depredations of mice, rats and other vermin. No wonder the ageing process overtook them early.

One day an old woman hobbled to the door, not in the morning sick parade, but in the afternoon when the labourers had finished work and gone home and Wendy and I were on our own. Her face was contorted in a grimace of pain; round one foot was a dirty, blood soaked rag. She had been working in her garden when the hoe slipped, almost severing the top of one toe. She mimed that she wished me to cut off the hanging remnant. To my shame I could not.

Instead I went to the kitchen and plunged scissors into the kettle of water kept boiling on the stove. When I considered them sterile I handed them to her to carry out the task herself. Which she did very bravely, hacking through flesh and a shard of bone. I put on antiseptic powder, bound it with clean rag and intimated in limited Chisukwa that she must come back in two days time. To my relief the wound healed well.

Another time a man with an unusual skin complaint appeared, claiming he had been bitten by a chameleon. These strange creatures were common in Misuku. We would see them poised on slender branches chewing very deliberately, then moving on slowly, ponderously lifting each leg in turn as if after much thought. To my disappointment, although they took on the camouflage of their immediate surroundings, they never changed colour suddenly or dramatically. One felt it would have been quite against their principles.

All the same, it was easy to see why the people invested them with nfité and avoided them at all costs.

Applying calamine lotion to the man's arms and legs I said doubtfully, by no means sure of my ground,

"Chameleons don't bite."

Enos translating said,

"Yes Madam, that is so. These creatures do not bite white people. They bite only Africans."

An older labourer leaning on his shovel nearby took up the matter at some length.

"He says Madam, that is right. He says also that in the days before women had cloths to wear his mother was bitten by such a creature and all her skin came off."

There was a further exchange as I digested this, then,

"He says also that other cirombo (creatures,) bite only Europeans but do not bite Africans."

Could this be so? Certainly Europeans seemed more prone to certain diseases than Africans, but this might mean that the latter had acquired a certain immunity over aeons of time. Patently my knowledge was too limited for me to judge.

"Did his mother die?" I asked.

"Oh yes Madam, she is dead."

But whether she died of chameleon bite or some other complaint, or simply of old age, was not clear.

Some days after this encounter, unusually in the sick line-up there were two young girls who did not look at all sick. On the contrary, their skin glossy with oil and good health, they positively blossomed as they chattered and laughed with the other women, casting me side-long glances as they did so, so that for once there was a light hearted air about the proceedings. As they wore coloured nsaru, I thought they may have come up from the coffee nursery.

"What can I do for them?" I asked reluctantly when their turn came, convinced this would be yet another occasion to which I could not rise.

Enos questioned the girls with mock severity, there was much giggling along the line.

"They say, Madam, that this one is new married," He indicated the plumper of the two, "And this one is her friend. The married one wishes to know if she has a baby in her belly."

This was quite as bad as I had feared. I stared at him, at the giggling girls, at the women who waited expectantly.

Enlightenment came with a rush and I burst out laughing. The girls were exuberant.

But how, I wondered, had the old women who were now smiling delightedly, divined my own pregnancy when I was not even sure of it myself?

"Tell them they must come back in three months time, I said, "And I will give them the answer."

They were right of course. All too soon the remembered nausea, disgust at the thought of food, but fortunately, thanks to Enos, I need have very little to do with the preparation and cooking of meals this time. Nor were we being tossed on rough seas, or contending with a gruelling overland journey. All the same the first three months were enervating enough, only Wendy's need of care and attention prevented self pity reasserting itself in a big way.

Ken and I discussed if or when we should make the journey to Mzimba to see the doctor there. But the thought of walking out to Kapoka, for this was well before completion of the Misuku track, was daunting. Nor was the timing propitious as with Wendy's birth, for the rains were with us once more and even the main road south could be in a parlous state. In the end the problem was solved in a most unexpected way.

One morning two strangers arrived unannounced. One was a new ADC who told us Noel had been promoted DC somewhere in the South, the other to our surprise, was a doctor straight out from England, newly appointed to Karonga and District. What a wonderful opportunity for a prenatal examination. Or rather, it would have been except that the doctor himself was unwell and in need of treatment. He muttered something with an unpronounceable name, but the symptoms were akin to common or garden dysentery. We put him in the rondavel and nursed him back to health with TLC and rice pudding, both of which he enjoyed, while the ADC went about his duty, visiting Chief MweniMisuku and inspecting some of the rebellious villages beyond Mughessé that Ken had reported for infringement of the Agricultural Department's land regulations.

When the doctor, Richard, recovered I asked him to examine me. Obviously lacking the perspicacity of the old women, he looked surprised, but agreed readily enough. He pronounced that all was well, rather wistfully I thought, for my own health now that the nausea had passed, was patently superior to his. He took a blood test for good measure however, and said he would get it analysed at the hospital in Karonga when he got back. Somewhere along the line it got lost and we never heard the result. Which perhaps was just as well for he had, perforce, sealed the test-tube over our Primus stove, causing the blood inside to boil merrily, which might have induced some strange phenomenon not known to medical science. Later we revised our first impression of Richard. Six weeks after that first visit, at the height of the rains, he braved the rigours of the Chendo, the Misuku track and the walk in to Katobo, expressly to come and see us again. Which, as Ken remarked, must have constituted some sort of record for a home visit. The mothers with sick children were glad to see him too.

Once the sickness had passed time went very quickly for there was plenty going on around, Notably the sell-off of the coffee seedlings in the nursery once more, and all it entailed; when that was over it was almost time to leave for Lilongwe.

Because I was well we judged it safe to stay on in Misuku to within one month of the birth date. Which, being more organised this time, I calculated to be at the end of April. The rains should be almost over by that time and we would be most unlucky to get held up on the roads.

Instead of spending time in Karonga as we had before Wendy's arrival, we would drive straight to Chisenga, overnight there and press on south the following day.

Curiously enough it was not thought of the journey that troubled me. No, it was the prospect of parting with Wendy that filled me with anguish. For she, not yet two, was to go to stay with the Udds till our return. They had been so kind to us at Christmas some four months before, but we had not seen them since. Would she remember them? Settle down there without us? Or would she fret? Had I known then of the psychological damage to a child subsequently attributed to such a parting - common enough at that time - I would have fought tooth and nail to take her with me.

As it was, on the day before we were due to leave, she went off happily in the tobacco basket with its carriers, escorted by Enos. Clearly to her it was just another ulendo.

In the event her unhappiness came some five weeks later at parting from Alice whom she had come to love, to return to parents she did not remember in the first moment of reconciliation.

The house was quiet after Wendy's small cavalcade left. Ken had gone down to Kapoka to check over the pick-up and, as we had had no rain for a week, drive it back as far as Chisi and pray no rain storm overnight would cause the Kalengé to rise and trap us on the wrong side.

Desolate, I wandered from room to room, unable to settle, tidying Wendy's toys, unnecessarily re-checking preparations made well in advance.

In early afternoon Enos returned with a note from Alice Udd to say Wendy had arrived safely and seemed quite happy. Ken came back in late evening.

Another sparkling morning. Accompanied by two carriers with our katundu - luggage - we went down the path to the nursery, crossed the stream and climbed up the opposing hill.

Already the journey had a sense of déja vu view about it. Once more the greetings of early rising village women. Again at the Court the group of men waited for Chief MweniMisuku to open the session and hear their disputes. Without doubt all knew the reason for our ulendo, without doubt, they all marvelled anew at the fuss the Asungu made over the everyday occurrence of childbirth.

As we approached the foothills of Wilindi, the sun not yet too hot, habitation dwindled and gave out leaving the countryside to the belled cattle and the boys who attended them. The summit attained at last we rested briefly before tackling the steep descent to Chisi. No rain thank God.

We came to the truck, the gear was stowed, we bid goodbye to Sutherland who had unexpectedly joined us near his house, and to the carriers; amid more handshakes and good wishes for our safe return, I climbed into the cab. Ken swung the starting handle then settled himself in beside me. Bodwin, the capitao of the region climbed up at the back - it was unthinkable for him to let us go unescorted - and we cruised off down the slope.

We passed what was left of the impoverished village of Chato where the villagers had been so kind to us on the night we had camped there prior to Wendy's birth. Even then it had had an air of impermanence, now there was no sign of life; Ken's forecast had proved only too true, the exhausted land had failed to support them, the people had moved on. A little further on we stopped to give a lift to an itinerant traveller.

At the Kalengé the water was running well below the bridge and we crossed without difficulty. At Kapoka Nelson and his clan welcomed us warmly as ever. Women and children gathered round and gave me the same wooden chair as before. I responded as best I could and sat in the shade while Ken, Nelson and Bodwin went off to inspect nearby gardens. When they returned we parted from everyone with yet more good wishes, and coasted off on the grass fringed track.

After a few miles we met up with the road to Chisenga. It was dry and dusty but we notched up a reasonable speed and arrived at the rest-house at dusk. Angus's house on the ridge was empty, deserted. Where was he now? I wondered. And what had happened to the deaf and dumb cook?

Early next morning the stretch of road skirting the Mafingé Hills, blue and mysterious at this hour, led us to the so-called Great North Road and we headed south. Fine dust percolated the cab; as usual we were enveloped whenever another vehicle passed. Mercifully a rare occurrence. The miles wore away with the day, uneventful, fatiguing.

Eventually we arrived at Mzuzu the night's stopover.

Mzuzu? What was this? Surely we were going to Mzimba? The name was unfamiliar to me, but ought not to have been for I remembered belatedly Ken's having told me some time before that Mzuzu had been chosen to replace Mzimba as the new Provincial Headquarters. Reasons for the move were never clear to me. Perhaps the latter was healthier. Certainly it was nearer to Lake Nyasa which not only meant that freight shipped up to the port of Nkhata Bay was more easily accessible, but more to the point, that Government officials and others were able to spend weekends there, swimming, boating, and sampling other delights of the lake shore.

Whatever the reason it was here that we were to spend a couple of nights with the new Provincial Agricultural Officer and his wife.

As yet Mzuzu was but an embryo township comprising a broad main street, (no tarmac,) on which stood the Boma, the Departmental H/Qs, notably Agriculture, and the ubiquitous PWD, plus administrative offices appertaining to them. A little way off, besides one or two small Indian stores, was the one building sure to be found in all places where the British held sway, namely the Club.

Later on Ken and I came to know Mzuzu rather too well. By which time there was an African hospital, school, one or two conventional shops, as well as two residential roads. The first, lined with spacious houses and large gardens, accommodated senior officers and their families; not surprisingly it was known as Quality Street. The second road with smaller houses known as Blackwood Boxes after the PWD engineer who had designed them, were for junior officials. Many and bitter were complaints by expatriates about these houses, quite unjustifiable not only to us, but to anyone who had experienced the primitive housing conditions in the Northern Province. For they had integral kitchens, running water and main drainage and were far superior to anything in Karonga. Let alone Misuku.[1]*

All this however lay unknown in the future on this our first visit to the place. On this occasion we noted merely that Mzuzu was not hot and humid like Karonga and other lake shore stations, being somewhat elevated and set in undulating countryside. On the skyline was the profile of two almost identical hills, rounded like breasts, known as the Sleeping Woman.

John Sandys the new PAO had taken over when Robert - he who had decreed Ken be posted to Fort Hill - had gone on leave. John was only too glad to escape bureaucracy and office routine and get about the Province. He came to Misuku early in his tenure of office and thereafter whenever he could, and grew to share our love of it. On his very first visit he arrived earlier than expected, as I was trimming Ken's hair, and given that barbers in the country were about two hundred miles apart he asked me to cut his as well. This became a custom whenever he came to see us. Of such trivialities are friendships forged.

We had not yet met his wife Naomi, we found her hospitable and lively, with a hectic social life. Although we could not know it at the time John and Naomi also became lifelong friends. Naomi died in England many years later; with John and his daughter Frances the friendship continues to this day.

Installed in their temporary home I lazed about in the mornings, admiring Naomi's energy and verve. Ken accompanied John either to the office or out on fieldwork.

As in Karonga and everywhere else, because of the early start, the official day was over at 3PM and the station came to life.

It began with the tea ceremony, often with an array of silver and fine bone china, see- through cucumber sandwiches (no crusts,) and small cakes. After this the

---

[1] They were in fact a distinct improvement on conditions still existing in parts of postwar Britain, where much of the housing stock consisted of bombed buildings hastily patched up to accommodate returning heroes.

physically fit and healthy indulged in cricket matches on an improvised pitch, or in tennis tournaments on bumpy ground intended for courts. Then came sundowners, dinner parties or a visit to the Club. This vital institution, the hub of Mzuzu social life, had naturally been given high priority in the transfer, the necessary accoutrements moved lock, stock and barrel. For the more cerebral there were bridge, chess, and for all I knew, tiddlywinks clubs. Also an amateur dramatics society, about which I heard much from Naomi who was one of the leading lights. For the indolent like myself there were comfortable chairs in which to sit around, chatting and drinking. It was all a far cry from Misuku.

On the day after our arrival I went to see the doctor, at this time dividing his time between a temporary surgery in Mzuzu and the established facilities of Mzimba. Again all was well, but he advised me not to delay before going on to Lilongwe.

Accordingly, rested and restored, we said grateful thanks to Naomi and John and set out once more.

South of Mzuzu the road had received a good deal of attention from a PWD road grader, which should have made for a smoother ride, but there was also more traffic, so no noticeable improvement. Also the disturbed earth surface was even dustier and hid deep pot-holes and corrugations. There was nothing for it but, literally, grit the teeth and endure the miles.

That we reached Lilongwe without incident would have been a cause for celebration for anyone less travel worn. As we encountered tarmac on the outskirts however, certainty of a comfortable hotel ahead lifted the spirits considerably.

We booked in to one of the now familiar rooms leading on to the common verandah; a bath, a good meal, and a soft bed did much to restore the tissues.

The next morning was one of leisure but to my dismay, in the afternoon Ken announced that on the morrow he must return to Mzuzu to his work with John Sandys. His annual leave was already in danger of being overrun, paternity leave was as yet a concept undreamed of. No-one thought to question this state of affairs; though women resented it they knew it went with the territory, that having made one's bed as it were, one must make the best of it.

So Ken kissed me goodbye once more, promising to return "In a few days or If anything happens."

Before he went he introduced me to a man met in the bar of the hotel, who had promised to drive me to the hospital if/when it should be necessary.

Whether the poor fellow welcomed such a commission was doubtful, but as he was cooling his heels prior to taking up a job at a tung station some miles out of town, he was probably glad of any kind of company or commission. At any rate he was friendly, obliging, and important to me, especially as the kind Apthorpes had moved on and I knew no-one else in Lilongwe.

In retrospect I was remorseful at having taken his kindness for granted, for he did indeed drive me to the hospital a few days later. But with the press of subsequent events I completely forgot him until many weeks had passed. Did not even known his last name so could not even write to thank him...

In the meantime conditions at the hotel were pleasant enough but I was now experiencing at first hand the feeling so acute in Alice Udd, that is the pain of being parted from Wendy. I missed her cruelly, the separation a wound that dogged me by day and invaded my sleep at night. There was nothing to be done about it except hope the new baby would not be long in coming.

To this end, having checked my booking at the hospital, (By phone!) I walked the golf course every morning. And when Sunday came round I went to church.

Inside the handsome building a shifting pattern of light and shade from high windows gave an impression of cool calm. I settled myself behind a pillar half way up the aisle where I could watch the congregation arriving. At the back many African men, women and children were already assembled, all colourfully dressed, talking, greeting friends and newcomers, enjoying themselves with only slightly less exuberance than their counterparts at the cinema in Mbeya. Presently the European contingency began filling up seats at the front, women hatted and gloved, men straining at their collars, children grudgingly quiet but fidgety. A hush fell as the priest entered and made his way to the pulpit, followed by a cross bearer and choir boys, Nyasan and English. Young and earnest, he preached on the Easter theme, somewhat belatedly I thought because by now April had imperceptibly slipped into May. As we sang a familiar hymn I wondered idly if the priest had got it wrong. But no. Rousing from torpor brought on by his eloquence and the heat induced by the press of bodies, I heard him say,

"Today is Palm Sunday. Do you know what happened on that day long ago?"

In case we did not he proceeded to tell us. When he had finished he said,

"Now you may all come up to the altar to receive your crosses. At this all the children surged forward. More sedately the adults followed. I stayed where I was hoping to be invisible.

When everyone had returned to their seats the vicar looked round the church and said firmly,

"Everyone must have their cross."

How true! I reflected. Then realised with horror that his eyes were searching me out.

There was nothing for it. Clumsily I got to my feet...

In the blur of subsequent events my amnesia regarding this occasion lasted even longer than loss of the name of my kind acquaintance at the hotel. Indeed the incident would have been erased from the mind for ever but for the palm cross remaining in my Sunday School Bible to this day. Fashioned from bleached palm reed, it exactly resembled the ones given us at Easter time at the Church of England village school in the far off days of my childhood.

When I was finally admitted to the hospital there was no kind Sister Hunt, but no Sister Schnabel either. Or alcoholic old lady. Cool competent hands attended the birth and in the early darkness of a Thursday morning our son Benjamin was born.

It was daylight when Ken came. He said,

"I'll be staying here this time. I'm taking a couple of days off. They won't be keeping you in very long."

He was right this time. Unlike Wendy, Benjamin earned my immediate and undying love by being of good size; there was no battle with the dreaded scales, no feeding problems, no other complications.

Also, a quiet revolution in post natal nursing care appeared to have taken place between the two births. Instead of bed rest for as long as possible, a mother was now encouraged to be on her feet after a day or two. This suited me admirably given my longing to get back to Wendy, but was, I thought, tough on overworked mothers in England with several other children at home to be cared for, often with very little help.

On the eve of our departure Ken arranged a celebratory dinner. Leaving the baby in the kind and capable hands of the nursing sister, we drove to the hotel and were met at the door by John, the major domo resplendent in white kanzu, red fez and red cummerbund round his ample waist. Like everyone else in the small fraternity he had heard our news, and greeted us delightedly.

At our table, to my surprise and pleasure the white cloth was bedecked with bouganvillea petals, pink, red, purple, interspersed with white frangipani. A work of art, beautiful, delicate, poignant, ephemeral. Briefly time stood still...

Reality returned soon enough. At dawn next day having said goodbye to the hospital staff, we cruised off and set off on the long journey back to Misuku. As we left the tarmac I became fearful for the baby's tiny lungs on the dusty road and wondered why I had not opted to take the Beaver to Fort Hill. Ken could have preceded me by road and met me there. That way also, as the plane put down at Karonga, I could have shown off Ben to all our friends.

Well it was too late for that now. Ben fell asleep at once, I tented a soft cloth over his head in an attempt to shield him from the sun and dust. Surprisingly, with overnight dew, the dust was not too bad for the first few miles. The road grader had been on this stretch too and ironed out the worst of the corrugations. At intervals boulders either side of the road had been painted white, which gave the journey some slight sense of a royal progress.

"Some visiting VIP I expect." said Ken absently.

Later we learned that a new Governor on a tour of inspection of the North had gone through a few days earlier.

The first day's journey went well. After that we were not so lucky. Indeed we went through fire and water, with a near death experience thrown in for good measure.

North of Mzuzu where we had over-nighted we came across an illegal bushfire out of control. Acrid smoke swirled across the road, penetrating the truck, cancelling out visibility. Flames fanned by a hot wind licked hungrily at either side of the road. I moistened the cloth over the baby with water from the flask and dabbed his eyes and mouth. It was no place to linger. Ken trod hard on the accelerator, and held to the crown of the road, praying we might not meet another vehicle as we careered through the murk.

At last we were clear. Ken stopped the truck, we got out, gulped fresh air, the baby cried vigorously.

"That will help to clear his lungs." said Ken.

As soon as Ben calmed down I fed him water from the baby bottle, we too had drinks.

We were most unlucky to encounter a flood that same day since the wet season was almost over and we had not seen rain for days.
It came without warning. One moment the sky was cloudless, the road clear. Then as we rounded a bend and coasted down a mild slope the way was blocked by muddy water. Even as Ken got out to assess its depth the heavens opened. Clouds which had disgorged their contents on the hills to cause this flash flood, regained strength and rolled toward us as if in some desperate last fling, knowing their time was up.
At once we were deafened, blinded, the truck totally assailed by the onslaught. There was no escape this time, nothing to be done but sit it out praying it would soon ease up. With the windows tight shut heat in the cab was excessive. Leaks appeared from unexpected sources, but this did not matter as the dripping water cooled us slightly. I mopped up the baby as best I could.
It took a long time for the rain to slacken and stop and longer for the water to go down. After what seemed like an eternity we were able to wind the windows down and move off cautiously, slipping and slithering on what was no longer a road, but a sea of mud, fearful of slipping into the ditch, the white painted boulders coated in sepia mud.

The brush with death came the following day in the hilly country of the North where traffic had once more become sparse to nonexistent. As ill luck would have it we were traversing a narrow defile when a bus approached at speed, raising a cloud of dust as it hurtled toward us. Ken sounded the horn well in advance. On almost any other stretch of the route he could have veered off into the bush at the side of the road to let it pass, here it was impossible. The driver did not see or hear us, either he was talking over his shoulder or else he had fallen asleep. Ken pressed the horn again and kept his thumb down. Still no response.
It is said that faced with death one's whole life returns in rapid flashback. It was not so with me. My concern was for the baby whose little life would be over, when it had barely begun. He in fact was crying again, either from communicated fear or because of the involuntary tightening of my arms around him.
At the very last moment the driver saw us, we had a split second glimpse of his terrified face as he wrenched the bus over as far as the rock face allowed. It missed us by a hair's breadth.
When the countryside broadened out once more. Ken stopped the truck, leaned over and took Ben from me. I got out and collapsed by the roadside.

The rest of the journey was accomplished somehow. There remains the vague memory of a night spent at Rumphi rest-house, another at Chisenga, of making our way back to Kapoka next day and receiving the congratulations of Nelson and his retinue. Then came the slow drive to Chisi where the carriers waited, jubilant at the birth of a male child.

Only when we left the truck and began the climb to Wilindi did reality reinstate itself.

When at last we reached the Court Chief MweniMisuku and the elders were waiting, the news having preceded us. They were likewise congratulatory, as were villagers along the way who waved or came across to shake Ken's hand. In this manner we came to our own house at last.

Oh the bliss of being home again! The welcome at Katobo was quite as gratifying as that on my return to Karonga after Wendy's birth. True the walk from Wilindi and across Misuku itself had been exhausting, but we were met by Sutherland and Enos, both beaming, by Akim, Trisom, and by the labourers who had lingered after the day's work was over. Some of their wives had also gathered. The men came forward and there were more handshakes. The women pressed round to catch sight of the baby, Akim in his soft insidious voice made a speech to the effect that the people were happy that Ken had begotten a son. Ken responded in kind, though in truth the baby's gender was less important to him than that the whole undertaking had come to successful conclusion.

As on my very first arrival at Katobo the house had been whitewashed throughout. This was a surprise, Ken not having authorised it. Certainly the walls had been in a bad way, the bare mud and laths of their construction visible in some places, while in others the tunnels of white ants could have done duty as a map of the London Underground. But surely this was of concern to ourselves alone?

The explanation? The women had insisted to Sutherland that, even though it had not taken place there, a house must be cleansed after a birth. Fortunately the work was not still in progress this time, but it was obviously only lately finished and a damp, sour smell hung over everything. Nor was the whitewash confined to the walls alone but slopped generously over floors and furniture as well.

No matter, the intentions were good. Tomorrow Enos would clear it all up. Tomorrow Ken would walk over to Mubula and bring Wendy back from the Udds.

CHAPTER 38

GOVERNOR'S VISIT

Next morning as daylight broadened I sat peacefully in bed feeding the baby and listening to the day unfold. The far off clink of cow bells from the cattle on the hills, the bad tempered hornbills in the tree by the rondavel beginning to stir, voices of early rising women going down to the stream to draw water. Through it all was my happiness at the prospect of being reunited with Wendy. Ken slept on - we had both been woken in the night by Ben - until the work clanger roused him. Enos brought in tea; when Ken had drunk his he got up with a groan, dressed and went outside to confer briefly with Sutherland, before coming in again to tackle the disconcerting mountain of mail piled high on the dining table in the adjoining room. Through the open door I could hear him ripping envelopes, screwing up the contents after a cursory glance and hurling them at the waist paper basket, to a commentary of oaths and unflattering comments about the bureaucrats down in Zomba as he did so, "Stupid lot!" "What a waste of time, why don't they just..."

Sometimes there would be pauses, when I knew from experience he was paying more attention to the ones which seemed important.

This had gone on for some time when I became aware of a pause which lengthened into an ominous silence. Letter in hand he appeared in the doorway.

"What's the date today?" he demanded.

"Er..."

I was startled. Unlike the seasons calendars played little part in our lives at Katobo. In the light of recent events, for me they had figured even less. Ben was born on 2nd May, I was quite sure of that. But had I subsequently been in the hospital for two days or three? We had spent a night at Mzuzu, then an extra one at Rumphi because of the fire and flood, and all that. And one at Chisenga.

"The seventh? I hazarded, "Or ninth?"

"Oh, never mind."

He withdrew as I struggled with the calculation. To judge by the commotion he was scrabbling through the debris on the table to locate his diary, found it, and was now flipping through the pages. Then with an expletive usually indicated in books by an asterisk, he shouted,

"But that's tomorrow!"

Still waving the paper he reappeared.

I looked at him in consternation. Nameless horrors ran through my mind. Not another language exam surely? Not an urgent summons down to Zomba because of some perceived misdemeanour? As usual I was way wide of the mark.

"The Governor. He's coming here. Tomorrow."

"The Governor? I echoed stupidly. "Here? He can't be. Are you sure?"

This exalted character, remote as the Queen herself, could have no possible bearing on our life here in Misuku. It must be some mistake. But wait. Vaguely I recalled the newly graded road as we travelled north, the white painted boulders and Ken's remark that some VIP must be touring the area. If we had not been so preoccupied with immediate difficulties we might have speculated as to who it could be, might even have wondered if he would get as far as Karonga. As it was the matter was forgotten. In any case it would never have occurred to either of us that we ourselves would be involved in any way.

Cautiously I asked, "Do you mean he's coming to Misuku? Or here to Katobo?"

"Yes to both, he said, " First to the Court to meet the Chief, then on here."

"But he can't. Not with the house in this state. All that whitewash and stuff. And we've got nowhere to put him. And no food.."

In actual fact neither of these statements were truly accurate; we had the rondavel

for guests, and we had of course stocked up with food before leaving Lilongwe. But although grammar and logical thought had deserted me, I knew beyond any shadow of doubt that nothing about the place would begin to approximate to standards expected by a governor.

"Oh, it's alright, said Ken scanning the letter again, "It's only for a brief stop after the business at the Court. Just a bit of a break before their return journey. Coffee and biscuits will be fine."

"They?" I queried faintly.

"Well he wouldn't be travelling alone now would he? He'll have a couple of aides I suppose. And the PC from Mzuzu, and the DC from Karonga , and the ADC perhaps. Maybe one or two others."

"But we haven't got that many chairs! Or cups. Or anything..."

He did not hear me.

"Of course he'll want to see the coffee. And the nursery. And the rest of the place most likely. I must go. Shan't be in for lunch, too much to do. Goodness knows what's been happening while I was away."

He was almost out of the door.

"Wait!" I called desperately sitting bolt upright and dislodging the baby who started to protest,. "Today you're going to Mubula to bring Wendy back from the Udds. You promised."

"Can't, he said briefly, "Too much to do. I'll be busy all day."

At this weakness and self pity washed over me like a tide and I burst into tears.

"Yes, go, I cried, "Make sure the coffee bushes are standing to attention. Paint a few boulders white while you're about it."

At first I thought he had not heard me then, slowly he came back. He sat down on the bed, took my hand and said,

"Look, I don't want this any more than you do. But it's important, don't you see? I'll go to the Udds tomorrow the minute they've gone."

He put his arms round us and kissed us both gently, then he left. I continued to sob into the baby's nonexistent neck.

Not for long however. There was too much to do, postnatal depression would have to wait.

Two things cheered me when I got up. Firstly Enos had made bread, the homely smell of it wafting across from the kitchen made me realise how hungry I was. Secondly he and Saxon the current kitchen boy, had already made a start on the house cleaning. Secondly, on our arrival the previous evening the red polished floor of the sitting room had been starred with whitewash, now it was pink all over. No improvement there, but as Enos explained,

"When it is dry Madam I will wash it again and after breakfast I will polish it and all will be the same."

I told him I would help him as soon as I could.

Yet again I thanked God for Enos. Temperamental as he undoubtedly was he never failed to rise to an occasion.

Assuredly news of the Governor's visit to the Court had reached Katobo in our absence and spread throughout Misuku. Everyone would have known about it. But notice of the visit to our house would have been restricted to the letter Ken had just opened. I shuddered to think of what would have happened if, in the press of other matters he had neglected to open the mail when he did. The Governor might have found himself helping to clean up.

As it was we had a few hour's grace. Fortified by new bread I went out to tackle the sick parade.

I had hoped to escape this chore for a day or two, but how was it possible when the women facing me were invariably up mudding and whitewashing the walls, and sweeping out their huts within hours of giving birth? And working at full strength next day.

The sight of the larger than usual crowd was dismaying, but it soon became apparent that most of the people were not sick, they had come to see Ben, who now slept peacefully in the tobacco basket to one side under the eye of the gentle Trisom. The few men present offered lengthy speeches of congratulation and goodwill, to which I listened ungratefully, containing my impatience as best I could, returning perfunctory thanks as I dealt with the genuine cases.

When at last everyone had gone, helping Enos and Saxon in the sitting room, I bemoaned the lack of chairs, cups etc for the morrow. Enos said,

"Madam I will go and see Sutherland when he returns to his house tonight. He will find chairs, also chicoppo (cups)."

Ken came back in late afternoon, by which time the house was more or less back to normal.

Next morning we were once again awake early, everything was quiet about the place. Yawning Ken got up and peered through the curtains.

But what was this? Instead of pale sunrise lighting up the hilltops, the fine mist which enveloped Misuku perhaps thrice in a year, had chosen this day of all days to make its appearance. As through a shroud labourers loomed up for work in ones or twos.

"It's sure to lift, Ken said, "It's early yet."

"Perhaps they won't come?" I suggested hopefully, thinking privately and a little guiltily, that in the circumstances a few white boulders along the way might not have come amiss.

The mist did not clear, the house was isolated, its shoreline the rim of the lower terrace.

After a hasty breakfast Ken in newly pressed khaki shirt and shorts, left for a last minute inspection of the place before going on to the Court with Sutherland. The clothes of the latter were identical with Ken's, but immaculate and he looked excited rather than harassed. He had once again earned my gratitude by arriving at the door accompanied by three men carrying wooden chairs and an assortment of patterned mugs.

At about half past ten very faintly through the mist, came the sound of engines approaching the Court. Excitement at Katobo mounted, my nervousness increased. I reckoned however that the visitors would not be with us for another hour for not only would the speeches be fulsome, but Ken would wish to show off the coffee terraces on the way back. All that could be seen of it them that is.

Meanwhile the house was presentable as it was ever likely to be. I had Saxon light the fire in the sitting room against the gloom and chill outside. It burned cheerfully and already Jack Spot, the most stupid cat in the world, was curled up in front of it. Sometimes he got too close and had several bald spots to show for it. The floor shone red again, the newly painted walls gleamed white except where the ever industrious ants had made new tunnels. Over the fireplace hung Ken's painting of chrysanthemums, on the bookcase was a vase of the dark red roses which had delighted me on my first arrival at Katobo.

I checked with Enos that everything was ready in the kitchen and posted Akim at the head of the lower terrace to alert us of the visitors' approach. Presently I laid the newly fed baby, in his crib, in a corner of the room where I could pick him up if he cried. As I did so a rush of love and tenderness welled up in me; so far in his week long life he had cried hardly at all.

A shout from Akim roused me from this maternal preoccupation. With alarming suddenness the visitors were upon us.

Ken led the way across the garden. So many people!

It was impossible to tell at this stage which one was the Governor but it was immediately apparent that our estimate of numbers had been too low. Clearly, even with Sutherland's reinforcements there would not be enough chairs. Or cups, or horror, biscuits. These and other jumbled thoughts ran through my mind as Ken made the introductions. Only one thing registered - relief that the Provincial Commissioner was one I did not know, Tycho must have moved on.

Most of the men were out of breath from the climb up the valley, that and the mist accounted for their silent coming. They filtered into the sitting room, the Governor , Sir Robert A......., pausing momentarily on the threshold, till one of his aides led him gently to the big armchair. The others seated themselves as best they could. The ADC from Karonga earned my undying thanks by declaring there was nothing he liked better than sitting on the floor. I shot him a grateful glance, surely he would go far. Others followed his example, Ken and Sutherland stood at the back of the room so that one way or another everyone was accommodated.

The Governor's aides readily adjusted to the situation, started up a conversation with customary expertise and soon the talk was flowing. After a moment or two I collected myself sufficiently to signal to Enos strategically stationed by the door. Presently he appeared, in borrowed plumes which almost certainly belonged to Sutherland his brother-in-law, bearing a tray of Misuku grown coffee and plates of newly baked biscuits. If the assortment of cups and mugs were not what the visitors were used to they gave no sign, The aroma of the coffee and the cheerful fire generated an air of bonhomie and everyone, including myself, began to relax. So far the Governor had taken little part in the proceedings. Now he was looking round thoughtfully. At the cat before the fire, the baby in the corner - both sleeping peacefully thank God, at the mist swirling beyond the red and white check curtained windows... Perhaps the scene reminded him of nursery days at home before he was banished at a tender age to face the rigours of an English public school. Helping himself to another biscuit he began to question Ken about the work of the Department, about the District and the Asukwa in general. He listened attentively and followed up with more personal matters. How long had we lived here? How did we get our water? And our general supplies? Then, abruptly he turned to me and asked how I liked living in Misuku. I replied truthfully that I liked it very much. His next question however, was less easy to answer as it was one I frequently asked myself,

"What do you do all day?"

And I could only stammer that what with one thing and another, the time passed very quickly.

This apparently struck a chord with one of the aides for he said,

"Actually Sir, do you think we should be getting along? It'll take us some time to get back to Chisenga. Especially in this fog."

His Excellency looked startled but roused himself and stood up. In the doorway he lingered. When it was my turn to shake his hand he murmured something about "The last homely house."

Had I heard aright? Could it be that even Governors were human? That this particular one occasionally read Tolkien to his grand-children at bedtime?

He turned, the others trouped out after him. He, they, disappeared over the rim of the garden as silently as they had come.

The miasma persisted all day, the Governor could have seen nothing of the splendour of Misuku about which he had undoubtedly heard so much. To him it would remain a formless limbo, forgotten as a dream. A dream punctuated with vague memory of a bright room, a baby, a cat sleeping on the hearth, the irresistible appeal of freshly ground coffee? Perhaps.

Ken came back after forming part of the escort of locals as far as the Court. He ate a hasty lunch then set out once more. This time for Mubula. Wendy came home at last and our family was complete.

Next day the sun shone as if it had never deserted us. A fortnight later we received a courteous letter of thanks from the Governor. Later still Ken had notification that he had been allocated funds to build a new house.

CHAPTER 39

"BUILD ME A WILLOW CABIN AT YOUR GATE"

Of course the go-ahead for a new house had not come about solely as a result of the Governor's visit. Ken had in fact been lobbying successive PAOs on the subject, along with that of the road, ever since his posting to Misuku had been officially recognised. But it is possible that at some dinner party for VIPs in Zomba, the Governor expatiating on his travels to the North may have let fall the name of Waterfield, a fellow living somewhat roughly in the Misuku Hills with his family. And if Dick Kettlewell the Director of Agriculture had been among those present, well, who knows?

As my attention was almost solely on the children at the time the news came through it was something of a shock as well as a surprise. With the passing of time and the improvements Ken had made, our present house had become home. Nevertheless there was no getting away from the fact that basically it was just a three roomed hut of wattle and daub in constant need of repair. And, as I had discovered over the last few months, far too small and inconvenient for a family of four. No doubt about it, the Governor's hypothetical remark was fully justified.

Therefore for the next few weeks when I should have been concentrating on practical matters, I fantasised on what the dream house should be like. Knowing electricity to be out of the question, running water and proper sanitation were my top priorities. Indeed it is not too much to say that the prospect of taps gushing water and a lavatory that flushed, brought a rush of blood to the head.

An integral kitchen was next on the list. Apart from the inconvenience of the present regime, the impossibility of maintaining an acceptable standard of hygiene and cleanliness was extremely worrying. Besides Enos deserved something better than the succession of the primitive mud hovels which had served us hitherto..

Then there must be at least one extra bedroom. Also a separate dining room and an office for Ken. Our present sitting room still combined both these functions, the dining table perpetually strewn with memos and official letters which must be swept aside before we could sit down to eat.

I should of course have foreseen that Ken's priorities were of quite a different order.

"The first thing is to pick out the site, he said, "Then I must get hold of some burnt bricks. And aluminium roofing sheets and..."

"Tin roofs are very hot, I put in, "And noisy in the rains."

I had come to love the soft thatch, its wild life notwithstanding, especially as we had by now a reasonably efficient ceiling. Moreover I recalled Jess' remark on the subject when she and I were inspecting Steve's new house under construction in Karonga.

"Well it doesn't get really hot up here in the hills, Ken reasoned, "And they're only

noisy when the rain is really heavy."
"Which is most of the time in the wet season."
"Alright, we can discuss that later. More to the point, where can I get hold of burnt bricks? And how will I get them up here when I've found them?
There was more, much more, in this vein.
Surprisingly the site was determined quite easily. After making forays about the station it became clear to us that the redoubtable Keen Hammerson had not only picked out the one bit of semi flat land on which to build, but by accident or design it was a spot which commanded one of the finest views in Nyasaland. Common sense dictated therefore, that with a bit more land levelling, the new house be built along side the old.
With Sutherland's help Ken began to take levels; this done he hired extra labourers to carry out the necessary groundwork.
Thereafter his evenings were devoted to drawing up plans, calculating dimensions, assessing the materials needed. Once he was sure of his figures he fired off requisitions to the PWD in Mzuzu for the crucial burnt bricks, roofing sheets, (I had lost the argument on that one,) timber, windows and frames, glass, nails, screws, cement, to mention but a few.

A deafening silence from the South ensued. Thus we had ample time to make our wishes and ideas known to one another. I did not get very far. What had seemed to me to be entirely reasonable necessities of life in the middle of the twentieth century, were, apparently, the height of extravagance and decadence according to Ken.
There could be no separate dining room for a start, or office. Yes we could have an integral kitchen if that was what I really wanted - he sounded dubious - and running water into the house shouldn't be too difficult so long as he could get sufficient piping.
"With a tap over the sink in the kitchen, I said firmly, "And a bath and wash basin in the bathroom with taps that actually work."
"Well, those chaps in Zomba haven't exactly erred on the side of financial excess you know."
"I'll bet they all live in houses with running water. Hot AND cold I shouldn't wonder."
He ignored this.
"What's this about a flush lavatory? Are you mad? Have you any idea what it would cost? And the expertise and labour involved?"
I had not but knew I was about to be enlightened. I sighed and stopped listening.
"So you see, he was saying as I gave him my attention again, "It's quite out of the question. Most of the money will have to go on..."
"Don't tell me. Burnt bricks and roofing sheets."

In the end the layout was not unlike that of the present house. Which is to say, the principle rooms would have the same incomparable views of the countryside as the old. But with bigger rooms and with an extra bedroom leading off the far side of an enlarged sitting room.

"That will give us two bedrooms, said Ken categorically, "Three counting the rondavel. That's quite enough, we get too many visitors as it is."
There was no question of a separate dining room. Ken-
"Certainly not enough money for that."
The kitchen and bathroom, together with a small store room, would be at the back, separated from the sitting room and bedrooms by a narrow corridor. Sanitary arrangements, alas, would be as before.

As with surveying, Ken was not entirely without experience in building work. As a boy in the 1939/45 war he had helped his over-worked father to build - sink rather - an Anderson air raid shelter in the back garden of the family home. At eighteen his afore mentioned service with the Royal Engineers had involved various practical projects. Furthermore, during his first tour in Nyasaland prior to our marriage, he had supervised construction of a dam out at Chinunka. He was therefore reasonably confident that building a house would not be beyond his capabilities.
Once the knotty problem of getting burnt bricks had been resolved that is. Needless to say there were none available in Misuku. Moreover, although some of the minor requirements ordered began to filter through, in the unlikely event of the PWD in Mzuzu supplying them, there would still remain the difficulty of getting bricks up to Katobo.
"The PWD truck wouldn't get any further than Kapoka, he said, "The track is too narrow and the surface not good enough, not even in the dry. And the Kalengé bridge would never take the weight anyway. So they would have to be off loaded at Nelson's place. Given the quantity involved it would mean endless journeys to and fro in the truck and even then they'd have to be off loaded at Chisi and brought in by carrier. No, it's just not feasible.
To me the problem seemed insoluble and I wondered if the whole enterprise would have to be written off. But apparently there was a solution. One that had been lurking at the back of Ken's mind for some time, simple in concept, difficult and laborious in practice.
"The bricks must be made here, he said, "And fired on site."
I stared at him.
"But how?" And what with? And..."
Into my head floated the memory of Jewish trade union leaders in the Old Testament complaining bitterly to their Egyptian overlords about lack of straw, a some what unlikely constituent one would have thought, without which they could not possibly be expected to make bricks. We had no straw either for that matter. Would dried grass do ? I wondered.
"Of course they would have to be made out of mud." Ken explained patiently.
"Ah. We've got plenty of that. In the rains at least."
"Yes. That won't be a problem, although of course we can't start till the rains are over. But we'll get on with making brick moulds. The idea will be to get them filled with mud and turned out like sand castles."
At this point I thought what a pity our children would not be old enough to join in.

"They'll be laid out in the sun to dry, then they'll have to be fired in a kiln." He made it sound quite easy, I was dubious but certainly could not come up with any other solution. In any case the silence from Mzuzu was broken a little later by a terse note saying the PWD had no burnt bricks to spare. So the matter was more or less settled.

There was no choice as to what sort of mud might be most suitable for brick making. Even had Ken been possessed of the geological expertise, which he was not, land pressure on and around the station was too great. So he chose a convenient spot up the hill behind the house, near but not too near the water furrow on which we all depended, which speeded down the hillside en route for the stream near the coffee nursery in the valley.

Rather than gouging out an unsightly and potentially dangerous pit, he told the men to dig a trench across the hillside, following the contour. This would kill two birds with one stone, as it could subsequently act as a storm drain, or bund, and help to check erosion.

Meanwhile he had been working on a prototype brick mould; it was very much the size and shape of Enos' bread tins. When he was satisfied with it, he made several replicas.

When the rains slackened sufficiently for work to start, the proceedings provoked much excitement and ribaldry among the men. With the trench dug out, the thrown up earth must be puddled to mud and, since mudding was women's work, a number were taken on, older ones mostly, some of them the labourers' wives. Needless to say they were less provocative than the girls tending the coffee seedlings in the nursery, nor did they wear coloured nsaru - even had they owned such things they would have been kept for going to church on Sundays.

Though the concept of brick making was new to these women, mud puddling was not. Indeed mudding the floors and walls of their huts was one of their regular tasks, had been so since time immemorial and they set to work with a will.

Soon the hillside became a pageant of men bent at work in the trench, with women
crisscrossing the garden, water pots on heads, depositing libations on the loose earth with a shuffling, possibly ritualistic, sort of dance, until it turned to mud beneath their feet.

In spite of the usual hilarity of the men at the presence of women, the latter took the work seriously. Albeit cheerfully with much chatter, buoyed up perhaps by the thought of actually being paid for their labour, even though their chances of keeping any part of their earnings were decidedly slim.

Each day when enough mud had accumulated the women settled down to help a few older labourers to fill the brick moulds. Among these was William our erstwhile cook. Really elderly now, but willing and eager as ever to please, he sat contentedly scooping, smoothing, and turning out elongated mud pies only too horribly reminiscent of the one and only loaf he had tried to make for us.

Women were in fact better at the job. Especially when one of the younger trench diggers who claimed formerly to have worked for the PWD down country, appointed himself tutor, showing them how to fill the moulds evenly, press down the mud to exclude air bubbles, then turn out their efforts, heavy as William's bread, in rows to dry in the dependable sun.

Meanwhile to the intense interest of everyone including myself, Ken and Sutherland had been measuring and pegging out markers for the foundations of the house. In the expanse of landscape it took a bit of imagination to visualise the final outcome.

"But it looks so small!" I protested, "Are you sure you've got the dimensions right? I mean, the kitchen and bathroom look very small, and the extra bedroom positively minute."

Ken said shortly,

"Yes I'm sure. Check them yourself if you don't believe me. Things always look smaller on the ground."

Sutherland said nothing, but Enos standing by was also dubious when he realised the kitchen would be attached to the house. True, if it were modern and well equipped it would not only make his work easier, but raise his status and give him more prestige as well. On the other hand he probably remembered from his experience in South Africa, that it would also warrant more attention from the Dona and cramp his style considerably. Gone would be the dim, smoky hut into which I ventured as seldom as possible, where his cronies squatted hugger-mugger, drinking cups of sweet tea as they performed small tasks for him. Greatly reduced would be the opportunities of receiving his wife and children, or his old mother, and sending them off with a biscuit or some other titbit. I felt almost sorry for him. But not sorry enough to change my mind, even though Ken's doubts continued.

"It'll make the house noisy, he warned, "The stove being made up, the clatter of saucepans and things. Not to mention the chatter."

I pointed out that the kitchen would be separated from the main rooms by the corridor, which would cut down noise so long as the doors were kept shut, and we left it at that.

When the sun had baked rows and rows of mud bricks to about half their weight, and lightened them in colour so that they now merged harmoniously with the dry tawny landscape, it was time to tackle the problem of getting them fired.

My knowledge of kilns was limited to remembrance of old abandoned brickworks dotting the countryside in England, left from the time when small builders commonly manufactured their own bricks, and of a school visit to a commercial pottery where the kiln was a huge metal affair with heavy doors clamped shut. Neither experience seemed relevant to the present situation.

Fortunately that did not matter, for Ken it seemed, had thought the matter through before the work started. Only one course of action was possible. The bricks must be stacked in a such a manner as to form their own kiln. A kind of self immolation in fact.

Accordingly he supervised the building of a railway tunnel in miniature, which is to say, merely some 4feet high, open at both ends, with air-vents in the roof at intervals.

This was far harder than it sounds. For a start most of - if not all - the men had never seen a tunnel of any kind and had no idea what was expected of them. Secondly there was nothing but staves and the bricks themselves on hand with which to support the underside of the arch as work progressed. Many, therefore were the false starts and collapsed attempts before some approximation to a form of corbelling was achieved.

Finally however the tunnel was ready. The next step would be to light a fire under the length of it, a fire which must be kept burning day and night until the bricks were thoroughly hardened and burnt. It would take a lot of firewood.

Like mudding, gathering and cutting nkuni - firewood - was women's work, a chore common enough to all of them, though one decidedly less congenial than brick making. Each morning they set off together up the hill behind the house and returned with their loads around midday. Soon a pile of wood the size of a respectable Guy Fawkes bonfire had been assembled.

"That will do for now, said Ken, "We may have to get more later, ideally the fire should burn for a week."

When everything was ready, that is, when Ken was reasonably sure the roof of the tunnel would not collapse, the wood was distributed evenly along it by means of long poles with makeshift prongs on the end, and the fire lit.

So began a time of high festivity. The people loved nothing better than a good blaze, be it a small one for a beer drink or an 'accidental', that is, illegal, one on the hillside to clear land for a new garden. To have a fire actually sanctioned by authority exceeded all bounds of expectation.

It was tended day and night not only by the labourers in turn but also by enthusiastic volunteer villagers anxious to share the occasion. The place took on an air of holiday and became littered with the remains of roasted corn cobs, sweet potatoes and other debris of alfresco feasts. Almost certainly beer was brought along after dark. Thus with the glare of the furnace from each end of the tunnel, pin-points of light from the air vents along it, and the singing, dancing figures prancing with their improvised tridents, the scene was positively Bacchanalian. We held the children up at the window of their darkened room - even the baby was old enough to take notice by this time - as we put them to bed. Would dreams of the scene remain imprinted on their minds, to be confused later with cold, frosty November the Fifth Bonfire nights in England? It seemed very likely.

To everyone's regret the firewood was spent after a week and the party was over. The cooling off period did not apply solely to the bricks. The labourers lounged around apathetically each day in spite of Sutherland's best efforts to get them working on more mundane jobs. Ken also suffered anti-climax, longing to test the results but knowing it vital to wait until the kiln was quite cold, which would take several days. Dismantling it when at last he judged it ready, was almost as difficult as constructing it and a good few bricks were broken.

To me the most surprising thing was their transformation in colour. They no longer resembled to the mud of their origin, nor that of their the un-baked state as they lay in rows drying in the sun, but were now an indefinable shade of ginger. No matter. Except for some of the ones forming the outer part of the kiln, they were indisputably burnt bricks, tough, and resonant when tapped with a trowel. Ken was delighted and said it did not matter about the near failures, or the breakages, as he had made a generous allowance for both in his estimates. In the event all were destined to be fired again subsequently, but we did not know that at the time.

Being closely involved with the building of a house is, one suspects, vastly different from hiring a builder to do it and inspecting the ongoing work at intervals. In the latter case, human nature being what it is, one would almost certainly detect faults and misunderstandings and criticise accordingly.

"That doesn't look very good. That's not what I meant at all."

But with everything going on under one's nose it is quite different. At least so it was in my case. The work of each individual labourer/builder - all of them engaged on tasks entirely alien to them - became familiar to me. I came to know for instance, which of them bore responsibility for slopping on too much cement and causing unevenness in a course of brickwork. Knew which of them had driven in the crooked nails above the window, and so on. Far from being dismayed however, I regarded any sign of progress as a triumph. So it was just as well that Ken's standards were higher, even though he often returned from regular agricultural duties in the district and order the work to be taken down and done again. But all this came later.

Meanwhile the most important matter was to get cement brought up, for without it building could not start. In those days cement was packed in one hundredweight paper sacks, stout and strong certainly, but only too easily gashed open, or dropped and the powdery contents dissipated like snow in September. Conversely, should it get wet it would arrive at its destination solid and useless. Ken took no chances. When the PWD reluctantly supplied several bags and sent them by lorry to Kapoka, he drove there to collect them, having previously alerted Nelson to get them all under cover. He brought them back as far as Chisi where they must be off loaded. From there he personally accompanied the carriers who brought the bags in the rest of the way. Only when they were all safely under cover at Katobo could everyone relax.

At last with vital materials assembled the work could begin. The self proclaimed ex PWD expert who had tutored the women in the art of filling brick moulds, now not only claimed knowledge of the function of a plumb line - in this case a stone attached to a length of chingwe - but of bricklaying as well. Even he, however, along with everyone else, was dismayed, when instead of starting to build up, Ken ordered the men to dig out more trenches. Yet another new concept. All were relieved when, foundations complete, the walls finally began to rise; though the burying of precious bricks in the ground where nobody could see them was considered a wicked waste.

As with the road, work slowed down when neither Ken or Sutherland were on hand to supervise it. Impossible to say for certain if this was due to fear of doing something wrong, for after all, not even the self styled expert knew for sure what was required, or from natural inclination. In any case the result was the same. The walls therefore inched up slowly indeed. Yet eventually, as the walls inched towards the eaves, it became necessary to construct ladders and scaffolding from bamboo poles lashed together with chingwe, rather rickety but serviceable enough. Before this however it was necessary to incorporate the chimney. This Ken did himself, with bends. Here the experience of re-building the one in the present house, after the old one had collapsed into the sitting room that memorable night soon after my arrival at Katobo, stood him in good stead. Mentally I measured development of the house with that of Benjamin. He was almost a year old when brick making was complete, a shaky toddler by the time the walls reached the eaves. On gloomy days I visualised his being able to read fluently by the time the whole thing was finished.. In all fairness, this was not entirely the fault of the workers. The PWD also played its part, of which more later.

When the doors and windows arrived from Mzuzu Ken sent for the carpenter of the pointed teeth and Arnolfini hat - he still had both - who came at leisure with his mate. We had seen neither of them since the early days when they had worked on Mary's rondavel and conjured up our blissful double bed. Not surprisingly I had fond memories of those days, forgetting as one is apt to do, all the discomforts and difficulties. This time they fitted the door frames and doors without too much trouble, which implied they had been plying their trade successfully elsewhere in the intervening years. Over the Songwe border perhaps, or in Tanganyika. With the PWD window frames in place, the carpentry finished, the brickwork up to eaves level, Ken closely supervised the fixing of wall plates and installation of the complex pattern of roof trusses and rafters. After which it was time to put the roof itself in place. The shiny sheets of aluminium were hauled up one by one and nailed securely on. The last sheet on, the last nail hammered home to much self congratulation among the workforce, the building at last looked like a real house and there followed the time-honoured, seemingly universal, topping out ceremony. Trisom climbed on to the roof with a green fir bough; to the cheers of the men and the brick making women who had come to watch, he tied it to the chimney. The rest of the day was declared a holiday.

Now that the roof was on, and the windows lately glazed by Ken, the house was secure, a dry place to store remaining materials and for men to work under cover as a second wet season of the project returned.

Probably I was not the first person to come to realisation that completion of the shell of a house is but half the work necessary to make it habitable. True our new home would lack refinements usually taken for granted in the twentieth century; electricity and sanitation for instance, would be conspicuous by their absence. The former would be served by the same assortment of lamps and candles as before, the latter by a new pit latrine outside. But there were floors to be concreted, ceilings to put up, installation of internal walls, and much more. There also remained what was to me the most vital modern convenience of all, the plumbing. Roughing it with buckets of water in the early days was one thing, with a family of four, two of them children, it was quite a different matter. I had lowered my sights somewhat by settling for cold water only, hot being less important in the tropics. And in truth there was a moral dimension to consider. Namely it would use up more precious firewood - always in short supply among the villagers. But taps gushing cold water to the bathroom and to the kitchen sink, I was determined to have.

The present hot water system was one of the 'improvements' Ken had put in on his extended ulendos to Misuku early on, when I stayed behind in Karonga awaiting Wendy's birth. It comprised a 44gallon drum raised on bricks over a fire box, a short distance from the back door, has already been described. Over the years it had served us well and could remain the same.

However cold water was still man-handled from the furrow, carried into the house and stored in various containers ready for the day's use. Now at my insistence, he had devised a more ambitious scheme. It would involve an extra drum sited higher up the hill, with an inlet and an outlet pipe to bring water directly down into the house by gravity flow. More pipes would conduct it to bathroom and kitchen to feed the gushing taps I craved so much. It sounded simple enough and it too should be foolproof unless the furrow got blocked by invading cattle, or some other Act of God which would cut off our water supply entirely. But as Ken said, "That happens anyway. I only have to send someone up the hill to clear it. "But, he added cautiously, "The pipes might get blocked up with time. So I'll need to get filters."

Along with the other building materials he had ordered from the PWD, were the pipes and accessories necessary to install this state of the art plumbing system. To no avail. Even after a note arrived stating that "Plumbing Requisites" had been despatched there was a long wait. At last Nelson sent word of their arrival at Kapoka and, as with the cement, Ken drove from Chisi to collect them. The pipes, the extra drum, were present and correct. Of the necessary elbow joints, filters, flanges etc, all specified in great detail, there was no sign.

He came back in a towering rage.

"How can I put a water system together with pipes and drums only? He fumed, "I'm not conducting a blasted orchestra. All very well those lazy lumps in Mzuzu knocking off on the dot of three. They should try living out in the bush for a change."

As usual there was a good deal more in this vein, some of it even true perhaps. He fired off another memo and wasted three more weeks.

"It's no use, he said at last, "I'll just have to make a quick dash to Mzuzu and get them myself."

Given the likely state of the roads, for we were by this time at the beginning of another rainy season, not to mention the walk to and from Chisi, a 'quick dash' seemed rather unlikely and I saw him off early one morning with misgiving. He expected to be away 'two or three days.' Another euphemism. It was after dark on the fourth day before he returned with the carriers. He was exhausted, muddy, but un-bowed, the PWD men now he had met them, transformed from lazy lumps to

"jolly decent chaps, very helpful."
As with the brick making, the work was protracted and difficult in practice. Suffice it to say that everything was in place at last, to be tested at a later date, when it should, in theory, work perfectly...

Virtually the last job on the house was the mudding and plastering of internal walls. Once again the women were called in. They were dubious about tackling brickwork instead of customary wattle and daub walls, and downright rebellious when Ken banned the use of cow dung.
The practice of mixing cow dung with the mud plaster was ages old. The Department of Agriculture frowned on it, urging people to use the dung to enrich their crops. A ludicrous, wasteful idea in which nobody believed. As everyone knew, cow dung was either for mudding walls, or when dried, as fuel for their cooking fires. There was a lot of angry talk.
"Sir, said Sutherland, "These women say that without cattle dung the plaster will fall off the walls."
"Rubbish." said Ken.
But I was whole-heartedly on the side of the women. The custom being so old, the extra work involved, implied a good reason surely. The outcome was unclear. Probably the women carried on regardless, with Sutherland turning a blind eye. We however could not wait to see the result. For we were going on a journey.

CHAPTER 40

THE SUNSET IN A PUDDLE

It now seems odd that I did not think to question Ken about home leave well before the end of his statutory tour of duty. The rhythmic turning of seasons in Misuku, Ben's birth, the Governor's visit, the new house, the ongoing drama everyday life on the station must have dulled the senses. Whatever the reasons I had overlooked it completely. Nor did Ken, for whom there never was a good time to leave, think to remind me until, at the height of the building work, a letter arrived from Zomba to the effect that his six months home leave, on full pay, fares included, was now overdue.

It could not be ignored.

"How can I leave now" he procrastinated, "The house is at a crucial stage. Then there are the coffee seedlings to be sold off again, not just here at Katobo but in the new nurseries starting up in the villages. If everything is left unsupervised goodness knows what I'll find when I get back."

"No-one's indispensable." I replied pompously. Having got a sniff of the idea of going home I could think of nothing else.

"And another thing, he went on, "It's now November. Remember remember? Who in their right mind would want to go to England in the middle of winter? Much better to leave it till the spring."

Reluctantly I was forced to agree. Recalling that dark and dismal month, and the ones that followed, I tried to dredge up the reality of that other life. During our years in Misuku our sole contact with it had been the letters from family and friends. Would they have changed as I myself had changed? I had left England pregnant certainly, but young and carefree withal. Quite a different person would be returning to the haunts of home.

And what about our children for whom Misuku was home, the only one they had ever known? How would they react to alien surroundings and strange people? So far they had known very few Europeans, Enos, Trisom and the people about Katobo were their surrogate family.

And what of my mother whose house we would be invading?

It must be admitted that valid as they were, none of these considerations weighed with me one jot, I was desperate to be there.

Quite apart from Ken's reluctance, practicalities would take a while to resolve. Notably the journeys. To our surprise we found we now had the choice of going by sea or air. The former I knew about; the nightmare of the voyage out had left a scar on my psyche and I was in no hurry to repeat the experience. Besides I wanted to take the quickest route possible. Ken on the other hand enjoyed sea travel.

"It's all very well for you, I told him, "You don't get seasick. Or pregnant."

282

"Yes, well it's a shame you were so ill. But you wouldn't be pregnant this time...."
"I certainly hope not"
"...And think of all those places you'd love to see again. Durban, Cape Town - Remember Camps Bay? St Helena? Or we could go via the Suez Canal, Stop off and see the Pyramids perhaps. You'd like that wouldn't you?"
"Yes, but that would take ages. Whereas if we fly, why we could be home in three weeks or so!"
The very thought of it brought a rush of blood to the head.
Here it should be said that actual flying time would amount merely to three or four days. The rest of the time would be taken up in getting out of Misuku, and driving south to Blantyre - though of course this would apply whichever route we took. If going by sea we must wait at Blantyre for the twice weekly train to Beira, there perhaps to incur further delay, then endure or enjoy, according to one's temperament, the six week long voyage. If by air, we would catch the plane to Nairobi which connected with the air liner that would take us on to London.

The sea option was out as far as I was concerned, but it must be admitted that the alternative was not without its hazards. By common consent the Nairobi/London flight was subject to disruption from a variety of sources. Sandstorms, flamingoes on runways, engine failure, to name but a few. Even so I was prepared to give it a go. We discussed the matter at length and at last reached a compromise. We would wait until March, go home by air, and come back by sea.

All this, though exciting, was still in prospect, and the intervening period would have dragged had there not been so much to do. There would be three more pay-days for a start. Another trip to Mbeya would be necessary. After that the coffee seedlings must be sold off.

The new house was finished at last; two days before we were due to leave the women completed the plastering with or without cow dung. The walls still wet - sometimes it seemed to me that all the significant events of our life in Misuku were accompanied by the sour smell of whitewash - we moved in. I had long since been separating out the things we would need to take with us on leave and our cases and bags were already full to bursting. That however was the easy part. Clearing out the old house and discarding the detritus acquired over the years was mind wrenching. Should one keep the terry-towelling lamb, now grubby and rather disgusting, that Jess had made for Wendy when she was a baby? Or the vase Trisom made from a short length of bamboo to hold roses from the garden? So many useless objects so dear to one's heart. In the end I made a pile and told Enos to dispose of everything, knowing full well that with the locals nothing was ever wasted. Everything else was packed in the two large trunks to be left behind.
The move itself at least was simple. The men carried the furniture the few yards from one house to the other and put it all down provisionally in much the same position as before. The old kitchen would be left for the time being. In our absence Enos, retained on half pay, would transfer everything to the new one to and sort

things out to his own satisfaction. Probably the DC and other official visitors would use the new place when they came on ulendo to Misuku, and he was instructed to be on hand to help them with water, firewood etc. just as Samueli, the Udd's cook had helped us in their absence.

To Sutherland was awarded the poisoned chalice of responsibility for all things agricultural while Ken was away.

Naturally there was much to be done on the day before our departure. Ken paid off the temporary labourers and the plastering women. All were regretful at the ending of such sociable work, no-one more so than old William, erstwhile labourer, brickmaker and cook.

In the afternoon while the children were resting in their new bedroom I went across to the old house, ostensibly to make sure nothing was left behind. On the threshold I stopped short, catching my breath at sudden realisation of all that these three small rooms had witnessed over the years.

The start of our married life, the climacteric of parenthood, the anguished post mortems on Ken's many setbacks and failures, the satisfaction of the few successes. Isolated incidents stood out, most of them shocks rather than surprises. My terror on the day Wendy pushed a canna seed high up her nose. The collapse of the first chimney in the early days. The arrival of the drenched carriers that stormy night, staggering under the weight of the big armchair. In imagination I saw again the coffee seedling which had erupted through the concrete of the sitting room floor. In the bedroom feelings, emotions too huge to recall. Only the night of the manyega - the soldier ants - came back with clarity. Waking in the dark to find the bed alive, the naked figure of Kalokhili laying about the intruders with his flaming fire brand, the neo Jackson Pollock created by Ken with insecticide on the earth floor - long since covered by concrete.

All would be obliterated, for the house was to be demolished in our absence, rather than be left as a blot on the landscape as it gradually fell down. Soon nothing would remain but a few curling photographs in the family archive. And remembrance of that time etched on our minds for ever...

At first light next day the assembled carriers hoisted up their loads and disappeared over the rim of the garden; Enos and Sutherland who had elected to accompany us as far as Chisi stood to one side, as did the men who were to carry Wendy and Ben in the tobacco basket. At last we were ready and set off on the familiar path down the valley. There was Mary's rondavel and the tall tree where the noisy hornbills roosted, there were the coffee bushes in serried rows on the terraces, their glossy leaves stirring in a light breeze. On down to the stream, no-one was abroad at the nursery.

Silently we negotiated the rickety bridge and climbed the opposing hillside with the light broadening. At the top I paused to look back. There stood the two houses side by side. A fleeting cloud fell across the old one, dimming its white walls, its dull thatch, so that it merged into the landscape submissively as if conscious of its fate. By contrast the rising sun shone directly on the new house, causing its aluminium roof to flash diamond like the morning windows of the princess' house in the children's book of fairy tales...

But travellers must fare forward.

The journey south was protracted but uneventful. We encountered rain, not unexpectedly as the wet season would not be over for another month or so. But there were no washed out culverts on the Misuku track and, thank God we were not troubled by the Kalengé river. Thus we attained the road south without difficulty. We over-nighted at Chisenga, and at Mzuzu where we rested for a day, with Ken reporting to the PAO on the state of agriculture in Misuku in general, and the coffee cooperative in particular. Then on to Lilongwe, and finally to Blantyre, not revisited by me since my arrival in the country seemingly so long ago. It was reassuring to find Ryalls Hotel exactly the same. A feeling reinforced for Ken because of his last visit which was when I was in Lilongwe hospital at the time of Wendy's birth. His purpose then had been to sell his old van; this time he was hoping to get rid of the pickup.

He was unsuccessful. As a compromise he arranged to leave it with his old friend Arthur Tomes, a wheeler dealer of the highest order, to get the best deal he could on it. I had met Arthur briefly on my first visit, but not his wife Billie. Now both were present and, as we must wait a few days for the plane, they invited us over for a meal.

They lived in a house somewhere off the road between Blantyre and Zomba. They now had a little girl called Sallie. To my gratification Sallie was also small for her age, although in her case it was because of a milk allergy, rather than to an unaccountable indifference to food in general as was the case with Wendy and Ben.

Billie and Arthur both had a keen sense of the ludicrous, which was just as well considering what life had handed out to them. During the 1939/45 war their house in London was bombed by the Germans, and sustained a direct hit which reduced it to rubble. Arthur's mother was killed outright. They themselves survived only because Arthur's brother with whom they had been drinking in the pub down the road a mere half hour before, knew they had gone home. He insisted that the rescue services dig down to the cellar in which they sheltered during air-raids. Arthur's injuries included a perforated eardrum, Billie wore the scars across her forehead like stigmata. Somehow this enhanced, rather than marred her fragile beauty.

Arthur had come to Nyasaland just after the war to take up a job similar to Ken's, but later had transferred to the PWD in the South, which was where Ken first met the two of them. Ken had gone on to the North but they had been posted to one God forsaken spot after another, including a stint on the dreaded Lower River. At Chirimba there were only two other Europeans, an elderly major, dour when sober, genial when drunk, which was most of the time, and his formidable wife, known to all and sundry as Auntie B. Auntie B habitually waited for her husband behind the door with a rolling pin when he came home drunk, late at night, which may have affected his brain a little.

She also invaded Billie's privacy whenever she had a mind to, walking in unannounced, inspecting cupboards for signs of extravagance, criticising her leniency with her staff.

Auntie B dyed her chickens green to deter hawks; there was no scientific evidence to suggest this. She also pierced the eggs she sold to her neighbours, so that they could not incubate them and raise their own stock.

One day as she was inspecting the said chickens for ticks, a constricting snake had the temerity to attack her, Starting with her feet it very soon progressed to what passed for her waist.

"Cut it off you fool!" she shouted to the garden boy who was watching in horror nearby.

Which he very bravely did. Unfortunately in the process he managed to rip off her skirt as well. It was the sight of Auntie B in her bloomers that really unnerved him.

"Oh God, you can't imagine how I hated that place Enid," Billie confided as we sat drinking tea while the men were outside looking at the sick vehicles that littered the garden, "Arthur and the major would be out all day and I was left with this harridan. Except at weekends that is. Then Arthur's friends would drive out from Blantyre - this was before Sallie was born thank God - and they sat around all day drinking and talking. And they wore those baggy shorts you know. My dear, a girl didn't know where to look. I hate men!"

They certainly did not hate her. As for me, I loved her for her humour and rueful ability to spread laughter. Qualities that never left her over the years of an enduring friendship.

There remained a short time till the plane was due so we checked out of Ryalls and drove to Zomba where Ken needed to report to the Agricultural Departmental headquarters. If possible, he wished to see Dick Kettlewell, the exalted Director. After which we intended to explore the Plateau, about which I had heard much. But, first things first.

We set out from Blantyre on the road taken on our epic journey up country at the start of my new life in the North. Morning freshness ruled now as then, smooth tarmac rolled before us. People trudging along with their loads, following the age old pattern of life, were identical with the ones encountered then. Perhaps some of them the very same ones.

On that first occasion we had skirted Zomba, now we drove into the town itself. Some way down a broad street shaded by jacaranda and quivering bluegum trees, we came to the complex of official buildings, to the ultimate Boma, the seat of Government. That is, the Legislative Council, an imposing edifice flying the Union Jack. Nearby were the various Departmental offices.

"I need to see Dick himself, said Ken stopping outside one of them, "And explain how vital it is for me to be based permanently in Misuku and not get posted somewhere else. I don't want to be messed about as I was when I came back after my last leave." The words had a familiar ring.

I knew by now the esteem in which Dick Kettlewell was held by those who had worked for him on the outstations. For he had constantly been out and about when he was PAO for the Northern Province, getting to know his junior officers, recognising the many problems and difficulties they faced and seeking to alleviate them. Such people are seldom rewarded by high office, but in his case, persistence and charm made advancement almost inevitable.

By chance, his time in the North had partly coincided with that of Tycho Hassett as Provincial Commissioner. Rumour had it they had served in the Guards together during the war, they must have made a formidable pair.

"I shall stress the importance of coffee to Misuku, Ken went on, "And tell him about the conservation work and so on. Dick will understand because he's been there. The trouble is though, he'll probably be away. Or too busy to see me. Then anything could happen. In any case it will take some time, so you'd better take the children for a stroll."

I did as he suggested and wandered down the shady street, the air still fresh and cool, resigned to a long wait. We had not gone far however when Ken rejoined us.

"Dick wasn't there?" I asked dispiritedly.

"He was there, but very busy. He saw me briefly though and said he wanted to hear more. So he's invited us to lunch at his house."

Gratified as I was on Ken's behalf, it was not good news. I knew full well that Wendy and Ben, having been cooped up by so much travel, tended to erupt when freed, and would almost certainly fail to attain the standard of behaviour expected of children in polite society. Keeping them in order would be a challenge in itself and I very much wished we could stay behind

"Couldn't you just go alone? I said, "You'd be able to talk without interruption then."

"Certainly not. He's invited us all."

In due course we presented ourselves at a spacious, gracious house set in a large garden well back from the road. Thus I was at last introduced to Dick Kettlewell about whom I had heard so much, and his wife Margaret.

Of the lunch itself I remember little, being too occupied with the children. When it was over Margaret suggested we have coffee in the garden,

"So that the children can run around."

Fearing for her flowers I agreed nervously. Margaret talked in an undemanding way of their own children away at boarding school in England, and I was able to give half an ear to what the men were saying. Ken, predictably, was stressing the importance, not only of the coffee cooperative, but also of the necessity of the Agricultural Department's continued presence in Misuku.

"There are many problems, I heard him say, "But land pressure and erosion are the most pressing of all. Already some villages have had to be abandoned. If things continue in this way the whole of Misuku will soon be over grazed, over cultivated, until it fails to support life at all."

There was a good deal more in this vein and he must have talked to some effect, or perhaps he was preaching to the converted, for Dick listened attentively and when he stopped said that, yes, assuredly Ken must go back and continue his work there. He also declared his intention of visiting us there after our return,

"If I can get away."

We all knew what that meant and in fact he never did come. Nevertheless a most unlikely and enduring friendship with the Kettlewells was born, carried on mainly by correspondence of necessity, as distances dictated, but subsequently encompassing visits to their home in Oxfordshire after Dick's retirement. The association ended only with Dick's death in 1994, Margaret having died some time before.

After leaving the Kettlewells we drove up toward Zomba Plateau 'on the clock', in accordance with a notice at the foot of a single carriage-way hacked out of solid rock, which sternly told travellers to go up on the hour, and down on the half hour. Or it may have been the other way round.

In truth the gradients were less severe than on the Chendo Track, or on the Misuku road, and the tarmac surface was infinitely superior to either. On the other hand there was far more traffic, also lush vegetation and tall trees on either side which obscured visibility, so the one way system was reassuring.

Our immediate goal was the Kuchawi Inn, a hotel nestling below the summit but high enough to command spectacular views of the countryside. Unlike Ryalls, the Kuchawe was new and stylish. We took tea on the terrace in very civilised fashion, relishing the cool, mosquito free air, taking in the wooded hills and hidden valleys stretching away below us, and the smudge of what might have been Mlangé Mountain away on the skyline. We sat on, the children playing within sight - Ben still uncertain on his feet - as the sky turned from bright to paler blue, to silver, streaked with bars of magenta, till daylight dwindled into to night.

In the morning we set out for the high plateau. Everyone familiar with it extolled the beauty of the place, but we had a special reason for wishing to see it. For, as was well known, such writers as John Buchan, Rider Haggard, Conan Doyle, whose works had thrilled our adolescence, had been inspired by the high places of Africa, Zomba Plateau among them. They had written books entitled King Solomon's Mines, Prester John, The Lost World, Children of the Mist, and the like. As it was love of books which had brought Ken and me together in the first place, it is no exaggeration to say that these particular ones had helped to shape our lives.

Alas, as we climbed, the weather closed in as on the day of the Governor's visit to Misuku. As in a bad dream, in eerie silence we drifted through a sea of fog, visibility limited to the dubious extremity of our headlights. At one point a lake the colour of steel was faintly discernible. We got out and found it teeming with fish, trout mostly, but whether they were a natural feature or had been introduced as sport for weekending Government officials, and food for the people unfortunate enough to inhabit the region, we never discovered.

A bit further on we came on a file of people walking in single file in the middle of the road. Startled by our headlights they moved over to let us pass. The patriarch leading the way and the men following after him carried spears, on which were skewered several fish. Behind them came women head-loaded with firewood; a gaggle of children brought up the rear. Children of the Mist indeed.

The fog persisted. But somehow that did not matter. Had we encountered the land laid bare in sunlight, the magic and mystery of the old books would surely have

been dispelled. As it was the spell cast on our adolescent minds was left intact, perpetuated by the gloom.
Next day we came down from the heights in every sense and made our way back to the Tomes' place. Once again they gave us lunch, cementing our friendship. In the afternoon Arthur drove us out to the airport.

The plane which took us to Nairobi was, of course, a good deal bigger than the Beaver. It also flew at greater altitude, but still low enough for us to pick out familiar features and landmarks. Once clear of the Highlands, in a cloudless blue sky we followed Lake Nyasa northward on a course which must, sooner or later, take us in the direction of Karonga, even perhaps, in the vicinity of Misuku itself. Thus accomplishing in two or three short hours the tedious journey to Blantyre that had taken us a week by road.
Looking down now on the smudgy landscape I recalled occasions at Katobo when a plane might be faintly heard, but never seen. Then I would pause in what I was doing, and try to recall that other world beyond the immediate. Was it possible that, even now, labourers leaning on their shovels, the butterfly girls in the nursery, village women going about their chores, would likewise pause to listen? Would Enos, who after all had made the flight to South Africa, conceivably connect the sound with ourselves? Assuredly not. All were at the centre of their own lives, and that was how it should be.

We spent a night at Nairobi in a hotel larger and grander than either Ryalls or the Kuchawe Inn. It was several stories high and boasted a lift, a first for the children. Nevertheless we were glad to leave it in the morning and transfer to the air liner which would take us on to London.
We were informed by the pilot in his speech of welcome that it had turbo-prop engines, a fact which meant nothing to me, and would certainly have passed me by but for what happened later.[1]
Surprisingly, due either to a dearth of first class passengers, or to spare others the unwelcome presence of our children, we were shown to a small compartment (cabin?) immediately aft the flight deck, where Wendy and Ben who, for reasons best known to themselves, had been on hunger strike for several days, might be induced to stretch out and go to sleep.

We were headed for Khartoum in the Sudan and I was very much looking forward to it. Khartoum, always coupled with the name of General Gordon, was yet another of the romance places of my youth. And Gordon another of my heroes.
Charles George Gordon, 1833/85, one of the foremost soldiers of his day, had performed deeds of great courage from China to Africa to the Danube in the service of his country. Not only that, in his meagre spare time he demonstrated his humanity by devoting himself to helping relieve the misery of the poor in newly industrialised England. I ranked him almost as highly as Lord Lugard himself. Unexpectedly in 1884 aged 51, with health impaired through long campaigning,

---

[1] Possibly a Lockheed Constellation.

General Gordon found himself in charge of a regiment of Her Majesty's army in the Sudan, at that time one of Britain's many outposts of Empire. His mission was to relieve a British garrison besieged by the Mahdi and his Dervishes at Khartoum. His efforts alas, were unsuccessful for he and his men, heavily outnumbered, were surrounded and were themselves besieged at the imperial palace.
The garrison held out bravely until a relief contingent arrived. Sadly it was too late to save Gordon. He had died fighting on the palace steps two days earlier.
A statue of Gordon seated on a camel had been erected in the main square of the town and I very much hoped to see it as we drove from the airport to the hotel where we would spend the night.
To my dismay we arrived after dark and did not go to a hotel. Did not go anywhere in fact, but spent several tortuous hours in the desert, in a stifling marquee at the edge of a runway, in heat unknown even in Karonga, We took off again at dawn, having seen nothing of Khartoum. Or of General Gordon.

Our next stop was Rome where, in contrast with the heat of Sudan, we were met by freezing fog and almost prevented from landing at all. A brutal reminder of March weather in the Northern hemisphere. The plane began the descent, circled the invisible airport, lost height rapidly but was thwarted of touchdown at the last moment. It climbed laboriously and circled once more. Finally a break in the cloud cover enabled the pilot to try again. Skilfully he side-slipped down to the runway, We had a fleeting glimpse of rooftops, a classical structure - the Coliseum perhaps. Then came a landing reminiscent of the Beaver at Karonga.
This should have been a brief stop for refuelling during which passengers would not disembark. But the time lengthened, due we were told, to engine trouble. We waited, the children still gritty with sand from the desert, became fractious, the cabin grew cold.

Presently Ken and I watched in disbelief, as in the sub zero temperature, a mechanic in shirt sleeves came running, waving a spanner. He climbed up on the icy wing of the plane to the engine a few feet away from our porthole, unscrewed part of the casing and extracted what looked suspiciously like a sparking plug. He brandished it triumphantly, gave it a rub and replaced it.

We took off five minutes later, but the drama of the journey was not yet over.
An hour or so later our attention was diverted from the drama of sunshine on snow as we climbed to overfly the Alps, by a cough from the recalcitrant engine. Sparks flew, the propeller outside our porthole faltered, slackened, stopped and hung motionless, the plane gave a lurch. For a timeless moment the Alps rushed up at us wickedly white. Then miraculously the plane levelled out.
A stewardess looked in to see if we were alright, saw the inert propeller, said "Oh my God!" and backed out again.
After an age the plane limped into Heathrow. Exhausted and dirty we were received into the bosom of our loved ones. Both families had gathered to greet us, my sister armed with hand knitted duffle coats for the children. Someone drove us through slushy snow and undreamt of stream of traffic, home to my Mother's house.

'Nothing is so beautiful as Spring.
When weeds in wheels shoot long and lovely and lush
Thrushes eggs look little low heavens,
And thrush through the echoing timber
Doth so rinse and wring the ear
It strikes like lightnings to hear him sing.'

Hopkins said it all.
The snow of our arrival quickly disappeared; in its place sunshine, racing clouds, fierce showers, rainbows, sky blue puddles, improbably long evenings. Celandines appeared in verges, then violets and primroses, followed by aconites and bluebells in the woods, daffodils in the gardens...

What we did for the next few months has no part in this narrative, except to say we made the most of our leisure, enjoying the company of family and friends, including Mary, who came with us on a visit to more friends in Germany.

One significant matter must be mentioned however. About a month into our leave a letter arrived from Arthur Tomes in Blantyre bearing the good news that he had sold the pickup. With the proceeds and our savings - after all there had been very little chance to spend money in Misuku - we were at last able to realise our dream of buying a land-rover. Ken who knew exactly what he wanted, went to the fountain head and contacted the manufacturers with a view to getting one built to his own specification. That is, a long wheel base version but with extra seating for carrying passengers in reasonable comfort, as well as the option of transporting goods. The makers were very helpful and in spite of this being the strike season, were confident of being able to deliver it 'within a month or two.' Which had a distinct sound of Africa about it.

After three months and many phone calls Ken was anxious.

"If this goes on it won't be ready before we have to leave." he said. After that he harried them every day.

At last he had the answer he wanted and as in Misuku with the pipes and drums, made another quick dash and collected it himself, as recorded. So for the time remaining we were able to take friends and relatives out and about in some style, in appreciation of all the hospitality and kindness they had lavished on us.

CHAPTER 41

"ONCE MORE UNTO THE BREACH'

At last the long summer evenings started to draw in. There was a nip in the air, soon would come the season of mists, mellow fruitfulness, and in our case painful parting. This time it would not take place at the local railway station with our loved ones lined up on the platform, but in the privacy of my Mother's home. Which would not make it one whit less painful, especially for her, at losing grandchildren who over the months, had wormed their way into her affections. I did not fully appreciate her feelings for another twenty five years when, as related, Wendy went back to teach in Nyasaland, which had by then become Malawi.

This time I did not make the mistake of thinking everything would be the same on our return, knowing by now that change is an inevitable part of life. All the same I prayed there would be no more gaps in the family circle.

The last goodbyes said, our worldly goods loaded in the land-rover, we set off through the home counties with their ever increasing urban sprawl, came eventually to the lovely lanes of Hampshire and thence to Southampton. We threaded our way through busy streets in which the ravages of war were not yet entirely eradicated, came on the familiar bustle of the docks, where another Union Castle liner waited.

After the usual delays our heavy luggage was collected. We watched in trepidation as the land-rover was winched aboard and swallowed up in the hold, not to be seen again until disembarkation several weeks later.

On deck the customary razzmatazz of departure. The same tug at the heart as the boat inched away, snapping the last streamers attached to loved ones on shore. The band played, the clock on the quay side pointed to 4PM precisely.

Rather than sailing to Africa ' the long way round' as on our last voyage, we had elected to take the East Coast route through the Mediterranean, the Suez Canal and the Red Sea, to arrive some six weeks later at the Kenyan port of Mombasa. Initially the passage was quiet and enjoyable. We called at Genoa and Gibraltar before heading for Port Said and thence to Suez, 1906 nautical miles away according to a framed map on the boat deck.

As we proceeded the temperature soared and our cabin became an inferno. We crept through the Suez Canal, so narrow as scarcely to give the boat clearance. Indeed at one point a shudder from stem to stern gave rise to the certainty that its paintwork would never be the same again. Progress was agonisingly slow, the children suffered painfully from prickly heat. The Red Sea was hardly any cooler. The British port of Aden 1310 miles from Suez - I had become obsessed with the map on deck by this time - promised to be a diversion. And so it proved. Although still hot, the bazaar was bursting with curios, souvenirs, exotic material, ingenious toys, and fripperies of all kinds virtually impossible to resist. After Aden remained the 1602 mile leg to Mombasa.

At what point of a journey does one stop looking back with yearning, and start instead to look forward, wondering what lies ahead? In my case that point was the nadir of Suez and the Red Sea during sleepless nights of tending the children for whom I could do little. Then my thoughts would turn to the future when we would once again be back in our own home in Misuku. Of the overland journey of 1000 miles or so we must make from Mombasa to Nyasaland to attain this goal, I preferred not to dwell. Except that is, for the first stage.
Due to the Williamson's leaving Nyasaland, perforce, on Andrew's retirement, after much discussion and one or two forays into neighbouring territories, they had chosen to settle in Tanganyika and had taken a house near Moshi with, as Jess wrote,
"A splendid view of Kilimanjaro."
Here she had resumed all her old interests. Here too Andrew had set up as a dowsing consultant. And it so happened by remote and happy chance, that this spot was but one or two miles off the road we ourselves would be taking.[1]*
The arrival at Mombasa was hailed with relief by most of those on board ship. But especially by people who, like us, had small children, the attractions of a lengthy cruise having long since faded.
The unlading of cargo began in its usual leisurely fashion, passengers' luggage and effects, as ever, taking second place to commerce.
Meanwhile ship to shore formalities were completed, goodbyes said to the crew and to passengers with whom we had developed the camaraderie of fellow sufferers, knowing it unlikely we would ever see them again.
Around noon the hold was opened up. With bated breath we watched as our precious land-rover was winched up by a seemingly casual operator, swung high over the side of the ship, then put down gently on the quay.
This was the moment we had been waiting for. The land-rover, thoroughly checked over before we left England, was loaded with our gear, at exorbitant cost by willing hands, the tank was filled at a nearby petrol pump facility. The engine fired at once, we were ready to set out on the next stage of the journey.

During all our travels in Africa I have no recollection of our ever having had recourse to a map. Partly this was because many of the regions in which we found ourselves had never been mapped in detail, and partly due to the scarcity of roads in general. There was seldom any choice, seldom more than one route in the direction one wished to go. If it happened to have a reasonable surface over most of its length, well, that was a bonus indeed. On this particular day the going was tolerable and we made good speed, heading west across the coastal

---

[1] Andrew had long been aware of his dowsing talent. We had witnessed it ourselves in Karonga, by holding on to him as he held the rod, feeling its power to buckle and bend if he came across underground water. See Tom Williamson, New Light On An Ancient Art, pub. Robert Hale, London, 1993

plain, gradually gaining altitude. Suddenly, to our surprise and pleasure, in gathering dusk we came across a road sign pointing to a track off to the right. It read,

A.C. WILLIAMSON
UNDERGROUND WATER SURVEYS
BY DIVINING AND GEOPHYSICAL METHODS
2 MILES

We turned off, and presently came to a house which might have been transplanted, so similar was it to their previous one in Karonga.

That we arrived at the Williamson's door unannounced was hardly our fault. For not only had Ken notified Andrew of the boat's arrival at Mombasa even before we left England, but we had followed it up with letters or postcards from various ports of call en route. Had even one of these got through on time, Andrew, not a family man, might well have gone on ulendo. As it was he put a brave face on it and merely asked how long we intended to stay. Jess on the other hand was genuinely pleased to see us.

Was she lonely or bored in this somewhat isolated spot? Not at all. Boredom was not in her agenda. She had lived in too many remote places in the course of her life, by now experience coupled with natural self sufficiency, enabled her to adapt to almost anything. Moreover she was delighted to find herself at last in a place favourable for establishing a proper garden. Already there were flowers, vegetables and shrubs growing in profusion.

Andrew too was fully occupied, and in great demand. As would anyone in Africa be who held out the hope of finding the precious commodity of water.

As with the exterior, the inside of the house virtually replicated the one in Karonga, so it seemed that little had changed. In the sitting room the same books occupied the same book shelves, the same pictures - scenes of places on various continents where Jess and Andrew had sojourned - hung on the walls. On the polished floor were the rugs Jess had bought in India when she was teaching young girls whose fate it was to be plucked early from school to become part of some rich man's zenana.

But darkness was upon us and a houseboy other than Umali carried in an extra lamp.

Andrew said,

"Pity you weren't here a bit earlier, you could have seen Kilimanjaro. But never mind, it's sure to be clear in the morning."

And so it proved. Jess had not exaggerated, there was indeed a splendid view of Kilimanjaro. In the distance the highest mountain in Africa rose up from a base said to be 100 miles in circumference. It was, and is a volcano, long extinct, or so the experts say. But who can wholly trust a volcano? Or an expert either for that matter. Be that as it may, there had been plenty of time for hardwood forests to become established on its flanks, for grass and vegetation to grow up, and cultivation to develop on the lower slopes.

We had in fact flown over it on the plane taking us to England on leave. But that was toward evening, and with shadows lengthening we had discerned only its smudgy bulk. Now we saw the shining slopes in broad daylight - unforgettable - and marvelled at the improbability of snow in Africa.

Our time with the Williamsons was short. All too soon the illusion that nothing had changed was shattered. Once more we must say goodbye and pack up and leave.

Of the rest of that journey only a hazy recollection remains. Night stops at places with names like Dodoma, Iringa come to mind, townships perhaps the size of Mzimba, with a hotel, a store, a bank, a commercial garage with petrol pump. One occasion does stand out. Going in to dinner at a nondescript hotel in one such place, isolated in bush country, it was disconcerting to meet another girl in a Marks and Spencers outfit identical to my own.

The general impression of that countryside was one of featureless scrub with no visible water sources or means of supporting life - no wonder Andrew's talents were in demand. Wildlife there was however. Giraffe were plentiful, family groups of them ambled across the road in front of us with little traffic to bother them; sometimes a troupe of monkeys raced away from us. The tawny veldt was also known to conceal lion and leopard. We did not see any, but early one morning overtook a secretary bird striding along the side of the road. This odd looking creature, about 4 feet high on long spindly legs, with sober grey/white plumage and a crested head with quills sticking from it, must, surely, have been named by Victorian explorers familiar with clerks in Dickensian London offices. Ill paid but obliged to look respectable in dark suits and clean shirts. These unfortunates, doomed to spending long days in grimy offices heated only by meagre coal fires, covering large ledgers with immaculate copperplate, or adding up laborious columns of figures, stuck sharpened quills behind their ears to make sure of having a good supply of (somewhat primitive) pens.

Imperceptibly we gained altitude, the bush gradually gave way to vegetation, the area grew more populace as the air became fresher. And with it a lift of our hearts for we knew Mbeya could not be far off and we would be virtually on home territory.

Great was the joy of our arrival at the Mbeya Hotel at last, familiar now because of our regular shopping trips, memorable to me of my very first visit and the unforgettable experience of Spartacus the Gladiator, at the cinema with Mary and Gerry Williams. It all seemed a long time ago. This time the staff and a few acquaintances at the bar, greeted us as long lost friends, which made it seem some- thing of a minor homecoming.

We had a day of rest and comparative relaxation. Ken went about the business of getting the car serviced, sending official telegrams to Mzuzu and Karonga, I ventured nothing more strenuous than keeping an eye on the children who embraced the freedom of the hotel garden in the manner of prisoners released from long confinement. In the evening I went out to gladden the eye of the 'open all hours' Indian storekeeper with a massive order of groceries. As usual he had it sent along to the hotel; somehow we crammed it in to the land-rover with all the other luggage, ready for the obligatory early start in the morning.

Next day the road was dusty and pot-holed as ever as we crossed the plain and climbed up the scarp. But at the top the nondescript bush country seemed less desolate and the people less aloof, simply because we were going home. At Mbosi we did not evade the customs post this time. The lofty Sikh at the customs post seemed to sense our urgency, stamped our passports with necessary clearance, then waved us through disdainfully.

Thus we made good time and reached Fort Hill in daylight. It had not changed. The same smoke haze hung above it, an identical crowd milled about the compound, on the runway stood a big WENELA plane. We did not stop but pushed on to Chisenga rest-house, there to sample once more the dubious delights of lamp light, and water carried in by hand to the enormous concrete bath Henryk Knight had built for his equally enormous wife.

Next morning neither Ken or I had difficulty in waking up early. With dawn breaking we cruised off on what had been part of Angus Day's road system - now somewhat neglected as no other resident engineer had been appointed. The air was invigorating. As the sun came up the Wilindi massif rising up hazily in the distance beckoned like the Promised Land. We passed Piccadilly Circus at the head of the Chendo and in an hour or so reached Kapoka.

Given the remoteness of the place, the vagaries of the postal service and our recent experience with Andrew and Jess, it seemed unlikely that Ken's letter to Nelson from one of the townships along our route, would have got through. Yet here he was, his good eye twinkling, his people gathered round him. We got out of the truck, the women exclaimed over Wendy and Ben who, though jaded by travel still retained something of the colour, the well-being, of months spent in a cooler climate.

When the cordial greetings were over Nelson told Ken he had received his letter. "Yes Sir, it arrived two days ago. A drum of petrol has also come from Mzuzu." This was good news indeed for the PWD down country could be as erratic as the mail, deliveries could never be taken for granted.

"Good, replied Ken, "I can't take it now, there's no room in the galimoto, but I'll drive down for it later. What is the road like?"

"Oh, very good Sir." (An understatement to put it mildly,) "And Mr Udd's new bridge is also very good. Also there was a meeting at the Court of Chief MweniMisuku."

"Oh yes?" Ken's mind was on the road, meetings at the Court were common enough, but Nelson went on,

"Yes Sir. A big Bwana Makubwa came from the South. Many people in Misuku gathered to hear him. Mr Udd and his grown son were also present."

This was intriguing and we paid more attention. Who could have commanded

such a wide audience? Surely the Governor had not come again? Still less the Governor General of the fledgling Federation of the Rhodesias and Nyasaland? "No Sir, continued Nelson at Ken's questioning, "This man was African but he could not speak our tongue. He spoke only English."
Nelson could give us no more information, not having been present himself, and we resolved to question Ragnor Udd next time we saw him.

In the event Ragnor walked over to Katobo a few days after our return.
"Yes, it was a big meeting alright, he told us, "Half the population of Misuku was there I should think. After a build-up by one or two locals, it was addressed by someone of the name of Banda.
"Dr Banda!"
I was galvanised, not by the name, that meant nothing to me, but by the designation Doctor.
"What! I exclaimed, "Are we to have a hospital here in Misuku? No wonder the people turned out for him!"
"Nono, nothing like that. This was political. He didn't come with the DC or any officials."
"But who is this African who speaks only English? asked Ken. Then as a thought struck him, "Oh, I suppose he was American?"
"Wrong again. He's a Nyasalander, born in a village near Lilongwe I believe. Rumour has it that he went to a mission school as a boy, a bright lad, and was sent on for further education in South Africa. After that he made his way to America where he graduated in medicine, subsequently achieving further honours at Edinburgh and Glasgow Universities. He then practised medicine throughout the 1939 – 45 war in Liverpool and later in London. He was away so long apparently that he forgot his mother tongue. Only recently returned to Nyasaland by all accounts."
"But the meeting..."
"Oh yes. Well he spoke quite moderately, but that chap Msepelé from Tialekanjeré - a trouble maker if ever there was one - made what you might call a free translation. He was much more radical. Forgetting, or perhaps not caring, that Rodney and I could understand both versions."
That was all Ragnor could tell us and the conversation moved on. Ken congratulated him on the splendid new bridge at the Kalengé, I added my own heartfelt thanks.
"Well I've got this new truck you know. Bigger than the last one."
Clearly our new land-rover would pale into insignificance beside it. But we did not grudge him his good fortune.
In the press of immediate matters demanding Ken's time and attention in the days and weeks that followed, the matter of the meeting was soon forgotten.

We said goodbye to Nelson and his family and continued on our way. The Kalengé bridge was indeed impressive. It stood well above river level, very robust, and with vastly improved approaches. Ken gave an appreciative whistle as we drove over and I felt a surge of relief. No longer would we be virtual prisoners in Misuku, hostage to the weather. Neither would we have to walk out to Chisi at best, or to Kapoka during the rains. The thought was barely believable.

After the Kalengé we traversed remembered brachystegia scrubland, meeting no-one but a group of young men walking out to Fort Hill. Highly excited, they told us they were going to sign up for the mines, clearly having no presentiment of what was in store for them.

The road had received little attention in Ken's absence, but even though he must be always on the watch for potholes or boulders, the surface was tolerable. The foothills of Wilindi did not trouble the land-rover and great was our rejoicing as we swept past Chisi. No need to park there now. Now for the ultimate test, the climb to the summit.

I held my breath as we wound round the narrow rock-face, hugging the track that became steeper by the moment. Then, quite suddenly, we were up and over. Ken pulled up and cut the engine.

The silence was broken only by the sound of cattle bells floating up to us. Below lay Misuku dreaming in sunlight.

Inevitably I was reminded of my first arrival, prior to Wendy's birth, when I had viewed this land from the top of Mughessé - discernible now as a smudge on the opposing skyline. On that occasion I had thought life in such a beautiful place must be idyllic. Now I knew better. For the people it was precarious at best. Not even beauty was assured. Poverty, disease, land pressure on their crops, the felling of trees for firewood, all took their toll. Erosion, if left unchecked, would put paid to cultivation, hunger would force people to move on, the old way of life would be gone for ever.

I roused myself from these gloomy thoughts. From our vantage point we could see the sprawling homestead of Joseph Mkumbwa, founded on coffee many years before at the time of Mr Lilford. Beyond was the school with its beaten earth patch where the boys played football, and the Court complex where perhaps, at this very moment MweniMisku was in session with the elders, dispensing his own brand of justice. Ken said,

"Look, you can just make out Katobo. Over there, he pointed, "Among the trees."

My eyes searched out the familiar whitewashed cottage we had left, and failed to find it. Then I realised with a pang it no longer existed. It was to the new house we were returning.

CHAPTER 42

CHANGES

Next morning we were woken once more by the discordance of metal striking metal - the signal for the men to start work - which in turn, roused the hornbills to their daily protestations in the big tree outside the rondavel. It also roused me from dreams of dustmen - refuse collectors - making an early round at my mother's house in England. The clamour heightened the sense of disorientation brought on by weeks of travel and It was some time before I recollected we were back at Katobo, and this was a working day.

The previous afternoon we had come down from the heights of Wilindi and for the very first time had DRIVEN the track across Misuku. To misquote Eliot once more,
"It was as you may say, very satisfactory."
That is, villagers along the way saluted the land-rover, as they did any vehicle passing through. When they realised who was in it they stopped, surprised to see us travelling in this way, and called out greetings in their usual friendly manner. Naturally we in turn stopped to reciprocate. Thus our progress was somewhat leisurely.
Boys at the school called out in English as we waved and drove slowly past. At the Court Chief MweniMisuku and the elders, who had as usual somehow discerned the time of our coming, welcomed Ken back with grave ceremony.
At Katobo Enos, Trisom and labourers who had remained after working hours, all seemed pleased to see us. If they had experienced a somewhat more relaxed atmosphere in Ken's absence and regretted its likely demise, they did not show it.

Why then, once adjusted, did I feel a sense of loss? The reason was simple. Realisation that the old house had gone for ever was hard to shake off, the new one in which we had spent the night seemed little more than one of the lodging places along the way.
Getting up I parted the curtains, cautiously - already the labourers were gathering - and looked across to the site of the old house. Coarse grass, unnaturally green, had already half obliterated it. Sighing I turned away. Ken was drinking his tea, I said,
"This place doesn't feel the same as the old."
"I should hope not. Less livestock overhead for a start." he replied, but getting up, added more kindly, Don't worry though, you'll soon get used to it. And when we get the water connected, why, you'll wonder how we ever managed before."
In truth he was right. Not only was the new house half as big again and a great deal more convenient, it was in fact not so very different from the old. Being so

near the other and occupying the same ledge on the hillside, it commanded the same splendour, the same panoramic scene which never failed to lift the spirit. In spite of myself romanticism gradually gave way to practicalities. The more so when the water was piped in. This did not happen at once, there were too many other matters demanding Ken's attention for that. When at last he had time to attend to it everything worked perfectly - and continued to do so. Moreover we no longer had tadpoles in the soup, or frogs in the bath. Of course the supply was limited to cold water only, hot water for the bath was carried in from the drum outside as before. But even to turn on a tap gave one a childish pleasure; a pleasure fully shared by Enos at the kitchen sink. During our absence he had arranged the kitchen to his liking, now he very soon devised his own method of entertaining family and friends, discreetly, as he worked. Appreciating him the more on our return, provided he restricted the number and the noise level, we turned a blind eye.

I myself spent more time in the new kitchen, but mainly on a Sunday, a rest day for the staff, when I could have the place to myself and make sure it was clean, hygienic and reasonably tidy.

This was easier still after the arrival of William 2nd, the latest in a long line of kitchen boys taken on by Enos, probably as a favour to a crony rather than any suitability for the job. However unlike William 1st who had nearly ruined our digestive systems, this one was young, a failed schoolboy who spoke a little English. He resembled his namesake however in being willing, eager to please and keen to learn, so that domestic matters ran relatively smoothly for once.

Alas it was not so for Ken. After breakfast on that first morning of our return there came a shock. He came back to the house accompanied by a well dressed African, a stranger to whom he introduced me, saying flatly,

"This is Pearson Msembwe the new Head Capitao. Sutherland has been transferred."

I held out my hand automatically but could not assimilate what he had said.

Sutherland gone? Impossible, I must have misheard. Sutherland was Ken's right arm, the prop and mainstay of all his work. Sutherland, a tower of strength in my early days and a helping hand ever since. Sutherland who had translated my culinary instructions to the unlikely first William, interpreted and largely diagnosed the complaints of the afflicted in the daily sick parade. Sutherland who had found Enos for us... Assuredly there was some mistake. Misuku without him was unthinkable as had been the prospect of Karonga without Jess and Andrew.

Yet even as I reasoned, such being the vagaries of Government - here I thought fleetingly of Steve - I knew it to be true. Bad as it was for me, for Ken it was downright disaster. A fait áccomplis about which he could do nothing. His work was hard enough already, without Sutherland's competent and reassuring presence about the place and in the District at large it would be well nigh impossible. Many years after when the events of this time were but a distant memory, Ken told me,

"Throughout most of my time in the North I had two strands of support. The first was Andrew Williamson in Karonga, the second was Sutherland in Misuku. When they left, one after the other, I felt like a cripple without crutches."

When I had recovered sufficiently I called Enos.

"Yes Madam, it is true, he said, " Sutherland has gone."

"But what about his wife who is your true sister? And the children...?"

"They remain in Misuku. My sister has gone back to the village of my father and mother and the children with her. My sister is sad too much."

"But why?" I persisted when Ken and I were alone. "I wondered why he wasn't here to greet us yesterday, but assumed he'd been held up on ulendo somewhere."

"Why indeed, agreed Ken, "I thought it odd myself. In fact I'd half expected him to be at Kapoka with Nelson. "It's possible he wanted a change and asked for a transfer. But far more likely someone further south transferred this chap for their own convenience. It's a blow to me I can tell you. Still, he added, "He seems pretty experienced. Perhaps it'll work out alright."

It did not.

The new man was capable, certainly, when he had a mind to be, but more often than not was bad tempered and uncooperative. He came from the South, was unfamiliar with the terrain and gave the impression of despising all and sundry. Subsequently we heard in a round about way that he had earned the reputation of being disruptive and had been moved on before. Clearly Misuku was the last dumping ground for undesirables.

And for this man we had lost Sutherland. Ken now had to rely solely on the District Capitaos to enforce the Agricultural Department's necessary, but highly unpopular rules and regulations. Committed as they were, they had not Sutherland's authority to back them up on his visits to their areas. Ken's ulendos, shared out over the whole region were necessarily, rare events, which meant the people would revert to their old ways. Soil conservation measures would be ignored, erosion would gain the upper hand, the people would become even poorer.

In due course Ken lodged an official complaint against Msembwe. After considerable delay he was informed that "matters were being considered". He heard nothing more; it was uphill work in every sense.

On the plus side, the local District Capitao had also gone. To me this shadowy figure lived in a village a few miles off, rather than in one of the capitaos' houses on the ridge, so that I saw him only on pay days. But I knew him to be inadequate, rather than a positive asset to the work force. His replacement, Ngomba, who did live on the ridge, was also an off-comer; he was young and inexperienced, but intelligent and hard working. Cheerful also, he got on well with the locals. Ken began to work with him more and more, by-passing Msembwe whenever he could.

With the rainy season well established we settled down once more to our cloistered existence, with expectation of no more than an occasional visit from the ADC who had earned my gratitude by obligingly sitting on the floor during the Governor's visit. We were surprised therefore by the arrival one day of a police officer from Mzuzu. Accompanied by two Askari he had driven his jeep as far as the blasted blue-gum, then puffed his way up the hillside to the house. Never before had we been honoured by such a visitation, as all the misdemeanours of the area were dealt with either by the Chief, or the DC in Karonga.

The officer introduced himself as Fitzherbert, and surprised us further by enquiring after Pearson Msembwe. Ken, gratified that notice of his complaint was receiving attention, gave a full and bitter account of that gentleman's shortcomings. Fitzherbert listened but made no comment. Instead he went on to ask if we knew anything about a man called Msopelé. Ken, echoing Ragnor, said,
"I do indeed. A trouble maker if ever there was one. Lives in the village of Tialikanjeré on the other side of Mughessé, quite a remote area. He was away for a long time, I don't know where, but came back while we were on leave apparently. I heard from my District Capitao there that he's been stirring up the people to flout the Department's regulations on conservation etc. - I intend to go there and read the riot act as soon as the rains ease off."
He went on,
"Then there was the business of the visit of a Dr Banda, also during our absence. Our nearest neighbour Ragnor Udd, attended the meeting. He's the missionary at Mubula some eight miles away, who speaks good Chisukwa. He gave us a full account of the proceedings. He said that Doctor Banda gave quite a moderate speech in English, but Msopelé translating, gave quite a different version. Highly inflammatory."
As an afterthought Ken finished,
"I reported it to the DC as soon as I heard."
Fitzherbert asked,
"How far is this village of - er- What did you say it was called?"
Ken spelled it out and said,
"It's about 10miles or so off. On foot of course, there's no road. And it involves climbing up over Mughessé, the ridge you see here, rising up behind the house."
At this Fitzherbert looked thoughtful and appeared to lose interest.
As with the PWD road engineer before him, we gave him lunch, after which he made his goodbyes and we saw him no more.

In spite of Ken's many other duties, getting things back in order at Katobo, completing the road, visiting villages within a day's reach, etc, he was still obliged to spend 14 nights of every month on ulendo. Not necessarily all at once fortunately. Mostly he took the small tent and camped for a night or two at a time, taking Enos to cook for him. If however he was making a longer ulendo to the outlying villages, circumstances permitting, which is to say that if there was the opportunity of camping in a mud brick church or school, and the weather reasonable, the children and I would go with him.
The pattern of these occasions did not vary. Every night was spent in a different village, every morning early Ken would go off about his work of inspecting gardens with the District Capitao, the village headman and the elders, then make his way to the next place.
For me it was more like a holiday. As usual I followed at my own pace, the children in the tobacco basket - a little more cramped now - with William 2nd and sometimes Akim as well. I stopped to chat with the women whenever I felt like it. Most of them in the more remote parts had never travelled further from their homesteads than their legs would carry them and were probably glad of

any diversion.

In this leisurely fashion we would arrive at the next village in the afternoon, by which time Enos, who had gone on ahead, would have everything organised and cups of tea at the ready.

Unfortunately however, these ulendos had become rarer with our expanded family. Glad though Ken was of our company, logistics were obviously more complicated than if he went alone. In either case it was hard work for Ken. He invariably came late to the night's destination and even then his work was not finished. His first job on arrival was to ensure the carriers had food, (poso,) and a place to sleep. His second was to hold a meeting with the headman and elders.

Inevitably lack of supervision encouraged the villagers to follow their natural inclination of cultivating right up to stream banks, neglecting to dig bunds across hillsides to check erosion; the land, as he had feared, was becoming more impoverished. The villagers, though friendly and hospitable as ever, were shamefaced, acknowledging their backsliding and promising to mend their ways. So much for promises, Ken had heard it all before.

Changes were also evident in the District at large, including at Karonga itself. Andrew had been replaced by not one, but two officers. Brian Stearn, a Cambridge graduate with further training at the College of Tropical Agriculture in Barbados, now lived in the Williamson's old house. He visited us often at Katobo. Until that is, he was joined by his fiancée, Pat, so another wedding. But one which resembled Steve's only in that Ken, having driven us all to Karonga for the occasion, officiated as Best Man, and that Wendy and I wore our best frocks.

After his marriage agricultural matters in Misuku did not figure quite so often in Brian's schedule.

The second appointee, Gordon Burridge, was based at Chisenga and lived in Angus Day's house. He too often came to Katobo for weekends until he too sent for a girl friend, Marian, to share his splendid isolation. As with Billie and Arthur Tomes, their type of humour chimed with our own and we had some hilarious times together. They too married, but that was when we were on leave.

The last notable change on our return was in Mzuzu. Our good friend John Sandys, the Provincial Agricultural Officer who visited us whenever he could, was promoted to Zomba.[1]

We first met his successor John Evans, and his wife Rosemary, on one of our rare shopping trips south. Hospitable and kind, we were destined to become better acquainted with them and their large family in quite different circumstances.

Soon after his appointment John came to see us as part of an exploratory tour of the Northern Province; because his time was short he flew to Fort Hill, where Ken met him, and drove him back to Misuku. They spent several days going round the villages, with John especially interested in the Coffee Cooperative.

At the end of his visit Ken took him back to Fort Hill to pick up the Beaver on its return journey south.

---

[1] He later became Director of Agriculture, Fiji.

But the plane never arrived at Mzuzu. Fears there mounted as it became overdue, No doubt the unspoken thought was that it had developed engine trouble and plummeted into the lake. It had not but the actuality was potentially almost as serious. The pilot had lost his bearings over the high Nyika and for some time followed a steep sided valley. Unluckily an adverse air current prevented his regaining altitude and the plane crashed into the hillside. Miraculously everyone on board escaped with minor injuries and managed to struggle their way to the nearest settlement. A runner was despatched to relay the news to Mzuzu and eventually all were rescued, not much the worse.

Opportunities for meeting colleagues were rare, but one such occurred when an Anglican priest from Likoma Island was due to visit Karonga and hold a service. The shifting ex-patriot population in the area continued to evince a complete lack of enthusiasm for church services, let alone the daily prayers so important to Captain Lugard and his men, but a new DC reputed to 'be keen on such things', circulated a memo throughout the District, urging everyone to go and take advantage of this occasion of spiritual sustenance. And, since most of the toilers in the field would consider a religious service a small price to pay for a convivial weekend in Karonga, it was a fair bet it would be well attended. As we now had the Landrover and the "road" in almost to the door, the Chendo Track not withstanding, we decided to go and have the children christened.

Oh the luxury of getting our baggage loaded on the Landrover almost on our doorstep, and instead of walking out to Chisi, able to drive the rest of the way. The heat and dust of the journey were the same as ever, but the Chendo held no terrors for the land-rover and we made good time.

The service incorporating the christening was held in Karonga's only formal meeting place, namely the open sided Courthouse near the DC's office with Captain Lugard's cannon outside. It was attended by friends and acquaintances as predicted, and by a throng of local people. Wendy and Ben were baptised by the priest, with the DC's silver soup tureen doing duty as a font, while I prayed fervently that God and the baby Paludrine tablets we forced down their throats every day would save them from the mosquitos also in attendance. A black and white photograph of the occasion remains in the family archive, of the four of us dressed in our best, in front of the living bamboo fence of the tennis court.

There followed the easy sociability as before, though Mary would have recognised none of the bachelors. Someone held a lunch party, with tennis in the afternoon to follow. We however opted to go down to the lake, where the seductive delights of lake water lapping on the shore, warm sand between the toes, the opportunity to immerse oneself as in a cooling stream, were enhanced by the pleasure it gave our children.

Again we met Richard, the doctor we had tended when he unexpectedly arrived ill at Katobo prior to Ben's birth. He was now living in one of the old surviving Colonial houses near the lake. To our surprise he had been joined at the hospital by a nursing sister and the hospital now burgeoned with unaccustomed cleanliness and the smell of disinfectant. Even the squatters in the compound had been reorganised to sit in rows.

The nurse, like Marian Burridge at Chisenga, was Scottish but there the resemblance ended. Not in the first flush of youth, she was severe and serious, rather like Sister Schnabel at Lilongwe. She was however, undeniably single so it goes without saying that she was pursued by all the unattached men in the District. Which must have made a pleasant change for her. She had the Cloverleaf house of which we had such pleasant memories. On the only occasion I had cause to visit her there I found the place transformed. Gone was any evidence of my own sketchy housekeeping, in its place the same regimented hygiene apparent at the hospital. No pot of drooping marigolds here, no books and papers scattered about there, no ant tunnels on the walls; even the hornets and other livestock lurking above the matted ceiling appeared to know their place. On the hitherto cool polished floor was a carpet - surely the first ever seen in Karonga - partly covered by a drugget. A clear case of 'Before you let the sunshine in/ Be sure it wipes its feet.' Naturally speculation ran rife that Richard the doctor would marry the nurse. But no. He went on leave to South Africa and had the good sense to come back with a gorgeous blonde. The nurse married a dour police officer from Mzuzu.

On this occasion our return to Misuku was uneventful. But on a subsequent journey from Karonga even the Landrover, by then not so new, protested at the state of the Chendo which, since Angus Day's departure, had been 'maintained' by road gangs. Sooner or later we were bound to have a puncture. Sure enough, on this particular day it happened a few miles up the Track. We got out and Ken put the spare on. After a few miles a different tyre blew. Ken patched up a puncture in the inner tube.[2] It held, but not for long. Several punctures and a good few miles later when all the patches had been used up, we were stopped yet again. Ken, desperate beyond cursing, packed the outer casing tightly with dried grass - the only material to hand - and thus we limped to the top of the Chendo and on to the Chisenga road.
Here the going was smoother but there was another hazard. The last stretch wound tortuously round the foot of the Mafingé Hills so that with a wounded vehicle, and the light fading, driving took the utmost concentration. One false manoeuvre would certainly have sent us over the edge. We arrived at Chisenga rest-house at last; Ken cruised over the car inspection pit in readiness for giving the land-rover a thorough checkup in the morning.

After breakfast next day he tightened nuts which had shaken loose, made minor adjustments to the engine and obtained more patches for the tyres at the small PWD depot. Helped by the capitao/mechanic in charge, he did what he could to the badly damaged tyre and put it on again. He also wrote out an order for two new tyres, which the capitao said he would 'post' on their next lorry going south to Mzuzu.
We were ready to go. Alas, as Ken drove to the front of the rest-house where the children and I waited, the steering wheel turned - but the land-rover went straight on.

---

[2] All tyres consisted of inner tube and outer casing at this time.

The cause was simple, potentially deadly. A concealed screw on the steering column had taken one bump too many and dropped off. Had this happened on one of the bends of the previous evening we would certainly gone over the edge, our fate sealed. The cause, simple or not, would have been of little comfort to our grieving relatives.
As it was we limped back to Misuku without further mishap.

In the matter of getting about our most regular outings were, of necessity, the shopping trips to Mbeya, which of course were infinitely easier with the land-rover. If necessary we could drive there in one day, though mostly we still preferred to overnight at Chisenga on both outward and homeward journey, the comparative leisureliness of benefit to us all. Thus, provided we did not get bogged down in mud or held up by some unforeseeable mishap outside our control, it was possible to spend a weekend at the Mbeya Hotel in civilised fashion.
Circumstances favoured us even more when, after a while, the Portuguese WENELA manager at Fort Hill was replaced by an English couple, Connie and Bill James, who were always happy to have us to stay with them. Moreover, having no children of their own they made much of Wendy and Ben.
Connie and Bill very soon became a byword for hospitality and kindness well beyond the call of duty. Beyond the means of mere Colonial Servants as well. Like the Udds they had a luxurious home and enjoyed a high life style, largely on account of the twice weekly recruiting planes which, at Connie's behest, brought in all manner of delicious foodstuff, and other luxuries, from South Africa.
I asked Connie how, even with such refinements, she could bear to live at Fort Hill virtually in the middle of the labour compound. She replied,
"Well we get very generous leave, and if it all gets too much for me between times I hop on one of the planes and go off on an exotic holiday somewhere. We consider it worthwhile putting up with the job for a few years because of the high salary. By that time we'll have saved enough to set up in a business of our own. Anywhere we like. We might settle on something in South Africa. Or we might buy a pub in England."
I saw her point but as with Alice Udd, felt no envy, well knowing nothing would induce Ken and me to live a moment in the hellhole of Fort Hill in the hope of jam tomorrow. It was always pure delight for us to get back to Misuku.

Very occasionally we over-nighted neither at Chisenga or Fort Hill, but detoured off the road in the never-never bush land between Fort Hill and Mbosi, at a place called Kamemé, where there lived a solitary American missionary called Clarabel. Clarabel, whose last name we never knew, was not connected with the Udd's mission. Indeed there were numerous individual Christian sects scattered about the country, each with their own dogma. Which was confusing for the local people to say the least. In Clarabel's case - the expression 'Muscular Christianity' springs to mind - this did not seem to matter for she appeared to transcend all creeds and dogma, and commanded wholesale admiration and respect.
Perhaps in her mid thirties, she was great in every sense. Well over six feet tall, with a wide smile and a bone crushing handshake, she left no-one in any doubt of

their welcome. She had arrived at Kamemé several years before to find nothing but an old mud hut by way of habitation. One night the roof of this hovel collapsed on her. Or would have done but for her prodigious strength. As it was she managed to hold up the bamboo beams and claw her way out.

But the limitations life imposes on most of us did not deter Clarabel. With boundless energy, and no doubt with generous financial support from the mother church in the USA, she supervised the building of a hospital, a church and finally, a proper house for herself.

Staying with Clarabel was akin to stepping into another world. Outside rampant bush was interspersed with homesteads of mud huts; there were no other Europeans for miles around. Once inside however, the house was entirely Western, awash with every convenience barring electricity. Like the Udd's place there were hooked rugs on the floor, patchwork quilts on the beds, embroidered texts on the walls, and other reinforcements sent out by a faithful congregation back home.

She had a refrigerator even bigger than the Udd's and a large wood burning stove in the integral kitchen. Clarabel loved to cook. She it was who first introduced us to Devil's Cake, a memorable experience after our spartan diet.

It goes without saying that Clarabel had experienced many dangers and disasters since her arrival at Kamemé. One of the more spectacular occurred when she was summoned to a village in the Luangua valley where the people were troubled by lion attacking their cattle and, latterly even prowling among the huts at night. An emissary implored her to come and shoot it/them before any lives were lost. Clarabel who was never without her rifle, promised go and see what she could do.

It was a poor area, once more she found herself housed in an old mud hut with an unglazed wind hole. She was woken in the middle of the night by a tremendous roar far too close for comfort.

"My Lord, she said, "I thought that old lion was going to jump right in through the window. I've never been so terrified in my life. I grabbed the rifle and took a shot, but missed I guess. Luckily that frightened it off though. In the morning we found it had dug up the body of a new born baby buried near one of the huts - that's the custom you know - and I said to myself,

"I'll sure get a shutter fixed over that wind hole before nightfall."

But then you know I went off to hunt it, without success unfortunately, and was busy all day until bedtime, and it was too late to do anything about it by then. But I thought,

"Oh well, the lion seems to have gone away and probably won't come back now it has plundered the grave of that poor child."

"I kept the rifle cocked though just in case. And sure enough around two in the morning there was almighty roar, and another. There must have been several of them and the vibration brought part of the roof down."

Clearly Clarabel was unlucky with roofs.

"I blasted away with everything I'd got and they were so close I couldn't miss this time. At dawn we found two of them laid out. The villagers weren't troubled after that."

People often came to Clarabel's hospital as a last resort when the medicine man's potions had failed and it was inevitable that she witnessed terrible suffering. She told us of one standard remedy meted out to sickly babies, that of opening up the fontanelle to insert fetishes - charms against evil spirits. There was little one could do against this sort of treatment.

The very last time we visited Clarabel we found a young baby, plump, beautiful, shiny black, asleep in a crib in a corner of the kitchen. The woman had been brought in haemorrhaging badly. The baby a girl - was born alive, but in spite of Clarabel's care and attention the mother bled to death. The father begged her to take the baby in, and for better or worse, she decided to do so and bring her up as her own child.

Not long after this, for reasons never clear to us, Clarabel was forced to leave Kamemé. We never heard what happened to her. Or to the baby.

CHAPTER 43

A SPARROW FALLS

The week began badly. That Monday morning the tea was brought in by William instead of Enos, which was not a particularly unusual occurrence or even one I would normally notice, having long since mastered the art of emptying the cup while still half asleep. This time however I woke up on the instant, fully alert to the sinking sensation that something unpleasant was about to happen. What was it? Ah yes, Ken was going on ulendo. Not just for a night or two either, but for the whole week, would not be back until Saturday evening in fact. As I contemplated this depressing prospect I became aware of William still hovering by the bed.

"Sir, he said to Ken's recumbent form, "Enos is not here. He cannot come, his child is sick"

Ken too was awake, he sat up groaning. Like me he was unhappy about the ulendo, but considered it imperative that he visit the impoverished, far-flung villages on the other side of Mughessé yet again. To add to his difficulties Pearson Msembwe, the surly Head Capitao who had replaced Sutherland, must go with him to provide back-up, a quality that gentleman had so far signally failed to display. And now this blow. Enos was also to have gone as cook, even now he should have been in the kitchen making all the necessary preparations.

"Typical, said Ken as he got up, "He probably wants to get out of the ulendo for some reason best known to himself."

This was unfair, as at a less stressful time Ken would have acknowledged. Enos had his faults but unreliability was not one of them. Besides he enjoyed going round the villages where the people regarded him as a person of some consequence.

Ken paused as he dressed, and said,

"If Enos really isn't coming I'll have to take William with me."

He went out, I got up quickly and went through to the kitchen to tell William to go home and get his things, then, impeded by the children who had wandered through from their room in search of something to eat, I began to pack pots and pans, tins of food etc, a routine by this time long established. When that was done there was the bedding roll to be made up.

William came back with his katundu - baggage - tied up in his sleeping blanket, he was in high good humour at the prospect of the unexpected outing. I asked him,

"Which of the children of Enos is the sick one?"

It was not an idle question for in truth I was interested in all the family. There were four children. The eldest, Winford, had been born before Enos went away to the mines, as had Linness, a little girl of five or six who sometimes came to play with Wendy. Then came another boy, Osman, whose birth I remembered clearly as a cause of great rejoicing; lastly there was a baby girl.

"It is the one they call Osman." said William.

"Ah."

On reflection I wondered momentarily if Ken was right in his suspicion that Enos was malingering, but dismissed the idea immediately, knowing in my heart it was not so. Sickness in all its guises was real enough, its presence and the constant threat of it, all around. There was never any need to invent it, the very thought of doing so might bring on bad nfeté, even to the point of bringing about the actuality.

By this time I had realised that with both Enos and William away I would be left without any domestic help. Not as serious a matter as formerly, for Trisom could help me in the kitchen as he had done many times after the first dubious occasion. With his assistance I could manage ordinary every day things well enough now that we had a proper kitchen with a stove. But there remained the perennial difficulty of my having no English speaker about the place in the case of emergency.

I put it to Ken when he came in for a hasty breakfast, He said between mouthfuls,

"Well I expect Enos will be back tomorrow."

"But if he's not? Of course I can do most things with Trisom's help, my Chisukwa is adequate for that. But I must have someone here who speaks good English. Just in case."

"Oh, I forgot to tell you, I've told Ngomba to confine his work to Katobo, there's plenty for him to do here. You like him don't you? His English is excellent. He can report to you every morning to help with the sick parade and you can call on him at any time if anything out of the ordinary crops up.

Ngomba the new young District Capitao who now lived in one of the allotted houses on the ridge, had settled in well and in some respects almost replaced Sutherland. Ken worked more and more with him.

Later than intended the head loads were lined up outside for the carriers. They consisted of Ken's suitcase, the small tent, the bedding roll, cooking pots , foodstuff wrapped in the collapsible bath and a shapeless bundle containing one hoped, all other necessities. At a signal from Ngomba the men came forward, adjusted their head rings, hoisted up their loads and moved off.

Back in the house Ken said,

"Did you remember the tin opener? Good. Here is a copy of my itinerary, though I don't suppose you'll need it. There's just one other thing. The mail must go off to Karonga this morning." He indicated the mail bag lying on the table. "Akim is outside waiting for it. It's all ready except for the pay vouchers. Msembwe should have brought them on Saturday but he didn't. And he certainly should have brought them this morning. But he's not even here. I can't wait any longer, he'll have to catch me up. He'll surely drop the vouchers in on his way. Akim can't leave until they've come, so I'll have to leave you to see to it. You can do that can't you? Just put them in with the rest of the mail and make sure the bag is sealed properly. I'm so sick of him!, he added, meaning Msembwe, "And I've got him round my neck for a whole week."

With that he kissed us and left. The children and I watched him go, waving him out of sight up the hill.

There was plenty to do. I went to the kitchen to make sure Trisom knew what was expected of him. Beside his garden duties he often helped William to chop wood and carry water in, now he must temporarily forego these chores - Ken had detailed a labourer to take over there. He could already make tea and do other simple things.

I found him hovering nervously, his Arab nose quivering. We had often consulted together in the garden and I knew we would manage pretty well together; not for the first time I thought what a pity it was that he had never mastered any English.

I mixed up millet porridge, set it on the stove and left him stirring it diffidently.

Akim, another non English speaker, loitered to one side; I told him rather sharply to make himself useful by keeping an eye on Wendy and Benjamin while I dealt with the sick, (although the women waiting in line gave them plenty of attention, along with their own children.)

Ngomba had already arrived. He questioned and translated, much as Sutherland had done and was a great help. But being less familiar with the task, he needed more time for consultation and an hour passed before the last sick person left.

It was over at last, I thanked Ngomba who left at once, then called Wendy to me, gathered up Ben and went back to the house, Akim close on my heels. I added one or two personal letters to the mail bag, sealed it securely and handed it over. Akim stuffed the bag in the battered satchel which served as his badge of office and we parted with the usual courtesies. He set off at a spanking pace, the children and I finally sat down to breakfast.

When we had finished I took them with me up to the vegetable garden. Angled at the side of the house and somewhat higher up the hill, the view of the countryside had a slightly different aspect which I often paused to admire. The daily tryst with Trisom whose province it normally was, was usually a pleasure, albeit a pleasure somewhat mitigated by the predations of chirombo - insects - for the vegetables on which we largely depended for our fresh food.

On this day as on so many others, tomatoes were flourishing, as were the corn cobs; the green beans looked sickly. The Asukwa considered our habit of picking things young and green to be wasteful, and so it was, but vital to our health.

Next I examined the experimental New Zealand spinach. It was yellowish, not at all like the picture on the packet, and the lettuces growing alongside were decidedly dog eared. Sighing I picked the best of the bunch and we returned to the kitchen, where I set out the ingredients for a simple lunch and explained to Trisom as best I could, what I would like done with them.

By this time the morning was well advanced and it was already hot; the children and I went through to the sitting room, looking forward to long cool drinks.

But what was this? Islanded on the expanse of the polished dining table close by the open door lay a bulky packet. Wonderingly I examined it. Then stiffened with horror. The pay vouchers!

But surely, while I was outside with the sick people Msembwe had come by and added the packet to the mail bag before he hurried off to catch up with Ken? True I had not seen him, but then I had been fully occupied. True I had not checked before sealing the bag, had indeed forgotten the whole matter. That he had not done so was now patently obvious. Wringing my hands almost literally, I cursed myself for incompetence. Cursed Msembwe also. Why had he not given the pay vouchers to Ken on the right day? Or brought them along yesterday? Why had he not been here with them, on time this morning to start out with Ken? Sutherland undoubtedly would have been. Only too well did I recall the mayhem one time when old Simbeyé and the Askari with him bringing up the wages from Karonga, had been held up by floods and arrived a day after the scheduled pay day. That would be as nothing if Akim returned with no wages at all. Even as I sought to excuse myself, fighting panic I realised that speculation was futile, only prompt action could save the day now.

But what action? Think positively. Of course. Someone must go after Akim. And quickly. But who to send? Instinctively my thoughts turned to the first William, erstwhile cook and brick maker, always willing and anxious to please. But William was elderly, and certainly not quick. Besides, I knew he had never been out of Misuku, he would be lost in every sense.

Who then? It would have to be one of the labourers. Having been part of our lives for so long all were well known to me. Would any of them agree to go? I had no authority to make them. Suddenly I remembered the self styled brick making expert who claimed to have worked for the PWD somewhere down country. He assuredly would know his way around, he would be the most likely. Swiftly I wrote a note to Ngomba, asking him to find the man and bring him here at once. I sent Trisom off with it, telling him to hurry.

Ngomba soon appeared, the brickmaker took longer to locate, so I had time to relate what had happened. Ngomba quickly grasped the implications. When the man appeared I said,

"Please ask this man if he would be willing to follow after Akim and give him this packet. Tell him also that he should be able to find Akim at the village where he will sleep tonight. But if he does not, then he must go on to Karonga and give the packet only to Akim or to the Bwana DC or the ADC. On no account must he hand it to anyone else."

I waited anxiously as Ngomba did so. The translation - the only words of which I could be certain, 'pay vouchers' and the names - was lengthy. With impatience I realised a preamble was necessary to lead up to the crux of the matter with the usual niceties, and that I in my haste had asked too much too soon. Had my requirements been presented in direct translation the man would surely have been scared off at once without his properly having considered the matter.

Even so he was startled when he understood the enormity of what was being asked of him. He stood very still. Clearly he was weighing up the burden of the responsibility of this onerous task against the prestige and status he would enjoy among his peers, many of whom had gathered round to listen, should he bring it to a successful conclusion. Perhaps he had hitherto enjoyed a certain reputation among them as a man of the world, much travelled, who had worked for the PWD about which they had heard much. Would that influence his decision? I fervently hoped so, but as the silence lengthened I felt sure he would refuse.

To my huge relief, when he spoke at last it was to ask how much nbombo - money - he would get for undertaking such a task. And when would he be paid?

I mentioned a hefty sum, determined to pay him out of my own purse if necessary, and said I would give half now, and half when Akim returned to Katobo with the wages. Still he hesitated, but the labourers, to whom a month without pay was unthinkable, urged him on. Indeed I would have felt sorry for him had not so much been at stake. When he spoke again it was to put the seemingly inevitable question, one which I should have foreseen,

"He says Madam, "What about poso?"

"Yes yes, tell him I will pay that as well. But he must go quickly. Now now!"

Even then he did not move, then,

"This man says he will do this thing. But first he must go to his house to get his sleeping blanket and his spear because of the leopard."

I sighed with relief, struggled with my impatience and said,

"Right. Please tell him to go at once and come back quickly."

In Misuku nothing happened quickly but the man was back within the hour. I gave him half the agreed money and handed over the pay vouchers telling him to take good care of them, reiterated the importance of his mission and the need for haste. Secreting the packet under the folds of his nsaru he listened soberly. This done, after the hand-shaking and God speeding without which no journey at all could begin, amid shouts of encouragement from the men he finally set out.

In the afternoon as the labourers made their way home, spades shouldered at the slope, they still discussed the matter and I had time to reflect on what I had asked of this surrogate messenger. Akim would be following the same arduous and dangerous route in reverse, that we ourselves had taken on the foot slogging journey up from Karonga before the birth of Wendy, and would stay in the same villages. This was the way the brickmaker must go. I very much hoped he would fall in with one or two fellow travellers and that he would catch up with Akim at the first stop.

From this point my thoughts turned to what would happen if the wages failed to arrive on time, or worse, not at all. Better not to dwell on that.

More to the point, who had left the packet on the table? Certainly the table was near the door and the door was always open... anyone could have reached in. Was it Msembe himself coming late, in a hurry to catch up with Ken? But why leave without telling anyone? Or was it his wife? Or one of his children? But there was no evidence of his having a wife or children in Misuku. The question hung in the air, adding to the minor mysteries of life in Misuku. And what use was speculation anyway? I had done what I could to rectify the matter, now it was in the lap of the gods.

Next morning there was still no sign of Enos. Trisom, either because he did not understand my questioning, or else chose not to, remained silent except for one word,

"Palebé." Which in this instant meant, "He is not here."

I was not left long in ignorance however. As the children and I sat having breakfast a discreet cough at the doorway heralded Ngomba. He said,

"Madam, the child of Enos is very sick."

I started up,

"Oh, what is it?" I cried. My own concerns having selfishly preoccupied me, I was alarmed for the first time..

But he too had nothing further to say, beyond telling me that Enos had gone to the Dispenser at the Court to get medicine.

Good for Enos, I thought. He knew my limitations too well to bring the child to me, he would automatically go to the Dispenser. And if his treatment failed, his wife would insist on calling in the local medicine man.

Wretchedly I wondered if I should go to their house in the forlorn hope of being able to do something. But Enos had gone to the Dispensary and his wife spoke no English... This afternoon then? I would have to take the children of course. And carry Ben most of the way. The village was about one and a half miles away over a hilly path. It would be hard going for Wendy as well in the heat of the day. In cowardly fashion I decided to leave it until next day.

But the following morning brought Ngomba again. He said,

"Madam, the child of Enos is dead."

"No!" I cried, "It's not possible!"

Even as I uttered them I heard the stupidity of my words. Of course it was possible. Only too likely in fact. Death was all round us. Why had I not long since acknowledged that it could strike close at hand?

I knew very well why not. This universal nightmare of mothers the world over must be stifled, smothered, locked away in the subconscious, never allowed to surface, never given credence lest it become reality.

"But what was it? What made him die?"

Again the futility of my utterance came back at me. Babies were born, babies, children, adults, got ill every day. Either they got better or they died. There was no knowing why.

Now this worst of tragedies, the death of a child. And this particular child, known to us from birth by the frequent visits of Enos' wife to the house.

Ngomba had remained silent. Now he shook his head and replied reluctantly,

"The people say his stomach swelled up."

I looked at him sharply. Another mystery. Was witchcraft suspected? Did someone have a grudge against Enos and taken it out on the son? But that I could not believe.

Later when I was once more capable of rational thought it seemed more likely that Osman had suffered some intestinal obstruction, or eaten poisonous berries, perhaps out on the hillside with his mother's back turned as she gathered firewood.

Ah, the mother! And Enos. What of them? A tide of misery washed over me.

The dismal day got under way, everyone about the place subdued. Later a single drum, distinctive as the passing bell of the church of my childhood village, sounded out the death. That night sleep was a long time coming. Waking was a relief - short lived as I remembered Enos and his wife for whom a new day would bring no relief, no hope. Today they must prepare the burial. Almost certainly it would take place near their hut so that the child's spirit would feel at home. People would come to mourn, there would be drumming, women ululating to drive away devils. Later there would be a feast.

Ken had assured me the week would go quickly. He was wrong. On the contrary, between the dramatic and the tragic events of the past few days when I had ardently wished him present, time had dragged painfully. However today was Thursday, Ken's ulendo was almost over I told myself, he would be back on Saturday.

Just before lunch came a pleasant surprise in the form of a letter from him, courtesy of a carrier/labourer. I tore it open eagerly, then paused, suddenly anxious lest it announced a delay in his return because of the dire conditions he had found in the villages. But it was alright. He began by saying how much he loved us and missed us and looked forward to getting home. Then however the tone changed.

"How are you all? Write back at once and let me know you are alright. The bearer will bring your reply to me at Tialikanjeré. Don't delay."

This was unusual, but then he was not usually away for so long. And what was familiar about the name Tialikanjeré? Ah yes. It was the village of the trouble maker Msopelé in whom Fitzherbert the police officer had taken such an interest when he had paid a surprise visit soon after our return from leave.

Clearly Ken was having a hard time of it, almost certainly getting little support from Msembwe. I went inside and wrote a note of reassurance. No need to tell him about little Osman, he would hear that soon enough, the messenger would certainly tell him, regale the sad news to all and sundry. I sealed the letter and handed it over, urging the man to make good time.

Later, in the dead time of the afternoon as I sat reading, the children resting, the labourers having finished their work, away to their homes, Trisom quiet in the kitchen, a strange thing happened. Out of the silence - bare feet make no sound - came a light tap on the open door. Startled I went to it, and found several men standing there, one carrying a spear. In my keyed up state it was a moment before I realised who they were. Then I saw the smiling face of Nelson Mwandofi from Kapoka, his brother Bodwin, and three or four other capitaos normally seen only on pay days. Also one or two strangers.

Automatically I exchanged polite greetings with them, trying to collect myself, wondering what had occasioned the visit. Had Ken overlooked a scheduled meeting? Possible, though unlikely. But if so they would all have learned of his absence well before they reached Katobo. What then, had induced them to walk so many miles at this particular time? No answer presented itself.

When the salutations and greetings had been prolonged to breaking point a silence fell. I searched my mind for something to say. Nothing came. Then, by great good fortune I recollected that sometimes at the conclusion of business on pay days Ken would tell Enos to bring tea for them. Nervously, wondering how they would react to being entertained by a woman, I invited them in.

They sat up very straight on unfamiliar chairs, I called Trisom to bring tea and biscuits and wondered what to talk about. I mentioned the rains, had it been a good season? Between them they agreed that yes, by and large it had been good and if it went on a little longer the people would have food enough to see them through the hungry gap later in the year.

At this point Wendy and Ben who had heard our voices, wandered through from their adjoining room, pleased to see new faces. This broke the ice, I asked after their own children. After that one man I had never seen before told me he came from the Kaseye valley, which accounted for the spear now resting by the door, which he would certainly need 'against the leopard.' But what was he doing so far from home? It was not even in Ken's area. I told him that sometimes when were going shopping in Mbeya, we went that way to visit the Dona Clarabel at Kamemé. Did he know her? Of course he did, everyone knew Clarabel. He told me she had gone away and taken the motherless child with her. No-one knew when she would come back.

When the biscuits had all been eaten, the strong, sweet, tea drunk, the men gravely turned their cups upside down on their saucers; conversation languished and finally died. Nelson, his good eye bright as ever, stood up, the others followed suit. We parted with expressions of goodwill and more handshakes. As the children and I watched them go I realised I was no wiser as to why they had come. All the same the visit cheered me till bedtime.

Friday at last. Of the brick making messenger there was no sign, by which I assumed he had not caught up with Akim at the first village and had been obliged to go on to Karonga.

In the afternoon I took the children for a walk as usual. When Ken was at home to carry Ben we would venture further afield, without him I was limited by Ben's nearly two year old legs. We could stroll the track leading to the capitaos' houses, formerly a favourite walk of Wendy's when there was a chance of playing with Sutherland's children, but less so after his departure. Or we could take one of the many paths radiating from the place, used as I have said, by the labourers going to and from work, and by women going up the hill to gather firewood. On this particular day I chose one of the latter.

Because they must go higher the women always went in groups and made as much noise as possible to scare off any leopard that might venture down from the forest on Mughessé, but there would be no danger to us at lower level among the homesteads. We were going merely a short way to a stand of straggly pines planted by the Forestry Department some years before, to look for fir cones.

As usual there were none, but the copse was shady, cool, silent, with an air of enchantment about it. The children shattered the silence, dodging in and out of the trees, scuffling up the carpet of pine needles, reluctant to leave when the time came.

We retraced our steps down the hill. I, heartened at the thought of Ken's return next day, exchanged greetings with women outside their huts kindling fires for cooking the evening meal, the only substantial meal of the day.

But the wretched week had not finished with us yet. As the children ate their supper I noticed a red blotch on Ben's leg just below the knee. I laid my hand on it, it felt hot. Was it also slightly swollen? I could not be sure. I fetched calamine lotion and told him not to scratch it.

Both Wendy and Ben enjoyed bath-time, and for me the novelty of water actually gushing out of the tap had still not quite faded. Not tonight however, for by now there was no doubt about the red swelling on Ben's leg. Smothering my alarm I scooped him out of the bath and examined him closely. Had he been bitten by one of the many unidentifiable insects that beset us daily? Had he been stung during our walk by a bee from a home-made log hive high up in a tree? But no, a bee sting was painful, he would have cried out.

What then? Could he possibly - the thought made my blood run cold - have been bitten by a snake as he played in the copse? Feverishly I searched the small body for signs of a lesion. Nothing. Nor did Ben show any distress. On the contrary he was quite unconcerned. I called Trisom through from the kitchen, foolishly hoping he could reassure me in some way.

"Do you know this thing?" I asked in Chisukwa.

His eyes widened as he looked at the leg, then he shook his head. No help there then.

I got both children to bed, Wendy with the usual delaying tactics, praying that the swelling would dissipate itself and be gone by morning.

Once in bed they both fell asleep readily enough and, encouraged by Ben's regular breathing I thought at first my optimism might be justified. But when I looked in an hour or so later a glance at the leg as I pulled down the sheet, caused my heart to miss a beat. The inflammation, the swelling, had increased dramatically. The knee had almost disappeared. A wave of panic swept over me. Was this a creeping poison which would eventually envelop the whole body and attack the vital organs? I pushed the thought from me. What should I do? A tourniquet? But that would wake Ben up. He would probably struggle to his feet and become agitated, which would make matters worse.

I must get help. But from whom? Well first of all from Ngomba. I called Trisom again and, forcing myself to speak slowly, knowing he would not understand my Chisukwa otherwise, I told him to go and fetch Ngomba from his house on the ridge. When he had gone I fetched water from the refrigerator and sponged the leg gently. Then I applied more calamine, Ben did not stir.

All the while I tried to think rationally. I must get a message to Ken. Yes, that was it. As I knew from his itinerary he would be spending this last night of the ulendo at a village about 10 miles away on the far side of Mughessé. But who would go for me? No-one travelled alone at night, especially on such a journey. It would involve climbing to the top of the mountain and submitting to the ordeal of traversing the forest, the home of the spirits of the chiefs, shunned even by day. I knew for certain no such messenger would be forthcoming.

Well then I must ask Ngomba to find someone who would go for me at first light. Ken would come at once and drive us down to Fort Hill and... Here my mind gave up, I sat down by the bed and prayed that Ngomba would be at his house and not out visiting friends in one of the villages.

In fact he appeared minutes later. Oh the blessed relief of being understood. Quickly I explained the position and led him through to the children's room. I drew back Ben's cover once more and with pounding heart said, "Do you know what has caused this? Have you seen anything like it before?" Startled he gazed at the leg, the silence lengthened. Then he too shook his head. At this despair gripped me so hard I was forced to sit down. Fool that I was. What had I expected? What could Ngomba do or say to help matters? He was no doctor, no magician. He was however saying something. Hesitantly he murmured, "Perhaps the Dispenser at the Court..."

The Dispenser? Why had I not thought of him? The reason, simply, was that he was simply the functionary to whom I referred the sick women if I could not help them. He had not figured in our own lives, indeed I had never met him. For the Dispensary, in spite of being part of the Court complex, was a little way off the beaten track and not visible when we passed that way. I knew it to be part of a network of Government medical institutions however, set up to serve rural communities all over the country, supervised by African dispensers qualified in some measure. To what standard I had no idea. No matter. Seizing on Ngomba's suggestion I said,

"Oh yes, he would be sure to know. Will you go and find him for me and ask him to come as quickly as he can? Take the lamp from the kitchen."

He left at once. I sat down again by the bed and calculated how long it might take the Dispenser to come. The Court was about a mile and a half away, and because of the terrain it took me about an hour to reach it. Ngomba would cover the ground in half that time. If he found the man at once they could be back quite soon. I looked at my watch, it was almost ten o'clock.

An hour dragged by agonisingly slowly. Surely they should have come by now? But wait, the Dispenser would most likely be asleep - in Misuku most people went to sleep once the cooking fires were out because they had no lamps. Or he might be out visiting and Ngomba would have to go and find him. Somehow I smothered my frustration.

Ben turned over in his sleep, the cover came away. The leg, really swollen now, not only the knee but the ankle invisible, lay inert alongside its fellow like a huge obscene slug. Hastily I drew up the cover.

Voices in the kitchen. I went through quickly. But found only Trisom there with Ngomba. He said,

"Madam I have found this man. He says he is busy. He says he will come later." At this red rage enveloped me. How could he be busy at this time of night? He was being deliberately obstructive. He had no intention of coming. My last faint hope of help had gone.

Only after many years could I bring myself to review the events of this night dispassionately and, realising the dilemma in which the Dispenser found himself, acknowledge that I had almost certainly, misjudged him. He and his kind worked on their own, often in remote areas, largely without support, just as Ken did. His remit was to serve his fellow Africans. He had nothing to gain and plenty to lose by attending a European. What if the child should die because of his ministrations? On the other hand it would not do to ignore the summons entirely. Almost certainly his delay that night was due to the need to rouse the Chief and elders and seek their advice before making any move.

As it was Ngomba said he would stay on in the kitchen. Vaguely I noticed he and Trisom had been joined by old Kalokhili the night watchman about to make his round. I told him to keep a sharp look-out. For what? The Dispenser would not come, no other terror coming out of the night could be as monstrous as the one before my very eyes.

Back in the children's bedroom I felt Ben's forehead. Was he running a high temperature? But the night was warm and I could not be sure. At any rate he was sleeping soundly. Too soundly? No thank God. As I turned him gently to apply more calamine lotion on what now only faintly resembled a leg, he stirred slightly. But I now saw that the inflammation was creeping up toward his groin. Into my head leapt Ngomba's words at the death of Enos' little boy,

"The people say his stomach swelled up."

At this my legs gave out and I collapsed on to the bed, pulling up the sheet once more as if obscuring the excrescence would make it go away. But I could not stay still. I got up, made my way through to the outer door of the sitting room and stood gulping in the night air. There was no moon, no stars even; total blackness outside mirrored the blackness of my mind.

Indoors again I sat down by the bed. In the sitting room the lamp hissed.

At first I thought the faint sound of voices were part of the nightmare. I had no idea how long I had slept, or indeed if I had slept at all, but alert now, I listened again. The voices were real. Crossing to the window I parted the curtains and watched as three dark figures, one of them carrying a guttering lamp, broke cover at the rim of the lower terrace. Hurriedly I went out to them, abstractedly conducted the obligatory courtesies which even now must be observed and led the men inside. One of them, carried a pair of enormous scissors, sight of which caused me nearly to faint. The Dispenser must suspect snake bite. This hideous implement was intended for an assault on my child's tender body.

I led the way to the bedroom, pulled back the cover to reveal Ben's leg and put the question yet again, "Do you know what this is? Have you seen anything like it before?"

The words hung in the air, the aura of our combined sweat filled the small room. The one I took to be the Dispenser silently stepped forward, felt Ben's forehead and checked his pulse gravely. This done he took the leg in his hand, examined it minutely and squeezed it slightly. Then he proceeded to go carefully over the rest of the body, which caused Ben to wake up. For a moment he lay gazing round, blinking in unaccustomed light. Then to my inexpressible relief he let out an indignant cry. Wendy also woke, very interested in what was going on.

The Dispenser straightened up and said slowly,

"I know this thing."

I stared at him wildly,
"What is it? Is it serious? What can you do for him?"
He disregarded me, there was a prolonged silence. Then he said,
"There is nothing to be done. At this time tomorrow, he paused dramatically,
"This child will be better."
With that he turned abruptly and swept out of the room, the others close on
his heels.
"Wait!" I called after them.
They paid no heed. By the time my tottering legs enabled me to reach the outer
door they were already striding across the garden. One by one they dipped down
over the terrace and were out of sight. A moment later Misuku was in darkness
once more.

Back in the bedroom Ben was now fully awake, crying angrily and struggling to
stand up. I gave him a drink, he was very thirsty, then I took him in my arms and
soothed him, talking softly and singing to him in a cracked voice. Very gradually
he quietened down and let me lay him down. Wendy took longer to settle.
All this time my mind was in a turmoil over the Dispenser's words. Could I trust
his diagnosis? I had to, there was nothing else to hold on to. In utter exhaustion I
lay down across the bottom of Wendy's bed.

I woke to complete darkness for the sitting room lamp had burnt itself out.
Again I had no idea how long the uneasy sleep had gripped me and I could
not read my watch. Holding my breath I leaned across and felt Ben's pulse. It
was faint but regular. Thank God! Stiffly I got up and drew back the curtain,
then sat down to wait for daybreak To my relief it was not long in coming.
By the first faint light I examined the leg. Did it appear, could it possibly be,
slightly less swollen? I could not be certain. Surely though it was no worse?
For the moment I must possess myself of patience. The light strengthened, the
inflammation really did seem less intense, I dared myself to hope. A faint tap at
the door heralded Trisom. He stood in the doorway apprehensively, I beckoned
him in and pointed. Slowly his expression changed and a smile lit his face. Ah,
so I had not been mistaken, he too had seen the improvement. Turning back to
me he said,
"Leta chai Madam?" I nodded.
Never had tea tasted so good. When I had drunk it I went through to the kitchen,
Ngomba was still there, jubilant at Trisom's report. Resisting an overwhelming
urge to throw my arms round him I burst into tears. When I was coherent I
thanked him again for his help and support. I also asked him to thank Trisom
for staying all night, and tell him he could go home now and have holiday till
Monday morning.

There was now no doubt that the swelling was subsiding. Amazingly Ben, apart
from being thirsty, seemed none the worse. Light-headedly I tried to keep him
from too much exertion. Throughout the day the improvement continued.
The cause was never discovered, never satisfactorily explained. Had he been

the target of an insect with a bite too small to leave a mark? Had he brushed against an irritant plant during our afternoon walk? Buffalo bean for instance, known to be common in the hills? Unlike fir plantations in England carpeted only with needles, the grove - always deserted as I now realised, and perhaps even shunned - supported low undergrowth and festoons of creeper, any of which could have caused a bad reaction on contact. Like other events of that tragic week the matter remained shrouded in mystery. Had I over-reacted? I did not think so. Certainly, to this very day, should anyone chance to ask, "What was the very worst time of your life?" I would answer unhesitatingly, "It was that night alone in Africa when I thought my baby would die."

CHAPTER 44

"OH WHAT IS THAT DRUM?"

Although the carriers started coming in around 10 o'clock on what was, by then, developing into an ordinary Saturday morning, I did not expect Ken until evening, for he would be working his way back through the villages as usual. Also he might call on the Udds as their place was close on his route. My joy and relief therefore were all the greater when he appeared shortly after lunch.

Wendy playing outside saw him first and ran up the track behind the house to meet him. He caught her up and brought her down on his shoulders, I met them at the back of the garden.

"Thank God you've come!" I said.

I took hold of his arm, lead him to the house and shut the door firmly. As he put Wendy down I threw myself into his arms. After a few moments he held me away from him and said,

"What is it?"

Incoherently I tried to tell him what had happened.

"Enos' little boy was sick. Well you knew that. But then later Ngomba came to say that he was dead. His stomach swelled up and he died. We heard the drum."

I paused, took a deep breath then went on,

"Then yesterday afternoon we went for a walk as usual and afterwards Ben's leg became red and started to swell up and it got bigger and bigger and I didn't know what to do. So I sent for Ngomba and he didn't know what it was either so he went to get the Dispenser. But the Dispenser wouldn't come at first and the leg kept swelling, but at last he did and he'd got this enormous pair of scissors... And I thought Ben would..."

Here I was forced to stop.

Ken held me close again, he said,

"And now?"

"Oh now thank God the swelling is going down, just as the Dispenser said it would."

We went through to the children's room. Ben had woken up and was playing placidly with the toys on his bed; at sight of Ken he started up and held out his arms. Ken picked him up, sat him on his knee and examined the leg. It was by now much reduced in size and the all encompassing inflammation had given way to red blotches.

"I can't see any sign of a bite or sting." he said, going over the rest of the body, impeded by Ben pulling at his beard, "And he doesn't seem feverish."

"No, he was very thirsty though. But he ate breakfast... "

"Well, try and keep him from too much exertion. It'll probably be gone in a day or two.

Now I must go and pay off the carriers. We'll talk later."

But when he was at last free and the children having their afternoon rest, we collapsed on the bed and both slept instantly, I suffering bad reaction from the night's events, he exhausted from the long and difficult ulendo.

William woke us half an hour later with tea. Shaking off torpor Ken told him he could leave and stay off till Monday morning. But then as another thought struck, Ken told him to wait a minute. He got up, fished in his pocket and gave him some money to take to Enos to help with cost of the burial. This cheered me a little. William said he would pass by that way as he went home. Enos, he assured us, would certainly be present on Monday.

When we were both fully conscious I asked Ken about the ulendo.

"It was miserable, he said, "Even worse than I feared. The villages were a shambles, all the regulations flouted. Not surprisingly the people were none too keen to see me. Some of them even boycotted the meetings, which is unheard of. As you know they're normally only to happy to have a good palaver and sit around discussing their affairs for hours. But not this time.

"Something else was different too. Food was scarce, not just for me but for the carriers as well, even when I got on to the village headmen. So you can imagine the capitaos and the men weren't happy either."

"That is unusual, I said, "Normally the villagers are so hospitable, it's part of their culture."

"Yes. But anyway I could see there was no point in prolonging things. And I heard the Udds were away again, so that's why I got home earlier today."

"I'm thankful you did."

I went on to recount the events of the week starting with the death of Osman, trying to convey the wretchedness I felt for Enos and his wife.

"Yes, a bad business." he said

But inevitably, selfishly, after a while I reverted to my terror over Ben's leg.

"If only you had been here it wouldn't have seemed so bad. You would have thought of something. But really, if you had seen it at its worst I'm sure you'd have been worried too. And driven us down to Fort Hill to catch a plane and..."

Here I was in danger of becoming incoherent again. I took a deep breath,

"I didn't know what to do. I couldn't get a message to you, or to the Udds, I knew no-one would go for me in the night. And anyway I heard too, just after you left, that they were away in Uganda. But Ngomba was a tower of strength, he stayed most of the night you know."

"He's a good chap, Ken said, and added bitterly, "unlike Msembwe."

"Oh and I've just remembered, I went on, "The capitao from Kamemé said that Clarabel had left. And no-one knows where she's gone or when she's coming back."

"The capitao from Kamemé? He looked at me in surprise, "I don't know the capitao there. Kamemé isn't in my area. Did someone come across him at Fort Hill or something?"

"No, he was here with the other capitaos."

So then I told him of the visitation and the tea-party, which had temporarily been driven from my mind by subsequent events.

"Yes, they came one afternoon - Thursday I think. And of course I assumed it was you they wanted, but were too polite to say so. So then I thought you must have arranged a meeting here and overlooked it, and they just wanted to show they hadn't defaulted on it."

"I hadn't arranged a meeting with them. As you know I only get them together on pay days, we sort out any other business then. It's too far for most of them to come between times."

"Well then, why did they come? You can't think of any reason?"

He shook his head, paused, then said,

"I'm not sure."

At supper that night Ken said,

"I've decided to go down to Karonga next week. On Monday if possible. All of us I mean"

I looked at him in surprise,

"But we're going to Mbeya next weekend, you can't have forgotten? Supplies are pretty low, I'm banking on it."

"All the same we'll skip Mbeya this time."

"But I can't get half the things I want at Andanis. And besides, there's the Chendo Track, and with the rains still on... And the rest-house isn't nearly as comfortable as the Mbeya Hotel."

"I need to see the DC and Brian Stearn about Msembwe. He has to go."

At this I knew it was useless to argue further. I sighed heavily.

When the children had gone to bed we settled down in front of the fire, lit for its cheer rather than warmth, Ken twiddling the knobs on the wireless trying to get BBC World Service. I in a state of torpid relief at Ben's recovery and Ken's return, sat over a book. Faint resonance of drumming drifted across the valley.

"It sounds as if the carriers are celebrating their first good meal for a week, remarked Ken, "And spending their earnings on a beer drink as well."

The battery on the radio was low, it being so long since our last shopping trip, and he was getting only static and muffled voices interspersed with whistles. Disgustedly he got up and switched it off, put a record on the gramophone and started to wind it up.

"Why doesn't someone start up a wireless station in Zomba or Blantyre? I wondered aloud, "Surely we'd be able to pick that up. It would be good to know what was going on in the rest of the country. We might hear the Governor now and again, or Dick Kettlewell. Or even Arthur Tomes, I'll bet he could tell a tale or two."

Ken said it might be a good idea but he didn't think it very likely.

The gramophone wound down the groove to silence. Beethoven gave way to the sounds outside, the festivities were hotting up. Sometimes the drums were louder, sometimes they faded as if the participants were on the move, as on New Years Eve when the people went from place to place including Katobo, celebrating late into the night. The influence of the Scots Missionaries without a doubt. I was reminded also of the Malipenga, sometimes known as the Mapanenga, which took place occasionally in the day time, and had its origins in recruiting drives for the King's African Rifles. As such the practice had long been discontinued, but in Misuku youths with nothing better to do, kept up the custom and occasionally wandered the villages in the sure hope of hospitality and flirtation with the girls.

The sound continued to waver among the hills, shifting all the time, louder, nearer now and I paid it more attention. Ken looked up and listened intently. I put the question I had been asking one way or another ever since arriving in Africa, "What is it?"
He did not reply. I went to the adjoining room and checked that the children were asleep, then as on the previous night I went to the window and parted the curtains. And froze. Ken joined me. Away to the right of the house on the track along the ridge came a rabble of men with torch flares, marching, shuffling rather, singing and shouting in time to the drums. This was no festive visit. Nor was there any doubt of the destination, the path led nowhere but to our own house.
"Wait here." Ken ordered as the noise grew louder still.
He strode through to the sitting room, picked up the lamp and went outside. Left in near darkness, I could now make out individual cries -
"Uhuru! Kwacha Africa!" - "The dawn! Freedom for Africa!" And in English -
"Down with Imperialism. Away with your Federation."
Trembling, I hovered irresolutely, positive thought gone. Then with an agonised glance back at the children I went to join Ken outside.
The mob reached the top terrace and fell silent, disconcerted perhaps at the sight of us standing at the doorway in a pool of lamplight. Their torch-brands cast shadows on black figures in black nsaru, about twenty-five or thirty men in all, some armed with spears, others with knobkerries or sticks. No gleam of white teeth slashed the darkness in a smile.
Still silent they stood in a semicircle round us, about ten feet off. Then one man stepped forward and made a speech which another translated into English,
"We have not come to frighten you..."
The incongruity of this was such that a hysterical laugh, instantly stifled, welled up in me.
"... But from this day no black person will come to work for you. If they do we will cut out their tongues. Many other bad things also will we do to them."
He continued in this vein, railing against the Agricultural Department, the Government, and particularly against Federation which, he said, was an organisation for stealing away their land.
Ken heard him out. When at last he ended his tirade Ken stepped forward. Ignoring the spokesman he addressed the men directly as at one of their own village meetings. The ringleader protested, Ken persisted.
Impossible now to recollect what he said. Incredibly, they listened to him in silence.
Then a babble of argument broke out,
The ringleader resumed his harangue, there were more cries of Uhuru and Kwacha. Ken countered, speaking slowly and reasonably. Again the majority gave him their attention, others appeared to be remonstrating with the leader who

was urging them on. To what? An attack? Nerves silently screaming, with huge effort I resisted the overwhelming urge to rush back to the children, determined if necessary to throw myself across them and defend them bodily to the last breath. Again Ken reasoned.

Suddenly there was a hush as if some stalemate had been achieved. The moment was pivotal, Ken held his ground.

Then, unbelievably, a man in the shadows to one side broke away, slipped silently into the night and was gone.

Hesitantly one or two others followed suit, then a small group. Thus it went on until only the leader and his henchmen remained standing alone. They faced us defiantly. Then they too turned away and left, still shouting their slogans, still banging a drum.

When it became apparent that, for the moment at least, we were to be left alone, Ken led me inside. I collapsed in the big armchair, but roused up at once,

"The children! They may have been frightened." I tried to get up.

"Stay where you are." Ken said sharply. He strode across the room and looked in at the bedroom. "Just as I thought. Both fast asleep."

He put his arms round me.

"It's alright. No-one's been harmed. It was just a drunken mob, I recognised one or two of the men. There'll have come to their senses by morning."

"But what if they come back?" I whispered.

"They won't."

Although he spoke decisively I was not convinced. Beside having no means of communicating with the outside world we had nothing with which to defend ourselves. Ken had shot crocodiles on the lake shore with a borrowed gun, but had never owned one. Had he had one could he have turned it on fellow human beings? Unthinkable then, unthinkable now. He was still talking,

"I suspected something was afoot when I was away. That's why I came back as soon as possible this morning and that's why I intended to get you all down to Karonga. I said nothing because I didn't want to alarm you. I don't know if the trouble is widespread, well, I'm pretty sure it's not, or we would have heard of it before."

Thus he sought to reassure me.

"Come, he went on, "You must go to bed, I'll come later."

"No no, I must stay near the children."

The thought of being separated from them by the sitting room with its unlockable outer door was insupportable. He considered then said,

"Alright we'll bring them into our room. You'll feel better if we're all together. I'll put up the camp beds, you can give me a hand."

This last was to distract me, but my hands were shaking so much that I was no help at all.

When the beds were ready he carried the children through, so carefully that even Wendy did not stir. He said again,

"Go to bed now."

I threw myself on the double bed and for a second night lay down fully clothed, fully awake.

The drum still beat across the valley. Clearly the mob had not dispersed but was winding its way round the villages. Delivering the ultimatum to the labourers, to the capitaos, to Akim and Trisom. And to Enos who had trouble enough already. How serious was the threat? How dangerous our position? Unbidden to my mind came thoughts of the Mau-Mau in Kenya who until recently had committed unspeakable atrocities, not only on Europeans but also on Africans loyal to them.[1]

Of course that could not happen in Misuku I told myself. These people were our neighbours, friends even, they would not harm us... But then, surely, not one of the expatriates in Kenya had dreamt of such a thing until it happened? How could they have foreseen that their workers, servants, long term associates would rise up and attack them, either from free will or under duress?[2] And indeed why not in Misuku? Ken had always known that the measures he must enforce were deeply resented. I myself, through ignorance, must have offended against many tribal customs. And in the wider context I knew dimly that Federation was regarded with suspicion, and even hatred. The people feared their land would be taken away by Europeans, and with good reason. Indeed that had been the case in Kenya and other African countries in the past. The Asukwa had good cause to be wary.

Had we been naive and blind? Observed anything untoward? But there had been no signs of unrest in Misuku. Here at Katobo everything was the same as ever. The labourers did their work, sick people lined up for medicine, villagers brought scant fruit or vegetables for sale. On ulendo - until this last one - Ken had been received kindly in the villages, the carriers had enjoyed the customary hospitality and revelry.

Should we have recognised the significance of the visit of Dr Banda at the Court which had attracted such a large gathering? Perhaps. But that had occurred during our absence on leave and we had merely heard about it from Ragnor. Had we been present it would probably have impacted more on us: as it was the immediacy of daily life had claimed our attention and in the course of time it had been forgotten.

Nor had we, cut off as we were in the rains, received any intimation from Karonga or anywhere else that trouble might be brewing.

Wait a minute though. What about the visit of Fitzherbert the policeman a while ago, and the interest he had taken in Flax Msopelé out at Tialikanjeré? That had registered with Ken certainly. He knew the area to be lawless, which was why he had paid it so much attention. He knew there was unrest as soon as he got there, and cut his ulendo accordingly. That was why he wanted to get us all down to Karonga as soon as possible. But certainly the events of the night could not have

---

[1] The Mau-Mau was a secret society of the Kikuyu people, banned by the British Government between 1950 and 1956. For further details see 'Nellie, Letters from Africa', Elspeth Huxley, 1973. And the history books.

[2] Tribal fighting broke out again in February, 2008

been foreseen beforehand. Such was the chaotic jumble of my thoughts in the darkness of the night.

The sounds outside receded and finally died away. Against expectation I drifted into sleep. A sleep so troubled as to be identifiable as such only by the dreams it engendered. One in particular kept recurring. It was not of rioters, not of Ben's swollen leg, not even of the death of little Osman, but of the pay vouchers. Against a leaden sky a dark figure in a long black nsaru stood at the open doorway, its face hidden. With outstretched arm it reached out an El Greco hand to lay a package on the polished table. Then it turned away, dissolved like smoke as if it had never been. But when at last, trembling, I approached the table and dared to open the package there came a putrid smell. Fearfully, with utmost loathing, I opened it and felt inside. In place of paper my hand touched something slimy, horrible, indefinably dead.

Ken it transpired did not sleep at all, but had sat up all night facing the outer door in the adjoining sitting room. As he told me later his thoughts went something like this:-
"This is different from anything I've come across before, it has a political dimension and that could be serious. How serious? And more to the point, how widespread? Are we in immediate danger or is it an isolated incident? Impossible to tell. We must get out though, that's certain. I don't think they'll try anything by day because they know they haven't enough support among ordinary people. And they wouldn't want to be recognised - but if the mob comes back tomorrow night I won't be able to hold them off a second time. Thank God we've got the track right up to the house. And thank God I brought up that new drum of petrol recently.
But where to go? Will the road be blocked or ambushed, up on Wilindi say? Or anywhere else for that matter. Unlikely, I don't think they're organised enough for that. What about the Kalengé bridge though? If that's been blown by insurgents down there we'd be stopped in our tracks. If not we could make for Fort Hill, that's the nearest place with good communications and other Europeans. Also we could cross the border if necessary and pray the trouble hasn't spread there.
But then there's the WENELA recruiting camp at Fort Hill, a hotbed of unrest at the best of times, it might be one of the first places to erupt. [3]
Should we go to Karonga then as I'd planned? But even if we got down the Chendo safely the road to Karonga could be blockaded. We could find the place under siege. And the air strip out of action and no way out except by the lake. And even that would depend on the Ilala coming to the Khambwe and sending boats to take people off the beach and... No, definitely not to Karonga.
The only other possibility is to drive out and go directly south down to Rumphi. But Rumphi's a long way off. Must be a couple of hundred miles. And if the road is blocked at any point we'd never get through.
What other option is there though? A new thought struck him. Could we walk out

---

[3] In this he was right. See the Daily Telegraph 27th February, 1959

then? Down to the Songwe and over the border into Tanganyika? But that's about twenty miles. Enid might be able to do it, but we'd have to carry the children - we wouldn't get carriers, the ringleader made that clear. Besides some of the villages along the way might be hostile - Tialikanjeré for sure. That chap Msopelé has been whipping up trouble there for some time... No, that's out. We'd never make it." By morning he had come to no conclusion.

CHAPTER 45

PILGRIMS' EGRESS

I woke to customary sunlight, roused by the children, surprised and excited at finding themselves in our room. For a moment I too was confused, my mind still on my dream, then the events of the night came flooding back. Outside all was quiet. Presently Ken came in with tea and drinks for the children - I had barely noticed his absence so engrossed was I in my thoughts. Sitting down on the bed he said,

"Listen, it's very important for us to behave normally, both for the sake of the children, and for the people. They will have been frightened too you know."

I gave a wan smile. Normality had been receding ever since the start of Ken's ill-fated ulendo, or so it seemed.

"It's Sunday remember, he went on, "No-one would have come to work today anyway. We always have the place to ourselves on Sundays, more or less, and I don't suppose anyone will come near us. But you never know. The Asukwa are an independent minded people, have had to be, not all of them are likely to take notice of the threats of a drunken mob. So we'll get up and have breakfast as usual, then we'll talk again."

The advent of daylight, Ken's matter of fact-ness, and the tea, did much to restore my morale. Before I got up however, the dream still weighing on me, I told him the saga of the pay vouchers, which subsequent events had blotted from my mind.

"I didn't think of them when I gave the mail to Akim, I admitted, "But even if I had I'd have assumed that Msembwe had come and put them in the bag with the rest of the letters while I was outside with the sick. The bag was on the table where you left it and the door was open as usual. Certainly I didn't see him or that would have reminded me to check. As it was I simply forgot. Then when I came indoors there was the packet lying on the table. Anyway, I did what I could." I finished lamely.

Somehow the matter, so vital at the time, had lost its significance. Ken seemed to be of the same opinion for he said,

"Well it's largely academic now. I dare say a lot off things will have been disrupted."

"But where is Akim? I persisted, "And the man I sent after him? They should both have been back days ago."

Ken looked thoughtful but did not reply.

Breakfast over, Ken having urged me to eat, said firmly,

"I'm sure we're not in immediate danger, those hotheads won't try anything by day, they know they haven't got enough support. All the same I think we should leave. We'll go as after dark, we'll be alright till then. And we just might have information that could help us decide what course of action to take.

Meanwhile it's absolutely vital to carry on as usual. If the people see us behaving in the normal way it will reassure them. Don't let the children out of your sight. I'll light the stove in the kitchen so that you can cook lunch, it's important to keep up our strength. Then I shall go and check over the land-rover - well I often do that on a Sunday anyway - and fill up with petrol. And you must pack the suitcases with essentials to take with us. And food and drink of course." Kissing me he added,
"We'll be alright, you'll see."

Normality it seemed, had indeed returned to Misuku. The sun shone, the hornbills squabbled in the tree outside the rondavel, everyday sounds drifted up from the numerous homesteads all round us. Were the events of last night just a bad dream?. Suddenly a drum beat, faint but insistent, caused my heart to lurch - until realisation dawned that it was the customary Sunday morning summons to church. Already on the ridge across the valley people were threading their way to the day long proceedings. Did they feel threatened or disturbed I wondered? Certainly there was no question as to what they would be talking about.
Two early incidents cheered. Firstly a youth came with a few potatoes to sell. A spy? Surely not, this was a common enough occurrence I told myself. Secondly Mwanjondé our sometime 'milk-man' arrived with his wife, as usual she carried the milk in an old whiskey bottle on her head. We exchanged the customary courtesies.
When they had gone, keeping a sharp eye on the children playing a few feet away near the kitchen door, I went through the ritual of filtering the milk through muslin - despite my best efforts the bottle, supplied by us, was none too clean - then boiling it to excess. Which probably reduced its food value to nil. Assuredly it was a normal Sunday.

Until, that is, there came the faint throb of an engine. My heart leapt. Ken coming back to the house, said,
"It could be that the DC has sent someone to escort us out."
We strained our eyes for signs of a jeep. In vain. The sound grew stronger but still we saw nothing. Suddenly a plane appeared almost over head, the first we had ever seen in Misuku. It was small, almost as small as the Spitfires so familiar to the skies of our wartime childhood. When it circled low over the house we could clearly see the markings of the Royal Rhodesian Air Force.
Unprepared, we could do nothing but stand in the middle of the garden with arms outstretched, knowing not only was there no level place for it to land, but that if by some miracle it should do so, it would be too small to carry us all away.
It circled once more, dipping its wings in acknowledgment then made off. Very likely it was near the extremity of its fuel range.
The sound of its engine died away leaving us with a feeling of abandonment and the discomforting knowledge that the trouble must indeed be wide spread.

Our fears were confirmed in the afternoon when a tap on the door heralded the arrival of Ngomba and one of the labourers. What had prompted this brave act of defiance? Loyalty? A stubborn refusal to be intimidated? The desire to help once more? We would never know.

The news was not good. Ngomba told us there was trouble at Fort Hill. Connie and Bill James had flown out on one of the WENELA planes. The border post and the recruiting compound were in rebel hands. He said also that Marian and Gordon Burridge had gone from Chisenga.

Ken did not question him as to his source. Thinking about it later it seemed likely that he had come by the news from the returned Akim, who was too frightened to approach us directly. Ken thanked both men for coming. Ngomba enquired about Ben's leg. Was it getting better? I assured him it was and thanked him again for his help and support in the matter.

We parted sadly.

Where now lay our escape? Ken, whose outward calm had been momentarily shattered by the appearance of the plane, now became strong in resolve.

"We have no choice, we must make for Rumphi. We'll go after dark as I said. Make sure you've packed everything then try and get a bit of rest. I'll join you later, there's a fair bit for me to do before we go."

I did as he said but rest was impossible, sleep a myth, as my mind grappled with the dangers of the journey to come. Ken had not yet divulged his thoughts of the previous night to me, but then he did not need to. I knew the route we must take, in the rains hazardous enough without the possibility of hostile actions. With this added danger...

Assuming we left Katobo without mishap and traversed Misuku safely, we must snake the narrow pass up and over Wilindi, with its sheer drops and likelihood of rock falls from the cliff face. Once down the other side we would ease along the track on the watershed to Chisi, thence on the long stretch down to the Kalengé. I knew the road surface to be poor at this time of the end of the rains; one of Ken's next jobs was to have been getting the road gang working on it as soon as the weather allowed. What if we should get a puncture? Or worse? And to the hazards of washed out culverts, hidden pot-holes etc, must be added the possibility of ambush or attack.

And what of the Kalengé itself? If the bridge had gone would the water be low enough for us to drive through? And the main road south, what of that? Rumphi was miles away; even if we got there safely it might be in rebel hands, hostile, armed...

Here my mind gave up, hysteria just below consciousness. In desperation I got up, checked the suit cases yet again, well knowing that for once bare necessities meant just that. The children's toys, our books, pictures, the gramophone and its records, mementos of our travels, everything that made a house a home, must be left behind. Going through to the kitchen I noticed the bread knife Ken and I had bought on our honeymoon in Austria. I picked it up and slipped it into one of the cases. We have it still.

When the cases were full, more as an act of faith than conviction, I made a bundle of the things we would need on arrival at our destination, clean clothes mostly, and wrapped it all in a blanket in the manner of villagers going on ulendo. Then I set about mustering food and drink to take with us, impeded by Wendy and Ben active again from their afternoon sleep.

When the time came we had some sort of supper. When Ken had eaten he went to lie down at last. I told the children to be quiet so that he could sleep. Wendy and I played snakes and ladders, Ben watching placidly, until it was their bedtime once more. Making some excuse for leaving them fully clothed, I eventually got them to settle down on the camp beds, as before.

With the children sleeping there was nothing to do but sit down to wait. As on the two previous nights time passed agonisingly slowly, my ears attuned now not to the arrival of the Dispenser, but to return of the insurgents.

After what seemed an age but was not, Ken woke up, having slept the sleep of exhaustion. He said,

"I'm going to have a look round outside."

Even as he spoke a disturbance close at hand made me cry out. Ken strode across the room and flung the door open. There stood Kalokhili the night watchman smiling his gap-toothed smile, reporting for duty as usual as if nothing untoward had taken place. Where had he been last night? I wondered hysterically. Old and deaf he assuredly was, but surely even he could hardly have slept through the whole proceedings? But - what did it matter after all? Putting down an uprising would hardly come within his job description. More to the point why had he shown up now? And would his presence hinder our plans? As he and Ken exchanged greetings I was glad for once of his aged sensibility and his custom of sleeping the night away in the shack that had once been the kitchen.

Another interminable wait. At last Ken judged it quiet enough to make a reconnaissance and went outside. For a third night I went to the children's room and looked out of the window. The cooking fires had died down. Thank God. I knew from experience of late home-coming ulendo that while the women and children slept early, on fine nights such as this the men would sit around talking, discoursing, as long as the embers glowed red. Turning, I fumbled and found a favourite toy for each child to take. Ken came back, he said,

"Just as I thought, Kalokhili's snoring in the old kitchen. Everything is quiet, it's time to go. Is everything ready? Good. Then I'll go and load up."

With that he slung the bundle over his shoulder, picked up a suitcase in each hand and went outside, adding,

"I shall only be a minute. Get the children ready."

I woke Wendy as gently as possible. Always a light sleeper she was instantly alert. I told her we were going on ulendo and she must be very quiet or she would wake Ben and he would start to cry. Back in the sitting room, the curtains drawn, the lamp still burning, I stood holding Wendy's hand. Looking about me the familiar scene became imprinted on my mind. There stood the big armchair hauled by the drenched carriers so laboriously from Kapoka on that dreadful night, there was the polished dining table - Enos' pride and joy. Ken's painting of the chrysanthemums hung over the chimney breast as it had done in the old house...

There was no time for anything else. Ken came back. He too looked round, but only for an instant; he said,

"Are you ready?"

I nodded. He scooped Ben up from the camp bed. Back in the sitting room he turned off the lamp, by the light of the dying fire we groped our way through to the backdoor and slipped outside. Ken shut it behind us firmly and said, "Wait."

So we stood in darkness until our eyes adjusted, then with Ben in his arms, he started off up the path. I leading Wendy by the hand stumbled after him, praying that no unseen eyes were watching, no hands poised ready to drum out a message, no dark figures waiting to intercept us. Never had the distance so between house and carport seemed so great.

When we reached it at last I lifted Wendy into the Landrover and pulled myself up after her, Ken handed Ben to me then got in the driving seat. With Wendy wedged between us, he slipped the hand brake. Without engine, without lights we cruised down the track, the night starry but moonless, ideal for our purpose.

Impetus took us on past the capitaos' houses - all dark and silent on the ridge - and on down past the coffee nursery to the stream in the valley bottom. Now the engine must be engaged to take us over the rickety bridge and up the other slope. The resonance was deafening, surely it would be our undoing? But the cooking fires were dead, nothing stirred in the darkness.

So on to the Court complex, that too was in darkness. Somewhere a dog barked, I held my breath. On past the church and the school to Joseph Mkumbwa's homestead with its coffee garden, cattle kraal and huddle of huts. Was that a shout? We could not be sure. On and on we went, through banana groves, past scattered hamlets, Ken hunched over the wheel, dispensed with lights wherever he could. In this way we left habitation behind entirely and reached the foothills of Wilindi.

Lights were essential now. The beam wavered as we wound our way toward the summit, pinning our shadow to the rock face for anyone to see. Yet another wartime image rose up in my mind - that of enemy bombers pinned by searchlights to the night sky, moving targets of anti-aircraft guns on the ground. We reached the top without incident however and began the treacherous descent, knowing one false move could send us over the edge. Knowing too that every twist or turn could present an obstacle, natural or otherwise.

Down to the foothills at last onto the track following the long ridge of the watershed and on through country we knew, with relief, to be sparsely populated. Past the erstwhile village of Chato, where we had camped before Wendy's birth, where the people had been so kind to us in their poverty. Where were they now? I wondered fleetingly.

Gradually the way became less tortuous as we lost altitude and it was possible to relax slightly. The next challenge would be the Kalengé river. Would the bridge be intact? Ken thought it would, or said he did in reply to my anxious enquiry.

"Although it's vital to us it's of no strategic importance to anyone else. Even if there are rebels in the area - which I doubt - preventing a few people getting in or out of Misuku wouldn't be high on their agenda. Also the bridge is pretty robust remember, thanks to Ragnor, cutting it would take a bit of doing." [1] He was right,

---

[1] It was destroyed later.

the bridge stood stout and strong as ever. With the water swirling a few feet below we swept safely over, thankful to our hearts for Ragnor's competence.

Somewhat reassured we went on toward Kapoka where, we hoped, Nelson that old campaigner and his extensive clan, would be sleeping peacefully, untroubled by threats or intimidation. And so it proved. At least there was no sign of life. We passed without pausing.

Ken's whole attention was on the track, mine throughout had been on trying to shield both children from jolts and knocks as we bumped and swerved along; now the track was flatter, dustier. Looking up for the first time I noticed clouds had gathered, or rather, that the sky was no longer starry. But the rain held off.

At last we came to the turn-off on to what was a recognisably a road, though it had deteriorated badly since Angus Day's departure. It would take us past the T-junction at the head of the Chendo Track known as Piccadilly Circus, thence on to Chisenga. Should we stop there? We knew the Burridges had left, knew too that Fort Hill further on was in rebel hands. Too risky Ken decided. In the event we saw lights shining out from the rest-house as we approached, but whether friendly or otherwise we did not wait to find out. Instead we pressed on and eventually we came to that main artery of the country known to us as the Great North Road. We headed south, knowing as we did so that if the uprising were general, we were now in the greatest danger since leaving Misuku.

The first road block was not long in coming, a tree-trunk across our path made an effective barrier. Without hesitation - for who knew if it was ambushed? - Ken slewed the land-rover over to one side and blazed a trail through the bush to circumvent the obstacle. Mercifully the sump hit no rock or tree root and regained the road, the bonnet strewn with foliage.

After that we encountered many such tree-trunks, but miraculously someone - police, an army patrol - had preceded us and moved them just enough to let vehicles through. This probably saved our lives. At the same time it gave further indication that the trouble was indeed widespread

Since leaving Katobo we had seen no-one. Time no longer existed, we were the only people left on earth, destined to drive through darkness to eternity...

In reality we passed somewhere near Njakwa with its lonely store, and skirted the Nyika plateau. Other land marks there surely were, to us they were invisible, therefore they did not exist.

The cab of the land-rover was very hot for we judged it dangerous to open the windows in case of a stray bullet. The children slept fitfully, we ourselves were assailed with drowsiness. We must have air at any cost. We wound the windows down a little, a shiver of dust laden air filtered in; it was not enough, we had to stop. One after the other Wendy and Ben woke up, We got out, gulped in air, handed round drinks and hurriedly moved off again.

The need for sleep returned all too soon. Desperately resorting to an old way of passing a long journey, we started to sing. We sang nursery rhymes, the children, wakeful now, joined in. We sang bed time songs, songs from children's records on the wind up gramophone - Little White Duck, Runaway train. We sang Christmas carols, anything we could think of, the engine drowning out our parched voices.

The milometer told us we must be nearing Rumphi. The road blocks still partially removed, were less frequent. Our chief fear now was that with senses dulled by fatigue, we might come on one unexpectedly on a bend. Or we might be less alert to other dangers. For the time being however the universe was limited to the interminable ribbon of road unwinding in wavering side lights.

The final stretch, though we did not recognise it as such at the time, was uneventful. Anti-climax even. Or would have been but for the sense of foreboding which drove out all thoughts of sleep and abruptly stopped our song. What we would find at the end of our journey?

CHAPTER 46

LAST POST

The first signs of daylight were streaking the sky as we drove into Rumphi. There were the scattered houses set against a backdrop of blue remembered hills. There was the Boma. And there, high above it, stirring in a slight breeze, fluttered the Union Jack.

In spite of the early hour the DC was at his desk. A stranger to us, he introduced himself as Jock Corrie. He looked as if he had been there all night which indeed he confirmed. Rumphi had been beleaguered for several days until a contingent of the KAR arrived. It follows therefore that he was as short of sleep as we were. He received the bedraggled group before him with weary kindness. Also with incredulity on hearing where we had come from and at our having got through unscathed. He expressed guarded surprise that no-one in Karonga had mounted a rescue mission, or at very least sent us warning when the first signs of unrest had broken out there. Probably it was only near exhaustion that allowed this implied criticism of a colleague to escape him, at any rate he quickly summed up our plight and did not waste words.

"Go across to my house, my wife will give you breakfast, he said. And to Ken, "Report to me when you've had some sleep."

Like her husband Barbara Corrie was also up and about. We learned in due course that she had refused to leave him when other wives were being evacuated. When we arrived she was the only woman in the entire place. She organised food, baths, beds, for us, but how, or in what order, was a blur in the mind.

Once again I was woken far too soon from the first untroubled sleep for a very long time. Resisting for as long as possible the children's efforts to crawl over me, I kept my eyes tight shut and tried to remember where we were. When at last I opened them I found we were in a room with several army type beds, set close together dormitory fashion, evidence of the refugee families from various outstations who had passed through Rumphi. Rumphi? Ah yes, that was where we were, could it be that the nightmare was over?

There was no sign of Ken. I had no idea of the time, or indeed of the day. My watch was no help for I had forgotten to wind it. The sun was high however, and the children were hungry. So at length, resentful of being disturbed, ungrateful, with the bad temper that often accompanies release of tension, I got up and unearthed clean clothes from the blanket bundle next to the suitcases standing in a corner.

When we were presentable we left the room, not knowing where to go, but attracted by faint sounds of voices, laughter.

At an open door a surreal sight presented itself. In an elegant drawing room a handsome, immaculate woman, dimly remembered as Barbara Corrie, presided over a table set with starched white cloth, fine bone china, silver tea service complete with sugar tongs and plates piled with sandwiches and little cakes. All this I took in at a glance. Clearly rebels and riots were figures of a fevered imagination.

Until that is, as we hesitated in the doorway, reluctant to spoil the pretty scene, it became apparent that apart from Barbara herself, the other dozen or so people assembled were all men, most of them in uniform.

Barbara caught sight of us and drew us into the room, made introductions then encouraged us to eat as much as we could. Gratefully we did so for we were embarrassingly hungry, even the children in good appetite for once.

After a while Ken and the DC came in. The latter told us we were to spend the night at the rest-house then go on to Mzuzu early next day under armed guard of the KAR.

So we said goodbye to the Corries with sincere thanks for their kindness, I especially grateful to Barbara, another unsung heroine of the British Empire which took the wives of its serving officers so much for granted.

Of the journey to Mzuzu next morning I remember little - the tented encampment of the KAR near the Boma as we left the township. The officer and the Askari with rifles at the ready who accompanied us in an army truck, the telegraph poles along the road leaning drunkenly or toppled to the ground, their wires trailing the dust.

Although we did not know it we were caught up in an eye-blink of African history which would, at most, warrant a single line in school textbooks - 'Independence Riots, Nyasaland, 1959'. Nevertheless the events of those few weeks would have significance not only for ourselves, but in a wider context unquestionably played their part in the dissolution of the Federation of Southern and Northern Rhodesia and Nyasaland. Which, in turn hastened the attainment of Independence in those territories.

We found Mzuzu transformed into a garrison town bursting with refugees like ourselves. It was guarded by troops of the Kings African Rifles, reinforced by a squadron of the Royal Rhodesian Air Force equipped with small planes like the one which had buzzed us in Misuku. There was no chance of our getting a room at the rest-house and we were nobly rescued by John Evans and his wife Rosemary. John was the Provincial Agricultural Officer who had narrowly escaped death by plane crash on the Nyika when returning from visiting us in Misuku some time before. The Evans' house was already full to overflowing with their own large family and with others from outlying areas fleeing south. Among them we were very pleased to see our friends Gordon and Marian Burridge and baby Ian, from Chisenga.

With food supplies disrupted catering for us all in crowded conditions must have been a nightmare for Rosemary. Like Barbara Corrie at Rumphi - she too must surely rank as a heroine of the British Empire, both probably unacknowledged by officialdom.

Shortly after our arrival in Mzuzu a State of Emergency was declared. A Security Force was set up comprising all able-bodied men including Gordon, John Evans and Ken. There-after we saw little of them; indeed but for the KAR officers and their men, the DC and his staff, Mzuzu became a place of women and children. After a while the flood of families from the outposts thinned as people moved on, many never to return; the Evans' household was reduced to Rosemary and her family, Marian and her baby, myself with Wendy and Ben.
Every morning we and a few other women who had chosen to stay, were shepherded with our offspring to the Clubhouse, under escort, there to spend the day, well guarded, trying and failing to amuse children of all ages who, when not at school, were used to running wild. One morning en route for this particular form of torture our convoy was stopped by what appeared to be another outbreak of violence and we were quickly surrounded by a hostile crowd. Whether it had a political dimension was doubtful. More likely it was to do with food shortages or with the curfew now in force. Whatever the cause the ADC in whose charge we were, had the unenviable task of standing up in his jeep and, struggling to be heard above the din, reading out the Riot Act, before ordering the Askari to disperse the mob.

Rumour was rife. One uncovered, apparently well founded, was a plot to kill all Europeans. Another proved to be authentic. Namely that about twenty Africans had been killed at Nkhata Bay some fifty miles away. The incumbent DC (coincidentally a friend of Ken's from early Karonga days,) had been confronted by rebels marching on the Boma. He too must read the Riot Act before any action could be taken. This he did as the insurgents advanced. But as it was incomprehensible to the majority as well as inaudible to all but the foremost, predictably it was ignored. The DC ordered the Askari to fire in the air. When this too failed to stop the onrush he had no choice but order his men to fire into the crowd.
Unknown to us, Ken had meanwhile been assigned a mission of air reconnaissance in the North, setting off one day in one of the aforementioned RRAF two-seater planes, the pilot navigating by the Great North Road over which we had fled. The intention was to refuel at Fort Hill, which by this time had been recovered by Government troops, before going on to Misuku. Unfortunately as they approached the Nyika a mist came down, obscuring not only the road, but the lake as well and they became well and truly lost. At the same time the plane's fuel gauge dipped alarmingly. Only at the last moment did the fog lift sufficiently for Ken to recognise a landmark or two. They landed at Fort Hill with, as the pilot cheerfully put it,
"A teacup of juice to spare."

When the weather cleared they set off again, first to Chisenga where everything appeared calm, then on to Misuku.

It lay peaceful and serene as ever under a clear blue sky. At low level they could see people getting on with their lives. In some instances ken could identify individuals, many of them paused, looked up surprised, then waved as the plane flew over. Only at Katobo was there any sign of former unrest. The place was deserted, our house a burnt out shell. I was filled with dismay at hearing this. Not at the loss of our home though that was painful enough, being far too thankful we had all escaped unharmed. Certainly not at the loss of goods and chattels which could be replaced. No, the over-riding sense of sadness was because it was now unlikely we would ever return to Misuku for Ken to carry on with his work. His efforts to improve the lot of the people by improved agricultural methods, and especially the establishment of the Coffee Cooperative, were now in jeopardy. Would the people be glad to be left alone? Assuredly they would not miss us (except for the staff at Katobo perhaps,) as we would miss them. The rest would go their own way, the land would deteriorate further.

But there was a sense of loss of the house itself and all that had gone into the building of it in the first place. The possé of women mud puddling earth dug out by the labourers. Their hilarity in the task of turning out mud pie forms that would eventually become bricks, under the eye of the self styled expert. The high spot of firing the kiln and the nightly festivity that accompanied it, the official stokers joined by half the neighbourhood.

And after this when building had at last begun, the wavering courses of brickwork which must be torn down and done again. The skewed nails, the less than perfect carpentry, the walls climbing slowly to the eaves. The nailing down of the aluminium roof sheets. And finally the excitement of the topping out ceremony and the half holiday that succeeded it. All gone as if it had never been...

The capitaos' houses on the ridge were also burnt down. A good deal later we learned that any capitaos there at the time were given half an hour to leave. As they attempted to pack up their belongings a mob gathered and began looting. This compounded my misery. What betrayal these loyal men must have felt at our leaving them! I was especially concerned for Ngomba, that tower of strength in my hour of need and earnestly hoped and prayed he had left well beforehand. Alas in the confusion we never had news of him, or of Trisom, William, Akim and the rest

Later still we heard that the Udd's place at Mubula, had suffered the same fate as our own. They too were away at the time; they had lost much more than we ourselves.

When it appeared that those of us remaining in Mzuzu were not about to be murdered in our beds tension began to ease. Women and children were no longer required to spend their days at the Clubhouse, though in practice we were under house arrest, able to go out only for necessities, under armed guard.

The Security force remained active, so husbands came and went. Gordon and Ken because of knowing the territory, were away in the North. One night very late, Ken came back unexpectedly. The Evans' hose was in darkness as he made his way round to what had formerly been our bedroom and somehow 'effected entry' - so much for security. It happened that I was now sharing it with Marian and it was pure coincidence that he got into my bed and not hers.

Gradually, Mzuzu took on the aspect of Waterloo after the battle of that name as depicted by Thackeray in Vanity Fair. Which is to say, relief at Napoleon's downfall was expressed in all manner of frivolities. There were children's parties with jellies and balloons, fancy dress balls and silly games for all ages. A mixed hockey match was dive-bombed with toilet rolls by the RRAF boys. Other excesses were of a more private nature.
Eventually the State of Emergency was rescinded, the Security Force disbanded and the men came back for good. Apart from the insurgents killed at Nkhata Bay and one or two deaths in the South, casualties had apparently been light.
It was at this juncture we met up with Gerry Williams again, last seen at the cinema in Mbeya, on the night of Spartacus the Gladiator, with Mary a long time ago.

Marian and Gordon left and it was many a day before we all met up again. We ourselves were allocated a house, no doubt to Rosemary's infinite relief.
Needless to say the place allotted to us was not in Quality Street, but in Mzuzu's only other residential road. It was by this time lined with bungalows known as Blackwood Boxes after the PWD engineer who had designed them, and because of the general exodus at the start of the troubles, many were now empty.
For reasons Ken and I could never understand, these houses were apt to be despised by their former occupants, some of whom should never have come to Africa in the first place. To anyone who had lived in Karonga, let alone Misuku, they were the height of luxury. True there was no electricity, but there was conventional sanitation AND running water. The integral kitchen not only had a stove but fitted cupboards as well. As usual there was spartan PWD furniture throughout the house, also brick built servants' quarters out at the back. Luxury indeed.
It took us no time at all to move in for we still had only our suit-cases by way of worldly goods. But new friends whose kindness we never forgot, notably Bobbie Brask the wife of a Danish PWD engineer, Jill Storer married to the Provincial Educational Officer, and Rosemary Evans herself, rallied round with kitchen utensils, curtains, cushions, and the loan of books and toys, so that soon we had the semblance of a home once more. (It was at this juncture that we met up again with Gerry Williams, last seen at Mbeya when Mary and I had watched Spartacus with him at the cinema. This time he was accompanied by a wife and baby.)
Why was it then that we did not feel settled, that we longed to be back in Misuku?

In due course we received a letter from Enos to say he wished to join us with his family. Ken sent money for the bus-fare from Fort Hill, though it was quite likely he would be able to beg a lift from a PWD lorry going south. We had not seen him since the beginning of that last, fatal week in Misuku when he had failed to turn up to accompany Ken on ulendo on that Monday morning on account of little Osman's sickness and subsequent death. I very much hoped his wife would benefit from the change of scene.

Life assumed a sort of routine. Wendy and Ben, so healthy in Misuku, caught measles and lay in a darkened room for several days. For good measure, as they recovered I managed to get foot and mouth disease. Ken was away again and so was the only doctor. Only the Veterinary Officer was available. I called him in. "It wasn't funny," I assured Ken on his return, "My lips and heels are still sore."

The rebellion fizzled out, the ringleaders were rounded up and soon it was all over. It had received too little support, been too ill organised to have any realistic chance of success. The English newspapers lost interest, the British Government, predictably, set up a Royal Commission of enquiry. Headed by Sir Patrick (later Lord) Devlin, it duly arrived in Zomba, then subsequently toured the country. Ken was summoned to appear before it in Mzuzu in May 1959. See extracts of his deposition in what became The Devlin Report,1960, at the end of this section.
Here it is necessary to stress that this deposition was pieced together with hindsight, against later knowledge of the political situation of the country at large, and of the extent of the African Congress' influence in Misuku itself. It gave only the bare bones of our situation there on the night of the uprising. Only during his last ulendo did he have evidence of the hold that Congress had gained locally.

Many months were to pass before the findings of the Devlin Report were published. Totally forgotten now, though copies of it probably still lie mouldering away in some dusty archive in Whitehall, the Devlin Report was eagerly awaited in Mzuzu at the time, its likely contents discussed endlessly by us all. Some people contended that, with minor changes, the status quo would be maintained and life for expatriates go on much as before. Others, including ourselves, judged this to be wishful thinking. Tardy as Ken and I had been to detect any signs of unrest in the splendid isolation of Misuku, it was not difficult, in the light of present circumstance, to visualise quite another future.
The uprising had been crushed certainly. But the heady concept of Independence had been established among the people. And not just in Nyasaland and the Rhodesias, but in many other territories as well. Indeed, as the British Prime Minister Harold Macmillan famously put it, the Wind of Change was blowing through Africa. In short, the 19th century Scramble for Africa was being unravelled.

EXTRACTS FROM KEN'S DEPOSITION TO THE DEVLIN REPORT 1960,

'Short description of Misuku

A stretch of country about fifteen miles square from 4000/6000 feet high, very short steep hills, a permanent stream in each valley. Rain forest on the main watersheds, densely populated. Coffee growing area in natural geographical isolation, but tenuously connected to the Chendo road by one of Nyasaland's most hazardous jeep-tracks.

I have lived and worked in the area of N.W. Karonga District since 1952, and in the Misuku area particularly.

In 1958 while I was on six months home leave the visit of Dr Hastings Banda in September raised the political temperature. However on returning from leave things were quiet. Then towards the end of January (1959) ulendo became difficult as food was refused both to myself and my staff, in some of the villages.

The last ulendo I did was from 15th-21st of February (959)in the Misuku foothills. Food became hard to get - sometimes people brought it at night. I had quite good meetings with an unusually large number of Congress members present, though no disturbances.

I completed the ulendo and returned home to Misuku at mid-day, Saturday 21st February.

About 7PM ... we heard the sound of people singing. Shortly (afterward) a crowd came into view and stopped outside our house.

The leader made a speech in Chisukwa and ... Nkhonta translated. The substance of which was,

"No black man will be allowed to work for you. If anybody does we shall cut his tongue out, and there are many other evil things we shall do also" .... (Ken omitted to mention his own remonstrances and speech at this point.)

"....They then shouted such slogans as "Kwaca", "Down with Imperialism", "Self Government today", sang their Kwaca hymn and went away.

"I learnt afterwards that each of my instructors, servants and labourers had been threatened in a similar manner.

Next morning a Beaver (type) aircraft circled us very low, this gave us reason to think that the disturbances were widespread and serious. Further rumours came through (on Sunday afternoon) about riots at Karonga and Fort Hill. We were out of touch with all other Europeans.

I was now very worried, we conjectured at the next step Congress would take. I had my wife and two young children to think of. I possessed no firearm.

I decided that if we intended to leave it would be unwise to delay. But it was not a decision easy to make as I assumed that road-blocks would be picketed. So we left at midnight (Sun. Feb. 22nd) with a minimum of noise, with a suitcase and haversack, in the land-rover. I did not switch the lights on.

We came across road blocks near Chisenga, but as someone had obviously preceded us (down country) and shifted them we managed to get round them. I thought it best to carry straight on to Mzuzu and deposit my wife and children there, and we had no further trouble on the way, to our great relief.

It may be asked do I consider our lives were in danger. The answer is, yes, they would have been had we stayed. The chief danger being from the alcohol with which the people primed themselves. And it would have been natural for the mob to set about us...

Five days after we left I returned with a small police patrol to try to rescue some of our kit. We succeeded in getting out one third of it... but could only spend half an hour in the vicinity as a crowd was gathering... But we did have time for a few words with the Sub-chief, who...had been personally threatened and assaulted by one of the Congress leaders...'

PRESS CUTTINGS FROM BRITISH NEWSPAPERS

THE TIMES February 21st 1959, Salisbury (Rhodesia)

Disturbances occurred early today at three widely separated points – Karonga, Fort Hill, and Rumpi. Crowds of Africans stoned buildings and installations on these airstrips, and at Fort Hill a European signals officer was injured. A statement by Sir Roy Welensky, the Federal Prime Minster, says that troops from the second battalion, The King's African Rifles have been moved from Zomba to the Karonga area, where the families of some African policemen have been attacked. Unruly crowds also attacked the lock-up at Karonga, releasing some prisoners. Un-official reports say it is believed that about 50 prisoners were released.

THE TIMES February 23rd 1959,
POLICE STONED IN NYASALAND
From our own correspondent, Blantyre, Nyasaland
Blantyre had a day of disturbances today as news circulated among the African crowds of last week's unrest in the Northern Province of Nyasaland. At a Nyasaland African Congress meeting in the town Mr. H.B. Chipenbere told a crowd of seven hundred that the Africans would fight on in spite of the "shooting at Karonga."
....
The Northern Province, where last week the demonstrators attacked Karonga and the Fort Hill airfields and where the police opened fire, wounding three people, was still uneasy today.

THE TIMES February 24ᵗʰ 1959
TENSE SITUATION PERSISTS
NORTHERN AIRFIELD NOT YET RETAKEN
From our correspondent, Blantyre
The situation in Nyasaland is still regarded officially as tense...
In all three provinces of Nyasaland particularly the northern province, uneasiness persists. Mr. Ingham, Secretary for African Affairs, said today that the police and troops had not yet retaken the Fort Hill airfield, in the Northern Province, from the mob, but were busy gaining control of Karonga. Crowds had been gathering at several centres in the country all day, but there were no reports of violence so far.

THE DAILY TELEGRAPH, 27th FEBRUARY, 1959
'No reinforcements can be flown to Nyasaland's Northern Province because Fort Hill airfield is blocked by barrels and tree trunks. The border post there is in African hands.
Troops would have to travel over 500 miles by dirt road from Blantyre to get there. The rains have made the road nearly impassable. ... The Nyasaland Information Department said in a statement that a convoy of the Kings African Rifles had met road blocks...
Police have escorted two American missionaries, Mr and Mrs Udd, from the Misuku area of Karonga district, Northern Nyasaland, to safety."
Ken and I did not hear of this last fact for many weeks after, since when the question,
"Why was no police patrol similarly mounted to bring the Waterfields out?'
has remained unanswered.

CHAPTER 47

END OF THE ODYSSEY

In common with others in Mzuzu and elsewhere Ken and I tried to visualise the future. My own Inclinations were entirely selfish, A problem that had preoccupied me long before the recent troubles, one which I had never been able to resolve, was now more acute.

Whatever happened in the country at large, I knew I was incapable of self denial such as Alice Udd's. Our children would need schools. Not even the best education in the world I felt, could compensate for loss of a happy home life. How could one agree to one's children going away to boarding school when day schools in England were accessible as daily bread? Already Wendy was coming up to school age, Ben would follow soon enough. There was little prospect of our returning to Misuku. There was no school in Mzuzu even if we stayed there, but it was far more likely we would be posted to some outstation. Certainly I could teach both children adequately for a few years wherever we were, but that would be no long term solution.

Fortunately Ken shared my feelings; the matter was however not one of his immediate concerns. His thoughts in general were of quite a different order.

That self government would come sooner or later seemed inevitable. How would the country evolve? How would we ourselves fit in? He could not tell.

One probable outcome however was not hard to guess. Even with continuing support from Britain, finance for Nyasaland was likely to be severely stretched, development curtailed, especially in outlying country regions. It followed therefore that the Agricultural Department, starved of funds, would perforce restrict its resources and activities to main centres within striking distance of towns or townships. Almost certainly Ken would be assigned to one of the latter. Life would be pleasant enough, with regular working hours, a high standard of living, time for rest and relaxation, sociability. In short everything would be much easier than if we had continued in Misuku.

And yet ... In his heart Ken knew we would no longer have close contact with the people. He would lose the possibility of making a difference to the lives of the most needy. The idealism which had brought him to Africa in the first place, would be gone for good.

We thought about it, discussed it long and hard. And decided to leave.

Sadly we faced up to the irrevocable loss of our way of life in Misuku. Its beauty, and the people who had been part of our lives for so long. We recalled how deeply we had felt the loss of Sutherland, Ken's support for many years and the stalwart of my early days. Now all must be relinquished. Ngomba, another tower of strength, Trisom the garden boy, always gentle and nervous, the first William, whose very willingness and desire to please had nearly wrecked our digestive systems. Then there was Akim the tricky one, who nevertheless could be relied on to rise to any occasion, and old Kalokhili, on whom our nocturnal security so precariously depended.

And what about Nelson Mwandofi at Kapoka, totally reliable and friendly? And his brother Bodwin and the other capitaos who had displayed their loyalty by visiting me in Ken's absence during that last fatal week prior to the troubles.

There were also the labourers, their wives too, who came sporadically to mud or whitewash the walls or do other jobs classed as women's work, and the old men and the women with sick children in the daily line-up for medicine. Even the pretty girls who worked down in the coffee nursery would be missed. The prospect of never seeing any of them again was sorrowful indeed. Remembrance of them, and others, would lodge in the mind for ever.

And of course there were the good times spent with European friends, many now scattered. Andrew and Jess, our good friend Noel Harvey, Angus Day, Steve Witting, Sue Maynard the DC's wife who had been so good to me on my first arrival in Karonga, and other valued acquaintances. Well at least there was the possibility of meeting up with them again in England.

Lastly, worst of all, was the prospect of parting with Enos. He had served us faithfully over the years and clearly wished to go on doing so, as demonstrated by his joining us in Mzuzu. That he and I had been mutually dependent was beyond question. It is no exaggeration to say that without him I might not have lasted in Misuku. Now he earnestly pleaded with us to take him to England.

How to explain that it was simply not possible? He could have no concept of the obstacles. The immigration rules, housing problems, finance, our own (only too likely) straitened circumstances, his polarisation at being cut off from his own kind, the weather, all combined to make it not only out of the question, but not necessarily even in his best interests.

There was nothing for it therefore but to make our sad farewells with assurances that we would never forget him. This was true; the effects his letters had on us in the years to come have already been described. The connection with him lasted some forty years, and with his family tenuously into the 21st century.

As it was, sorrowfully, suitably recompensed he prepared to make the long journey back to Misuku with his wife and children.

Reluctantly Ken handed in his resignation, reluctantly he sold the Landrover that had probably saved our lives. Our passage home confirmed, our boats were metaphorically burned. We said goodbye to the friends remaining in Mzuzu who had been so good to us in our time of need, and promised to keep in touch.

On the appointed day we piled our meagre belongings into the Chevrolet put at our disposal by the DC. And with heavy hearts took the road south.

The End

347

POSTSCRIPT

In the fullness of time the Federation of Northern and Southern Rhodesia and Nyasaland was dissolved, the constituent countries became independent but chose to stay within the British Commonwealth of Nations. In 1964 Nyasaland became Malawi with Dr Hastings Banda as its first president.

In spite of poverty and recurring famine, in spite of a massive influx of refugees from Mozambique during that country's period if civil strife, unlike many, if not most, of the countries of post colonial Africa, Malawi has to this day remained peaceful.

FEBRUARY 2008

NUMBERS

1. modzi,
2. wiré
3. tatu,
4. nai
5. jehanu,
6. sikis
7. jehanuawiré (5 + 2)
8. tatuawiré (5+3 etc.)

GLOSSARY

NOTES:-
1. Some of the words included may have been derivative and not pure Chisukwa, but were in common use in Misuku in the 1950s.
2. Accents have been used in some cases to represent the closest pronunciation available; but may not be 100% accurate in all cases.

African Soldiers - Askari

Beans - Malima

Beer (home brewed) - Moa

Boma - Administrative Area

Bride Price - Libola (Pro: Liwola)

Bring - Leta

Carry - Tenga

Chicken, Cockerel - Nkoko

Chicken house-miniature nkokwe raised on stilts, with rickety ladder for access

Child - Mwana

Cloth worn by both sexes - Nsaru (perhaps from sari)

Coffee - Kahawa

Cough - Kakora

European - Msungu, pl.- Asungu

Fire, Fever - Moto

Firewood - Nkuni

Food in general - Tkudya, Chakudya

Food money, in lieu of hospitality - Poso or Posho

Giant Millipede - Bongololo

Grain store - Nkokwe: small round mud hut raised on stilts

Headache - Mutu

Greeting (& thanks) - ndaga, mawomba

Hospital - Chipitala

I am well - Éya makora

I don't know - Kaya

Insect – Chirombo

Journey, Safari - Ulendo

Lion – Nkaramu

Madam - term of address - Dona (from Portuguese?)

Bad Magic - Nfiti or Nfété

Maize - Firombé

Maize meal, flour - Ufa

Meat, animal - Nyama

Medicine - Mankwala

Millet (porridge) - Mlesi

Money - Ndarama
Money/paid work - Nbonbo

352

Missing, 'There is (are) none' - Palebé

Pit latrine - Chimbuzi

Potatoes - Kartoffé, (German?) Mpatata

Soldier ants - Manyega

Stomach, Middle - Pakati

Sunday - Sabati

Vehicle - Galimoto

Work - Mbombo or Nchito

Work force boss - capitao

Pineapple - Chinanass (from German?)

Plane, bird - Ndegi

Rain - Ifula

Sore - Chironda

String from bark or tough vine
Chingwe

Tea - Chai

V.I.P. - Bwana Mkubwa

Yes – É or Éya

PLACE NAMES

BLANTYRE - The commercial 'capital' of Nyasaland and the first European settlement in the country, it was named after David Livingstone's birthplace in Scotland.

CHISENGA - The Northern most Public Works Department depot.

FORT HILL - The Northern frontier and customs post between Nyasaland and Northern Rhodesia. It was also the centre, with airfield, of a native labour recruiting company.

KARONGA - Situated on the lake shore in the far North of the country, it was said to be the oldest settlement after Blantyre. Originally established by Mandala, the African Lakes Company, it became an Administration H/Q (Boma).

KATOBO (pro Katowo) - The Agricultural Station in Misuku, at the foot of Mughessé. Our home for several years.

KHAMBWE LAGOON - Deep water anchorage c 3 miles from Karonga where a massacre took place at the end of the 19th Century. In the 1950s it was the site of a cotton market.

LILONGWE - The Administration H/Q of the Central Province. (Birthplace of Wendy and Ben.)

MBEYA - Small market town and Admin H/Q in Tanganyika, about 160 miles from Misuku.

MISUKU HILLS - c 60-70 miles north of Karonga. An enclave with permanent streams, contained between Mughessé and Wilindi Ridges at an altitude of c 5000/6000 feet.

MZIMBA - former Administration H/Q of the Northern Province.

MZUZU - Subsequent Administration H/Q of the Northern Province.

MWENITETÉ - Cotton market on the lake shore c 10 miles north of Karonga.

RUMPHI - Small township and Boma on the North Road c half way between Mzimba and Karonga.

SONGWE RIVER - north of Misuku, it formed the frontier between Nyasaland and Tanganyika.

ZOMBA - The administrative capital of Nyasaland.

NAMES CURRENT, 2007

CHITIPA - formerly Fort Hill
MALAWI - formerly Nyasaland
TANZANIA - formerly Tanganyika
ZAMBIA - formerly Northern Rhodesia
ZIMBABWE - formerly Southern Rhodesia

SOME QUOTATIONS AND MIS-QUOTATIONS

A Land where it seemed always afternoon.. Thomas de Quincey
For the leaves were full of children.. T S Eliot
Does the road wind up-hill all the way? Christina Rosetti?
The Hill called Difficulty.. John Bunyan
The Ship had somewhere to get to and sailed calmly on.. W H Auden
And then the lighting of the lamps.. T S Eliot
The Moon was a ghostly galleon.. Alfred Noyes
There was a birth certainly.. T S Eliot
Oh what is that drum?.. W H Auden?
And we the bridal path will travel.. Sir Walter Raleigh
It is a truth universally acknowledged.. Jane Austen
The river once bridged ceases to be a barrier.. T S Eliot
I will lift up mine eyes unto the hills.. The Bible, Psalm, Old Testament
Mary, Mary.. Anon
Light the candle, deck the tree.. Anon
Speaking in tongues.. The Bible, New Testament
Unwillingly to school.. Shakespeare
Genesis of a road.. GK Chesterton
Thursday's child has far to go.. Nursery Rhyme
Build me a willow cabin at your gate.. Shakespeare
Once more unto the breach.. Shakespeare
But oh the bliss of the double bed, after the hurly-burly of (the camping equivalent)
the chaise longue! Mrs Patrick Campbell 1865-1940

ABBREVIATIONS

DC - District Commissioner
ADC - Assistant District Commissioner
KAR - Kings African Rifles
OHMS - On Her Majesty's Service
PAO - Provincial Agricultural Officer
PC - Provincial Commissioner
PWD - Public Works Department
RRAF - Royal Rhodesian Air-Force